UNITED STATES SOVIET RELATIONS

UNITED STATES SOVIET RELATIONS

Karl W. Ryavec

Department of Political Science
The University of Massachusetts at Amherst

Longman
New York & London

United States-Soviet Relations

Longman Inc., 95 Church Street, White Plains, N.Y. 10601

Associated companies:
Longman Group Ltd., London
Longman Cheshire Pty., Melbourne
Longman Paul Pty., Auckland
Copp Clark Pitman, Toronto
Pitman Publishing Inc., New York

Senior editor: David J. Estrin
Development editor: Marylyn Marshall
Production editor: Elsa van Bergen
Text and cover designer: Joseph DePinho
Production supervisor: Judith Stern

Library of Congress Cataloging in Publication Data

Ryavec, Karl W.
  United States—Soviet relations/by Karl W. Ryavec.
    p. cm.
  Includes index.
  ISBN 0-582-28587-9 (pbk.)
  1. United States—Relations—Soviet Union. 2. Soviet Union—Relations—
United States. I. Title.
E183.8.S65K9   1988   87-35380
327.73047—dc 19   CIP

ISBN 0-582-28587-9

89 90 91 92 9 8 7 6 5 4 3 2

Dedicated to
André L. de Saint-Rat
Professor of Russian, Emeritus

and to
Richard E. Gustafson and William J. McNiff
Professors of History, Emeriti
of
Miami University
Oxford, Ohio
teachers and wise counselors

Contents

Preface

This book's purpose is to present an overview of the main features of the Soviet-American relationship and to provide a sense of the differing views and controversy surrounding it in the United States. The author has tried to mask his own viewpoint, although "reading between the lines," that inevitable accompaniment of political studies and a mainstay of Sovietology, will reveal it soon enough.

The writing of the book was prompted by several causes. The author noticed that, although there are many fine histories and interpretations of the superpower relationship and also many excellent works on specific aspects of it, there was no reasonably up-to-date book available in English surveying the whole range of the relationship and its major constituent topics. Secondly, this book was written because its author, a specialist in Soviet domestic politics, found that he was spending much of his "worry time" thinking about the problems the United States and the Soviet Union have in dealing with each other.

Moreover, the two standard explanations of the American-Soviet contention—competing great power interests and opposing ideologies—have not been convincing to him. This book is the first result of an attempt to clarify for the author and for others what is at work in the United States-Soviet relationship, both on the surface and below it. Essentially, my perspective is more a cultural than a political one. As a child of working-class, immigrant parents belonging to a tiny ethnic group without its own state from that intermediate part of Europe labeled unsatisfactorily and pejoratively as either "Central," "Eastern," or "Southeastern," I cannot but feel that both the United States and the Soviet Union are playing unnecessary and possibly dangerous games, and certainly playing from unrealistic positions, in their rivalry-relationship. I also hold that the United States-Soviet connection cannot be a full-scale relationship with a high degree of mutual understanding, trade, people-to-people contacts, and "live-and-let-live" attitudes and policies until, and if, one or both systems change significantly. However, I do not at all think the two countries are doomed either to war or to bitter conflict. If the leaderships and key interests on both sides can calm themselves and become more realistic, that is, accepting of inevitabilities and unavoidabilities, the United States and the Soviet Union can come to enjoy a limited (limited underlined several times) and somewhat mutually profitable relationship.

Our world is now one of specialization and specialists, although real expertise and anything approaching wisdom remains rare. Most writers on the superpowers' relationship specialize in one or a few related aspects of it. Their predilection for focus and detail gave me an opportunity I hope I have not wasted. Many of their works are cited, both in the text and in the bibliographies at the end of each chapter.

The topics covered have been the most important ones: the history of the relationship, the relative power of the United States and the USSR, their military competition, their successes and failures in arms control, their rivalry in the Third World, the trade between them, the process and effects of their domestic politics, their contrasting cultures, their perceptions of each other, the diplomacy and negotiation occurring between them, and the difficult issue of American strategy toward the Soviet Union. Predictions about the future are only tentative or implied.

The author has tried always to be realistic and also to treat the United States not as "we" but as an "other" in an attempt to look at Soviet-American relations from the perspective of a third party who, as a fellow "earthling," will inevitably be affected by an exacerbation of the superpowers' conflict. The author has also tried to excite thought among readers. If disagreement or even anger is produced, so much the better. They go with the topic.

Many quotations from many people are included in order to convey a sense of the discussion and debate. Anything between quotation marks attributed to anyone is quoted exactly as said or written. The main lines of debate on various pertinent issues in the United States today are also included.

Finally, it is hoped this book, whatever its limitations, will encourage some of the students of today to become the specialists, scholars, and perhaps even stateswomen and statesmen of tomorrow. Certainly, the American-Soviet relationship could use more good people involved in improving it. Improvement is too big a job for a few.

Karl W. Ryavec
Amherst, Massachusetts
January 1988

Acknowledgments

My primary debt is to David J. Estrin, Senior Editor of Longman, Incorporated, who believed in the idea of this book and kept the faith during its unduly long gestation period. David deserves my thanks, too, for his many welcome and helpful notes of encouragement. I am also indebted to the readers, still unknown to me, who read the manuscript for Longman, and to Elsa van Bergen, the Production Editor. Their comments were often incorporated but always useful in my writing of a revised draft. They saved me from some of the embarrassment of error. Any errors that remain are my responsibility.

My thanks are deserved also by present and former colleagues who read and commented upon either chapters or sections of the book: Professors Jean Elshtain, Edward Feit, Franklin Houn, Harvey Kline, M. J. Peterson, and Anwar Syed. M. J. deserves special thanks for her efforts with my chapter on superpower rivalry in the Third World.

Former students, now professionals in their own right, were dragooned into reading chapters as well. Colonel George R. Hofmann, U.S.M.C., helped me greatly in improving the military chapter as did Peter Kracht with Chapter I, Dr. Christine H. Teixeira with the chapter on trade, and Bernard C. Victory with the chapter on arms control. Having former students like these is a reward indeed.

Friends, too, were brought into reviewing chores above and beyond their own work. Professor Paul Marantz made useful comments on the section on cultural differences, as did David Powell on Chapter I. The research assistance of Harry Koolen is also appreciated.

I am also indebted to the Russian Research Center of Harvard University, its Director, Adam Ulam, and its Associate Director, Marshall Goldman, for providing me with an office during the spring of 1986 and for the typing assistance of Treacy Curlin and Rose Dibenedetto. Patricia Bashand and Mary Mireault typed parts of the manuscript at my university.

I am particularly appreciative to Doris Holden who typed much of the manuscript twice and whose help was crucial in meeting the deadline. Donna Dove also put in long hours typing during the "big push" of August, 1987. Stanley Radosh, the Slavic Bibliographer of my university's library, and the staff of the library's Reference Department were very helpful in many ways.

Chapter 1

The Nature
of the Relationship

PROBLEMS OF PERSPECTIVE AND STUDY

For the past forty years, American foreign policy has been preoccupied with the relationship between the United States and another of the world's great powers—the Soviet Union. The American people have been fascinated, repelled, and often alarmed by the images received from the media about the aims, ideological beliefs, and motivations of the Soviet Union and its people. As a result of the media's tendency to ignore, overemphasize, or distort world events we may miss important issues affecting Soviet-American relations and misinterpret others. In addition, we cannot detach ourselves fully from our own cultural values and ideological beliefs, which makes it even more difficult to put problems in perspective and look forward to improved relations with the Soviet Union. Yet we can try to be objective. It is in such a spirit of "critical involvement" that this book is written.

It is not surprising that a veteran journalist writes of the "fickle" nature of Soviet-American relations: "What seems attainable one month looks beyond hope the next, and in the shifting moods that govern relations between the two powers, no real sense of dependability evolves."[1] Every time the relationship improves, something happens to make it worse. In 1986, for example, it was difficult to arrange a summit meeting because of the Soviet arrest of an American journalist in response to United States expulsions of Soviet diplomats for spying. In 1987 relations were disrupted by the U.S. Marine spy scandal at the American Embassy in Moscow. Another problem is the lack of consensus on the Soviet Union in American politics.

The Soviets themselves present serious obstacles to the study of the Soviet

1

Union. The biggest problem is traditional Russo-Soviet secrecy about goals and decision-making, which further aggravates American guessing and sensationalism about Soviet objectives. As an American Secretary of State has put it: "While we can define their alternatives, we cannot decipher their intentions. To a degree unequalled anywhere else, Russia in this respect remains a secret."[2]

If the Soviets were more open about their actions, the public mood in the United States would be less unstable and less virulently anti-Soviet. Ironically, Soviet spokesmen claim they are open in stating their goals. This is only partially true. The Soviets speak in very general terms and in their own "code-language" of "scientific socialism." Most Americans find it impossible to decode this language. Not only does Soviet official language obfuscate Soviet intentions but decisions are made in total secrecy and only official explanations, if any, are issued. There is no independent investigative journalism in the Soviet Union that could try to clarify what government is doing behind the scenes. And politicians' memoirs are rarely available to tell us what finally happened. Although Mikhail Gorbachev, the general secretary, has promised to be more open about Soviet affairs, it will take time for this new *glasnost* policy—if it continues—to have any far-reaching effects.

This problem of secrecy and "miscommunication" is compounded by a host of questions concerning Soviet foreign policy. For example, is Soviet power still growing internationally? What are the outer limits of Soviet international expansion? Are the Soviets "defensive" or "aggressive" in their foreign policy? And, perhaps most important to Americans, what are the Soviet Union's ultimate objectives with respect to the United States?

Soviet power is still growing internationally, partly because the USSR is the richest country in the world in raw materials, but has relatively low levels of personal consumption. It can afford a greater international involvement. It also grows because it is invited into areas such as the Middle East by states that want its military aid. Another reason is the perennial search by Soviet leaders for greater security in a world that is still heavily non-Communist. But this spread of communism has brought the USSR into conflicts with other Communist systems. Some become anti-Soviet (China and Yugoslavia) while the peoples of others rebel against the Soviet pattern (Czechoslovakia, Hungary, and Poland). The USSR continues to try to outflank and contain its hostile Communist neighbor, China, and maintain Soviet-type systems in East Central Europe.

The USSR stands to lose a great deal from a status-quo or "sit-tight" policy. It must maintain an active international involvement just to keep its present power and influence. This unavoidably brings it up against the American tendency to favor a stable, relatively unchanged international environment in which American business and trade can operate well and of course against American anti-communism. The big question is, what are the outer limits of Soviet international expansion? There is no easy answer to this question and the uncertainty surrounding it generates considerable tension. Because of Soviet repression of dissent and military actions in Eastern Europe and Afghanistan, Soviet foreign policy seems to some like "a carefully constructed series of nasty practical jokes."[3]

There are other unanswerable puzzles. For example, what is the ultimate source or motivating principle of Soviet foreign policy, particularly in terms of the United States and its allies? If the Soviets are motivated primarily by defensiveness, possibly defensiveness of an intense, even paranoid sort, one might try to calm them and give them less reason to feel so insecure. This strategy is rejected by those who feel that aggressiveness is behind Soviet foreign policy and that a cooperative stance would only encourage that aggressiveness. Others give a mid-range or compromise answer to this puzzle, seeing the Soviet Union as "defensively aggressive" or "aggressively defensive." One American analyst speaks of "the offensive essence of Soviet defense."[4] The disagreements on this issue can be intense.

Another puzzle is the nature of the aims of Soviet policy toward the United States and the persistence or drive behind them. There are four general aims the USSR might have toward the United States in the context of their present conflictful relationship: (1) appease the United States; (2) block or limit the United States; (3) harass or injure it and so try to reduce its power; and (4) effectively eliminate its international power or even destroy the United States. Those who take Soviet propagandistic rhetoric seriously tend to see Soviet aims as "hard" and limitless and would opt for aims (3) and (4). But those who talk to Soviet citizens or rely on Soviet scholarly or policy-makers' writings tend to lean toward a "soft" or limited set of Soviet aims; i.e., aims (1) or (2).

A fundamental question is whether one sees foreign policy actions as the result of rational thinking and planning or of accident or mere reaction to the actions of others. Soviet and American spokesmen and apologists often present their own side's actions as unavoidable responses to overt hostility. Clearly, there is some validity to such claims. But some foreign policy actions are taken because of nonrational feelings, emotions, or fears. Any country tends "to use foreign policy in nonrational ways to express current hopes and fears."[5] The nonrational is reflected in both American and Soviet foreign policies; each side, for example, spends billions on military programs as extra "insurance" that is probably not needed but reflects "worst-case" fears.

Nationalism, Marxism, or Realpolitik?

Still another mystery centers on the relative weights of Soviet Marxism, "Russianness," and *realpolitik*[a] in determining Soviet foreign policy. Since a Russian elite is dominant politically in the Soviet Union, Soviet society and politics have come to be a unique mixture of Russian culture[b] and Marxist language and dogma. Often Russianness is dominant in Soviet policy and

---

[a] A non-ideological, realistic approach to politics; a policy of pure national interest—very rare.
[b] The term "culture" is used here in the anthropological sense: thinking and action in accordance with the traditional ways of a people.

Marxism or ideology is mere verbiage. Certainly the Soviet hold on Poland (a traditional enemy of Russia) is dictated as much by Russian national feeling and national interest as it is by considerations of building an international Marxist system. The same feeling must also be present vis-à-vis Germany, part of whose former area, Prussia, has been attached to the Soviet Union, and toward China. Emotion cannot be eliminated from politics, particularly when it reflects a people's history.

Culture often affects a nation's foreign policy. Americans, for example, are strongly attracted to the "underdog," particularly a people struggling for national independence. American culturally based actions can be a problem for the Soviets. For example, Soviet officials seem not to have understood American concern over the Soviet invasion of Afghanistan. At least they do not accept this American sympathy toward the underdog as sincere. American aid to Afghan guerrillas may be seen by the Soviets as purely an attempt to embarrass or harm the USSR. As a member of the Soviet Central Committee, the Americanist G. A. Arbatov, put it:

> I am well aware that our actions with regard to Afghanistan were used to spark a whole storm of emotions and denunciations in the West. But political judgments should be based on facts, not emotions. The official American argument that the reason for the current deterioration [of relations—KR] lies in events in Afghanistan holds no water....[6]

Realpolitik is also seen as motivating Soviet foreign policy. In the quotation above, Arbatov may be saying, in effect, that the Soviet invasion of Afghanistan was unavoidable in terms of Soviet national interest and was being hindered by American aid to anti-Communist Afghans only for purposes of American national interest. Many of the USSR's actions are more *realpolitik* than anything else. The decision to support Ethiopia and abandon Somalia, Ethiopia's smaller neighbor in the Horn of Africa, is a good case in point. Of course, to the person who sees ideology as the sole motivating factor, the invasion of Afghanistan and the shift to the larger Ethiopia serve the Marxist goal of spreading communism throughout the world rather than protecting Soviet national interests.

Underneath all this uncertainty about Soviet intentions is the hardest question of all: Where is Russia as a system heading? Is it ever going to change internally in what Marx called a "qualitative" (total) sense? Will it at least "loosen up" or relax? Many Americans seem to hope that the Soviet Union will change in some fundamental way in a direction that makes it more like a liberal democracy. Such an attitude is another typically American cultural standpoint. Gorbachev, the new leader, is often looked on as a liberalizer when he may only want a more efficient economy. Americans have often thought "the Soviets were not to be bargained with but converted, won over to the virtues of free elections, independence, disarmament, and peace."[7] This may happen, but there is no sign of it yet. And this lack of movement toward democracy is painfully difficult for change-oriented Americans to accept. Americans might choose to express their frustration with Soviet rigidity by anti-Soviet actions based more on annoyance and rejection than on realistic service of American national interests.

Each of these "mysteries" of Soviet foreign policy can be explained in various ways. Emotionalism will rule at times. It may be hard for us to realize that international incidents of great concern to people in the United States may not be having much effect, if any, in the Soviet Union. In the United States, television can project all sorts of troubling and even horrifying images, while in the USSR, because of censorship, those images may never appear at all or may be subject to opposing interpretations. Compare, for example, the difference between American and Soviet TV coverage of events in Afghanistan and Nicaragua, or of the Soviet downing of a Korean passenger plane in August 1983.

Superpower Competition and International Context

It is important that the United States look beyond the crisis of the moment at the "big picture" in our relations with the Soviets. We need to keep in mind that the two nations became so-called superpowers not as a result of deliberate planning by either country but because of the aggressive actions of other nations during World War II. That war, brought on mostly by the militant expansionism of Germany, Japan, and Italy, resulted in the defeat or the serious weakening of the traditional great powers and Japan. In short, superpower status for the United States and the Soviet Union came out of war, and was artificially inflated by the results of war, although as we shall see, it has come to be weakened by subsequent events.

With the passage of more than forty years since the end of World War II and the emergence of bipolarity[c] the world has been returning to a power arrangement somewhat like the one that existed before the war. Nations other than the USSR and the United States have gained or, in some cases, regained a real measure of international significance. India as an international power is new, but France is old. Even small powers such as Iran, Libya, and South Africa have definite regional importance and some effect on the superpowers. In short, superpower status is less "super" than it was in 1950 or 1960. Moreover, the overall capabilities of the USSR have always been less than those of the United States and are likely to remain so unless the USSR undergoes radical change. "The Kremlin is more isolated than the United States and in many ways more vulnerable." [8] But the United States, too, is less powerful than it was. According to a French view:

> Although the United States is likely to remain a very powerful country ... it will not be able to retain its role of unchallenged world leader.... Europe and

---

[c] Bipolarity: a situation in which only two countries, hostile to one another, dominate international affairs.

Japan have now reached the level of development and wealth which would probably have been theirs if the world wars had not taken place.[9]

In 1986 a leading Soviet foreign affairs specialist emphasized that the super-powers face the emergence of a world in which they cannot control events even if they try.[10] We are certainly living through a new historical period. The world has been largely decolonized, but it has not yet taken a definite new form with a regularized pattern of relationships. In this unclear and sometimes violent context, the United States-Soviet relationship is bound to have rough moments.

Although the relative power of both Russia and America is declining in this world situation, "there is scarcely an aspect of international life that is not affected by their relationship and that would not be made more difficult and more dangerous by a high level of Soviet-American tension and unregulated competition."[11] In addition to making life uncomfortable for smaller powers and for international organizations such as the United Nations, the USSR and the United States each retains the power to raise almost any issue to a superpower confrontation and force the local actors to compromise or withdraw.[12] This happened in the Middle East War of 1973 (the Yom Kippur War to Israelis). They can also impede the solution of international problems.

It is generally known that a war between the superpowers would devastate them and much of the northern hemisphere. An

> attack on the urban societies of the United States and Soviet Union would . . . require only a very small fraction of the more than 50,000 nuclear weapons currently in the arsenals of the two superpowers. . . . An exchange of a few thousand of these weapons could kill most of the urban population and destroy most of the industry of both sides.[13]

If general war between the United States and the USSR is avoided, as it probably will be,[d] and the level of their conflict is reduced, they could, in spite of smaller powers' increasing freedom of action, help create a more orderly world.

> They alone have the power, through collaboration, to put limits on the world's turbulence, to prevent great conflicts and contain small ones, to curb the excesses of nationalism and ambition . . . and by so doing to make the world as safe as it can be made in the thermonuclear age.[14]

Although the superpowers cannot eliminate wars, if they agreed to restrict arms exports to the Third World, conflicts such as the one in Lebanon would

---

[d] Since a United States-Soviet nuclear war would destroy each side, there are good grounds for thinking such a war will not occur, as it has not for a third of a century. "Proxy-wars" with conventional weapons, however, are clearly another matter, as the examples of Korea and, to a degree, Afghanistan, show.

eventually run into ammunition shortages and become less destructive. Other sources could not make up for the lack of American and Soviet weapons.

The actions of the two superpowers affect each other's domestic politics as well. The Soviet invasion of Afghanistan may have helped embarrass President Carter and so aided in electing Ronald Reagan president. Similarly, after President Kennedy forced First Secretary Khrushchev to remove offensive missiles from Cuba Khrushchev was undercut domestically and later removed from office. This political interpenetration will continue. In their actions and statements, the superpowers speak politically to each other.

International Environment

People of opposing ideological positions seem to agree that the Soviet-American competition tends to worsen an unstable international environment. In addition, some of the smaller powers use the unstable international situation and the superpower rivalry to their own narrow advantage, and the superpowers are sometimes prisoners of this "coercive power of the weak." A leading Soviet Americanist has warned, "If we are in a situation of confrontation, many forces around the world could use this situation to play us off against each other and even make all kinds of trouble in different parts of the world."[15] It is rumored that Syria, which has great quantities of Soviet weaponry, has several times refused Soviet suggestions to be more cautious in its policy toward Israel and Lebanon. The United States, too, has found that some of its foreign associates refuse requests to moderate their policies.

The superpowers are now operating in a world politics context undergoing fundamental change. States are no longer the only international actors. International organizations, political movements, and multinational corporations are increasing in number and significance. Small groups and even individuals are engaging in international relations apart from the states of which they are citizens. Political life can no longer be firmly divided into domestic and international spheres. The study of international relations has become the study of world society.

The Soviets are fully conscious of the realities of the new world situation. They often note that international relations are becoming more and more "complicated," offering both "dangers" as well as "possibilities" and creating a need for a more precise definition of common interests and increased cooperation between the United States and the Soviet Union.

Despite the changes in international politics now taking place, "there is no evidence of spontaneous movement toward the kind of world the Kremlin leaders would choose." The world's most common ideology is nationalism, often a primitive ethnic-centered nationalism, not Soviet-type socialism. The United States, the more adaptable superpower, is best suited to make an accommodation to this tumultuous world.[16] But despite its potential adaptability and general flexibility, the United States often tries for an unattainable stability and shows itself a poor manager of international crises and critical situations. In contrast, although the Soviet Union's domestic policy is quite rigid, it has a long imperial history of conquering and ruling diverse peoples and has acquired from this experience "much skill in manipulating social privilege and social conflict."[17] Still, dynamic forces for change, such as Islamic fundamentalism and nuclear proliferation, continue to develop largely outside both superpowers' control.

This international fluidity and the declining relative power of the super-powers, as well as their inability to cooperate fully to promote stability, has helped make the 1980s a time of war, or rather, of wars. Several wars have occurred in recent years: between Iran and Iraq, the Lebanese Civil War (with Syrian, Israeli, and American involvement), the Soviet attempt to control Afghanistan, and the British-Argentine war over the Falkland/Malvinas Islands. No war of the 1980s has fully involved a major ally or "proxy" of one of the superpowers, such as Cuba for the Soviet Union or Pakistan for the United States. However, at least nine (so far sharply limited) superpower proxy wars have flared up since 1945, six involving the United States and three the Soviet Union and there is no certainty another such proxy war will not occur. Soviet military actions in Afghanistan sometimes have spilled over into Pakistan, while American-backed operations in Nicaragua may involve Honduras or Costa Rica in a war.

Regardless of the risks, neither superpower is going to drop out and let the other try to be the main "manager" of international affairs. Both have shown, despite great embarrassment and troubles stemming from their international involvement, that they are determined to remain key actors on the world scene.

THE NATURE OF THE SOVIET-AMERICAN RELATIONSHIP

A Limited Relationship

Fundamentally, the United States-Soviet relationship is a limited one, even a "non-relationship" to a large degree in comparison with many of America's other foreign ties. The United States has ties with many foreign countries. Some are generally friendly, e.g., Britain, while others are not, e.g., Libya. The distinctive feature of the United States-Soviet relationship is that it has so little content but is discussed with so much emotionalism and fear.

If we look at the various possible aspects or levels of Soviet-American relations, it becomes apparent that, although there is a great deal of talk in the West *about* them, there is very little *in* them. A leading American analyst lists seven "planes" or levels of the Soviet-American relationship: (1) strategic military competition, (2) conventional military competition, (3) political competition, (4) economic competition and trade, (5) ideological conflict, (6) cultural relations, and (7) functional cooperation, e.g., joint projects.[18]

Not much interaction occurs in any of these areas. Even in the military sphere, the superpowers do not intend actual war (for that would involve their mutual destruction) but instead are trying to maintain relatively equal prestige. Some of the conventional parts of the Soviet military machine exist for possible use against revolution in Eastern Europe, while American military power is much more likely to be used in the Third World than against the Soviet Union.

The picture is similar in other areas of interaction. The political relationship is more posturing than substantive negotiating; the economic sphere involves little more than trade in grain and "high tech"; the "ideological conflict" is made up heavily of propaganda no one reads; cultural relations until recently involved only a few big-name groups and fewer than a hundred scholars of each country per year staying any length of time; and functional cooperation has been moribund for a decade. A quick look at United States-Soviet trade in 1986 shows that the United States imported only $601 million worth of Soviet goods, and the Soviet Union only $1.2 billion worth from the United States. This is very low compared to United States-Japanese trade. In short, the Soviet-American relationship still is quite limited in interchange, content, and contact.

Realistically, however, even full-scale relationships do not insure peace. And there is no reason to think that a small-scale relationship by *itself* brings war closer.

Some of the friction between the two superpowers is generated by individuals on both sides who deliberately create tensions for their own purposes. In so doing they make the rivalry appear both more dangerous and more important than it is. And some of the seeming danger in United States-Soviet relations is caused by words and actions of both enemies and allies of the two superpowers, e.g., Syria and Israel. Such actions force the superpowers to support their allies and result in an appearance of more serious United States-Soviet conflict than in fact exists.

Why should anyone expect the USSR and the United States to get along in the relatively friendly way the United States gets along with, say, its old ally Britain, or even in the sometimes difficult but mannerly way it relates to France? The senior American scholar-diplomat of the relationship puts it this way:

All in all ... the Soviet regime never was, and is not today, one with which the United States could expect to have anything other than a complex and often difficult relationship. It is a regime marked by a relatively high sense of insecurity. It has a tendency to overdo in the cultivation of military strength. It is unduly sensitive to the slightest influence or involvement of outside powers in regions just beyond its lengthy borders. It has a neurotic passion for secrecy and, as a product of that passion, a positive obsession with espionage, both offensive and defensive—an obsession that has interfered with its relations with the West, and has even damaged the regime's own interests, more often and more seriously, than the regime has until lately brought itself to recognize.[19]

We will deal later with the many ways in which the two countries' normal ways of thinking and acting grate on their relationship, always tending to push them apart. Keep in mind though that, just as the Soviet Union frustrates, annoys, and repels many Americans, so the normal functioning of the United States is quite a nuisance and sometimes a threat to the Soviet government and the elites that support it. The United States is, compared with the USSR, rather volatile and changeable. Now one group and philosophy seems dominant in the government and then another. At times the Soviet Union seems not to be a special target of Americans and at other times it is seen as an enemy. The United States never seems to settle down to one general opinion of, and policy toward, the USSR. As a result, the Soviets never know what approach will "work" in improving relations or whether it is worthwhile trying any approach at all.

Yet this volatility or changeability in the United States-Soviet relationship operates within real limits. The cold war never produced a superpower war. None of the wars of the early 1980s produced a superpower confrontation. And in no area are the two countries in total or stark opposition.[20] A sort of unpleasant continuity has persisted as the norm in the superpowers' relationship. What is at issue is not how to avoid having a difficult relationship but how to avoid one that is extremely costly and possibly destabilizing and destructive to both states and to the world.

Asymmetry

The American and Soviet societies are so different from each other that they are asymmetrical or lacking a common measure. The concept of asymmetry seems to apply to any United States-Soviet comparison that is carried deeply enough—weapons systems, defense thinking, political elites, social stratification, bureaucratic behavior, mass values, etc.

> At its root, the rivalry between the United States and the Soviet Union is more than the sum of its parts. It is more than simply an ideological difference..., more than competition between great powers. The two societies are fundamentally different. The one is peasant-based; it is still rural..., although it has strong industrial bases...; it has a long history of authoritarian rule and a complicated mixture of admiration and disdain for Western culture; and it is based on a tradition of collectivist values powerfully reinforced by its official Marxism-Leninism. The other society is urban and has moved beyond the traditional structures of industrialism; its frontier experience has left an indelible imprint of individualism; its centers of economic and political power are pluralist. Such complicated asymmetries provide a rich breeding ground for misperception and require the modest restraint in policy that genuine humility dictates in the face of imperfect understanding.[21]

The two countries, although they are both industrial and military giants and have outward similarities such as mass urbanization and schooling and ethnic and racial tensions are nonetheless fundamentally different in sociological and cultural bases and politics. A difficult relationship is unavoidable.

This asymmetry exists in other ways as well. "The Soviets and the Americans confront each other at different stages of their international history and are out of phase with each other." The USSR is still a growing power new to parity with its main rival, while the United States is weaker than it once was and has a somewhat jaded attitude toward world politics. Their international goals are also different—the United States strives for stability and the Soviet Union for fluidity (outside of its own sphere).[22] Even the advent of the Reagan and Gorbachev administrations has not changed these fundamental differences.

This deep conflict in goals need not produce unyielding conflict, much less war. Asymmetry means only that problems, disagreements, and difficulties are inherent in the Soviet-American relationship and that the relationship will be a limited one. A former presidential adviser says that, although for decades the United States-Soviet relationship will be one of "not entirely peaceful coexistence," "the United States is no longer the number one enemy of the Soviet Union.... The United States ... remains the number one rival...." This is matched by the "parallel, gradual American redefinition of the Soviet Union from America's principal enemy to America's principal rival."[23]

The idea of Soviet-American relations as a conflictful but not necessarily deadly rivalry is increasingly reflected in American academic thinking.[e] The superpowers are even seen, from the perspective of the arms race or of the problems of late industrial society, as in a common predicament. There are thinking people on both sides who are asking, in effect, where is the profit in being a "superpower" if this status is pushing one's society and economy backwards?[f] Clearly, the United States must find a foreign policy for dealing with the Soviet Union that prevents the communist ideology from spreading further and also avoids self-impoverishment. And the Soviet Union, too, must find a way to relate to the United States without depleting resources needed for its economic revitalization.

HISTORICAL PERSPECTIVE

Conflict and Non-Conflict

To accurately assess the potential for an improved relationship between the United States and the Soviet Union, it is necessary to view the relationship from

---

[e] Note book titles such as *The Rivals* by Adam Ulam and *Soviet-American Rivalry* by Thomas B. Larson as well as *Neither Cold War nor Detente?* edited by Richard A. Melanson.

[f] Note, for example, the article by W. K. H. Panofsky, "The Mutual-Hostage Relationship between the United States and Russia," *Foreign Affairs* (October 1973), 109–118; and the essay by the Nobel laureate Andrei Sakharov, "Progress, Coexistence and Intellectual Freedom."

a historical perspective—to look underneath and beyond its present shape and dynamics. For example, have the two countries had a long-term conflict of historic dimensions that has created bad blood between them? Does each feel the other owes it something material or visible, such as territory or people? Are there ongoing elements of confrontation and conflict in their relationship that seem aimed at mutual injury or total distruction? If so, the prospects for improvement are bleak, at least in the short term. However, if we look at the record, we cannot automatically consign the United States-Soviet relationship to one of long-standing conflict. There have been no territorial disputes such as those between China and the Soviet Union or between Hungary and Rumania. The superpowers do not covet the same natural resources. Neither has lost a part of its population to the other. None of these problems, so common in the history of international politics, exists between them. There have been no border shooting incidents, such as those between Vietnam and China. In fact, although the appearance of major conflict between the two superpowers continues to exist, a fundamental feature of the Soviet-American relationship is the lack of war or even violent clashes between the two powers. It is unfortunate and surprising that the significance of this fact is so often unrecognized.

If Americans have had no major confrontations with the Soviet Union, why does the mood of conflict persist? One reason may be the relative absence of long-term opponents or rivals in American history. The Europeans, in contrast, have a higher tolerance for conflict. They are accustomed to wars and clashes with their neighbors, in some cases centuries-old hostilities, such as those between Greece and Turkey. Europeans have a different historical consciousness from Americans since they have long faced serious opponents.[g] In addition, "Americans often show a greater and less-controlled fear ... of communism than do people who have lived more closely under its shadow."[24]

Some observers of the international scene say war has been avoided only because a nuclear war would have destroyed both nations. But this assertion displays more cynicism than reason. A nuclear exchange involving the survival—perhaps complete survival—of one of the contenders was once possible. The United States could have attacked the USSR without suffering nuclear retaliation before 1948 or 1949 and perhaps even later. Yet it did not do so. And the Soviet Union could have destroyed the United States if it had been bent on it. Instead, both nations showed restraint. It is often forgotten that strong intent, if it exists, will find a way. The fact that each of the two militaries has had plans for a nuclear attack on the other proves only that times have been very tense. All militaries must make contingency plans for the worst.

Clearly, whatever feelings of dislike, fear, and hostility may have existed between the two countries, those feelings were not of the order of that blind hatred that leads to war. Only once, during the Cuban Missile Crisis of 1962,

---

[g] The difference between the Americans and the West Europeans over the Soviet pipeline issue in 1982 and 1983 can be seen partly in this light.

did it seem that a war between them might be imminent.[h] But there seems to have been little corresponding fear of war in the Soviet Union at the time, according to a Soviet defector.[25] With hindsight, that useful aid to scholarship, we see that in other crises between the two superpowers one or both avoided exacerbating the situation.

More attention could be paid to conscious crisis reduction or limitation by the United States and the USSR since World War II.[26] Perhaps too much has been written emphasizing the intractability or deterioration of Soviet-American differences. True, crises seemingly threatening war between the two superpowers did occur, but they were reduced before escalation to military action. Instead, proxies or allies of the principals have had all the bad luck. For example, the United States did nothing to oppose the Soviet Union's invasion of Hungary in 1956 and the Soviet Union did nothing to prevent the United States from fighting in Vietnam, although it did supply North Vietnam. More recently the United States did not make the Soviets pay a high price in Afghanistan, and in 1982 the USSR did not oppose the actions of Israel in Lebanon or immediately get in the way of American attempts to manage the crisis there.[i] Obviously, there is a curious sort of give-and-take in the United States-Soviet relationship even in its worst moments.

Thus we must conclude that the two countries' difficulty in getting along is due less to irreconcilable goals and nonnegotiable demands than to resentment related to events during and after World War II, and the profound differences in the cultures, political attitudes, and political systems of the two peoples. The USSR and the United States are not enemies in a totalistic sense, but rather rivals for power and influence in an increasingly fluid world political arena. The roots of this strong rivalry are diverse. Aside from simple fear or unacceptance of difference, there is concern in each country that the other will cut it off from the outside world or from its allies and material needs there. This relates to a feeling of vulnerability. For the Soviet Union this is especially true in the East European buffer zone and for the United States in the Persian Gulf oil region and in Central America and the Caribbean. When persons or groups with strong feelings on these issues get into the political limelight, the Soviet-American relationship can seem more one of enemies than of rivals, especially if a move is begun to push back one or the other physically or actually reduce its power or influence. The Reagan administration has made moves of this sort in Afghanistan and Angola by aiding indigenous guerilla movements.

The appropriate historical parallel for this rivalry is perhaps less that of deep, almost irreconcilable differences between hostile neighbors such as those between Poland and Russia and between France and Germany, but rather that of long-term antagonisms between distant powers whose expansionism occur-

---

[h] The Soviets call it the Caribbean Crisis.

[i] By 1983 the USSR did support Syria's objections to the United States plan for Lebanon and put its own anti-aircraft units into Lebanon, but it still did not threaten offensive military action.

red without much reference to each other and eventually brought them into conflict. The historic rivalries between Rome and Persia or between the Christian states and Islam are examples.

The United States and the Soviet Union have gotten along, although with an antagonistic relationship, for at least forty years. This in itself suggests they can continue to coexist on the basis of some sort of tacit acceptance of each other that might eventually grow into a better, fuller relationship.

Bases for Agreement

There are real bases for building an improved relationship. In the first place, the foreign policy establishments of both sides have some of the same priorities—remaining superpowers and avoiding a general war. Avoiding a general war means superpower politics must be both restrained and yet effective enough to prevent the other state from becoming dominant. Because of the fear the two superpowers have of a nuclear war between them—a war that would destroy them both—they have engaged in a sort of tacit collusion to prevent general war. This has meant each has occasionally "sold out" forces loyal to it in order to maintain an upper-level stability for itself. For example, the United States has never intervened significantly on the side of East European rebellions against Soviet power and the Soviet Union did not intervene militarily or break relations with the United States when it blockaded Haiphong Harbor in Vietnam and when, reportedly, American bombs killed Soviet seamen.[27]

Avoiding a general war is complicated by the natural tendency of both sides to prevent the other from becoming superior and thus being able to dictate terms. A leading scholar referred to this problem in the 1950s as that of the "two perils" and stated the necessity "to avert the one without backing into the other."[28] Besides the general interest in survival, avoiding war, and keeping their conflicts within bounds, both powers have other common interests—discouraging nuclear proliferation and preventing local wars from becoming global ones. By now they may even have a common interest in opposing terrorism.

And they sometimes take similar conservative positions. In the negotiations producing the new international treaty on the law of the sea, both successfully argued for a limit on the width of territorial waters since both have large navies with which they occasionally influence other states. They tend to take other common positions to resist Third World desires. They also both limit and perhaps manipulate their allies and clients to a degree. The USSR has not given its East European associates ("satellites," in cold war language) complete or modern military systems. It has left important gaps in their military capabilities which only it can fill—air transport and nuclear weapons, for example. Similarly, the United States has kept South Korea from having enough gasoline to think of launching its own war against North Korea. Even Israel has been denied certain military items, at least for a time. Neither superpower, in short, has fought the cold war wholeheartedly or helped its clients fully. Both could even be said to be maintaining the division of Germany. A united Germany could be the major power of Central and Eastern Europe. A divided Germany magnifies the power of the superpowers, particularly in Western Europe for the United States and in Eastern Europe for the Soviet Union.

We can now consider a list of those factors held in common by the two superpowers:

1. no direct war has taken place between them;
2. they have no mutual territorial claims;
3. both peoples have many positive images of each other;
4. both peoples share the belief that problems can be solved through reason and science;
5. both are mistrusted by many states;
6. both face common problems of industrial societies; and
7. the power of both, though growing militarily, is declining vis-à-vis their allies and enemies.[29]

In essence, the two superpowers are somewhat similar urban industrial societies. It is in their political systems that their great differences lie. This difference and the fluidity of today's world make the two rivals.

But, despite their rivalry and its likely continuation for a long time, the two powers have actually taken a number of concrete and meaningful steps to reduce the intensity, content, and danger of their competition over the past quarter century. These formal steps include agreements that (1) limited strategic nuclear weapons (never ratified but observed in the main); (2) lessened the risk of accidental nuclear war (e.g., the "hot line" agreement); (3) fostered cooperation in functional areas like the environment; and (4) broadened cultural exchanges.[30]

The two countries had about 110 agreements in effect during the 1970s. Besides the major strategic ones such as SALT I and II, they have had functional agreements "on the environment; in medical science and public health; and on space, science and technology, agriculture, oceanography, energy, transportation, atomic energy, artificial heart research, and housing and other construction."[31] Significantly, the two navies concluded a maneuvering agreement in order to avoid collisions while carrying on close surveillance of each other's activities.[j] The superpowers also have concluded specialized agreements against certain deployments of nuclear weaponry, notably on the sea bed and in outer space.

This large number of agreements clearly shows that the United States and the USSR have been able to overcome some of the antagonism caused by their rivalry. Ideological and other political differences are not an absolute obstacle

---

[j] It prohibits, among other things, simulated attacks.

to reducing tensions and establishing the potential for a better relationship. The Soviet Union has never had trouble in dealing realistically with opponents. In 1941 it concluded a neutrality treaty with militarist Japan which held for most of the war, thus sparing the USSR a second front and allowing it to move its Siberian troops to the defense of Moscow. Its 1939 treaty with Nazi Germany (which Germany violated) gave it part of Poland and other territory, and influence in Eastern Europe. The United States, also, despite its leaders' verbal attacks on communism, has often put aside its ideological objections to the Soviet system in the interest of cooperation.

Cooperative Competition

In addition to actual agreements, there is another connection between the superpowers—tacit, unintended, or covert mutual aid. It might even be called "adversarial symbiosis."[k] One example of this pattern of mutual support is the cooperative competition between the two militaries. "The military establishments in the United States and the Soviet Union are no doubt each other's best allies." [32] Each side feeds upon the strong statements and new weapons systems of the other. Copying is fundamental to weapons acquisitions of both sides. This has been a part of great power rivalry in the past, e.g., the British-German battleship-building competition before World War I. "The military-industrial establishment on both sides cites the research and procurement of the other to justify its own demands for larger budgets and allocations." Soviet and American counterpart groups may be, in effect, bureaucratic allies and pacers of each other. More than one observer has deplored the possible "Sovietization" of American foreign policy.[33] An amusing example of cultural copying is the making of an "anti-Rambo" film in the USSR.

Nikita Khrushchev, when he ruled the Soviet Union, talked about this problem with President Eisenhower. Both leaders agreed they were reluctantly being forced to allocate more funds than they preferred to weapons programs because of their respective militaries' mutual fears for national security.[34]

Good examples of this sort of adversarial alliance are the development by the United States of MIRVs (multiple independently targeted re-entry vehicles or multi-bomb missile projectiles). The Soviets followed with them as soon as they could and eventually even developed a medium-range mobile missile that is a MIRV, the SS-20. A retired Soviet colonel has said to this author, "You are making a terrible mistake in deploying cruise missiles. We will build them, too. They won't be as good, but we'll make more of them! Where will you be then?"

Sociopsychological-Cultural Context

A variety of cultural and emotional factors affecting the Soviet-American competition are associated with the origins of the cold war. Americans were

---

[k] Symbiosis—"Association of two different organisms ... which contribute to each other's support." *The Shorter Oxford English Dictionary.*

shocked and angered to find themselves facing a new opponent only a few years after fighting a major war. They had thought victory would bring democracy, not Soviet domination, to Eastern Europe. Similarly, the Soviet leaders, in all probability, had assumed that the United States would withdraw to the Western Hemisphere after World War II. Roosevelt had said as much to Stalin at Yalta in early 1945. The Soviets also thought United States aid to them would continue. Both powers now found that the postwar period was not to go the way they had anticipated. This produced a base of frustration, anger, and puzzlement in the relationship. The cold war that followed was almost unavoidable.

In addition, both societies did not realize some of the wartime hopes of their inhabitants. Some Soviet citizens thought Stalin and the political apparatus would ease up on them since they had fought so gallantly (for Mother Russia, to be sure, not communism) and because the leadership had stressed nationalist, not Marxist, themes during the war to get support. They were rudely disappointed, however. Stalinist inflexibility and harshness continued. In the United States, World War II brought "staggering social and political upheavals." After 1945 "small-town America was disappearing.... For many Americans the life of the farm, the close family, and the rooted community were over. America was reaching for a new identity."[35] Although postwar prosperity cushioned this process, it could not stop it nor prevent its societal effects. The unexpected addition of a major foreign competitor increased its political impact. Small-town America was now faced with a Muscovite-Marxist state, an antagonist much harder to get rid of than the American grizzly bear or Comanche warriors. The cold war became for some a way of not dealing with the unwanted problems of a new kind of America.

This unsettled American domestic sociopsychological context has made the relationship with the Soviet Union subject to sharp swings or disturbances. It gets tangled up in the process of American efforts to find stability in the midst of the turbulence of post-industrial society.[1] Some of the pressures of post-industrial America were vented into the cold war and against the Soviet Union. Fending off the USSR gives some Americans something to do other than resolving domestic issues, both those of long standing such as racism and those caused by post-industrial life—increased leisure, drug addiction, unemployment, etc. Similarly for some of the Soviet leaders, the rivalry with the United States takes up energies and justifies the superior position and extra benefits of the "new class" that governs the country, especially those of its members who are in heavy industry, weapons development, and the military itself.

The differences between the two countries' elites still contribute to the intensity of the antagonism. American corporation executives, bankers, and

---

[1] Post-industrial society is a way of life deriving from an economy in which the service sector has a bigger share than manufacturing, resulting in the growth of nonmanual work and science and technology.

small-town politicians start with a very different set of premises and experiences from those of the engineering-trained Communist party bureaucrats who define Soviet interests. Accordingly, "some monumental misunderstandings about one another were bound to occur."[36]

Another cause of the emotionalism of the competition was the realization that the Soviet Union stands in the way of what former Secretary of State Vance calls the "pervasive fallacy that America could have the power to order the world just the way we want it to be."[37] Americans tend to be an idealistic people, and many of them feel that "The American Way" could be introduced around the world or that American aims are benign.

A leading Soviet Americanist has commented rather starkly on a fundamental psychological mechanism of the Soviet-American rivalry. He claims, with some truth, that the United States has lost its former security from attack and, therefore, has a "feeling of insecurity," and accordingly acts with "illusions, maybe even fantasies" to try to regain security. But, he says, "You can never regain [your] former security. . . . Whatever you do, we will catch up . . . because we are not going to talk to America as if we were a second-rate country. . . . Only on the basis of equality are we prepared to talk with the United States."[38] This is a common theme in serious talks with loyal Soviets. The author remembers a Russian worker telling him in a matter-of-fact way, "Next time you won't be able to hide behind that ocean." This "position of total vulnerability . . . creates an unprecedented trauma in American public life and a shocked response to the unaccustomed reality of American exposure to danger from abroad."[39]

The American people are troubled by this vulnerability. Their entire history has been one of relative security from foreign attack and invasion. To know one's entire people and socioeconomic system is open to serious destruction is still a new and disquieting idea with which many Americans have not yet come to terms.

The Nature of the Players. Soviet-American cultural and political differences created real friction and definite resentments even during World War II when the two countries shared a common cause. Without that shared purpose, their fundamental differences were bound to cause much greater friction. A thoughtful and experienced scholar of Russia observes:

> It is the very nature of their general approach to foreign policy that makes it so hard for the United States and the Soviet Union to carry on a meaningful diplomatic dialogue, let alone solve some of their outstanding differences. On the Soviet side, the obsessive secrecy in which decision-making is veiled and the camouflage thrown over their real hopes and fears, and, on the U.S. side, the excessive volatility of American foreign policy and the diffusion of responsibility for its conduct, combine to undermine that mutual credibility which is a basic condition of fruitful negotiations.[40]

The USSR does not fear the United States only because the United States is powerful and opposed to it but also because the United States is unconsciously but naturally very dynamic. The USSR cannot compete in a friendly way with the United States without changing not only its politics but its culture as well—an impossibility. The two cultures are so different that the two peoples—Russians and Americans—are bound to be in some opposition to one another. They are too different fundamentally to compete within the same set of rules. At the least, the cultural differences prompt some suspicions of each other.

Many serious analysts of Soviet foreign policy consider the USSR to be a cautious power that has a strong aversion to taking risks. As a German observer puts it, "Moscow is no friend of hasty developments and the risks they entail. Its aim is to become the world's paramount power—in the long term." An Israeli scholar puts it this way:

> Soviet leaders act according to the proverb: "If you don't know the ford, don't step into the river." They do not plunge into contests blindly; they rarely gamble, unless they feel the odds are overwhelmingly in their favor.

An American writer notes: "The Leninist state thrives on conflict and confrontation, but real conflict would endanger the very comfortable existence of the ruling elite. Peaceful coexistence is easier, pleasanter and more profitable."[41]

The United States, on the other hand, is less predictable. It will do unpredictable things in foreign affairs—whatever the administration. The Vietnam War was a product of a Democratic administration, the invasion-liberation of Grenada was carried out by a Republican administration. Unpredictability has even been used as an instrument of foreign policy by United States governments. Former Secretary of State Henry Kissinger shrewdly used to tell foreign politicians he did not know what President Nixon would do if agreements were not reached. An American colonel sympathizes, in a way, with Soviet problems of trying to assess a United States government's actual position on an issue. "Predicting U.S. *intentions* must be . . . bothersome, partly because the Soviet inner circle has seen American strategists 'blunder' into wars that (from their perch, at least) made little practical sense."[42]

No two players who are so different—one secretive, cautious, and plodding; the other willing to take risks and act unpredictably—can get along easily or well. The reasons for their disparate natures are to be found in their cultures and domestic politics and societal situations, topics examined in Chapter 8.

The Nature of the Contest.   "Everybody recognizes that this is fundamentally a competitive relationship."[43] But, as has been pointed out, the United States-Soviet contest is not one of deep-seated hatred and non-negotiable issues. Each threatens the existence of the other only potentially. There is plenty of "safe space" between them. For example, they face each other in a massive array of military force only in Central Europe, but they both know an aggressive move there would lead to total war. They also know that they have faced each other in that arena without a war for over thirty years—a sure sign their conflict is manageable and can be reduced. In short, the two are not up against each other in any "close-in" combat. They themselves oppose each other at a distance, although allies of both are in situations of intense animosity and even military operations, e.g., North and South Korea and Syria and Israel. Nevertheless, despite the long-range nature of the struggle, the level of charge and counter-charge is so high that it envelops the rivalry like a cloud, allowing little of its actual content to be visible.

Although noisy and showy posturing is often about all there is to the Soviet-American relationship, this phenomenon often intensifies and sometimes becomes so threatening that people may fear a physical clash is imminent. Ironically, attempts to reduce the American conflict with the Soviet Union increase the noise level and perhaps even the competition. Arms control, for example, is often a competitive, and not a cooperative venture. Similarly, although establishing a relationship of greater content, e.g., more trade, with the Soviet Union may eventually bring us closer to a better relationship, it will not do so in the short run as both systems will remain as they are internally. However, additional contacts hold potential benefits. A relationship of greater communication and content makes it easier to resolve conflicts lower on the scale of threat and violence than would be possible in a situation of "nonre-lationship" between the two states.

The Soviet-American relationship is a dynamic process. Whenever one major issue is settled or recedes into the background, another one crops up. Why does this happen? There are a number of reasons. For example, Soviet aid to anti-American forces in the world and American aid and encouragement to anti-Soviet forces in Eastern Europe, Africa, and Afghanistan are always potential irritants, as are Soviet negative propaganda about American society and a combative, often anti-Soviet, media in the United States. If one or more anti-Soviet groups in American politics are quiescent, still another will rise up to affect American foreign policy toward the Soviet Union. Similarly, in the Soviet Union, either an internal opposition or one in Eastern Europe will periodically trigger Soviet repression, consistently opposed by the United States. In short, there is always a problem in this relationship. Periods of calm come again and again but do not last for long. When one side is able to make an agreement, the other is not politically capable of it. The two systems are usually out of phase.[44] The movement toward limited agreement in 1987–88 may not last.

The two contestants have varying advantages and disadvantages. Here, too, they are asymmetrical. The USSR's advantages in the competition include: staying power and a willingness to wait; a lack of an open public opinion, thus leaving foreign policy to the policymakers; a large military with huge amounts of equipment; a willingness to accept a competitive world with enemies; a supposedly better central geographical position; and a relatively young (in historical terms) and experienced and rather unified political elite with a strong expansionist drive without effective competition from other elites. The advantages of the United States include: a lack of a strong general fear of war (since the population has had no experience of it); freely aligned allies with some power of their own; a political system with a high degree of natural popular support and lacking a significant revolutionary opposition; an economy, despite its difficulties, of great capabilities in high technology and a potential for massive output, if needed; high-quality military products, although their number is limited; and an experienced navy with strong capabilities.

Ironically, even if the two superpowers could reach agreement on substantive issues, some things would not change much. The world would remain a contentious place with some of the less-developed countries being very poorly off. (But some would not be able to get aid simply by siding with one or the other of the "giants.") It may be too late for the superpowers, even if their contention were minimized, to alter the nature of world politics, though they could lower its intensity and reduce its dangers. Not all that much would change in the economic sense, either. The two will never be big traders with each other (although the United States' agricultural and high-technology sectors would gain greatly). Reducing outlays for strategic weaponry would not reduce defense budgets much as the USSR would retain a large army and the United States would maintain a large (and increasingly expensive) navy to protect its access to Third World raw materials.[m] Agreement would still be important, however, since it would improve the international climate and reduce the danger of a general nuclear war. In the long run, agreement could also reduce regional wars if it resulted in a United States-Soviet treaty to reduce weapons exports to quarrelsome and unstable Third World countries and to cooperate in helping solve regional conflicts.

Some Unresolved Issues

The United States and the Soviet Union are not deadly enemies. They are more like mutually unwanted and puzzling competitors in an unstable environment who want both not to lose anything and to make gains against each other and yet prevent that environment (world politics) from falling apart. Many Soviets admire the United States in some ways and want to copy it. In this sense, America has already won to a degree, much to the consternation of the Russian nationalists in the Soviet elites. What, then, is actually at issue between the superpowers that involves them alone, independent of the fractious nature of world politics today?

Issues do exist, including American inability, perhaps refusal, to conclude a strategic arms limitation treaty with the Soviet Union and American unwillingness to accept the USSR as a long-term part of the international scene. Soviet

---

[m] The United States strategic arsenal is paid for by only a fourth or less of the defense budget.

officials are annoyed by the lack of help from the United States in creating through arms control and trade a climate in which the Soviet Union could devote less to weaponry and more to economic reform and other domestic needs. Is American policy beginning to change?

On the Soviet side, there has been little attempt to be cooperative in matters other than arms control and trade. For example: In 1973 the USSR did not reveal that it knew Egypt would attack Israel. "The Soviet Union knew the war was coming . . . but did nothing directly to alert the United States. Once the fighting began, Moscow . . . refused to cooperate with the United States . . . to stop the fighting."[45] As a result of this pattern of non-action, anti-Sovietism in the United States has received a big boost.

Will Gorbachev cooperate more with the United States?

Another source of animosity has its roots in the very different goals of the two nations. The United States must, to maintain its material standard of living, be able to trade throughout the world. This means it prefers political systems that do not exclude it, as well as an open world ocean. Thus, the United States tends to favor the status quo. The Soviet Union must be against the status quo for at least two reasons. In order for the Soviet Communist Party to claim it is the legitimate ruler of the Soviet Union, it must take positions against systems that can be called non-socialist or capitalist. By appearing anti-capitalist abroad, the entire Communist ideology can be safely spirited outside the USSR, "exported" to foreigners, most of whom do not want it (as the recurrent restiveness and dissent in Eastern Europe suggest). The second reason the Soviet Union is basically against the status quo (except in its own sphere) is that in order to achieve peace and quiet in its own sphere, it must limit competing modes of existence, particularly those that are attractively differentiated from it by private property, elections, and civil liberties.

This Soviet pattern of seeking security through expansion must clash with the American need to trade everywhere and to maintain the freedom of the seas and the status quo. In short, the most fundamental needs or "life urges" of the two countries as systems bring them into conflict. "The Soviets' deeply ingrained and fundamental opposition to the international status quo has many negative consequences for Soviet-American relations . . . it puts the Soviet Union and the United States on a collision course."[46] Perhaps General Secretary Gorbachev's relaxation of Soviet governance and his encouragement of some private enterprise will eventually make the USSR feel less threatened by the outside world and thereby reduce Soviet antagonism to it.

There are still other unresolved issues. The two sides have never agreed on the meaning of détente. The Soviet definition has been a limited or narrow one, centering on the reduction in the danger of nuclear war through arms control and increasing Soviet-American trade. In contrast, the American public has tended to think it meant a phasing out of the Soviet-American conflict as a whole. These differing definitions of détente led to the American introduction of "linkage" into the Soviet-American relationship. Improvement of relations was to be linked to specific changes in Soviet behavior, an idea the Soviets rejected out of hand, with great vehemence and even contempt. One Soviet commentator has defined "linkage" as "making the difficulties of all the main problems interfere with the resolution of each."[47] Yet to many Americans linkage seemed a natural outcome of any concessions the United States might make to the Soviet Union. Compromise, a key American value, was to become a central feature of the relationship. The Soviets have always disagreed, saying that the "ideological struggle" between "socialism" and "capitalism" would continue unaffected by détente. To Americans this promise of continued competition seemed to render the idea of détente meaningless if not worse—a "Trojan horse" idea covering up continued Soviet expansionism.

> With such opposed ideas on détente, it is understandable that the two countries have quite different agendas in dealing with each other. The Soviets want arms control agreements and trade without strings; they reject the United States belief that human rights or disputes over Soviet actions in other regions . . . are appropriate issues between major powers. Conversely, the United States has consistently taken the position that arms control and trade policy cannot be considered independently from the degree of Soviet internal repression and external aggression.[48]

These differences naturally extend to the most serious matter of war.

> The view that prevails in the West is that East-West war—even if waged in other countries and by proxy—should be prevented . . . The USSR, on the other hand, views only a direct East-West war and the attendant danger of world-wide nuclear escalation as worthy of prevention.[49]

A leading Soviet spokesman says no issue of the conflict is as important as "the main issue"—"prevention of nuclear war."[50] And, since they differ over the question of war and what is "defensive" or "offensive," there is no objective way for the superpowers to separate genuine security awareness from competitive actions. The Reagan administration's Strategic Defense Initiative is a case in point.

With such differences over fundamentals (see Table 1.1), it is no surprise that both states have come to have a series of grievances vis-à-vis each other. A Secretary of State gives an American listing:

1. continuing Soviet quest for military superiority;
2. unconstructive Soviet involvement, direct and indirect, in unstable areas of the third world [where the Soviets often try to play a] spoiling . . . role in areas of concern [to the United States, e.g., the Middle East];
3. the unrelenting effort to impose an alien Soviet model on nominally independent Soviet clients and allies [e.g., Poland]; and
4. stretching a series of treaties and agreements to the brink of violation and beyond.[51]

TABLE 1.1. UNITED STATES-SOVIET ISSUES

Fundamental or Long-term
Ideological differences
Differing roles of the individual in politics
Lack of clarity over relative capabilities
Lack of delineation of spheres of influence
Poor ability to deal with each other
Unacceptance of each other as each is
Consideration of "victory" over each other
Fundamental commitments, e.g., Western Europe for United States and Eastern Europe for USSR

Short-term
Particular military actions
Antagonistic public moods
Incidents
Propaganda
Specific claims by allies

The Soviets have similar concerns. The continuing American application of high technology to weapons threatens to render obsolete the weaponry the USSR has developed with great effort over the past two decades. American propagandistic and diplomatic approaches toward the still-not-stabilized systems of East Central Europe are also very troubling to the Soviets. Without them "attached" to her, the Soviet Union would be decidedly poorer and almost without allies, not to mention bereft of a buffer zone on her western border. In addition, the Soviets see themselves frozen out of American plans for a settlement in the Middle East and are particularly irked by the American attempt to draw China into an anti-Soviet alliance. American radio broadcasts to the USSR also concern the Soviet elite. No wonder that, given the worldwide involvement of the superpowers, there is recurrent friction between them in the many regions in which they operate.[52]

To understand how the superpowers arrived at this uncomfortable and tension-ridden situation, a brief look at the history of United States-Soviet relations is in order.

REFERENCES

1. *New York Times*, 30 March 1978. The author, David K. Shipler, was then assigned to Moscow.
2. Secretary of State George P. Shultz before the Senate Foreign Relations Committee, 15 June 1983, *New York Times*, 16 June 1983.
3. Naomi Bliven, *The New Yorker*, 1 July 1985, 96.

4. U.S. Senate, Committee on Foreign Relations, *The United States and the Soviet Union: Prospects for the Relationship*, a staff report (Washington, D.C.: Government Printing Office, 1983), 4.
5. Robert Dallek, *The American Style of Foreign Policy* (New York: Knopf, 1983), xix.
6. Georgi A. Arbatov and Willem Oltmans, *The Soviet Viewpoint* (New York: Dodd Mead, 1983), 2.
7. Dallek, *American Style of Foreign Policy*, 198.
8. Richard J. Barnet, a book review of David Calleo, *The Imperious Economy* (Cambridge: Harvard, 1982), *The New York Times Book Review*, 18 July 1982, 15.
9. Jean-Francois Briere, letter to *The New York Times*, 1 November 1982.
10. Henry Trofimenko at the University of Massachusetts, 10 December 1986. Author's notes.
11. Marshall D. Shulman, "Overview of U.S.-Soviet Relations," *Statement*, Department of State, 26 October 1977, 2.
12. Lawrence T. Caldwell, "The Future of Soviet-American Relations," in *Soviet-American Relations in the 1980s*, Lawrence T. Caldwell and William Diebold, Jr. (New York: McGraw-Hill, 1981), 26.
13. Spurgeon M. Keeny, Jr., and Wolfgang K. H. Panofsky, "MAD VERSUS NUTS: Can Doctrine or Weaponry Remedy the Mutual Hostage Relationship of the Superpowers?" *Foreign Affairs* 60 (Winter 1981/82): 293.
14. J. William Fulbright, "The Significance of SALT," *AEI Defense Review*, August 1978, 13. Quoted in Seth P. Tillman, *The United States and the Middle East* (Bloomington: Indiana University Press, 1982), 271. Senator Fulbright was Chairman of the Senate Foreign Relations Committee.
15. Valentin M. Berezhkov, "The U.S. and the USSR: What Future Ahead?" in *The United States and the Soviet Union: Confrontation or Cooperation in the 1980s?*, ed. Nish Jamgotch, Jr. (Charlotte, NC: The University Forum Council, 1981), 22. Berezhkov was an interpreter for Molotov and Stalin.
16. John Lewis Gaddis, "Containment: Its Past and Future," in *Neither Cold War nor Detente?*, ed. Richard A. Melanson (Charlottesville: University Press of Virginia, 1982), 20 and 23.
17. Richard Pipes, "Russia's Mission, America's Destiny," *Encounter* (October 1970): 8 and 10.
18. Marshall D. Shulman, "Toward a Western Philosophy of Coexistence," *Foreign Affairs* 52 (October 1973): 36–40.
19. George Kennan, "Reflections: Breaking the Spell," *The New Yorker*, 3 October 1983, 45.
20. Strobe Talbott, *The Russians and Reagan* (New York: Vintage, 1984), 34; and Norman Graebner, "The Soviet-American Conflict: A Strange Phenomenon," *The Virginia Quarterly Review* 60 (Fall 1984): 568.
21. Lawrence T. Caldwell and Alexander Dallin, "U.S. Policy toward the Soviet Union: Intractable Issues," in *Eagle Entangled: U.S. Foreign Policy in a Complex World*, ed. Kenneth A. Oye et al. (White Plains, NY: Longman, 1979), 215.
22. Seweryn Bialer, "The Psychology of U.S.-Soviet Relations," 1983 Gabriel Silver Memorial Lecture, Columbia University, 14 April 1983, 9.
23. Z. K. Brzezinski, speech in Ottawa, 7 September 1983. *New York Times*, 9 September 1983; and "U.S.-Soviet Relations" in *The Next Phase in Foreign Policy*, ed. Henry Owen (Washington, D.C.: Brookings, 1972); reprinted in *The Conduct of Soviet*

Foreign Policy, ed. Erik P. Hoffmann and Frederic J. Fleron, Jr. 2d ed. (New York: Aldine, 1980), 329.

24. David Riesman, *Abundance for What? And Other Essays* (Garden City, NY: Doubleday, 1964), 8.
25. Vladimir Sakharov with Umberto Tosi, *High Treason* (New York: Ballantine Books, 1981), 84.
26. See Bertil Nygren, *Cooperation between the Soviet Union and Three Western Great Powers, 1950–1975* (Stockholm: Swedish Institute of International Affairs).
27. For a list of "non-actions" by both powers, see John Spanier, *American Foreign Policy since World War II*, 7th ed. (New York: Praeger, 1977), 258–259.
28. Henry L. Roberts, *Russia and America: Dangers and Prospects* (New York: New American Library, 1956), 241.
29. Alvin Z. Rubinstein, *Soviet Foreign Policy since World War II* (Cambridge, MA: Winthrop, 1981), 264.
30. United Nations Association, *A Strategy for the '80s*, 27.
31. U.S. Department of State, "US-USSR Exchanges," *Gist*, September 1978.
32. Richard J. Barnet, *The Giants: Russia and America* (New York: Simon and Schuster, 1977), 106.
33. Caldwell and Dallin in Oye, *Eagle Entangled*, 223, citing Colin Gray, "The Urge to Compete," *World Politics*, January 1974; Edward L. Warner, "The Bureaucratic Politics of Weapons Procurement," in *Soviet Naval Policy*, ed. Michael MccGwire et al. (New York: Praeger, 1975); and see Daniel Patrick Moynihan, *Loyalties* (New York: Harcourt Brace Jovanovich, 1984).
34. N. S. Khrushchev, *Khrushchev Remembers: The Last Testament*, trans. and ed. Strobe Talbott (Boston: Little, Brown, 1974), 411–412.
35. Barnet, *The Giants*, 56.
36. Ibid., 14.
37. Cyrus R. Vance, speech at the Harvard commencement, 1980, *New York Times*, 6 June 1980.
38. Berezhkov, "The U.S. and the U.S.S.R.: What Future Ahead?" 20–21.
39. Bialer, *The Psychology of U.S.-Soviet Relations*, 36.
40. Adam Ulam, "U.S.-Soviet Relations: Unhappy Coexistence," *Foreign Affairs: America and the World* (1978), 567.
41. Dieter Cycon, "Capitalist System Crisis Is Untimely for the Kremlin," *Die Welt*, 24 February 1975, trans. in *The German Tribune*, 6 March 1975; Hannes Adomeit, *Soviet Risk Taking and Crisis Behavior* (London: Allen and Unwin, 1982), 54; and Robert Wesson, *The Aging of Communism* (New York: Praeger, 1981), 94.
42. John M. Collins and Elizabeth Ann Severns, "Essentials of Net Assessment," in *U.S.-Soviet Military Balance*, Report No. 80-168S, Congressional Research Service, July 1980, 23. There was no document stating a United States intention to intervene in Korea in 1950. The decision was made by President Truman.
43. Marshall Shulman, quoted in *The New York Times*, 3 April 1983.
44. For a discussion of this phenomenon in the history of the cold war, see Zbigniew K. Brzezinski, "How the Cold War Was Played," *Foreign Affairs* 51 (1972): 181–209.
45. Alvin Z. Rubinstein, "Soviet-American Relations," *Current History* 67 (October 1974): 146.
46. Bialer, "The Psychology of U.S.-Soviet Relations," 21.
47. *New York Times*, 30 March 1978.
48. U.S. Senate, Committee on Foreign Relations, *United States and the Soviet Union*, v.

49. Gerhard Wettig, "The Mix of Interests in East-West Relations," *Aussen Politik* (English ed.) 33 (Jan. 1982): 76.
50. Arbatov and Oltmans, *The Soviet Viewpoint*, 90.
51. Secretary of State Shultz before the Senate Foreign Relations Committee, 15 June 1983, *New York Times*, 16 June 1983.
52. For a discussion of "intractable" or fundamental long-term issues between the United States and the USSR, see Caldwell and Dallin, "U.S. Policy toward the Soviet Union: Intractable Issues," in *Eagle Entangled*, ed. Oye et al., 199–227, esp. 205–219.

SELECT BIBLIOGRAPHY

The American Committee on East-West Accord. *Détente or Debacle: Common Sense in U.S.-Soviet Relations*. New York: Norton, 1979.

Arbatov, Georgi A. and William Oltmans. *The Soviet Viewpoint*. New York: Dodd, Mead, 1983.

Barnet, Richard J. *The Giants: Russia and America*. New York: Simon and Schuster, 1977.

Brzezinski, Zbigniew K. *Game Plan: A Geostrategic Framework for the Conduct of the U.S.-Soviet Contest*. Boston: Atlantic Monthly, 1986.

Caldwell, Dan, ed. *Soviet International Behavior and U.S. Policy Options*. Lexington, MA: Lexington Books, 1985.

Caldwell, Lawrence T. and William Diebold, Jr. *Soviet-American Relations in the 1980s: Superpower Politics and East-West Trade*. New York: McGraw-Hill, 1981.

Garthoff, Raymond L. *Détente and Confrontation: American-Soviet Relations from Nixon to Reagan*. Washington, D.C.: Brookings, 1985.

George, Alexander L. *Managing U.S.-Soviet Rivalry: Problems of Crisis Prevention*. Boulder, CO: Westview, 1983.

Horelick, Arnold L. *U.S.-Soviet Relations: The Next Phase*. Ithaca, NY: Cornell University Press, 1986.

Larson, Thomas B. *Soviet-American Rivalry*. New York: Norton, 1978.

Melanson, Richard A., ed. *Neither Cold War nor Détente?* Charlottesville: University Press of Virginia, 1982.

Nye, Joseph S., Jr., ed. *The Making of America's Soviet Policy*. New Haven, CT: Yale University Press, 1984.

Pipes, Richard. *U.S.-Soviet Relations in the Era of Detente*. Boulder, CO: Westview, 1981.

Sivachev, Nikolai V. and Nikolai N. Yakovlev. *Russia and the United States: U.S.-Soviet Relations from the Soviet Point of View*. Chicago: University of Chicago Press, 1979.

White, Ralph K. *Fearful Warriors: A Psychological Profile of U.S.-Soviet Relations*. New York: The Free Press, 1984.

Chapter 2

The American-Russian Relationship in History

The United States had only an intermittent involvement in the main currents of great power politics until 1941 and its entry into the Second World War. And, although Russia had been a regional power since the 1600s and a fellow player of the Western European game of power politics since at least the late 1700s, it was not one of the preeminent actors in international affairs until 1943. It was then clear Germany was going to lose the war and that the USSR might be able to dismantle Germany as she had Poland and other states earlier. It was only during the Second World War (1939–1945 in Europe) that the United States and the Soviet Union came into highly significant and serious contact. As we know, the result of that contact was the cold war. But this was not the first time contact between the two countries led to conflict.

In the nineteenth century, when Americans became conscious of the Russian system of exiling dissidents to Siberia, and again in the early twentieth century when the Russian government fomented public attacks on Jews (the pogroms), the American reaction was negative. In the latter case, the United States government took retaliatory actions such as the imposition of economic sanctions. What the Carter administration (1977–1981) called the issue of human rights has long been an irritant in Russian-American relations.

There seems to be a pattern of contact-repulsion in this relationship—a pattern that cannot be blamed solely on actions of one side toward the other. Is it not common in human relationships, too, that getting to know another person cannot at times be carried beyond a certain point because of fundamental differences of outlook and action? Soviet spokesmen have often complained of American inconsistency and weakness in not sticking with agreements and of American failure to discourage anti-Soviet statements in the United States.

Americans have often demanded that the Soviet Union change its domestic political practices.

IMPERIAL RUSSIA AND THE UNITED STATES

Although there were those who predicted the rise of the United States and Russia to great power status, it was the mistakes of other powers that brought this about. Russia and America became "super" powers when they did partly because Nazi Germany, Japan, and their allies failed to evaluate correctly the difficulties inherent in a world war of conquest—a war in which the Soviet Union and the United States might be allied against them. Their risk could have been reduced if America had not been attacked, had been attacked more effectively, or if the axis powers had attacked Russia together—a strategy that occurred to the Japanese but apparently not to Hitler.

Those who predicted, as did the French aristocrat Alexis de Tocqueville in the 1830s, that America and Russia each "seems called by a secret design of Providence to hold in its hands one day the destiny of half the world," [1] were correct even though the pattern was not yet clear. For more than a hundred years, the United States and Russia did not relate to each other directly as major world powers but as component parts of the existing system of international relations. They dealt with each other as they thought necessary because of pressures on them from third parties such as Britain. Diplomatic relations between them were established in 1808–09 with each aiming to create a rival to Britain. Already we can see the beginnings of a pattern of Russian-American relations: They have been good only when both feel vulnerable to a third party—at first Britain, then Germany, and most recently China. For most of the time until 1941 and the Nazi attack on the USSR, the two countries generally pursued their foreign policies separately and in their own different regions of primary interest. (See Table 2.1.)

TABLE 2.1. SOME RUSSO-AMERICAN CONTACTS PRIOR TO 1917*

Year(s)	Nature of Contact
1781	Dana mission arrives in Russia
1808–1909	Diplomatic relations established
1824	First agreement (on trade and territorial disputes)
1832	Treaty (on trade and navigation)
1863	Visit of Russian fleets to United States (during American Civil War)
1867	Sale of Alaska to the United States
1904–1905	United States favors Japan in Russo-Japanese War
1911	United States abrogation of treaty of 1832
1914–1916	United States firms making weapons for Russia (World War One) and United States banks loaning money to Russian government

* By 1911 thirteen treaties had been concluded.

During the early twentieth century Russian-American relations were unstable and changeable, for a variety of reasons. Various writers emphasize the anti-Russian policies of leading American capitalists and the pressure from firms wanting greater economic concessions in Russia than the Tsarist government would allow. Others emphasize the widespread abhorrence in the United States of Tsarist practices against dissidents, especially the fomenting of violent acts against Jews. (Here Soviet writers, who are government employees, claim a great influence for Zionism in American politics.) In any case, even before Russia went Communist, American-Russian relations showed some rather definite shifts and left a heritage of suspicion on both sides of a relationship not firmly grounded in widespread continual contact or mutual understanding. Notably, the emigration from Russia to the United States was mostly of Jews, many of whom were fleeing persecution. No large population of Russian-Americans ever became established to serve as "interpreters" of Russian actions, which might have limited anti-Russian feeling in the United States.

THE COLLAPSE OF TSARISM TO WORLD WAR II

The fall of the Russian autocracy in early 1917[a] produced in the United States a general assumption that Euro-American liberal democracy would automatically follow in Russia. This view now looks naive but was a natural reflection both of the optimistic faith in progress then held by Americans in general and of the simplistic belief that World War I was the "war to end all wars" and would "make the world safe for democracy." But each nation, each culture, works out its future in terms of its own history, traditions, and possibilities. Russia had never known anything approximating Western conceptions of democracy while it was under the rule of the tsars, and other somewhat representative Russian political patterns had been completely quashed centuries previously. The Provisional Government of mid-1917 undercut its image by remaining mired in a lost and dislocating war, and the new, populist Soviets allowed the Bolsheviks, the "hard Communists," to use them as a cover for their coup against the government in November 1917 (the "October 'revolution'").[b]

It is no surprise that a victory of Russian radicals, which would serve German interests in a war that was still going on, was a profound shock to public opinion in the United States, as well as to other publics in the West. To be sure, there were those in the West who welcomed the Bolshevik assumption of state power as the beginning of a world socialist revolution. Many of these

---

[a] For a sense of the wide diversity and the changeability of American views of Soviet Russia over time, see two collections of writings: Peter G. Filene, ed., *American Views of Soviet Russia, 1917–1965* (Homewood IL: Dorsey Press, 1968); and Benson Lee Grayson, ed., *The American Image of Russia, 1917–1977* (New York: Ungar, 1978).

[b] In 1917 the old Julian calendar used by Russia was thirteen days behind the Gregorian calendar used by Western Europe.

would undergo a shock years later, when Stalin's ruthless aggrandizement of power rendered the term socialist inapplicable to the authoritarian Soviet Union.

In short, the Bolsheviks' violent destruction of a fledgling democracy in Russia created in America a confused mood of disheartenment, anger, and fear. Two cartoons of the period reflect the popular reactions. One cartoon of 1918 shows a man with a smoking rifle sitting on the Tsar's throne with the caption, "What's the Difference?" (between Tsarism and Bolshevism). Another cartoon reflects the fear of Marxist radicalism that has been with us, more or less, ever since. It shows a bearded figure in a cossack coat, holding a saber and with bloodied hands pushing open a door marked "civilization." [2]

The initial contacts in 1917–18 between the new Bolshevik government of Lenin and the Wilson administration in the United States (in office 1913–1921) were greatly affected by the politico-military context. The democratic Provisional Government had been overthrown; the Bolsheviks were nationalizing property and eliminating opposition with their new "soviet" government and security service;[c] and, most upsetting to the western allies, the Bolsheviks were soon negotiating with the Germans and trying to get out of the war. A Russian-German peace could only expose France to a strengthened German army before the American troops sent to Europe in mid-1917 had an effect.[d] Despite the tensions of the time, early Soviet-American discussions dealt with the possibilities of American aid, Soviet payment of the Tsarist war debts owed to Americans, and even the concept of President Wilson's peace program, the Fourteen Points.

This time of war proved too tense and violent for the establishment of a normal relationship. And the existence of an anti-capitalist ideology on the Bolshevik side plus a feeling on the American official side that the Bolsheviks were only a temporary force and possibly even German agents[e] did not give the early ties a favorable basis. It is not surprising that Wilson eventually succumbed to French pressure to intervene, though justified partly by his idealistic concern that Czech prisoners-of-war be able to leave Russia to fight for the allies.

Intervention

The Intervention has been an issue to this day. Originally, it was intended to prevent allied military supplies from falling into German hands. But the

---

[c] Since the many opponents of the Bolshevik takeover who were members of the Congress of Soviets walked out in protest, Lenin's small group of followers was able to appropriate the populistic term "soviet" for itself.

[d] Although the first elements of the American Expeditionary Force arrived in France in June 1917, the force was not engaged in a major way until May 1918, after the Bolshevik treaty with the Germans had freed more German troops for use in France.

[e] Lenin's return to Russia in 1917 had been facilitated by the Germans as part of an intelligence operation intended to get Russia out of the war. During World War One *Pravda* was printed by the German government.

interventionist forces—Americans, British, French, Japanese, and others—lent support to anti-Bolshevik groups. Once these groups were defeated by the Bolsheviks in the civil war, the Intervention ended (1920). Significantly, two Soviet writers, in a book cleared by the Soviet government, say that the American army in Russia was "not a very large force," totaling fewer than 20,000 soldiers, and that "it did not engage in any major battles with the Red Army." An army that suffers casualties only in the hundreds can hardly have been historically instrumental. This shows the United States made no serious attempt to bring down the new Bolshevik government. But the image of the United States as part of an anti-Russian force of conquest and oppression is utilized by the Soviet government even today when it suits its purposes.[f]

The Intervention achieved some successes for the West. Although it did not prevent the Bolsheviks from reconquering most of the Tsarist empire plus Outer Mongolia, it aided in achieving the independence of Poland, Finland, and, until 1940 and Soviet conquest, that of three republics on the Baltic Sea: Estonia, Latvia, and Lithuania. The Bolshevik government, like any new force in the world, expanded to its allowable limits.

The Intervention had other effects as well. It gave the Bolsheviks increased confidence as well as increased mistrust in the West and strengthened both the militaristic and the totalitarian tendencies of the movement. But large-scale revolution in Germany, so necessary for the fulfillment of the Marxist vision, did not occur. Marxism in power was "Russified" and not "Germanized." This great failure suggests why the Intervention is still an issue between the Soviet government and non-Soviets.

After the end of the Intervention, Soviet Russia[g] and the United States had an unusual relationship. There was no formal diplomatic recognition; an atmosphere of mutual suspicion existed, but nevertheless significant trade was going on. The lack of diplomatic relations did not mean there was no communication. The two governments either used third parties such as France as "message bearers" or they communicated through the press or press releases. It was "relations without relations." The American Relief Administration provided free food to the Soviet population. American food saved many lives in Russia during the famine of 1921–22. "Of all the capitalist countries, only America showed us major and real help," stated a Soviet official journal of the time.[3] Neither country then saw the other as its major foreign rival. The USSR warily watched Britain and the United States eyed Japan with concern.

Various offices were set up in the United States to facilitate trade, and several American private firms built plants and operated businesses, so-called "concessions," inside Russia or provided technical aid to Soviet government-

---

[f] It was brought up by a Soviet diplomat in a talk to American professors in June 1987.

[g] It became the USSR only in late 1922.

owned industry. Hundreds of American firms traded with Soviet Russia. It was then that the legendary Armand Hammer got his start in United States-Soviet trade. Soviet Russia was a large market since it was enlarging its industrial base and paid in gold. Objections to such trade within the United States government were weak and easily overridden by new business lobbies that promoted trade with Russia.[4] (Significantly, some American business interests today are just as willing to trade with the Soviet Union, disregarding moral or strategic objections to such trade.)

During the early 1920s domestic American government harassment of persons with left-leaning views did not affect the rapidly developing economic ties. To be sure, Americans were not the only foreigners involved in the Soviet economy during the 1920s. But American economic ties seem to have been favored by the Soviets, partly because they were then less likely than European connections to have anti-Soviet ideological content and effect. America was an important contributor to Soviet economic, and hence military, development. Stalin said, "We have never concealed that in the sphere of techniques we are the pupils of . . . first and foremost, the Americans."[5] Most of the American aid was profit-oriented, although some individual Americans did go to Russia to take part in what then looked like a humanistic transformation of mankind. (Indeed, some groups of Americans emigrated to Soviet Russia during this period and during the depression of the 1930s.) Possibly the book that most graphically conveys the developmental pressure then operative in Russia and the role of American technology in supporting it is John Scott's *Behind the Urals*. Scott was an American who worked on the construction of the then new iron and steel complex Magnitogorsk. He noted, among other things, in "an immense" steel mill a large American motor which moved ingots rapidly and "which had received the full benefit of several decades of the best electrical engineering experience in the United States."[6] He also pointed out that Magnitogorsk's ten million tons of steel "will make a great many tanks. . . ."

United States exports to the Soviet Union, mainly machinery and equipment, reached their peak in 1930 and 1931, at a value of between $104 million and 114 million. This "represented only 2 percent of total United States exports; yet Soviet imports from the United States formed a respectable 25 percent of total Soviet imports."[7] Clearly, the Soviet-American economic relationship of the 1920s and early 1930s was much more important to the USSR than it was to the United States. Ironically, the United States provided the USSR with some of the things it needed in order to play "catch up" with the West. The United States still plays this role. This important source of Soviet equipment and technology was tapped without benefit of diplomatic recognition and the formal niceties of international relations. Indeed, hardly any American diplomats of the time showed interest in the Soviet Union. The same avoidance was typical of the American academic community.[8] The United States did not recognize the Soviet Union until 1933 when Franklin Roosevelt's first administration came to office.

UNITED STATES RECOGNITION AND THE 1930s

The 1930s still affect the American-Soviet relationship. Isolationist America refused to take part in collective security against militaristic fascism in Germany, Italy, and Japan. Official Soviet writers have implied strongly that isolationism, or a rather low American profile in European matters, was not a natural outgrowth of American culture and experience but rather part of a conscious policy intended to allow the fascists to destroy the Soviet Union. America's isolationism, they say, "led the aggressors right up to the borders of the USSR." [9] However, since isolationism put the United States in jeopardy, the official Soviet view is more polemics than a reasoned, factually based position. Nevertheless, the United States can be criticized for not having been realistic about fascism and for not taking timely and effective defensive action in concert with fascism's main opponents—Britain, France, and the USSR.

In this dispute many Americans ask: Why did the Soviet Union sign a treaty with Nazi Germany in 1939 that freed that aggressor from a potential second front and enabled it to move more easily against Western Europe? The Soviets respond, with some apparent plausibility, that "our country could not remain indefinitely in the dangerous position of appealing for collective security without support from the Western powers." [10] But since the Soviet Union gained a good part of Poland, including most of the Ukraine not under Soviet rule, it is equally apparent that the Soviet Union acquired significant benefits from this treaty and kept itself out of World War II for almost two more years, partly by supplying the Nazi war machine with raw materials. The USSR did more than try to save itself; it consciously "went about removing every possible point of future friction" with Germany. It even turned over a Soviet naval base to Nazi Germany for use by its submarines. [11] In effect, then, both the United States and the Soviet Union failed to stand up to Hitler until he actually attacked the USSR and, later, declared war on the United States. It is difficult for people in both countries to face up to this fact.

The 1930s produced other irritants in the two countries' relations. The Soviet Union unsuccessfully invaded small Finland in 1939–40 (the Winter War) and it forcibly absorbed three independent and democratic states in 1940—Estonia, Latvia, and Lithuania. All four countries had supplied emigrants to the United States. These invasions triggered that American concern for the "underdog" and politically activated both immigrants in America and perennial anti-Communists. The USSR gained a buffer against a possible German attack (which did occur only a year later) but inevitably raised legitimate concern in the United States that it was an aggressor not very different from Nazi Germany. Chalking up such behavior as a normal aspect of European great-power politics was not realistic for most Americans in 1940. The great purges and executions of the mid-1930s that brought Stalin to absolute dominance of the Soviet system did not help the Soviet image in the

United States either. Soviet territorial conquests and domestic politics were costly to the image of the Soviet Union in American eyes, while American refusal (until 1941) to participate fully in great-power politics tended to give added ammunition to the ideological and self-protective anti-Americans in the USSR. The culmination of events of the 1920s and 1930s was that the component parts of Europe and its major relatives—America and Russia— broke up into four opposed units and allowed a massive bloodbath to take place. These four units were (1) Britain and France, (2) the United States, (3) the Soviet Union, and (4) Nazi Germany and Fascist Italy.

The American diplomatic recognition of the Soviet Union was bound to occur. Because of the wearing effect of the Great Depression, which began in 1929, and its massive unemployment and human misery, the value-based and ideological oppositions to recognition of the Soviet Union had lost their political force. The American people and their politicians were now interested mainly in improving the economy and getting people back to work. (A similar shift in emphasis in American foreign policy took place during the mid-1980s and for analogous reasons.)

For some years, several groups of Americans had favored recognition: businessmen desiring a market and profits; pro-Soviet "fellow-travelers" and Communists, whether openly so or not; very liberal Americans who felt the Soviet Union ought to be better treated; and "realists" who saw it as a stable state, notwithstanding its revolutionary verbiage. In the late 1920s delegations of American trade unionists and students visited the USSR. Some of them published reports on their visits that had some political effect. People who were to be important in the Roosevelt administration were members of some of these delegations. This nongovernmental foreign policy could not fail to have eventual effect in the pluralistic United States, particularly in a context of increasing support for United States-Soviet trade in business circles.[12] To this movement of opinion favoring recognition was added the implied promise of the new Democratic administration of Franklin D. Roosevelt that it would adopt a new and less hostile position toward the Soviet Union as part of its broad change of policies. It was "unnatural and abnormal" for two large and important countries not to have diplomatic relations. But it would have been better if recognition had arrived with "less exalted hopes and calculations as to its effects."[13]

Soviet goals in achieving American diplomatic recognition apparently were: (1) to eliminate the last significant suggestion that the Soviet Union was unacceptable to the international community of states, (2) to obtain additional trade and economic aid, and (3) to gain an additional significant international counter-weight to Germany and especially Japan. The Soviet Union was not at all ideologically averse to a new and better relationship with the West. As early as 1925 Stalin, soon to be the key figure in Soviet politics, noted that "a certain period of 'peaceful coexistence' had been established."[14] A leading Soviet official of the time stated that the maintenance of "friendly relations with nations that differ from us socioeconomically . . . does not alter our social and political nature."[15] Similar Soviet statements are made today.

Japan had been considered a problem by both the United States and the Soviet Union for some time. Certainly, both the United States and the USSR had a common interest in getting together to limit Japanese expansion.[16] For the United States "the effect, if not the design of this move was to redress appreciably the balance of power in Eastern Asia."[17] "The Soviet government proceeded from the assumption that Japanese militarism was a threat to both the USSR and the United States. Therefore it formed its policy counting on the real interest of the Americans in the Soviet Union as a factor in stabilizing the situation in the Far East."[18] But despite this common interest, no joint policy toward Japan resulted. Soviet assumptions of American rationality and realism were not matched on the American side, as is also still often the case.

Despite some mutuality of Soviet and American interests, the United States government could not become fully and consistently involved in international affairs at that time, and certainly not with the Soviet Union. Although again a third party had brought the United States and Russia closer, isolationism was still the watchword, and the Soviet Union still seemed a violent, even a criminal, power to some Americans. To the United States government, Russia did not seem as important a power as Germany, Japan, Britain, or France.

American-Soviet negotiations did get under way in November 1933, more than half a year after the Roosevelt administration came into office. Although they resulted in mutual formal diplomatic recognition on November 16, they did not settle all the outstanding issues clearly. Indeed, they could not. Only systemic change in one or the other country could have done that. As it was, the main irritants of the past were only papered over with diplomatic documents. The United States was still troubled by the outstanding Imperial Russian debts and Communist propaganda and revolutionary activity ("Communist subversion" as it was later called), while the Soviets were concerned by the damage done by the Intervention, the harboring of anti-Soviets, and the lack of American loans. The Soviet government, under American pressure, was willing to suggest publicly that the debt issue could be discussed after recognition and to pledge to restrain its organizations from committing anti-American acts and not to harbor anti-American groups.[19] This paper pledge did not affect Soviet intelligence operations inside the United States, and the Soviets did not get the aid they wanted until World War II.

Of their three main goals for obtaining American recognition, the most the Soviets got was further acceptance into the international community. But this was undercut by continued refusal of the United States to become a member of the League of Nations, a decision that left it outside of the limited system of collective security and helped render that system ultimately ineffectual against Axis aggression. But even if the United States had been added into the European equation along with the USSR, the outcome might have been the same: war. The desire to avoid a war was so general among the non-fascist governments that Hitler might still have been able to bully and threaten his way forward. Significantly, the Soviet Union did not aim at punishing aggressors but, like the United States, at staying out of war.[20]

THE COMING OF WAR

Most of the Soviet-American diplomatic activity after diplomatic recognition involved exchanges of notes concerning trade. Still, recognition did not raise trade above the level of 1930 when diplomatic relations did not exist.[21]

The Soviet Union, being much closer to Germany, did become more involved internationally, but still in a limited way. It joined the League of Nations in 1934 and signed treaties of mutual assistance with France and Czechoslovakia in 1935. The USSR adopted the Popular Front policy in 1935 and, through its Comintern or Communist International, ordered Communists everywhere to associate themselves with democratic forces. These activities added up to a Soviet image of anti-fascist opposition that was not matched by significant military preparations. On the contrary, the Soviet military officers corps was being decimated by the purges of 1935–1938. Still, this anti-fascist image made the USSR appear more active than the democracies and contributed to the adherence to Communism of some persons in the democratic countries. (A few of these individuals became operatives of the Soviet intelligence service. Their discovery led to near-hysteria in the West about "Communists in high places" after World War II.)

Although the Soviet image of anti-fascism was important to some in the United States, others saw the Soviet Union in this period as an ineffectual but expansionist power. The execution of most of the top military men of the Soviet Union in 1937 and Soviet signing of a nonaggression treaty with Nazi Germany in 1939 and a neutrality pact with Imperial Japan in 1941 could not help but have a negative effect on the Soviet image. The negative impression was strengthened by the Soviet Union's taking of Polish territory in league with Germany (1939), its attack on Finland (1939), and its incorporation of Estonia, Latvia, and Lithuania (1940).

Soviet writers imply that the United States wanted the weakening of the Axis, the Anglo-French coalition, *and* the USSR, and charge that the United States rejected the Soviet suggestion of a Pacific-area nonagression pact and also had some sort of active part in "channeling" Hitler's aggression "to the East, in the direction of the USSR."[22] They even go so far as to suggest that the pact between Hitler and Stalin, which doomed Poland, could have been avoided if the United States had agreed to "concrete decisions on mutual commitments to oppose possible aggression." This placing of blame for the Hitler-Stalin pact and for World War II on the Western democracies and the United States has also been voiced by some Western liberals who argue either that the democracies were excessively fastidious or rigid in not making an arrangement with the Soviet Union or even wanted to encourage a Nazi attack on it.[23]

This charge seems improbable. Stalin, absolutely dominant in the USSR, had been interested in a deal with Hitler for some time, possibly even since 1935, notwithstanding Soviet policy of an anti-fascist Popular Front and ostensible Soviet commitment to Marxist beliefs. "From the Soviet point of view . . . the Nazi-Soviet pact represented the optimal objective. . . . The Soviet Union could hardly have acted much differently in the summer of 1939."[24]

> Stalin was not seeking merely to gain time . . . there was near unanimity among the Western embassies in Moscow that Stalin had a higher regard for the Germans than for the other Western powers, and that he certainly trusted them more. The speech which Stalin delivered in March 1939 revealed these feelings directly. . . .[25]

"Though officially neutral as far as the war in the West was concerned, the Soviet Union had a pro-German tilt. . . ." German naval vessels were outfitted in the USSR; critical raw materials were supplied to Germany; and British ships were detained.[26]

Stalin was actively committed to a pact with Hitler, the only arrangement that could give him territory in East Central Europe and eliminate the danger to the Soviet system of competing and more attractive political systems. It suffices to add that Molotov, Stalin's lifetime close associate, called in the German ambassador in June 1940, after the forced British withdrawal from France at Dunkirk, to express "the Soviet Union's warmest congratulations on the Wehrmacht's brilliant success."[27]

This Soviet complicity in the destruction of the political arrangement established by international treaty after World War I, carried further by the Soviet attack on Finland, certainly did not improve Soviet-American relations. President Roosevelt, in a speech in early 1940, described the Soviet Union as a dictatorship which has "allied itself with another dictatorship and . . . invaded a neighbor so infinitesimally small that it could do no conceivable, possible harm to the Soviet Union"; he added that "American sympathy is 98 percent with the Finns."[28]

During the late 1930s the Roosevelt administration prepared for the coming war as best it could, in light of the intense opposition from both the Congress and the public to any United States military involvement with Europe. In May 1937 Congress passed a Neutrality Act, which provided for an embargo on arms to belligerent powers and prohibited American citizens from traveling on their ships. Yet in early 1939 preparations were made for American fortifications in the Caribbean and Pacific possessions and France was permitted to buy more planes. American military forces were enlarged somewhat and maneuvers became more realistic. In April 1939 Roosevelt wrote to Hitler and Mussolini requesting assurances they would refrain from aggression and suggesting arms reductions. When the German and Soviet invasion of Poland came in September, the American government secured from the belligerents a promise not to bombard open cities and then proclaimed its own neutrality. Roosevelt allowed Britain to buy more war material and informally encouraged British resistance. He also took British aid in establishing the first American foreign intelligence organization. These moves laid the groundwork for the national security apparatus of the United States. America was taking on the remaining accoutrements of a great power but still holding back from large-scale military action.

WORLD WAR II: ALLIANCE OR SEEDS OF ENMITY?

The United States and the Soviet Union might never have been military partners in World War II if Germany, which was at war with the Soviet Union after its surprise attack of June 22, 1941, had not declared war on the United States. Already enraged by the Japanese surprise attack on the U.S. military installations at Pearl Harbor on December 7, 1941, the United States Congress declared that "a state of war exists" between the United States and the German *Reich* (an action already taken toward Japan). Americans were now in the war.

The overall military situation in early 1942 was grim. The British were falling back in North Africa; the Germans were close to Moscow; and the United States had lost some of its battleships at Pearl Harbor, could not reinforce its forces in the Philippines, and was not certain there would not be a Japanese landing in Hawaii or even California. The American defense plan, such as it was, called for an immediate pullback to the Rocky Mountains in the event of an invasion. Action was demanded—any action that might slow down the Axis powers. The United States had to play for time in order to build a military force for war and also become the "arsenal of democracy." Aid to the USSR was now necessary as it was the country engaging the bulk of the German army.

The American aid effort had begun even before Pearl Harbor. Within a week after Germany attacked Russia, a committee representing all American shipping and supply agencies was formed to send weapons and food to the USSR. Although there was strong opposition in Congress and among the public to aiding a dictatorship, an admiration of a valiant Russian defense against a German invasion began to develop in the United States. Military expediency and the need to preclude a separate Soviet agreement with Nazi Germany justified the aid policy.[29] However, a basis for future discord in American politics was created nevertheless.

The Lend-Lease Act gave the President the power, at his discretion, to sell, transfer, lend, or lease necessary war supplies (including food, machinery, and services) to nations whose defense was vital to the defense of the United States. Repayment was to be "in kind or property, or any other direct or indirect benefit which the President deems satisfactory."

The aid given the USSR was enormous in amount and of great diversity. Soviets tended to be critical of the United States for the time it took for Lend-Lease aid to arrive. Yet the USSR acknowledges the receipt of 9,600 cannon, 18,700 planes, and 10,800 tanks as well as raw materials, food, and trucks and locomotives. Stalin expressed his "sincere gratitude" for this aid.[30] Americans, naturally, tend to give fuller descriptions and to emphasize the crucial significance of such aid. Deane mentions 427,284 trucks, 35,170 motorcycles, 2,328 artillery service vehicles, 1,900 steam locomotives, 9,920 railroad flatcars, and 1,000 dump cars. In addition, almost five million tons of food were sent, enough to supply each Red Army soldier with more than one-half pound of fairly concentrated food per day.[31] More than one Soviet citizen has spoken with gratitude to this author of the "brown cans" (of processed meat, for example) that kept them alive. The Soviets do not mention that the aircraft sent in 1941–42 were "absolutely crucial to the Russians during those dark days."[32] Also left unsaid is the fact that without American vehicles the Soviets would have had little mobility and severe supply problems. "By the end of World War II, the Red Army owed its mobility . . . very largely to Lend-Lease trucks, boots and food."[33] The author once gave a ride in an old Jeep to an emigré Czech professor who noted, "The Russians entered Prague in these in 1945." American aid thus facilitated the Soviet domination of East Central Europe and also the attainment of Stalin's political purposes. He removed several nationalities of the USSR from their homelands in Studebaker trucks (the Balkars, Chechens, Ingush, Kalmyks, Karachai, and the Crimean Tatars).[34] Already it was apparent that aid to the USSR would be used for purposes most Americans find undesirable or even abhorrent, a problem that continues to exist.[h] One crucial fact stands out. President Truman noted that "the money spent for Lend-Lease unquestionably meant the saving of a great many American lives."[35]

American aid to the Soviet Union was presented as part of a "re-packaging" or change of image of that country into some sort of gallant fighter for democratic freedoms and supposed friend of the United States. The United States government made propaganda films extolling the Soviet Union. Even Soviet propaganda films were shown in American theaters. And since the aid was begun without any general United States-Soviet treaty setting forth its conditions, there was no debate in the Senate or anywhere in American politics on whether anything other than resistance to Nazism was expected of the Soviet Union. In fact, the United States had the very American goal of political self-

---

[h] United States aid even included espionage materials, e.g., special cameras, transferred under an arrangement between the O.S.S. (now the C.I.A.) and the NKVD (now the KGB). See Bradley F. Smith, *The Shadow Warriors* (New York: Basic Books, 1983).

determination and independence for Eastern Europe's peoples and it expected the Soviets to relinquish control of the area at the end of World War II. But by 1945 the USSR had been in military occupation of most of the region for a year and had already taken several steps toward its control there, e.g., the establishment of a pro-Soviet army and government for Poland.

Thus the seeds of the later cold war were contained in American aid to the Soviet Union from 1941 and 1945. This was probably unavoidable. All energies in the West were focused on survival. Aiding the Soviet Union, whatever its ideology and political practice, was then squarely in the interests of the United States. If the Russians had been conquered or forced to surrender, the Nazis would have been able to turn their full efforts to invading Britain, taking the Middle East and its oil, and driving through to South Asia and a link-up with Japan. In that event, the game would have been over and a "fortress America" would have had little recourse but to await the final battle. Albert Speer, Hitler's Minister of Armaments and War Production, wrote later that Hitler would not have rested "before achieving domination over America." [36]

We can see then that the "special relationship" that arose in 1941 and 1942 between the United States and the Soviet Union was based on one factor only: they had a common enemy. It was suggested by Sidney Hook, a leading American philosopher, that the Soviet Union should be considered a "co-belligerent," not an ally, of the United States during the war. Certainly, the United States and the Soviet Union had not become "friends," if that is possible for states, nor had they formed a firm and full-fledged alliance. They were instead self-interested states that looked to each other for temporary assistance against the fascist states and so formed outwardly good relations only for the duration of the war. Relations were not smooth even then.

A lasting feeling of dissatisfaction grew out of Lend-Lease for both sides. The Soviets expected full-scale aid immediately, not understanding America needed time to gear up to full production. Nor did they appreciate the practical difficulties involved in shipping the aid over thousands of miles of often stormy waters patrolled by German submarines. American dissatisfaction developed, too, particularly within the military, where it was felt the Soviets were at times either not utilizing equipment or asking for more than they needed. [37] Roosevelt had to put a protective executive mantel over Soviet aid to get all of it delivered. The Soviets could be suspicious about American motives, saying, for example, that "Lend-Lease was merely a western tool to further imperialistic ambitions." [38]

Larger Soviet realities and political purposes also had a role in creating tensions. American, as well as British, personnel involved in Lend-Lease were put off by Soviet secrecy—a secrecy so general and endemic that it often seemed mindless to persons from more open societies. "The principle of *quid pro quo* was not applied ... American military planners knew more ... about the Luftwaffe than they did about the Soviet Air Force." [39] This general secrecy tended to create or exacerbate anti-Soviet political views among some westerners involved with Lend-Lease. Deane accepts Lend-Lease as "vitally essential" but claims "it was the beginning of a policy of appeasement of Russia from which we have never fully recovered" and adds that by the war's end it had led to excessive demands and incorrect assumptions by the Soviets.

> The Soviet leaders became more and more demanding. The fire in our neighbor's house had been extinguished and we had submitted ourselves to his direction in helping to extinguish it. He assumed that we would continue to submit ourselves to his direction in helping to rebuild the house. . . . He allowed us to work on the outside and demanded that we furnish the material for the inside, the exact use of which we were not allowed to see. Now that the house is finished, we have at best only a nodding acquaintance.[40]

Deane's imagery of a "nodding acquaintance," penned in 1946 or 1947, is not far off the mark even today.

It was never made clear to the Soviets, or to the British for that matter, that Lend-Lease was intended only to aid in achieving victory over Germany and that it would terminate with the end of the war. (The Soviet Union received about $11 billion in Lend-Lease aid by August 1945 but the account was never settled.) And no attempt was made to use Lead-Lease to get political concessions from the USSR, although it was suggested within the Administration. Even if it had been tried, the result probably could not have led to a diminution of the postwar Soviet role in East Central Europe—a major irritant leading to the cold war. This area was of preeminent importance for Soviet security interests.

There were other frictions in the relationship as well. One was the fear of each side that the other would abandon the war or even sign a separate peace with the Axis. The Soviets remembered the Munich agreement of 1938 and the British and Americans, the Hitler-Stalin pact of 1939.

Another problem was the lack of total agreement between the British and the Americans. The Soviets became aware of this and capitalized on it to a degree. The British had long been aware that allies can later become enemies and thought in terms of maintaining the balance of power.[41] Inevitably, "the Americans darkly suspected the British of being 'motivated more largely by political than by sound strategic purposes.'"[42] Roosevelt even tried to get Stalin's further cooperation by making fun of Churchill in his presence—an attempt at personal politics right out of the American political tradition but having an unintended effect in hard international bargaining. Stalin now saw that the Americans could be used against the British to Soviet advantage.

A third problem was the Western Allies' delay in establishing a second front in Europe. This caused serious East-West strains and gave Stalin a psychological lever to use in his negotiations with Churchill and Roosevelt as well as propaganda advantages.

Difficulties also centered on differences between the Americans and the

Soviets over the future of Germany. If the Soviets had had their way, Germany would have become some sort of agricultural and de-industrialized slave state. (Ironically, some Americans shared this aim, expressed in the so-called Morganthau Plan.) The Americans ultimately agreed that Germany would pay reparations and that its political system would be changed but did not agree to the destruction of the German economy or the German state, much less to Stalin's suggestion of executing German officers.

The problem that was to be the most irritating and demoralizing for the Americans and also most productive of the already emerging cold war was the political content and shape of the several countries of East Central Europe: Finland, Poland, Czechoslovakia, Hungary, Romania, Bulgaria, Greece, Yugoslavia, Albania, and Austria. Before 1945 these countries, most with established cultural and political traditions and institutions, had never been seen as a unit or fundamentally similar in any way. And, except for Finland and part of Poland, they had never been connected with Russia or considered apart from the rest of Europe.

Some of them were now to become more like the Soviet Union, a real break in their histories, and cut off from Western Europe. Only Greece, Bulgaria, and parts of Romania and Yugoslavia were Eastern Orthodox in religion. Hungary and Poland were heavily Roman Catholic and had always been oriented westward in culture. Hungarian intellectuals learned French, German, and English, rarely any Slavic language. Poland had once been a large imperial kingdom, stretching from the Baltic all the way to the Black Sea. These societies had been rather traditional in their structures and with very little leftism or communism in their politics, except for Czechoslovakia, which had also been clearly democratic in the Western sense. Once Soviet troops were inside these countries, they began to make them more like the Soviet Union. Finland, Greece, Albania, Yugoslavia, and Austria were, in various ways, kept apart from this process of Sovietization. But the others, as well as the eastern third of Germany, came fully into it. There were no practical ways to prevent Sovietization from occurring there. The Soviets entered the region as they drove back the German army. Hardly any western forces got into the area although they could have been rushed into parts of it ahead of the Soviet army as some of the British proposed. However, such an action was seen by American leaders as likely to alienate the Soviet Union, whose troops would be needed, they thought, against a German last stand and also against Japan. (The atomic bomb was still an untested project.)

The Americans did not accept Sovietization for Eastern Europe then, and probably have not accepted it even now. The destruction of ancient ways of life by a Soviet military occupation came to be seen in the United States as an American failure somehow marring American military successes. That one cannot have everything did not sit well with American public opinion. It was never understood in America that the Soviet Union might exact a price for carrying the main burden of the fight against Hitler, thereby reducing American war losses. The United States Army had needed fewer than half the number of divisions pre-war plans had called for.[43]

It has been suggested that a firm diplomatic stand at the top-level conferences of World War II, especially at Tehran in Iran (1943), might have kept the USSR from imposing its system on Eastern Europe. We shall never know. No such Anglo-American stand was ever taken. Poland, for example, was dealt with by Roosevelt in Stalin's company only as "an issue of American politics," that could cost him votes at home. Roosevelt asked only that some sort of vote be allowed "some day" in the Baltic republics and elsewhere in the area for the sake of "world opinion." Inevitably, Soviet methods would guarantee a particular outcome to such a vote. Ironically, the Tehran Conference was the highpoint of East-West wartime cooperation.[44]

So the Soviet Union took control of the politics of East Central Europe, though it incorporated relatively little of that territory into the Soviet Union, except for major parts of East Prussia and Poland. (Czechoslovakia, Hungary, and Romania lost smaller areas to the Soviet Union.) The area became a sovietized buffer zone and sphere of interest. This was a great success for Soviet arms and further legitimized the Soviet system, at least in Russians' eyes. Seven hundred years of German expansionist history had been reversed. Russia now stood further west than any Russian tsar had thought possible.

Yet, for some in the USSR this was not enough. Having accomplished so much at such cost, they felt the USSR deserved full equality in the world. Stalin asked for a role in the occupation of Italy and Japan. He asked for two eastern provinces of Turkey. He also asked for military bases in the Turkish straits and on the Aegean Sea, as well as a United Nations trusteeship in Africa, in the former Italian territories, in parts of which the USSR is involved now. But the United States said "No" to this.

This successful blockage of the USSR where it was possible, a policy to be pursued again later (Greece and Yugoslavia), was never fully appreciated in the United States. This was so because of the effects in American domestic politics of the impositions of Soviet rule over lands from which many Americans had emigrated, of the nativistic American dislike of leftism, of liberal abhorrence of dictatorship, and, most important, the later "loss" of China to communism. This last event, occurring in 1949, made it appear that Soviet communism was "winning" on a huge, Eurasian scale and masked the fact that it had taken over only where the Red Army was in control and that it had been blocked elsewhere. Sovietization had very little popular support, as the string of upheavals in Eastern Europe since then proves. The retreats of Sovietism from 1946 to 1955, under some western pressure, were also not fully appreciated in the United States. The USSR gave up some Finnish territory, withdrew from northern Iran and ended its support of the Kurdish minority there, and eventually terminated its occupational role in Austria.

Yet considerable gains had been made by the USSR, gains that were used to convince the Soviet people that the sacrifices of the war (many of them the fault of the Soviet government) had brought a "profit" of sorts, not just a restoration of the way things had been before the war. But whether Western Europe was to be a later target is still a matter of dispute. Some emigrés from the Soviet Union say Soviet military officers and others spoke of going westward all the way to the Atlantic Ocean. Soviet gains in World War II had excited that unique and powerful combination of Russian messianism and Communist revolutionary feeling. Did not the victory over Germany, one of the most advanced nations of the world, mean that the Soviet Union had a natural right to dominate much of the Eurasian continent? To a Russian veteran of World War II who went through so much, was East Central Europe enough? Clearly, more, much more, could have been gained if the Americans, who in Russian eyes have no natural right outside their hemisphere, had not decided to draw a line to the Russo-Soviet advance.

A few days before he died, President Roosevelt sent a long message to Premier Stalin. Roosevelt said: "So far there has been a discouraging lack of progress made in the carrying out ... of the political decisions which we reached ... particularly those relating to the Polish question."

Roosevelt closed by pointing out that ultimately the Soviet-American relationship would depend on the views of the American public. "The American people make up their own mind and no government action can change it." In his reply, Stalin made clear that the Soviet government was going to "ensure" "friendly relations" between itself and Poland by allowing involvement in Polish politics only to Poles who accepted a Polish-Soviet frontier favoring the USSR and by weighting representation at consultations in favor of the Soviet-controlled Polish provisional government.[45]

The United States and the Soviet Union were contesting territories and peoples whose orientation was of utmost importance for the security and power of the Russians. (Would the United States allow Mexico and the Caribbean to come under the control of an opposing system?) Although by mid-1945 the cold war was not yet clearly apparent and some cooperation between the two states was still to occur, the cold war was already present in basis and outline; it just went unrecognized.

THE COLD WAR: PAST OR PRELUDE?

One of the most controversial issues in the history of American diplomacy has been the origins of the cold war. The cold war has been defined in several ways but all of them connote tenseness of the international climate, salience of military moves and thinking, and a widespread belief in the easy possibility of a full-scale "hot" war. The atmosphere of the cold war is conveyed well by a veteran American reporter who served in the USSR during and after

World War II. Here he is writing about the time in 1953 just before Stalin died:

> [The] country frozen in terror, the winds of cold war so sharp I seldom exchanged a word with any Russian outside of official circles. . . . What was it that frightened me and the three other American correspondents still in Moscow, our ranks thinned by the cold war at its height? Simply that no one knew what Stalin would do next. We were waiting for the 1930s to repeat themselves, for the purges to happen again, for a return of the time when the revolution was turned inside out, the heroes were declared villains and darkness fell at noon.[46]

And this mood extended to America. Some people cast good sense aside and saw enemies everywhere. In some strange way, the Americans' experience with anti-democratic Nazi Germany and cruel Japanese militarism followed by confrontation with Russia led by its ultra-suspicious leader, Stalin, prompted them to give in to some of the same paranoia and distrust that had permeated those systems. McCarthyism and a new "red scare" were one result.

What is meant by "Cold War"? One definition is: competitive attempts by the superpowers to alter the balance of power without general war. Another is: a state of superpower relations in which all means of confrontation are used except those that could cause nuclear war. Each side subordinates everything to the main aim of trying to weaken the other side and make itself supreme. It has been called "an armed truce, precarious and dangerous." Some ask whether it is "still today, the central and defining fact of international life."[47]

It is this issue of "end or continuity" of the cold war that gives it a special edge even now. Is it really over or is it only dormant and able to "bloom" again like a nuclear-tipped thorn bush? Certainly the cold war is part of the beginnings of our own time.[48] And, as with all origins, they tend to stay with us, in the background, and can be called into active play by particular events, politicians, and public moods.

But, whatever happens in the future, no "new cold war" can occur that is just like the old one. That intense antipathy toward the Soviet Union that arose so quickly and spread so harshly in the postwar United States can never be duplicated. America was still a "young" country in the 1940s. It was not yet jaded by the inevitable disappointments and failures of international involvement. Americans were shocked and repelled to learn about the harrowing details of Stalinism. By now, unfortunately, the cruel actions of modern dictatorship have broken out in all too many countries. Americans no longer believe that authoritarian propensities and practices can be rolled back by moralism and militarily defensive tactics. Nor can there be the hope that a war could destroy communism without much harm to the United States. For these and other reasons, talk of a "new cold war" lacks a real basis. The Soviet-American antagonism can intensify, of course, and at times it will; but it can never again have that full "holy war" feeling it had in the years immediately following World War II until the 1960s.

Despite the lack of full-scale hostilities, the cold war permeated world politics for two decades. It helped produce the Korean and Vietnam Wars and the Soviet military interventions in Hungary and Czechoslovakia. If one superpower acted in the world arena, the other reacted as if that action was a serious threat. A sort of autonomous or self-running process of conflict came into being independent of the importance of the actual issues involved. Actions were taken just to head off the possibility of other actions. Foreign policy was turned over to "cold-warriors" and third parties were able to draw one or the other superpower to their sides. One example of this "coercive power of the weak" was Afghanistan's ability to get American aid in the 1950s. Although the United States Joint Chiefs of Staff concluded that distant "Afghanistan is of little or no strategic importance to the United States" and that the USSR could bring it under its control whenever it chose, Soviet aid to Afghanistan led the U.S. Department of State to designate Afghanistan an "emergency action area" and begin its own aid program there. One ironic result was a Soviet-built grain elevator in Afghanistan filled with American wheat.[49]

All this suggests that the term "cold war" can be quite broad, even a catch-all phrase for all of Soviet-American relations. Like the proverbial elephant being examined by several blind men, the cold war has meant very different things to different people depending on what aspect, period, or event is being viewed and upon how it is being viewed. In short, what philosophical view of the origins of international political action does one favor? Does one believe particular people make things happen or do events emerge out of a process of their own? There are several general ways or models of explaining political events. They include:

1. The conscious actor model. (A person or group knowingly makes things happen.)
2. The ideology model. (People's beliefs determine their actions.)
3. The bureaucratic politics model. (Events are determined by the needs of organizations and their ways of doing things.)
4. The "flow of events" model. ("One thing follows another" apart from people's intentions.)

Most "explanations" of the cold war follow one or another of these models. For example, "revisionists," who tend to see many of the cold war's origins in American actions, usually adhere to either Model 1 or 2 (the conscious actor or ideology models). This book, on the other hand, follows Models 3 and 4 (bureaucratic politics and the "flow of events" models) in lodging the origins of the cold war in the events of World War II. No one approach is fully satisfactory.

In the United States there have been three general views of what "caused" the cold war and whether the Soviet Union or the United States was primarily responsible for it. These three perspectives can be labeled as: (1) the traditional-ist or orthodox, (2) the revisionist, and (3) the post-revisionist or realist. But not all writers' views fit neatly into these slots.

The orthodox group was first on the scene with its writings.[50] It saw the origins and responsibility for the cold war in Soviet expansionism. Some of its writers feel the United States reacted to this expansion moderately and well. Others view American conduct as ineffectual and too slow in response. In short, the orthodox writers are not all alike ideologically; some are liberal and some conservative. A succinct example of the orthodox view is that of Adam Ulam debunking the revisionist position.

> Stalin's behavior—which is synonymous with Soviet policy—between 1945 and 1953 can by no stretch of the imagination be considered that of a man afraid. . . . We did not scare him; he scared us. It is *because* we were scared that there occurred the "militarization of policy toward Russia."[51]

This quotation is a response to a key aspect of the revisionist perspective—that American actions triggered the cold war. Revisionists have charged that the use of the atomic bomb on Japan was a threat against the Soviet Union; difficulties with Lend-Lease were conscious attempts to harm the USSR; and the Marshall Plan was a try at undermining the Soviet position in East Central Europe. Whereas the orthodox might consider the Marshall Plan, which was offered to the Soviet Union and the states of Eastern Europe, as a renewal of American aid under a new formula, revisionists can see it as American economic expansion with anti-Soviet political motives and implications. They can even see it as an American attempt to control the Soviet and East European economies. They tend to see economic factors as central in American foreign policy and an anti-Soviet position as lacking a justifiable foundation.[52]

Despite the great difference between the orthodox-traditionalist and revisionist positions, their accounts of the cold war's origins "are virtual mirror images of each other."

> Traditionalists . . . portray American diplomacy as defensive and not parti-cularly effective—precisely the way revisionists describe Stalin's approach. Traditionalists depict the USSR as expansionist. . . . Revisionists reverse the charges. . . . Revisionists find the roots of American expansionism in American society, particularly in the institutions of capitalism. Traditionalists contend Soviet imperialism reflects Marxist-Leninist ideology, traditional Russian xenophobia, and the logic of totalitarian rule.[53]

Clearly, each of these perspectives has some validity. Traditionalists tend to ignore the extent to which the United States limited and slowed down Soviet expansionism. "Revisionists almost always employ a double-standard: Rus-sians' actions are justified or explained by reference to national security or

Realpolitik, Western actions are measured against some high ideal and found wanting."[54] The scholars of the cold war called "post-revisionists" are still an emerging and diverse group. The post-revisionists believe neither the Soviets nor the Americans were without responsibility for the cold war; each was victim as well as villain.[55]

Some writers suggest that some degree of fundamental agreement on the cold war now exists. A picture has emerged "of wartime understandings between the Soviet Union and its Western allies—understandings based largely on Western illusions, or at best the most fragile of hopes—breaking down within a few months of the end of hostilities."[56]

A big question concerning the cold war is the date it ended. (Of course, it can be claimed it has never ended.) Still, when did the cold war lose its quintessential qualities: the promise of actual "hot" war and the firm, hard edge of seeming permanency? There were several events that seem to have triggered a disappearance of these qualities. The death of Stalin in 1953 is one. The summit meeting of 1955, the first since 1945, stands out as re-establishing some degree of direct communication. The 1959 visit of First Secretary Khrushchev to the United States also seemed to presage an end to the cold war. But this thaw was refrozen by the U-2 incident of May 1960, a C.I.A. overflight of the USSR for which President Eisenhower accepted responsibility.

The earliest date at which one can realistically suggest the cold war lost its seeming permanency was in 1963 when the nuclear test ban treaty was signed and the "hot line" for crisis communications between the two governments was set up. The near-clash in the Cuban missile crisis a few months before had made both governments take measures, atmospheric and substantive, to defuse or reduce the implicit threat of war. Accordingly, 1963, the last year of Kennedy's presidency, was "a watershed in Soviet-American relations." One journalist observed at the time that superpower relations had finally "been brought down from the realm of ideology to the familiar precincts of traditional diplomacy."[57] Although this was too optimistic a view, a new stage in Soviet-American relations had been reached. Some would consider 1972 as more meaningful, when President Nixon, the first American President to go to Moscow, signed there the SALT I agreement limiting anti-ballistic missiles (ABMs).

There will always be some who feel strongly that the cold war has never ended; that instead only perceptions of its apparent ending have now and again become widespread. In fact, until the relationship is changed fundamentally for the better, there will recur tense moments that suggest the harsh rigidity of the early cold war. For example, in March 1983 General Secretary Andropov said that President Reagan had spoken an "untruth" (*nepravda*) concerning Soviet missile deployments, a personalized political attack that quickly brought a rough edge back to the relationship. President Reagan's calling the Soviet Union an "evil empire" at about the same time also exacerbated the atmosphere. Because the cold war has been such a major part of the Soviet-American contact, the memory of it never fades completely away. This lingering memory occasionally allows events to trigger the thought that the cold war will return. The American military intervention into Vietnam in early 1965 and the Soviet invasion of Afghanistan in December 1979 are both examples of actions that brought back some of the cold war "feel." Actions and events yet to come[i] may do the same for quite some time.

DÉTENTE

Détente is now in the past. It flowered briefly, perhaps from 1972 and the signing of SALT I to 1975 and the Soviet involvement in southern Africa and Ethiopia, although it can be said to have lasted until 1979 and the Soviet invasion of Afghanistan. Détente's problems began with the term itself. It is a French word of several related meanings, all of which were probably unclear to many Americans. It was meant to suggest the relaxation of tension ("de-tense"). The Soviets never used the word but instead the formulation, in Russian, "relaxation of international tensions." Unfortunately, the idea in operation was seen differently by the American public and the Soviet elite. To the Americans, détente was to mean an end to Soviet expansion and growth of military power. To the Soviets, it meant an elimination of the danger of war between the superpowers—"military détente"—but the continuation of ideologically-based conflict as expressed in anti-Western propaganda and aid to anti-Western movements and states.[58] When this difference of operational definition became apparent and it was seen that détente did not limit the growth of Soviet power, the questions arose in the United States: What is détente for; why is the United States following it; and what is its difference from the old policy of containment?[59]

The origins of the détente policy lay, for the United States, in the self-limitation of American military interventionism resulting from the failures of the Vietnam War, Nixon and Kissinger's recognition of the limitations this imposed on American foreign policy, and the signing of the SALT I Treaty. For the Soviets the origins were in the growth of Soviet power and confidence and the new political security of Brezhnev and the Soviet elite.

Presumed benefits of détente included, for the Americans, aid to the economy from trade with the USSR and reduced military expenditures, and less political wear-and-tear on government. (Nixon eliminated the military draft.) For the Soviets it seemed as if more trade with the West would allow the Soviet economy to develop without need for reform and its disruptive administrative and political effects. It also seemed to them that détente would allow American disengagement and Soviet expansion to proceed more smoothly and with less

---

[i] The shooting down of a Korean airliner by the USSR in 1983 brought about a similar atmosphere as did the mutual arrest of certain persons for spying in the fall of 1986.

danger of war and would allow the western acceptance of the Sovietization of Eastern Europe.[60]

American defenders of détente claimed it was a long-term process. One could not expect to see its benefits immediately. Henry Kissinger argued that détente would develop as the Soviet Union came to have a solid stake in economic interdependence and a better relationship with the United States. He and Nixon assumed they would have the political power to brandish military force occasionally to prevent the USSR from taking advantage of détente. In this they were undercut by the post-Vietnam American aversion to military interventionism and the Watergate scandal's effects on the Nixon presidency.

In addition to détente's fundamental problem of trying to limit a growing power with limited means, it failed to produce many visible and quantifiable benefits for the United States as a whole. Although some American firms made good money out of its increased trade, détente led to noticeable costs for the United States. The price of bread went way up. Some blamed higher energy costs on it, too, since the USSR supported OPEC, which drove up the price of oil. It did not end or limit Soviet expansionism in the Third World or the growth of Soviet weaponry. In addition, some Americans with political clout did not like the assumption of parity in power with the USSR implied by détente. They preferred superiority and were able to get this issue onto the political agenda.

The Soviets, too, were somewhat disappointed in détente. It did not bring American loans to the Soviet Union, or even most favored nation status (MFN) in tariff rates. It did not result in large-scale American development and purchase of Soviet natural gas. Nor did it bring the Japanese or the United States into solving Siberia's economic problems. In short, détente did not open the developed world's arms in welcome to the Russians.

Détente lacked the qualitative substance that had been promised. There was no transformation of international politics into a world with friendly and restrained superpowers reducing the scope and intensity of problems and disagreements. "True détente," if it were possible, would require the Soviet Union to have restrained the growth of both its international role and of its weaponry. As Zbigniew Brzezinski, President Carter's national security adviser, put it, détente should have become both "reciprocal" and "comprehensive," with the Soviet Union helping to make the world more orderly and with both superpowers reducing their nuclear weaponry and consulting with each other on their strategic plans.[61] That this did not occur is not surprising. During the 1970s the Soviet Union was finally attaining the power and influence that Stalin had envisioned in the 1930s. And the men whom Stalin had then picked to run the system were now in control of the country. Why should they put reins to the continued progress of their life's work—the expansion of their power and that of the Soviet Union?

The actual "killing" of détente was the Soviet involvement in the establishment and expansion of new pro-Soviet regimes in Ethiopia and former Portuguese colonies in southern Africa as well as the Soviet invasion of

Afghanistan in late 1979. These actions offended a United States already put into a no-nonsense, anti-foreign mood by: the huge energy cost increases brought about by the OPEC oil embargo of 1973, the ignominious withdrawal from South Vietnam, years of inflation and price rises, and finally the holding of American hostages by Iran. All this created an America determined to stand up to the outside world, including the Soviet Union which came to be seen by some as behind this weakening of America.

Détente came to be seen as not only working against America's interests but also as another Russian trick against the United States and perhaps even against American ideals. Was détente a way for Moscow to exploit domestic weaknesses and hopes for peace in America? Was it, too, as the ex-Soviet dissident Sharansky has charged, a secure way for the USSR to continue to head toward world Communist domination?[62] Senator Bob Dole has said that détente is a "dangerous myth" based upon a "phony premise"—that cooperation with Moscow will create self-generating Soviet goodwill. In addition, détente, he says, breeds unrealistic expectations that lead to "shattering disappointment" and a "self-imposed pressure for unilateral concessions." Instead, he argues, the Russians can be negotiated with best and the world will be a safer place after they are stood up to and put on the defensive.[63] This point of view is not acceptable to some, but it seems to represent a widely held American position on détente of the early 1980s.

POST-DÉTENTE

This period can be divided into two parts: "Reagan I" and "Reagan II." The first subperiod lasted until 1983 or 1984 and the second began then. It was still with us in early 1988 coinciding with the leadership of Gorbachev, the new and dynamic Soviet general secretary since March 1985. The period 1981–1984 was a harsh one in Soviet-American relations. President Reagan began a major and expensive effort to strengthen American military power and also tended to speak out strongly against the Soviet Union and its belief system and actions. The aging and ill Soviet leaders were affronted and perhaps even angered, by Reagan's statements and policies and were unable to counter them effectively. But, by 1984 and the presidential elections, Mr. Reagan had modified his expressions of anti-Sovietism, partly under domestic political pressures and partly under the natural moderating effects of holding office. He even began to move toward some sort of limited accord with the Soviets. They, however, were unable to respond well until the emergence of Gorbachev and the resolution of their long-drawn-out leadership succession process in 1985. Then, a younger, more confident, and realistic Soviet elite took over. They wanted some relief from the superpower rivalry in order to cope with the serious economic and other problems of the Soviet Union. Amazingly, the two systems were no longer terribly out-of-phase with each other. By late 1987 they concluded an accord on mid-range missiles that could lead to a new treaty on strategic arms, began an exchange of visits of the superpowers' leaders, and possibly launched a more orderly and mutually profitable relationship within their continuing rivalry.

The present state of Soviet-American relations—whether it is called "relative peace," "relativistic competition," "flawed détente," "limited détente," "neither peace nor war," or some other formulation—is not at all like the cold war. The very fact that no new term is generally used now suggests we are in a new phase of Soviet-American competition. Adam Ulam has called it a "very indeterminate period." William G. Hyland, a longtime staff member of the National Security Council, has said, "We are a long way from a new cold war . . . both sides have been much more cautious in behavior, and . . . each has made almost desperate attempts to stay in contact." Perhaps the two giants have learned something.[64] It naturally took time to adjust for two powers unused to world power and to each other as rivals. New views of international relations and of diplomacy, even a new language and new practices of interaction, had to be developed. Even if one focuses on the progress that still might be made in the United States-Soviet relationship, no one can doubt the two powers have covered some real distance in improving that relationship and can well cover more.

A summary of United States-Soviet relations since 1945 follows.

TABLE 2.2. HIGHLIGHTS OF UNITED STATES-SOVIET RELATIONS SINCE YALTA

Yalta Conference February 1945	Potsdam Conference July–August 1945	Berlin Blockade April 1948–September 1949	Korean War 1950–1953	Hungarian Revolution and Suez Crisis October 1956	U-2 Incident May 1960	Cuban Missile Crisis October–November 1962
*Roosevelt	Roosevelt died April 1945	Truman 1945–1953		Eisenhower 1953–1961		Kennedy 1961–1963
**Stalin	Stalin died March 1953			Khrush-chev and others 1953–1957	Khrush-chev 1957–1964	

| Test Ban Treaty and "Hot Line" 1963 | Soviet Invasion of Czechoslovakia August 1968 | Arms Agreements May 1972 (ABM) and June 1979 (SALT II) ⟶ | Soviet Invasion of Afghanistan December 1979 START | Martial Law in Poland December 1981 |

*Johnson 1963–1969   Nixon 1969–1975   Ford 1975–1977   Carter 1977–1981   Reagan 1981–1988

Brezhnev 1964–1982   Andropov 1982–1984

(*Continued on pp. 56–57*)

TABLE 2.2. (Continued)

Flight 007 downed September 1983	First U.S. cruise missiles arrive in England. West Germany approves deployment of mid-range missiles November 1983	Soviets suspend arms talks	U.S. and USSR agree on upgraded hot line July 1984	First formal U.S.-Soviet arms talks in 15 months begin March 1985
			Chernenko 1984–1985	

*U.S. president
**Soviet leader
SOURCE: Adapted and updated from *The New York Times*, November 13, 1982

| U.S.-Soviet trade agreement reached May 1985 | Reagan and Gorbachev meet at Geneva November 1985 | Reagan and Gorbachev meet in Iceland October 1986 | Reagan and Gorbachev meet in Washington, D.C. and sign a treaty limiting intermediate nuclear missiles December 1987 |

Gorbachev
March 1985–

REFERENCES

1. Alexis de Tocqueville, *Democracy in America* (*De la Democratie en Amerique*) edited and abridged by Richard D. Heffner (New York: Mentor, 1956), p. 142. I prefer the translation of Thomas Larson used in his *Soviet-American Rivalry* (New York: Norton, 1978), 31.
2. For examples of these cartoons, see Benson Lee Grayson, ed., *The American Image of Russia, 1917–1977* (New York: Ungar, 1978).
3. *The Bulletin of the Commissariat for Foreign Relations*, June 1922, 19. Quoted in Adam B. Ulam, *Expansion and Coexistence: The History of Soviet Foreign Policy, 1917–67* (New York: Praeger, 1968), 148.
4. See Antony C. Sutton, *Western Technology and Soviet Economic Development: 1917 to 1930* (Stanford: Hoover Institution, 1968), 287–289. Events described by Sutton have some resemblance to events of the early 1980s, e.g., American machinery bought by non-Soviet buyers "making its way" to Russia.
5. *XVI S"ezd VKP(B)*, (sixteenth Congress of the Bolshevik Party), 106.
6. John Scott, *Behind the Urals: An American Worker in Russia's City of Steel* (Bloomington: Indiana University Press, 1973), 143 and 170. Originally published in 1942.
7. Philip S. Gillette, "American-Soviet Trade in Perspective," *Current History* (October 1973): 158.
8. See Gordon Brook-Shepherd, *The Storm Petrels: The Flight of the First Soviet Defectors* (New York: Ballantine Books, 1977), 150–153. See also the first volume of George Kennan's *Memoirs* for a description of the scantiness of American government information on the Soviet Union at that time.
9. N. V. Sivachev and N. N. Yakovlev, *Russia and the United States* (Chicago: University of Chicago Press, 1979), 141, 142, and 150.
10. Ibid., 149.
11. Adam Ulam, *Expansion and Coexistence: Soviet Foreign Policy, 1917 to 1973*, 2d ed. (New York: Praeger), 283 and 285.
12. These unofficial ties are discussed in Sivachev and Yakovlev, particularly on pp. 90–92.
13. George F. Kennan, *Russia and the West under Lenin and Stalin* (Boston: Little, Brown, 1960), 299–300.
14. J. Stalin, *Works* 7: 295, quoted in Sivachev and Yakovlev, 76.
15. A. A. Gromyko and B. N. Ponamarev, *Istoriya vneshney politiki SSSR, 1917–1976* (*History of the Foreign Policy of the U.S.S.R., 1917–1976*), 2 vols. (Moscow, 1976), vol. I, 198–190. Quoted in Sivachev and Yakovlev, 76.
16. Ulam, 212.
17. A. Whitney Griswold, *The Far Eastern Policy of the United States* (New Haven, CT: Yale University Press, 1938), 441.
18. Sivachev and Yakovlev, 102.
19. Ulam, 213, citing Jane Degras, ed., *Soviet Documents on Foreign Policy*, III, 1933–41 (London and New York: Hippocrene Books 1953), 36.
20. Ulam, 217.
21. Kennan, *Russia and the West*, 299.
22. Sivachev and Yakovlev, 124, 144, and 146–147.

23. Referred to in Herbert S. Dinerstein, *Fifty Years of Soviet Foreign Policy* (Baltimore: Johns Hopkins University Press, 1968), 14.
24. Ibid., 14–15.
25. Hans Herwarth, *Against Two Evils* (New York: Rawson, Wade, 1981), 162.
26. Alvin Z. Rubinstein, *Soviet Foreign Policy since World War Two* (Cambridge, MA: Winthrop, 1981), 25.
27. *Akten zur Deutschen Auswärtigen Politik 1918–1945*, VIII (Baden Baden, 1961). Quoted in Vilis Skultans, "The Takeover of the Baltic States in June 1940," Radio Liberty Research, 13 June 1980, 5.
28. For a partial text, see Grayson, 150–152. Max Eastman, in a book published in the same year, called the Soviet system "worse than fascism." Excerpts in Grayson, 144.
29. Raymond H. Dawson, *The Decision to Aid Russia, 1941* (Chapel Hill: University of North Carolina Press, 1959), 290–291.
30. Sivachev and Yakovlev, 210.
31. John R. Deane, *The Strange Alliance: The Story of Our Efforts at Wartime Cooperation with Russia* (New York: Viking, 1947), 93–95. General Deane was a member of the U.S. Military Mission to the USSR.
32. Richard C. Lukas, *Eagles East: The Army Air Forces and the Soviet Union, 1941–1945* (Tallahassee: Florida State University Press, 1970), 232. See Lukas's Appendix A for a detailed list of American aircraft exports to the USSR.
33. William H. McNeill, *The Pursuit of Power: Technology, Armed Force and Society since A.D. 1000* (Chicago: University of Chicago Press, 1982), 354.
34. See Aleksandr M. Nekrich, *The Punished Peoples* (New York: Norton, 1978).
35. Harry S. Truman, *Memoirs*, Vol. I (Garden City, NY: 1955–56), 234.
36. Albert Speer, "On the Nazi Invasion of Poland—1 September 1939," *New York Times*, 31 August 1979.
37. Lukas writes of "over kill" in aircraft given the Soviets by lend-lease and Deane reports American diesel engines rusting in the open air. Lukas, 232; and Deane, 96.
38. Lukas, 231. And see his footnote 44, ibid., where three Soviet sources expressing this view are listed.
39. Lukas, 50–51.
40. Deane, 89 and 90–91.
41. Ulam, 357. Ulam sees a "fissure" between the two western allies (pp. 351 and 357).
42. John L. Gaddis, *The United States and the Origins of the Cold War, 1941–1947* (New York: Columbia University Press, 1972), 67. "Suspicion of British motives was widespread among American military officials at this time [1942—KR]."
43. Ibid., 79–80.
44. William Taubman, *Stalin's American Policy* (New York: Norton, 1982), 67–68, quoting United States Department of State, *Foreign Relations of the United States: Tehran*.
45. *Stalin's Correspondence with Roosevelt and Truman: 1941–1945* (New York: Capricorn Books, 1965), 201–204 and 211–213.
46. Harrison E. Salisbury, "The Days of Stalin's Death," *The New York Times Magazine*, 17 April 1983, 38.
47. See Marshall Shulman, "Changing Appreciation of the Soviet Problem," *World Politics*, X, 4 (July 1958): 510; referring to G. L. Arnold (pseud. for George Lichtheim), *The Pattern of World Conflict* (New York: Dial Press, 1955), 228–235;

Ranko Petković, a book review, *Socialist Theory and Practice* (Belgrade), 10 (October 1984): 85–86; Daniel Yergin, *Shattered Peace: The Origins of the Cold War and the National Security State* (Boston: Houghton Mifflin, 1977), 6.

48. Yergin, 410.
49. Henry S. Bradsher, *Afghanistan and the Soviet Union* (Durham, NC: Duke University Press, 1983), 20, 29, and 262.
50. See, for example, the works of Herbert Feis, e.g., *Churchill, Roosevelt and Stalin* (Princeton, NJ: Princeton University Press, 1957). Feis once worked for the United States Department of State.
51. Adam B. Ulam, "The Cold War according to Kennan," *Commentary* Vol. 55 (January 1973): 68. Ulam here is reviewing George F. Kennan's *Memoirs 1925–1950* (Boston: Atlantic-Little, Brown, 1967).
52. Revisionist works include: Gabriel Kolko, *The Politics of War: The World and United States Foreign Policy, 1943–1945* (New York: Random House, 1968); and William Appleman Williams, *The Tragedy of American Diplomacy*, rev. ed. (New York: Dell, 1962).
53. Taubman, 6–7.
54. Robert James Maddox, *The New Left and the Origins of the Cold War* (Princeton: Princeton University Press, 1973), 7. Maddox reviews works of six revisionists.
55. Taubman, 7.
56. Michael Howard, "Reassurance and Deterrence: Western Defense in the 1980s," *Foreign Affairs*, Vol. 61, 2 (Winter 1982/83): 309–310.
57. See Ralph B. Levering, *The Cold War, 1945–1972* (Arlington Heights, IL: Harlan Davidson, 1982), 99–100.
58. David Holloway, "Foreign and Defense Policy," in Archie Brown and Michael Kaser, eds., *Soviet Policy for the 1980s* (Bloomington: Indiana University Press, 1982), 42.
59. Stanley Hoffmann, *Primary or World Order: American Foreign Policy since the Cold War* (New York: McGraw-Hill, 1978), 60.
60. Adam B. Ulam, *Dangerous Relations: The Soviet Union in World Politics, 1970–1982* (New York: Oxford University Press, 1983), 61, 63, and 88ff.
61. Zbigniew Brzezinski, *Power and Principle: Memoirs of the National Security Adviser, 1977–1981* (New York: Farrar, Straus, Giroux, 1983), 147 and 150.
62. Natan Sharansky's testimony before the Commission on Security and Cooperation in Europe, 1 May 1986.
63. *New York Times*, 10 November 1986, A-18. Based on Bob Dole, "Grappling with the Bear: A Strategy for Dealing with Moscow," *Policy Review* Vol. 38 (Fall 1986).
64. *New York Times*, 3 April 1983.

SELECT BIBLIOGRAPHY

Balfour, Michael. *The Adversaries: America, Russia and the Open World, 1941–1962.* London: Routledge and Kegan Paul, 1981.
Brzezinski, Zbigniew. *Power and Principle: Memoirs of the National Security Adviser, 1977–1981.* New York: Farrar, Straus, Giroux, 1983.
Gaddis, John L. *Russia, the Soviet Union, and the United States: An Interpretive History.* New York: Wiley, 1978.

——. *Strategies of Containment: A Critical Appraisal of Postwar American National Security Policy.* New York: Oxford University Press, 1982.

Garrison, Mark, and Abbott Gleason, eds. *Shared Destiny: Fifty Years of Soviet-American Relations.* Boston: Beacon Press, 1985.

Garthoff, Raymond L. *Détente and Confrontation: American-Soviet Relations from Nixon to Reagan.* Washington, DC: Brookings, 1985.

Halliday, Fred. *The Making of the Second Cold War.* London: Verso, 1983.

Herring, George C. *Aid to Russia, 1941–46.* New York: Columbia University Press, 1973.

Herz, Martin F. *Beginnings of the Cold War.* New York: McGraw-Hill, 1969.

Hyland, William G. *Mortal Rivals: Superpower Relations from Nixon to Reagan.* New York: Random House, 1987.

Kennan, George F. *Russia and the West under Lenin and Stalin.* Boston: Little, Brown, 1961.

Kissinger, Henry. *White House Years.* Boston: Little, Brown, 1979.

——. *Years of Upheaval.* Boston: Little, Brown, 1982.

Laserson, Max M. *The American Impact on Russia—Diplomatic and Ideological—1784–1917.* New York: Macmillan, 1950.

Lukacs, John. *A New History of the Cold War.* New York: Anchor Books, 1966.

Maddox, Robert James. *The New Left and the Origins of the Cold War.* Princeton, NJ: Princeton University Press, 1973.

Mandelbaum, Michael, and Strobe Talbott. *Reagan and Gorbachev.* New York: Vintage Books, 1987.

Mastny, Vojtech. *Russia's Road to the Cold War: Diplomacy, Warfare, and the Politics of Communism, 1941–1945.* New York: Columbia University Press, 1979.

Melanson, Richard A., ed. *Neither Cold War Nor Détente? Soviet-American Relations in the 1980s.* Charlottesville: University Press of Virginia, 1982.

Pipes, Richard. *U.S.-Soviet Relations in the Era of Detente.* Boulder, CO: Westview Press, 1981.

Sivachev, N. V., and N. N. Yakovlev. *Russia and the United States.* Translated by Olga A. Titelbaum. Chicago: University of Chicago Press, 1979. A Soviet history of the relationship.

Snell, John L. *Illusion and Necessity: The Diplomacy of Global War, 1939–1945.* Boston: Houghton Mifflin, 1963.

Talbott, Strobe. *The Russians and Reagan.* New York: Vintage Books, 1984.

Taubman, William. *Stalin's American Policy: From Entente to Détente to Cold War.* New York: Norton, 1982.

Ulam, Adam. *Dangerous Relations: The Soviet Union in World Politics, 1970–1982.* New York: Oxford University Press, 1983.

——. *The Rivals: America and Russia since World War II.* New York: Viking Press, 1971.

Weisberger, Bernard A. *Cold War Cold Peace: The United States and Russia since 1945.* New York: American Heritage, 1984.

Yergin, Daniel. *Shattered Peace: The Origins of the Cold War and the National Security State.* Boston: Houghton Mifflin, 1977.

Chapter 3

American and Soviet National Power

Once one looks beyond the military factor, the weight of the Soviet Union in world affairs is quite modest for a country of its size, population, resources, and industrial development.
Lawrence T. Caldwell and William Diebold, Jr.

Our influence in the world has lessened in relation to what it was in the first decade or two after World War II.
Andrew J. Goodpaster, LTGEN, USA, Ret.

What challenges American primacy in world affairs is less the power of the USSR than the capacity of West Europe and Japan to outstrip the US in major areas of industrial efficiency.
Norman A. Graebner

Power is a key question in any political relationship. Who is the more powerful? Who, if anyone, can make another do what he wants? Who can outlast another in a contest? It is difficult to answer such questions with reference to two countries as different as the Soviet Union and the United States, and particularly when both refrain from exercising all their power. Neither state wants to pose a full-scale challenge to the other, risking nuclear war and massive destruction. Unexercised power is untested and unmeasured power.

Yet an examination of Soviet-American relative power is necessary, however difficult the task and uncertain the conclusions. It is important to know what varieties and degrees of power are available to each in order to predict the intensity, duration, and nature of the contest between the two nations. Power in politics, however, is not a visible thing, subject to exact measurement. Errors of evaluation are common.

The term "power" implies the probability that one party can get something it wants from another despite resistance.[1] This does not apply to the Soviet-American relationship since neither side has sufficient power to force its will on the other. However, both the United States and the Soviet Union have enough power to force smaller countries to adopt policies they favor. Even so, the naked exercise of coercive power by the superpowers is rare. Each tries to foster an image of itself as responsible and peaceable. Images are also an element of power, as is the ability of a state's propaganda effort to create and maintain them.

Limited exercise of power, depending on its form and amount, is often designated not by the word itself but by one or another associated "power term," such as influence, inducement, or compulsion. Whatever term is used, the central idea is that the behavior of one actor in a relationship depends to some degree on the behavior of another actor in the same relationship. In United States-Soviet relations this means that (1) each superpower tries to use its power in the international arena to reduce the power of the other and (2) although neither superpower can force the other to do something it does not want to do, each will try to maneuver the other superpower into actions or nonactions that cause it to lose power. For example, the Soviet Union can make the United States appear weak by aiding in the creation of a challenge that the U.S. is unlikely to counter, e.g., Soviet aid to Syrian-backed forces in Lebanon. The United States is very reluctant to use large-scale military force except in a clear case of defense of vital interests. The United States can in turn discredit the Soviet Union. For example, publicizing dissidents and food problems in the USSR undercuts its claims to success and apparent power.

In short, each superpower uses third parties to maximize its own power vis-à-vis the other. This does not mean that other powers are not able to resist superpower wishes or that third powers never use whatever power they have against the superpowers. In 1984 it was difficult for the Soviet Union to prevent the head of East Germany from visiting West Germany, though it eventually succeeded in this. The United States has not been able to prevent Israel from building Jewish settlements in Arab areas of Israel. In 1987 Kuwait was able to get both superpowers to help protect its oil tankers. Even when the superpowers have gone to war, as in Vietnam and Afghanistan, they have been unable to enforce their wills. As Henry Kissinger once said, "As power has grown more awesome, it has also turned abstract, intangible, elusive." It can even be said that "utmost strength now coincides with utmost vulnerability."[2]

No one state, even a superpower, has most of the power in existence. In fact, the awesome power commanded by the superpowers together is declining relative to the rest of the power in international politics. Other countries are growing in power. Syria and Israel are two states whose power has grown partly because of aid from the superpowers. The powers of China and Brazil promise to grow (and lead to further reduction in American and Soviet power).

Accordingly, the national power of the superpowers is in decline relative to that of others. And it is likely to continue in decline unless one or more of the elements of national power they command can be increased. The usual ways of increasing power—adding a new ally, making a major technological break-through, or developing a "wonder weapon"—are all unlikely to be monopolized by one superpower alone. Each is quick to respond to challenges to its power position and each has proven it can compensate to some degree for additions to the power of the other. An American "star wars" system will be countered by a Soviet one, Gorbachev has warned. Although the two superpowers have different mixes of the elements of national power and are asymmetrical as total systems, the overall power of each is not superior to that of the other. "Parity" or equality of power exists, at least in a rough overall sense. And, because of the nuclear weaponry of each state, neither will ever intentionally challenge the other to a military showdown or try to take maximum advantage of the other.

Superpower status is increasingly costly. Large military budgets cause fundamental problems for their economies. Foreign aid programs are resented by the populace. Political dissatisfaction grows as faith in the prevailing arrangements weakens. As problems multiply, inter-ethnic and inter-racial conflicts intensify. One's allies and clients go their own ways and even get in one's own way. Superpower status is, accordingly, increasingly frustrating.

PROBLEMS OF EVALUATION

There are several problems and typical errors in evaluating a state's power in world politics.[3] First, no evaluator can be certain he or she has listed all the possible elements of power, much less evaluated their combined weight correctly. There may well be unknown factors that prove important, even decisive. Second, the elements of national power are always changing—in amount, relationship to each other, and significance. What was crucially important in one context or application of power may be inappropriate in another. Third, the evaluator cannot be certain the evaluation will be valid over time. The future can be full of surprises. In addition, a single factor may prove much more important in a real situation than it seemed in the abstract. For example, a weak country may have a determined leader or elite able to muster resistance so strong that the superior country cannot win. Or special tactics may be used that the supposedly superior state cannot overcome. Every strength can be turned into a weakness in a particular situation. Similarly, trickery or surprise can be decisive and can favor the weaker state.

Outright errors of evaluation can be made. A particular nation's power can be seen as an unchanging absolute even though it has declined. A particular factor can be taken as permanent, when all factors are subject to change. Or a single factor can be considered decisive when it is not. It must not be forgotten that "the concept of power of nations . . . resolves itself into a series of hunches, of which some will certainly turn out to be wrong while others may be proved by subsequent events to be correct."[4] Finally, a state's power is strongly affected by the attractiveness of its purposes and justifications, the strength of the beliefs that support it, and the value of its deeds. Power in the purely material sense may have no long-term effect.[5] Skill and motivation also affect power. Even after the passage of centuries, historians disagree as to why a particular state lost its contest with another. Is it any surprise that contemporary evaluations of national power evoke disagreement?

THE ELEMENTS OF NATIONAL POWER

A nation's power is affected by a variety of factors, including its military preparedness and its technological capabilities. While it may seem that military force (or at least its image) lies at the heart of Soviet power, and that technological capability is at the core of American power, other national resources may be equally important. Thus, to determine how powerful the superpowers really are in relation to one another, we shall compare the two nations not only in terms of their defense systems and technology, but also with respect to some less obvious national characteristics. These include geography, natural resources, industrial capacity and economic power, population, national character, national morale, and diplomacy.[6] (Several of these factors, including geography, natural resources, population, and national character are relatively stable.)

These comparisons are made under the assumption that neither the Soviet Union nor the United States is able to act completely apart from the constraints of international politics; that the context of world politics offers each superpower certain opportunities unavailable to the other; and that, although there is a lack of clarity about the extent of Soviet power it is fairly clear that American power is no longer growing.

Geography
Some key geographical factors that affect a nation's power are: size of territory; location and distance from opposing states; the presence or absence of natural boundaries; the relative danger of invasion; and climate. The USSR is about two-and-one-third times the size of the United States (8,600,329 square miles versus 3,628,062 square miles). The area of the United States is 42.2 percent that of the USSR. All of the contiguous states of the United States are located below 50° North latitude, whereas only about one-fifth of the USSR is that far south. The latitude of the middle of the Soviet Union is about the same as that of Alaska. The United States borders on only two countries—Canada and Mexico—whereas the Soviet Union borders on twelve, with eighteen more lying within five hundred miles, and has a much longer border. Concern for politics in neighboring countries is naturally greater in the USSR than in the United States, particularly since the USSR has very poor relations with some of these neighbors.

FIGURE 3.1. LATITUDINAL POSITION OF THE US RELATIVE TO THE USSR

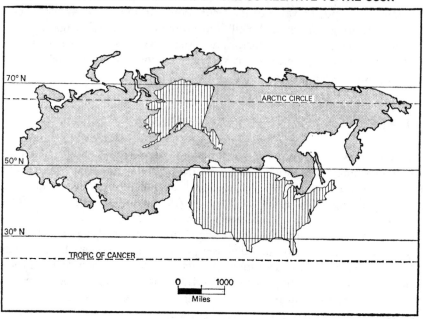

FIGURE 3.2. RELATIVE AREAS SHOWN AS SQUARES

SOURCE: W.H. Parker, *The Superpowers: the United States and the Soviet Union Compared* (London: Macmillan Press/Macmillan Ltd., 1972), 40 and 94 (opposite).

FIGURE 3.3. ANTI-RESOURCES

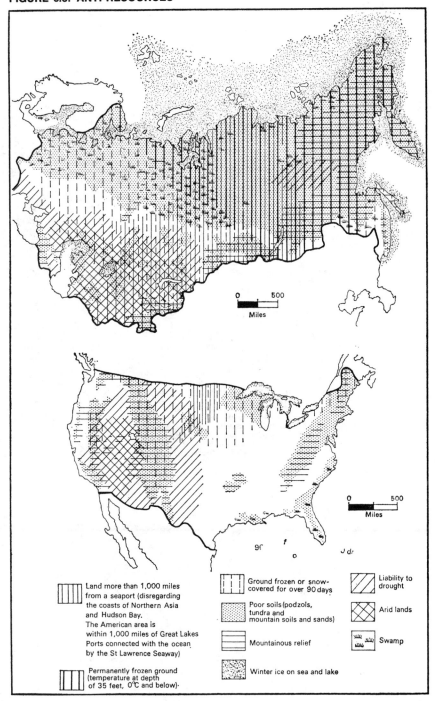

Land more than 1,000 miles from a seaport (disregarding the coasts of Northern Asia and Hudson Bay. The American area is within 1,000 miles of Great Lakes Ports connected with the ocean by the St Lawrence Seaway)	
Permanently frozen ground (temperature at depth of 35 feet, 0°C and below).	
Ground frozen or snow-covered for over 90 days	
Poor soils (podzols, tundra and mountain soils and sands)	
Mountainous relief	
Winter ice on sea and lake	
Liability to drought	
Arid lands	
Swamp	

FIGURE 3.4. US-USSR MILITARY ACTIVITIES WORLDWIDE

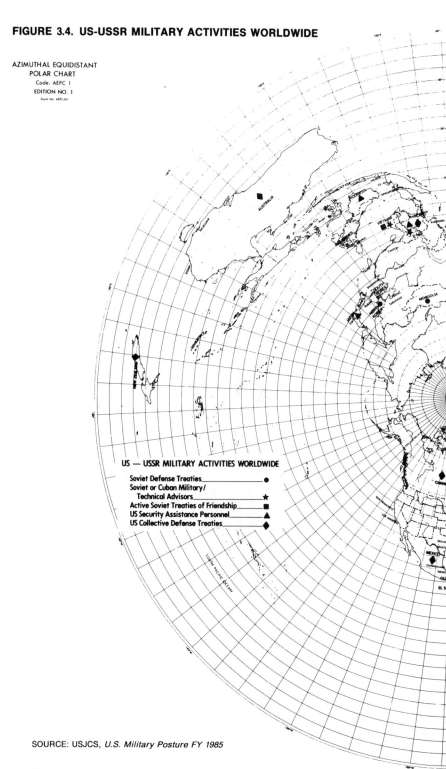

AZIMUTHAL EQUIDISTANT
POLAR CHART
Code: AEPC 1
EDITION NO. 1
Stock No. AEPC801

US — USSR MILITARY ACTIVITIES WORLDWIDE

Soviet Defense Treaties	●
Soviet or Cuban Military/ Technical Advisors	★
Active Soviet Treaties of Friendship	■
US Security Assistance Personnel	▲
US Collective Defense Treaties	◆

SOURCE: USJCS, *U.S. Military Posture FY 1985*

68

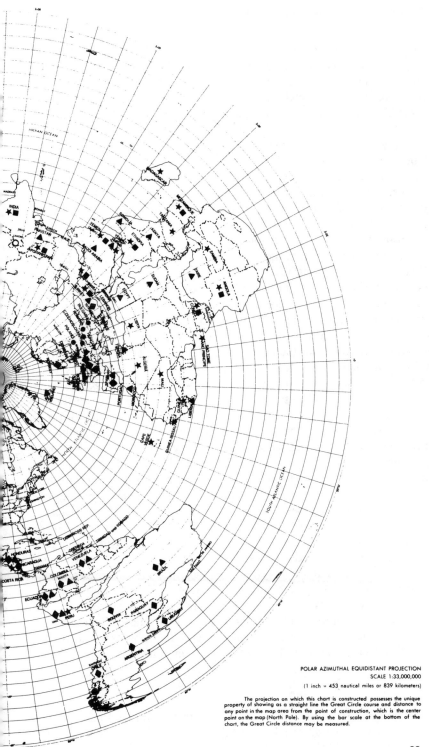

POLAR AZIMUTHAL EQUIDISTANT PROJECTION
SCALE 1:33,000,000
(1 inch = 453 nautical miles or 839 kilometers)

The projection on which this chart is constructed possesses the unique property of showing as a straight line the Great Circle course and distance to any point in the map area from the point of construction, which is the center point on the map (North Pole). By using the bar scale at the bottom of the chart, the Great Circle distance may be measured.

69

The two superpowers have had very different patterns of relationships with hostile foreign powers. The United States has enjoyed the relative security of distance and the "moats" afforded by the two bordering oceans, whereas the Soviet Union has never had such an advantage. It has been invaded several times and the historic home of its civilization was conquered once. (Russia was held by the Mongols or Tartars for almost two hundred years.) Although intercontinental missiles have made the United States vulnerable to destructive attack, Americans may still have a sense of relative security based on historical experience that is lacking in the Soviet Union. Certainly, the United States is remote from Soviet conventional military power and any other likely major opponent. The Soviet Union has to be concerned with Chinese military power and with potentially serious political developments in bordering states such as Poland and Iran. A high Soviet party official once said, "I recently suggested to a group of American senators that the United States change geographical places with us. They were quick to turn the idea down."[7]

The climates of the two countries are very different. The United States is much warmer and wetter and hence more conducive to agriculture than the USSR. And each has a particular climate almost unknown in the other—a humid temperate climate in the American South and a humid arctic climate in the Soviet North. In addition, the Soviet Union is plagued with more "anti-resources" (factors that hinder development) than is the United States. These include permafrost, large areas of swamp, and poor soils. One geographer notes that the burden of anti-resources means "the Russians are constantly at war" with their environment.[8] Almost all the USSR, but only one-third of the United States, has three months or more each year with the average mean temperature below freezing. Some writers have seen the struggle with harsh conditions of nature as at the root of a primitive determination to survive in Russian culture and government. The fact that the Russian people are the largest group of people living under these harsh climatic conditions does suggest a real degree of success in adaptation. It is clear then that the territory of the United States is easier to live in than is that of the Soviet Union; and its smaller size makes internal communication, travel, and transportation easier than in the larger USSR. The length of paved roads in the USSR only equals that in Pennsylvania and creates severe logistics and transportation difficulties. The factor of greater size does give the Soviet Union the possible advantage of greater defensibility and military maneuverability in war as well as more natural resources. But the inter-ethnic tensions resulting from the large number of unassimilated ethnic groups, as well as the harsh living conditions brought about by its far northern location and the lack of natural obstacles to invasion, tend to undercut these advantages.

Natural Resources

Here the two nations are in opposite situations, with the United States having more than enough food and the USSR enjoying the greatest store of raw materials of any country.

Food. This is an elemental power factor. A country that is self-sufficient in food can pursue a more forceful foreign policy more confidently than one dependent on food from abroad. Although both countries are self-sufficient in food, only 15 percent of Soviet territory is arable land and the northerly latitude makes farming a risky business. (In the early 1980s there were four bad harvests in a row.) Consequently, there are years—perhaps one in every three—when food has to be imported in order to maintain the standard of living to which the Soviet people have recently become accustomed. Important in maintaining this standard is importing enough corn for cattle feed, plus some grain. But since the USSR is a major producer of gold, oil, and natural gas, it can always pay for grain imports. And, since there are many sources of grain in the world besides the United States—Argentina, Australia, Canada, and France—the USSR is not dependent on its chief competitor for grain. Still, the recurrent need to import grain is an embarrassment for the USSR, although it produces more wheat than the United States.[9] Tsarist Russia was a major grain exporter, but Leninist socialism has harmed agriculture. And grain imports take foreign exchange that the government would rather use for other purposes, notably the import of high technology and machinery.

The Soviet food problem is not so serious that it involves the danger of starvation. Yet there *is* a Soviet food problem. It arises from the recent improvement in the Soviet living standard and a new mass assumption that there will be meat and a diversity of food, i.e., a balanced diet. If this expectation is not met, morale will suffer and disaffection may result. There are still important differences in the diet of Americans and Soviets. Although the respective intakes of fats and oils, dairy products, and sugar are similar, 44 percent of the Soviet diet is grain and potatoes compared with 26 percent of the American. And the Soviets eat less than half the meat and fish Americans do. Even this diet can only be met through imports—of fruits and vegetables from southeastern Europe (Bulgaria, Hungary, Romania, and Yugoslavia) and citrus fruit from Greece and Morocco. The need for grain cannot be fully met anywhere in Eurasia; it can come only from other continents. Hence, there is a need for a merchant fleet as well. In addition, one-third of Soviet animal protein comes from fish caught off other countries' coasts, not a secure source.

The only way the Soviet food problem might be solved is to abandon collectivized agriculture and allow farmers to own some of the land and machinery again and to sell their products at market prices. This would increase incentives to produce. A Soviet farm worker now feeds only about ten people. This is only a slight improvement over his ability to feed seven people in 1965. Recent Soviet attempts to improve farm output have had little result as yet.[10] A full return to private enterprise in agriculture would be a severe embarrassment to the Communist party and ultimately a political threat to it. Thus it is unlikely to occur in the near future, although Gorbachev is making limited moves in that direction.

The food situation in the United States has problems as well, though very different sorts of problems as far as most Americans are concerned. There is no food shortage for the country as a whole, but a certain percentage of people—the poorer and less educated—may not enjoy a balanced diet. Not everyone has the money for sufficient food. The government gives away certain foods that it holds as surplus stocks and also provides food stamps to low-income people. A new problem, only a decade or so old, is that of expensive food. The United States grew on cheap food, a boon that is no longer present. Ironically, a big boost in bread and baked goods prices resulted from a grain deal with the Soviet Union in 1972. Since then grain exports have been regulated by the government. The American food problem has been contained, but at a higher problem level than in the past. How the current farm problem will affect the food picture is unclear.

Raw Materials.   Here the shoe is on the other foot. The Soviet Union is more than self-sufficient in almost all industrial raw materials, whereas the United States must import large percentages of many of them. And the USSR is the world's largest oil and natural gas producer. It is the only major industrialized country other than Britain to be more than self-sufficient in energy. The USSR's daily output of oil in 1983 was 12.5 million barrels, whereas the United States produced 8.6 million barrels per day, two-thirds of Soviet output. In 1987 the United States was importing 38 percent of the oil it used. By 1995 the proportion may well be 50 percent and the oil more expensive.[11] The United States economy is vulnerable to a slowdown or stoppage if the supply of raw materials were interrupted. If needs to maintain a large sea-control navy designed, among other tasks, to keep the sea lanes open so as to protect access to sources of raw materials. The USSR does not need to keep sea lanes open to keep its economy going but only be able to keep in touch with some of its Third World allies. Instead, its problem is to extract its raw materials under harsh Siberian conditions and then to transport them from Siberia by rail and pipeline thousands of miles to the European USSR for processing. Table 3.1 gives an idea of the enviable resource position of the USSR.

The United States is very poorly supplied with some key minerals, e.g., chromite, manganese, and nickel—all three of which are listed as "strategic and critical materials" and are among the eighty items stockpiled by the government.[12] Stockpiles can last only for a short time if foreign source is not available. The United States has a net import reliance of greater than 50 percent for nineteen minerals and metals, many of them coming from southern Africa, an unstable area (see Table 3.2). Fortunately, it has been able to pay for these despite a declining dollar.[13] Until recently the United States imported some resources from the Soviet Union, e.g., 33 percent of its titanium, a lightweight, heat-resistant metal used in military aircraft. When the USSR stopped exporting titanium, the United States was faced with a shortfall until in 1980 it found that China could provide the required amount.

Some observers claim Siberian raw materials will eventually be able to command high prices and give the USSR a new leverage in world politics.[14]

TABLE 3.1. ESTIMATED SOVIET RESERVES OF SELECTED FUELS AND NONFUEL MINERALS

Item	Share of World Reserves (Percent)	Years to Exhaustion (at 1980 production)
Natural gas	40	65
Coal	27	230
Iron ore	40	250
Manganese	40	250
Chromite	10	80
Copper	7	28
Nickel	18	48
Gold	35	20
Tungsten	11	24

SOURCE: Henry Rowan, a CIA briefing to Congress, December 1, 1982.

TABLE 3.2. UNITED STATES MINERAL IMPORTS AS PERCENTAGE OF APPARENT UNITED STATES CONSUMPTION (1980–1988)

Mineral	Percent
Asbestos (95% of imports from Canada)	75
Bauxite, Alumina (37% from Jamaica, 36% from Guinea)	95
Chromium, Ferrochromium (7% from USSR, 55% from South Africa)	86
Cobalt (37% from Zaire)	94
Industrial Diamonds (worst situation) (57% from South Africa)	100
Manganese Ore (31% from Canada)	99
Nickel (38% from Canada)	74
Platinum Group (13% from USSR, 49% from South Africa)	86
Tin (23% from Malaysia, 30% from Thailand)	75
Zinc (best situation)	63

SOURCE: U.S. Department of State, *Atlas of United States Foreign Relations*, 2nd ed. (Washington, DC: USGPO, June 1985), 61.

Although such sensational predictions rarely come true, it is clear the USSR is not dependent on foreign countries for industrial raw materials while the United States is. What is not clear is how much the two countries can reduce waste and to what extent they, particularly the United States, can devise or discover substitutes for scarce minerals. But whatever happens, superpower status can be retained only with sufficient raw materials to maintain a modern military and powerful industrial economy.

Industrial Capacity and Economic Power
Even an abundance of raw materials does not enable a country to be a great power. It must also possess a modern industrial system with the capability of producing all the latest machinery and technology and a full line of up-to-date weaponry. It is clear that

The Soviet Union, while having been potentially always a great power, became one in fact only when it entered the ranks of the foremost industrial powers in the 1930s, and it became the rival of the United States as the other superpower only when it acquired in the 1950s the industrial capacity for waging nuclear war.[15]

Although the Soviet Union and the United States both have large industrial economies unmatched by any others, there are big differences in their guiding principles and operating procedures. The economies of the superpowers, being different, support their national powers in different ways. The Soviet and American degree of support of the defense effort differs. At most, 7 to 8 percent of the United States GNP (see Table 3.3) goes to the military, whereas in the Soviet Union the percentage is at least 12 percent. Since the Soviet GNP is about half the American, the economic resources going to defense seem about the same. But all such comparisons are misleading. The two economies are very different in military specifics. The Soviets get more "rumble for the ruble" since many of their military personnel are draftees and receive very low pay. Also, since Soviet defense plants are state-owned, they need not make a profit. In addition, Soviet officers are able to dictate to their defense industry.

The American military spends half its budget on pay and retirement. Not much is left over for weapons, operations, and maintenance. (Supposedly, the United States has ammunition for only thirty days of conventional war, whereas the USSR has a much larger supply.) The American military may be subject to "technology pull" originating from the defense industry—acquiring fancy weapons systems of great capability but expensive to make and not easy to use and maintain. The devastating results of the Iraqi attack on the U.S.S. Stark in 1987 show both the power and the limitations of high-tech weapons.[16] The United States's main industrial strength is its high level of technology, but its weakness lies in low utilization of its potential, its lack of readiness for high output of military equipment and weaponry, and the high cost and complexity of its products. The Soviet Union's main industrial strength lies in the high quantity and low cost of its production and the integration of its military's

TABLE 3.3. GROSS NATIONAL PRODUCT, 1980

Country	Billions of Current Dollars	Constant (1979) Dollars Per Capita
United States	2,614.1	10,408
Soviet Union	1,423.8	4,861
Japan	1,152.6	8,946
Italy	368.1	5,855

SOURCE: U.S. Bureau of the Census, *Statistical Abstract of the United States: 1984* (Washington, D.C.: 1983), 865, No. 1509; and George T. Kurian, *The New Book of World Rankings* (New York: Facts on File, 1984), 96.

needs with industrial production and planning. However, it has a real weakness in the low-technology content and low quality of many of its products.

The big question is whether the superpowers' economies can continue to bear the military and other burdens of superpower status at the same levels as before. Both economies are now growing slowly and intermittently. Both are subject to strong demands for a shift of priorities to the civilian sector. In effect, the superpowers' economies are finding it harder to maintain their present output and international standing. What efforts will they have to make if the arms race takes a new spiral upward into a "star wars" phase?

Although the American economy is still the biggest in the world and continues to achieve extraordinary spurts of growth, it has slipped relative to others in many ways. Japan was rated the most competitive industrial nation each year from 1980 to 1984, while the United States was rated third; it now achieves only mediocre ratings in industrial efficiency, although it is rated first in human resources. America's competitiveness has been slipping for twenty years and its rate of productivity growth lags.[17] The American share of world manufacturing exports (a good index of industrial viability) has declined from about 21 percent in 1955 to less than 12 percent in 1978, a 45 percent drop. Similarly, its share of world industrial output dropped from 59 to 40 percent over the thirty years from 1953 to 1983. This decline has had an impact on Americans. Between 1972 and 1982 real family income dropped by 8 percent or more and since 1979 two million manufacturing jobs have been lost. In addition, because of the large American federal budget deficit, the inflow of foreign money to take advantage of high interest rates has made the United States the leading debtor nation.[18] On top of this, many of the new jobs being created by the growth that *is* occurring are less well paid than the jobs that have been lost through "deindustrialization." Clearly, the United States is a different and less healthy country economically than it once was. The creation of new companies and many new jobs does occur, but on a weaker economic foundation. Inflation and interest rates were forced down by the Reagan administration but they could climb again. Although American economic growth for 1984 overall was almost 7 percent, the biggest annual increase since 1951, it grew at only a sluggish 2 percent in 1985—close to the low Soviet rate of 2 to 2.5. The rate for most of 1987 was better—about 3.5 percent, and the unemployment rate was low—5.7 percent.[19] American economic decline began in the 1950s, exactly when it seemed America was on a "roll" that would never end. One historian puts it this way:

> It was during the mid-fifties that the competitive quality of American manufacturers began to decrease. It was then that the cities of the nation began to deteriorate and actually to lose population.... It was then that the often senseless cult of "growth" became an unquestioned American shibboleth, without any thought given to the affinity of ... growth and inflation.[20]

Can it be that a similar process of serious economic decline exists in the Soviet Union? Can it be that the Soviet Union has gone about as far as it can go in economic development using its present strategy and methods? Mr. Gorbachev seems to think so and calls for a major economic reform. There are numerous indicators that the Soviet economy is in a no-growth stage that has all the signs of being permanent unless—and this is very unlikely—it shifts to new economic principles and processes more appropriate for efficiency and the production of high-quality goods at reasonable cost.

The USSR is rich in natural resources and a trained and educated population. It was bequeathed an industrial base by the tsars and has been adding to it for over fifty years. Yet its GNP, if divided up on the basis of the number of its inhabitants, gives a per capita GNP less than that of Italy—not one of the world's economic giants. Although the USSR can loft space stations into orbit, it loses a noticeable percentage of its harvested grain because it has to be transported in open trucks over rough roads. Although the Soviet Union outproduces all other countries in weaponry, it still has not met its people's demands for consumer goods. At some point, these and other economic deficiencies will have to be overcome in order for Soviet economic power to become a solid base for its international position.

Military Preparedness

The problem of assessing military power[a] is particularly difficult when considering superpowers in a nuclear age. Nuclear weapons may have "destroyed the previous direct correlation between military capabilities and political power."[21] Nuclear weapons are a serious danger even to the state that employs them. The superpowers' possession of numerous nuclear weapons and massive capabilities for their delivery makes war between them disastrous and also masks their usable military power. For military power that is not used (and perhaps is unusable) is really not military power but a sort of potential threat, a "psychological" power. Since both the United States and the Soviet Union try to derive some power from the support of other states and try to influence these states, the two superpowers are usually reluctant to use military power in a naked sense even against the smallest of countries. Their respective invasions of Afghanistan and Grenada are exceptions that "prove the rule." Afghanistan had long been in the Soviet sphere of influence while Grenada had been denounced as adventurist by the Soviet press.

The perennial problem of assessing differing kinds of military power also arises. This asymmetrical difference is a natural outgrowth of the superpowers' differing geographical situations and historical experiences. The Russian state has long had large armies supported by a military draft. This is necessitated by the relative lack of natural boundaries and Russian rule over large numbers of

---

[a] The next chapter is devoted to the superpowers' military rivalry.

unassimilated non-Russians. The United States has long been a leading naval power, using land power in small areas through amphibious operations. Only in the Civil War and World War II has it had large armies. Whereas the United States borders only on two relatively weak countries with which it has nonviolent relations, the USSR is surrounded by antagonistic countries, some of which are in anti-Soviet military alliances, e.g., Norway, Turkey, and Japan.

For the United States, military power is only one of its international capabilities. Its economy is itself able to serve the United States as if it were military power. The United States can utilize a whole array of economic capabilities to influence other states: loans, aid, food, technology, sales, and gifts of weapons (as well as the denial of any or all of these). The USSR has more limited economic influence, with the important exception of weapons aid. This means the Soviet Union is constrained by definite limitations on its military force.

Since Soviet power is great only militarily, it may never be able to stabilize its sphere of influence. And only the most endangered, and conveniently located, of its client states can expect assistance because the Soviet economy is too weak to provide high levels of aid to many countries. Z. K. Brzezinski has called the USSR a "one-dimensional" world power "essentially incapable of sustaining effective global dominance." It is, he says, "a global power only in the military dimension." [22]

Although the Soviet Union could be called a solely military power, this does not mean it cannot do much to further its interests and goals by displaying its military potential. That is, even unused military force has a certain influence if it is feared sufficiently by one's opponents. As a Japanese diplomat once put it, the Soviet Union is adept at the "peaceful uses of force." In effect, the Soviet Union is so heavily armed its very existence intimidates or at least inspires great caution. No power, even the United States, can view casually the prospect of setting the Soviet military machine in motion. Accordingly, protected by the concern and fear its military power inspires abroad, the USSR is free to wait for opportunities to arise in which its military force can be used to its advantage. Given the large number of states in the world and the turbulent nature of international politics today, suitable opportunities are not rare, as the examples of Angola and Ethiopia show. In recent years the Soviet Union has begun to display its military force for intimidational purposes, e.g., mock bombing runs into Norwegian and Japanese air space, submarine operations in Swedish waters, and overflights of American aircraft carriers at low altitudes. Still, the Chinese have shown that the Soviet Union can be taunted militarily, at least to a degree. In 1969 the Chinese massacred a Soviet border patrol without provoking a war and in 1979 China invaded Vietnam, a Soviet ally, and stayed for three weeks despite Soviet threats of retaliation. The United States invaded Grenada and opposes Nicaragua without fear of Soviet military opposition. This indicates the Soviet leaders are reluctant to use military force freely or on a large scale at any distance. Even in its war in neighboring Afghanistan, the Soviet military involvement, though brutally directed against civilians as well as combatants, has been rather small in scale and has been plagued by problems of morale and tactics. In early 1988 Soviet spokesmen announced the intention to withdraw.

The United States, too, engages in symbolic displays of power. Its navy has long been used to "show the flag" around the world. The United States has deployed units of varying sizes to many different areas in order to deter actions by other states. The United States has deployed nuclear weapons in tense international situations at least nineteen times since World War II. In four of these cases, the "message" was directed at the USSR, e.g., in 1962 during the Cuban Missile Crisis.

United States-Soviet military preparedness can be summed up as follows: Soviet preparedness is higher than American, since it has a very large military force. The United States active-duty military is only about half as large as the Soviet (2,167,000 vs. 5,130,000).[23] The Soviets have the advantage of many trained reservists as a result of compulsory military service, whereas the American forces lack this depth. Soviet industry is much more oriented to military production than is American and its output is greater. In addition, all Soviet industry has specific wartime production plans, whereas American industry does not.

However, a decided advantage of the United States is its allies and their support and power. NATO countries other than the United States provide 60 percent of anti-Soviet ground forces and tactical airpower in Europe. The Soviet Union has no militarily significant allies with it in the Warsaw Pact,[b] and most of the ones it has are unreliable, with the possible exception of Bulgaria, a minor military power at some distance from the East-West border in Germany. Still, the USSR could probably get ready for war rather quickly, whereas the United States could only reach a comparable level of mobilization in two years or so. Although the state of actual Soviet readiness is not known in the West, American deficiencies are. A 1984 report of the House Appropriations Defense Subcommittee found that the United States was not close to being able to fight a sustained global war on several fronts. The navy could operate against the USSR for only a week. Shortages of ammunition and parts were general, and the situation was not improving overall. Significantly, this situation existed even after increases in military budgets of the Carter and first Reagan administrations.[24] These increases were spent mainly on contracts for new weapons systems, not on fuel, ammunition, and training.

Military Technology. Although not necessarily decisive, this factor has become very important in this century, during which several technological

---

[b] NATO (the North Atlantic Treaty Organization) and the WTO (the Warsaw Treaty Organization) are the main military pacts led by the United States and the USSR, respectively.

developments have given (or appeared to give) one state or another temporary military advantages. The tank, nuclear weapons, ICBMs, and even technological capabilities such as the maintenance of communications and the breaking of codes have had military significance. The fear of technological breakthroughs by the opposing superpower has forced both the United States and the USSR to devote great scientific resources to military-related research. In addition, each side spies on the other's scientific activity, and the USSR steals technology from the United States if it is unable to buy it either directly or through third parties. The prospect of the United States developing a better anti-satellite system than the Soviet one and of developing a better anti-missile system based on laser or "star wars" technology, even though their military effectiveness is doubtful, had a role in prompting renewed Soviet-American arms control negotiations.

The usual view of the technology factor in the Soviet and American militaries is that American weaponry is often technologically superior to Soviet but that the number of weapons available to the United States is usually smaller. The possible technological difficulty with American weaponry is its complexity and difficulty to maintain and repair, particularly under combat conditions. This high level of technical sophistication is defended by the argument that it is the only way to match or overcome Soviet superiority in numbers. Yet the crucial questions of reliability and effectiveness of operation and "repairability" remain open. No one can know how well or long these technological "wonders" will work in a war. Other serious American problems are poor military procurement and high costs. Phenomenally overpriced items continually come to light.

These related issues of weapons technology, procurement, and cost have become political issues in the United States and are likely to remain so. At some point, politics may force a reevaluation and redirection of policy in these areas. The Soviets, too, will have internal disagreements over these matters as they raise the technological levels of their weapons systems and run into some of the same problems encountered by the Americans.

Military Leadership.   This is a crucial factor; without it, an otherwise excellent military can be useless. Leadership is a very difficult variable to discuss, partly because its worth can only be discerned in an actual war and partly because its effectiveness depends on other factors, e.g., political support and general as well as military morale. An American colonel notes, in writing about the Vietnam War, that it was "an obvious fallacy to commit the army without first committing the American people." That was the politicians' task and one in which they never "delivered," thus undercutting everything the army did in battle. The same colonel criticizes the American military leadership at the time for having lost touch with reality.[25]

The Soviet Union has not had a "Vietnam," but seven years of unsuccessful war in Afghanistan (longer than the USSR was in World War II) has cast doubt on the abilities of the Soviet leadership—both political and military. Just as the Americans in Vietnam, the Soviet leadership has neglected to commit the resources required for victory in Afghanistan. Unsuccessful wars eventually carry large price tags, political as well as economic.

Important, too, is the military leadership's knowledge about and experience of war. Some military leaderships have this only secondhand or from study. Here the United States, which has fought two wars since 1945, was once ahead of the Soviet Union. The USSR has only the experience in Afghanistan and its involvement through its advisers and observers in certain restricted conflicts in the Middle East and Africa. However, much of the familiarity with war gained by the American military leadership has been lost through retirements.

Knowledge of war can be undercut by rigidity of thought and tactics. Intense debate rages in both Soviet and American thinking about war, particularly the possible shape and content of a war between NATO and the Warsaw Pact. The Soviet military leadership has been oriented very strongly toward the offensive in its thinking and preparations. By 1984 the military leaderships of the United States and NATO had changed NATO's stance from a purely defensive one to one oriented toward counterattacks intended to disrupt the Warsaw Pact's supply lines. This "active defense" strategy may force the Soviets to think more about defense and is a way of capitalizing on the weaknesses commonly seen in the Soviet military: rigidity of command; excessively centralized communications, control, and command; and poor logistics. This takes us to the related issues of military quality and quantity.

Quantity and Quality of Armed Forces.   These factors can cancel each other out. Quantity can overwhelm quality and quality can do the same to quantity. The relative positions of the superpowers in the matters of military quantity and quality can be summarized as follows: The most obvious immediate difference is one of a real disparity in quantity—the USSR has more than five million men on active duty, whereas the United States has only about half that number. The disparity is increased by the much larger Soviet-trained reserve force derived from the military draft, which the United States does not have. See Table 3.4.

Quality is very difficult to judge. What criteria are to be used? If we consider intelligence, overall education, and acceptance of the military life and role, we can say that the quality of the United States military is now satisfactory. About 80 percent of new army personnel are high school graduates. Yet many American enlisted men today have been educated in schools in the poorest areas of the United States and are not prepared for using high-technology equipment. They need a re-education in the basics, "the three Rs," before technical training can be provided to them. The navy has found that only 9 percent of high school graduates have had a year of physics and only 3 percent have had a year of algebra.[26] Those who are well educated can avoid military service, since there is no draft. Quality in the Soviet military could be

TABLE 3.4. SOME INDICATORS OF UNITED STATES AND SOVIET MILITARY POWER

Indicator	United States	USSR
Military draft	No	Yes
Numerous trained reservists	No	Yes
Total armed forces	2,167,000	5,130,000 (plus 400,000 border guards and other special troops)
Estimated defense expediture	$284.7 billion (1985)	$295 billion (1984) (officially $19 billion)
Growth in expenditure	4.4% (1984) 2.2% (1985)	3.3% (1984) 3.0% (1985)
Inflation	4.3% (1984) 3.6% (1985)	−0.9% (1984) −1.6% (1985)
Personnel on active duty:		
Army	781,000	1,991,000
Air Force	606,000	453,000
Navy	581,000	451,000
Marine Corps	199,000	18,000
Strategic Nuclear Forces	—	298,000
Air Defense Forces	—	371,000
Forces abroad	525,600	214,210
Total nuclear warheads	26,000	34,000
Deliverable megatonnage	2,649	5,790
Deliverable nuclear warheads	10,398	9,544
ICBMs	1,026	1,398
ICBM warheads	2,126	6,420
SLBMs	640 (in 34 subs)	908 (in 80 subs)[a]
Bombers	297	250
Bomber warheads	2,544	1,000

[a] Soviet subs are deployed at a low rate, perhaps 20 percent.
SOURCES: International Institute for Strategic Studies, *The Military Balance, 1986–87* (London: IISS, 1986), 15–46; and, for the figures for warheads, a United States Defense Department estimate given in *The New York Times*, June 18, 1984, and ibid., January 7, 1985, 9, updated by use of: U.S. Bureau of the Census, *Statistical Abstract of the United States: 1987* (107th ed.) (Washington DC 1986), 325.

satisfactory because the draft pulls almost all men of an age group into the armed forces. Also, the Soviets may get more high-quality people in their officer corps than do the Americans because of the higher social status and privileges of military officers in the USSR. But there are real problems: poor knowledge of Russian (the language of command) by many non-Russian recruits, an increasing part of the army, and the resentment unavoidably felt by draftees anywhere. In addition, Soviet forces seem plagued by serious morale problems. Besides attacks on officers and defections to West Germany, there have been mutinies on warships, unheard of in the United States Navy. Soviet deserters from the war in Afghanistan have revealed that officer–enlisted man relations are very poor.

These morale problems may stem partly from the harsh conditions of life in the old-fashioned Soviet military—deprivation, brutality, rigid discipline, and an absolute gap between officers and enlisted men. This approach may tend to produce, as do conditions in Soviet society as a whole, a willingness to endure and suffer hardship. American forces, on the other hand, are accustomed to a relatively soft life with little attempt being made to regiment them into conformity. Instead, it is assumed that the American soldier will automatically perform very well in combat if he has been well trained. In the Vietnam War no American units either surrendered or were captured. On the Soviet side, we see the consequences of a harshly treated multi-ethnic army—large-scale desertions. In 1945 one of every seven soldiers in the German army was an ex-Soviet. But to what degree this World War II experience is still pertinent is unclear.

Population
The nature of a country's population unavoidably affects its national power. A century ago the size of a country's population and the amount and diversity of traditional production (food, handicrafts) were about all that mattered about a country's population. By World War I, however, other factors came into play, as Russia found out the hard way. Russian industry then could not provide sufficient weapons and ammunition for its huge army, and the Russian government was too inefficient to distribute enough food for the people in the cities. The result was rebellion, political collapse, and revolution.

In this post-industrial age, factors other than the size of a population are important. General educational level, technological training, overall health, infant mortality and death rates, life expectancy, geographical distribution and density are some of the factors that indicate how well a population contributes to national power.

But size still tells us something worth knowing. Without a large population, a state cannot support the economic, bureaucratic, and military bases of national power in the modern age. Still, the population ought not to be so large as to drain the country of the ability to maintain and increase its power. The large populations of countries like India and China inhibit the rapid development of national power. This is not true, or at least not very true, of the Soviet and American populations, both of which, though large, are much smaller than those of China and India. Both the American and the Soviet populations are still under 300 million. And, although they differ in size, they are comparable: about 280 million for the USSR and about 242 million for the United States. The American population is increasing, partly due to immigration into the United States.[c] In contrast, the Soviet Union's growth from immigration is negligible, the Soviet infant mortality rate is relatively high, and its life expectancy has declined. Although the Soviet Union has a pronatalist policy

---

[c] About one-fourth of the annual population increase of the United States is due to emigration from other countries.

and rhetoric favoring larger families backed up by child allowances, it is not achieving the desired effect. The population is growing significantly only among the Moslem inhabitants, a growth that may eventually cause serious tensions. One of every three potential military conscripts may be a Central Asian Moslem by the year 2000. (Almost one in five people in the USSR is Asian.) Since the European population is largely urbanized, educated through the secondary school level, and has no objections (as do Moslems) to birth control, it grows hardly at all.

Distribution.   Here there are notable differences between the two nations. The United States population is distributed in population centers throughout the country. The Soviet population, on the other hand, is still heavily rural and not evenly distributed. About 40 percent still lives in rural areas, a higher share than in any other industrialized country. About two-thirds of it still lives west of the Ural Mountains. This works against the economic future of the USSR since all the new sources of raw materials and energy are in Siberia, east of the Urals, where there is insufficient labor. The population of the European part of the country is slowly drifting southward, toward the warmer climate of the Black Sea, against the country's economic requirements.

Trends.   Although the United States population also has problems that detract from the country's potential, such as "dropping out" of school, drug use, violent crime, teenage suicide, unemployment, and abandonment of industrial plants, the American population problem as it relates to national power is different from that of the USSR. (The United States does have a special challenge—reintegrating into its prosperous postindustrial sector those people who have been "left behind" in urban ghettoes and "rust-bowl" cities.) The American problem is one of maintenance of its already generally high standard of living, about three times higher than the Soviet on the average, while the Soviet Union still faces the final challenge of a developing country—attaining a "European-North American" level. Doing this is now even further off than it was ten or twenty years ago, as the list of societal statistics in Table 3.5 suggests.

What is striking about these statistics is the poor Soviet showing in infant mortality and life expectancy despite the USSR's decided advantage in physicians. Even the life expectancy of American blacks is higher than the overall Soviet life expectancy. This does not mean that some United States vital statistics are not worsening to a degree. Teenage suicide rates are very high. The United States leads the industrial world in homicide rates. The high American violent death rate has been called a major public health problem.[27] Still, the United States has cut its infant mortality rate to only 10.6 deaths per one thousand live births and increased its average white male/female life expectancy to 74.7 years—real achievements.

Although it is not possible to explain fully the poor health situation of the USSR, demographers offer some possible causes. Two prenatal factors are

TABLE 3.5. SOME UNITED STATES AND SOVIET SOCIETAL STATISTICS (AT COMPARABLE TIMES)[a]

Item	United States	Soviet Union
Population	(1980) 226,504,825	(1982) 268,800,000
Natural increase	(1977) 0.7%	(1976) 0.9%
Births per 1,000 population	(1980) 16.2	(1977) 18.1
Total fertility rate (2.12 is the "replacement" rate)	(1980) 1.8	(1979–1980) 2.3
Infant mortality per 1,000 live births	(1977) 14.0 (1984) 10.6	(1981) 44.0
Crude death rate per 1,000 population	(1980) 8.9	(1980) 10.3
Life expectancy, males	(1978) whites 69.5 blacks 65.5 (1982) whites 71.5 blacks 64.9	(1980 61.9 est.)
Life expectancy, females	(1978) whites 77.2 blacks 74.5 (1982) whites 78.8 blacks 73.5	(1980 73.5 est.)
Physicians per 1,000 population	(1977) 176	(1976) 346
Percentage of males	(1979) 48.7 (normal percentage)	(1979) 46.6 (abnormal percentage)

[a] It is difficult to find comparable statistics for the same years.

SOURCES: U.S. Bureau of the Census, *Statistical Abstract of the United States, 1981* (Washington, DC: Bureau of the Census, 1981); *World Almanac, 1983* (New York: Newspaper Enterprise Association, 1983); Murray Feshbach, "The Soviet Union: Population Trends and Dilemmas," *Population Bulletin*, Vol. 37, No. 3 (Washington, DC: Population Reference Bureau, Inc., 1982); and *The New York Times*, October 14 and 20, 1984 and February 12 and October 12, 1985. Also see U.S. Bureau of the Census, *Rising Infant Mortality in the USSR in the 1970's*, Series P-95, No. 74. International Population Reports (Washington, DC: Bureau of the Census, 1980).

mentioned: the influenza epidemics and growing pollution in the 1970s. In addition, the breakup of the extended family and the increase in divorce, now 50 percent in some urban areas, combined with a continued high rate of full-time employment by women "may have caused a deterioration in the quality of child care." Alcoholism must have a negative effect. And, even though "the USSR has more physicians than any other country both absolutely and . . . relative to population size," they are not evenly distributed and their facilities have not been improved.

> The problems are those of a generally demoralized service: doctors, mainly women, are poorly paid, earning less than the average industrial wage, standards of hygiene are low, hospitals are impersonal, post-surgical care is very limited, medicines and medical equipment outdated and often unobtainable. But on top of this there is a crushing indifference, an absence of responsibility at all levels, and a lack of personal care and attention. Frequently

the only way to get a doctor to attend to your case properly is to offer a substantial bribe....[28]

Past food shortages, too, may have had a negative effect on health. One also has to wonder at the possibly harmful effect of chemical additives in processed food. Soviet food packaging does not list ingredients. Gorbachev is beginning to tackle this problem. He has attacked high alcohol consumption and has raised the pay of medical personnel.

National Character

National character[d] or national culture refers to those relatively enduring patterns of thought and action that are common and central to a people; that is, the ways of doing things they tend to think are "natural." What one people tend to think is normal may be seen as abnormal by another people. Still, there are those who reject the idea of national character out-of-hand, considering it either too vague or prejudicial. They ask, how can one type or label an entire population of millions of people? Others see the concept as racist and reminiscent of the fascist ideology of Hitler.

On the other hand, the idea of national character is widely accepted, especially by those who are familiar with other cultures. "The observer of the international scene who attempts to assess the relative strength of different nations must take national character into account, however difficult it may be to assess correctly." Its "qualities set one nation apart from others, and they show a high degree of resiliency to change." For example, what Tocqueville wrote in the 1830s about American willingness to cooperate with one another still applies well, and Bismarck's observation of the "elementary force and persistence" of the Russian nature also continues to apply to Russian foreign policy.[29] Those who write about Stalin point out his effective political use of Russian attitudes. Despite his crimes, there are still Russians who miss his presence.[e] The reelection of Ronald Reagan to the United States presidency in 1984 is attributed partly to "his identification with America's myths ... a nostalgic view of America, rooted in small-town values of hard work, patriotism and neighborhoods."[30]

A nation cannot live without myths widely accepted as fundamental values. "Every society is held together by a myth-system—a complex of dominating thought-forms that determines and sustains all its activities."[31] They give its inhabitants something to hold onto together and thereby become more than their sum.

---

[d] This topic is discussed at greater length in the last chapter.

[e] "Russian attitudes" or Russian national character mean Soviet attitudes, in effect, since the Russian people dominate Soviet society and politics. "American attitudes and national character" no longer refers to any one United States ethnic group since no single ethnic group dominates the United States now.

The differences in the way Russians and Americans think and act cause friction in United States-Soviet relations. At the same time, similarities are often noted in the two cultures—suspiciousness of foreigners and foreign ways and thinking, for example, as well as a common appreciation of technology and the joys of building huge projects.

A list of American and Russian cultural differences pertaining to foreign policy and their interrelations might look like Table 3.6.

Although some deny there are any cultural differences between the Russian and the American peoples, how else can we explain the following statement, made in 1977 to the author, by a Soviet scholar: "Ever since the time of the ancient Greek city-states, it has been a government's duty in its relations with other states to ensure that its citizens go along with its decisions." The Russian had been complaining about the U.S. government's claim that it could not sign an arms control treaty because of popular pressures. To many Americans, his statement puts things backwards, placing the people below their government. But to the Russian it is normal for a people to accept their government's decision (or to be made to accept those decisions). Another Soviet scholar, visiting the site of Shays' Rebellion (1786), said he assumed that Shays had been executed. I said, "No," pointing out that, though Shays had had to leave Massachusetts, he lived out his days a free man in New York State. But he did not believe me.

Americans tend to try to push their government to turn "relations with other nations partly into a quest for democracy, freedom, personal fulfillment, social harmony, and universal justice." Americans, with one lawyer for every 390 persons (more than three times as many lawyers per capita than England) tend to turn every political question into a legal one. This may work within the "lawyerized" American society, but it faces failure in the semianarchic international context in which many cultures are not legalistic. (Alexander Kerensky, the head of the Provisional Government of Russia before it was overthrown by the Bolshevik coup of late 1917, once told me that there is "no such thing" as international law.)

Also creating difficulties is an unconscious nonacceptance of each other by the Russians and Americans. Since in each society leading groups of people see their own society as the special and desirable one, the views and needs of the other society are unacceptable. This attitude became even stronger in United States policy when the Reagan administration came into office, since it has emphasized American uniqueness, power, and anti-foreignism (not only anti-communism). And, of course, since the Russian leaders talk as if their society is a Marxian socialist one and a pattern for the future, they must act as if the United States is an illegitimate power that will have to give up its international position to the Soviet Union. This is the stuff of which conflicts are made. "The dominant culture of neither the Soviet Union nor the United States has much understanding of, and probably has strong prejudice against, the political and economic systems of the other."[32] It is no wonder that in early 1984 there was a

TABLE 3.6. COMPARISON OF CULTURAL/POLITICAL ATTITUDES

United States	USSR
"legalism" and litigiousness	"politicism" (acceptance of political ways as autonomous)
short-range goals	long-range goals
dislike of conflict	(reluctant) acceptance of conflict
individualism	collectivism
assuming all differences can be resolved (compromise is highly desirable)	assuming all differences cannot be resolved (compromise is tentative and temporary, and perhaps a sign of weakness)
volatility (at a superficial level)	rigid continuity (sociopolitical change is slow)
"quickness" in action	"slowness" in action
sentimentality and moralizing about politics	realism and cynicism about politics

"nasty mood in Moscow ... rooted in a climate of extreme anxiety and anger" and in Washington a "sense of vulnerability mixed with anxiety." [33] The United States has run up against an adversary whose anti-capitalist ideology is buttressed by the staying power and harshness granted by a long and difficult history of suffering, defensiveness, and conquest. In dealing with the Soviet Union Americans face a fundamentally different view of politics: a view with a longer historical span and greater psychological depth, one of an old civilization that may have been updated, but was not uprooted by ... a radical social ideology. [34]

But the Russians face difficulties, too. Soviet actions may precipitate anti-Soviet moods in the United States that turn government policy away from accommodation, negotiation, and even communication with the USSR. Soviet pressure during the October 1973 Arab-Israeli war undercut détente. The Soviet invasion of Afghanistan in 1979 had a similar effect. It is not at all clear whether the Soviet leaders understand that their actions can challenge deeply held American values. Two American scholars caution that "note should be made of the pervasive responsiveness of the American public, of the media, and of politicians to anti-Communist and anti-Russian themes." Another points out that "the Russians, by their rhetoric and deeds, traditionally help American critics of rapprochement ... Moscow ... will probably persist in actions Americans find abhorrent." [35] Similarly, American actions can have an anti-American effect on Soviet policy. The USSR is no longer run by a Stalin who can ignore what high-level people think. During 1977 I was told by several Soviet citizens that American campaign rhetoric about the USSR in 1976 made them angry. They were especially disturbed that President Carter met with a prominent ex-Soviet dissident in the White House and sent a letter to the scientist Sakharov in early 1977. President Reagan's public statement that the Soviet Union was the "focus of evil" in the modern world may have had a similar result. Too many important people in the Soviet Union now know about American developments for the Soviet leaders to ignore such statements.

National Morale

"National morale is the degree of determination with which a nation supports the foreign policies of its government in peace or war." This intangible and elusive factor is still of crucial importance to the power of a nation. Country A may be better armed than Country B, but its government may still not be able to pursue its policies effectively without mass popular support and high national morale. "Without national morale, national power is either nothing but material force or else a potentiality that awaits its realization in vain."[36] Although Americans disagree vocally about government policy, they tend to support their government massively and firmly in a crisis. Despite the dissatisfaction with the Vietnam War displayed by large numbers of Americans during the 1960s, it seems that the American government can still depend on significant, albeit not necessarily enthusiastic popular support for its foreign policies.

Public protest in the United States, though made known to all by the communications media that are independent of government, tends not to be general or overwhelming. Even the public protests of the Vietnam War period, big as some of them were, involved only a very small percentage of the population (and even of the college population). Government policy, if presented and pursued differently, might have undercut or even eliminated much of the antiwar protest. The United States government never pursued the war strongly or clearly and it was apparent that government officials themselves were only reluctantly in favor of the war. Clearly, the U.S. government could have done more to improve national morale during the 1960s and 1970s. After the election of Ronald Reagan in 1980 however, it seems as if American national morale improved, at least as far as it affected foreign policy, until the Iran-Contra hearings of 1987. During the second presidential debate in 1984, Walter Mondale, Reagan's opponent, actually congratulated the President for helping to improve national morale. Clearly, what government does and how it does it can improve national morale, and even without making life better materially for many.

Soviet national morale is to some degree a puzzle; but, to the extent it has been visible, we see a mixed situation with higher "highs" and lower "lows" than in the American case. During the early days of World War II, probably in response to the terrible deprivations Stalin had put his people through during the government takeover of the land (collectivization) and the mass arrests and killings during the mid-1930s (the great purge), hundreds of thousands of Soviet soldiers joined the invading Germans. But, because the invaders' policies were no gentler than Stalin's, support for the Soviet system solidified, particularly among Russians. Once Stalin began to appeal to Russian nationalism and muted Communist phraseology, national morale rose to powerful intensity. The Germans were driven out of the USSR even before the Western Allies landed in France. The wartime appeal to Russian nationalism has been propagated in the USSR ever since, but with uncertain effect on national morale today.

One problem in assessing Soviet national morale now is that it is not possible to determine whether a myth keyed to one ethnic group, the Russians, will be accepted in the multiethnic Soviet Union during a national crisis. We now know, for example, that the Soviet military garrisoned in Hungary during the Hungarian Revolution of 1956 had to be withdrawn because they could not be trusted to fight the Hungarians and that another Soviet army had to be sent in to put an end to the revolution.

The Soviet people are under great strain, which is likely to have a negative impact on national morale. True, they have been under great burdens for a long time and have a capacity for endurance. Yet, as a popular song puts it, "Why are we, who were first in line [for socialism] still not at the head of the line [in terms of economic well-being]?" Although Soviet output per head of population (labor productivity) rose from just over a third of the United States level in 1965 to almost a half in 1975, since then it has fallen further behind that of the United States. In addition, food rationing now exists in many Soviet cities. The USSR has 16.2 people per thousand in the active duty military (all male), whereas the comparable figure for the United States is only 9.1. The Soviet economy is severely strained.[37] One indicator of low national morale is the present commonness of crime, against both persons and property, and of corruption. The Soviet Minister of Internal Affairs has spoken quite openly of these problems. He broke sharply with the standard Soviet explanation of crime, "vestiges of the past and of capitalism," and gave striking examples of the high scale of crime. For example, about half of all thefts from the railroads "are committed by transport workers themselves."[38] Although no firm conclusions can be drawn, it is not difficult to surmise that Soviet national morale is low.

Since the 1960s and the social disturbances connected with American blacks' quest for increased civil rights and the opposition to the Vietnam War, many observers have felt that the United States was undergoing some sort of sociopolitical malaise. Although some social indicators—crime and unemployment, for example—have begun to improve and have raised the level of confidence (a factor that aided in the reelection of President Reagan in 1984), it may be that conditions of life are worsening for a large minority of Americans. The unemployment rate for blacks is more than twice the rate for whites. Perhaps the United States is again becoming a country of two societies—one relatively comfortable and accordingly confident and with high morale overall, and another that is left out of or behind the majority society's favorable situation. One study finds a "two-tiered economy" with "the second tier dying." The poverty rate grew faster in the early 1980s than in any other comparable period since the 1950s. (In 1983, 15.2 percent of the population lived in poverty, while in 1985 thirty-three million Americans, about 14 percent, were classified as poor with another twenty to thirty million classified as needy. Only 2 percent of the population held 28 percent of the nation's wealth.)[39] Farm foreclosures grew faster in the 1980–1983 period than at any other time since the Depression of the 1930s. It will be a serious matter for American national power if this division into "two Americas" becomes permanent and depresses national morale.

The Quality of Diplomacy

By the term "diplomacy" we mean more than formal verbal exchanges between professional diplomats sitting around conference tables in elegant surroundings. Diplomacy[f] refers as well to the ways in which foreign policy is formulated and executed. In the United States and the Soviet Union, diplomacy is a product of other politicians, the military, the intelligence agencies, and influential people, in addition to the foreign service. In the United States diplomacy is carried out as well by individuals[g] and groups not connected with, or even opposed to, the administration, by the news media and, of course, congressmen and congressional committees. For example, during the SALT negotiations, individual United States congressmen took an active part in the proceedings. The Soviets were often told that any United States-Soviet strategic arms agreement must be approved by Congress; that administration approval is insufficient. The Soviet leaders understand this. In the United States diplomatic power is quite dispersed. In effect, then, diplomacy is no longer the exclusive preserve of diplomats. In the age of instantaneous communications and the "back channel" that bypasses foreign services, diplomats and entire diplomatic staffs can become mere "fronts" for governments and their real diplomacy.

Diplomacy, however changed from the earlier form, is still significant. It is still an art that can integrate the factors of national power into an actual foreign policy. If successful, diplomacy can increase a state's power beyond what it would otherwise be. It can even help defeat superior national power. "Diplomacy . . . is the brains of national power, as national morale is its soul."[40]

In comparing American and Soviet diplomacy, we are immdiately thrown into the old argument concerning the supposedly superior advantages of dictatorships over the supposedly inferior qualities of democracies. The Soviet leaders, it is said, do not have to fend off hostile public opinion openly expressed and the challenges of opposing political parties. They can, it is also said, calmly choose their goals and the policies that are most likely to realize them. In addition, they are said to have a long-range point-of-view, whereas democracies supposedly can think only of the present. Further, they can accept defeats without having to change policy. It may even be true that, because the Soviet

---

[f] This topic is discussed at greater length in the last chapter.
[g] Armand Hammer is one example.

leaders have maintained themselves in power for seventy years through "ceaseless watchfulness and repression," the "realism, cynicism and cunning bred by such an experience ... make the Soviet leaders skilled diplomatic practitioners.... The West, by contrast, is indolent because it can afford to be."[41]

Today Soviet foreign policy has to be the result of many possibly conflicting wishes. Compromise takes time and does not necessarily produce the best policy. And, during the first years of a leader's tenure, policy may be difficult to make. In any case, Soviet diplomacy has not been able to defeat the United States or even weaken it seriously. The relative decline of American power is the result of general world developments, not of the power or diplomacy of the Soviet Union.

The United States does have certain advantages supporting its diplomacy. For one, despite occasional attempts at destabilizing governments, the United States generally tries to support peace and stability in the world. Secondly, the United States tends to support its alliance partners and does not switch sides for temporary advantage as the USSR has done. And the United States has freely aligned significant allies, a factor lacking in the Soviet case. Finally, although American governments find it difficult to use large-scale military force in support of their policies, they do have a sufficient degree of real popular support for the maintenance of long-term policy, e.g., the alliance with Western Europe and opposing the most egregious Soviet expansionist acts. As Henry Kissinger points out, "the management of a balance of power is a permanent undertaking, not an exertion that has a foreseeable end."[42] Although American governments will never find the domestic politics of foreign policy all to their liking, if they are prudent and explain their goals well they will have sufficient support for the conduct of foreign policy, including contending and cooperating with the Soviet Union. Although the United States will not be able to eliminate the Soviet Union as a serious rival some sort of dynamic but manageable balance, more or less acceptable to both superpowers, can be achieved through diplomacy.

CONCLUSION

What has the national power of the two giants brought them? Have they achieved their aims or only prestige and notoriety? Neither has been able to eliminate the other as the major rival and contender; and, logically, neither could eliminate the other without committing national suicide. Is this troublesome balance likely to change? History suggests not. "Since the emergence of the modern state system in the fifteenth century, no single nation has succeeded in imposing its will for any length of time upon the rest of the world by sheer material force alone."[43] Potential hegemonies have no friends, only vassals and sunshine allies. Consider the fates of Napoleon and Hitler.

Both superpowers have been partly successful in exercising their national power on the world scene. Ironically, each has been aided, though unintentionally, by the other. The USSR is dominant in East Central Europe, partly because the United States allowed it to be; and the United States is backed by a massive anti-Soviet alliance flanking the USSR in both Asia and Europe, partly because the USSR has frightened its neighbors by its internal nature and by its military might and potential. A state can have too much power for its own safety and comfort. The United States could lose a degree of its allies' support if the Soviet Union adopted a less-threatening posture and policies. This has been happening, to a degree, over the past few decades, though not smoothly. Certain Soviet actions have periodically interrupted détente in Eurasia and helped keep the American alliance system intact.

For the Soviet Union, "by the 1970s many of the national dangers of the past had been dispersed.... In possession of a great buffer zone in eastern and central Europe and equipped with nuclear weapons, the Soviet State enjoyed the most secure position in its history." This is clearly a significant accomplishment and a demonstration of the national power of the Soviet Union. Although the Soviet Union is under pressure from many difficulties, it is not in a desperate situation and is now "much too strong and its elites much too proud to accept American terms that are blatantly one-sided."[44]

Similarly, the United States, despite the limitations imposed on it by the Soviet Union and a slight decline in its relative power in recent years, is clearly still a superpower with a great potential freedom of action throughout much of the world. True, it faces new limitations such as terrorism and serious economic competition, but these have not been able to immobilize it. It copes fairly well despite its isolationistic tendency not to be comfortable with the exercise of power unless faced by a crisis or the need to defend itself. All countries, including the Soviet Union, still find it useful to have relations with the United States.

But, as has been noted, both states face real limitations on their national power. "The Soviets attempt military solutions to problems that they lack the economic capacity to resolve, while the West seeks to exercise economic influence while lacking a country-balancing military force."[45] Basically, "the great Soviet arsenal has not brought commensurate political gains," says an experienced foreign correspondent. She goes on to note that, although the USSR regained a role in the Middle East in 1983 with huge arms shipments to Syria, it did not thereby get real influence there. Although the USSR irritates the United States by supplying Cuba and Nicaragua, thus far there have been no major successes for it in Latin America.[46]

The United States is finding it has to live in a world that does not go its way in many respects. The big question for United States power is whether it will adapt to a world of competing powers, some of which are better able to function economically. Although the United States still profits politically from a general world fear of the USSR this situation may not last. If the new generation of

Soviet leaders is able to reform the economy and also make the Soviet Union appear less threatening, the United States may be asked to withdraw its military forces from bases around the world. Moreover some of America's own allies have become competitors, sometimes politically as well as economically. They have been able to obtain high technology, combine it with cheap labor, managerial drive, and a national economic plan with broad political support, and push aside American products in world markets. The result in the United States is an economy and a society potentially not able to support American international power at its present level.

REFERENCES

1. This definition is similar to Max Weber's in *The Theory of Social and Economic Organization*. See Robert Dahl's discussion of "Power" in *The Encyclopedia of the Social Sciences*, vol. 12 (London: Macmillan and Free Press, 1972), 405–415.
2. Henry Kissinger, *American Foreign Policy: Three Essays* (London: Weidenfeld and Nicolson, 1969), 61; and J. H. Herz, *International Politics in the Atomic Age* (New York: Columbia University Press, 1959), 41.
3. Here I am indebted to the classic work by Hans Morganthau, *Politics among Nations*, 4th ed. (New York: Knopf, 1966), Chapter 10, "The Evaluation of National Power."
4. Ibid., 149.
5. See Martin Wight, *Power Politics* (London: Penguin, 1978).
6. Morganthau, 106–144. Slightly modified.
7. Jonathan Steele, *Soviet Power* (New York: Simon and Schuster, 1983), 8.
8. W. H. Parker, *The Super-Powers* (New York: Wiley, 1972), 98.
9. In 1983 the USSR produced 80 million tons of wheat, more than the American harvest of 65.9 million tons and very close to the Chinese yield of 81.4 million tons. Source: International Wheat Council.
10. Henry Rowan, a CIA briefing to Congress, 1 December 1982; and Thane Gustafson, *Reform in Soviet Politics* (Cambridge: Cambridge University Press, 1981), 155.
11. *Wall Street Journal*, 9 June 1983, 37; *New York Times*, 23 February 1986, D-1, citing a study by the National Petroleum Council for the United States government, and *New York Times*, 19 November 1987, D-6.
12. Parker, 79.
13. U.S. Bureau of Mines data, cited in *Strategics Review* 4 (1980): 12.
14. Daniel I. Fine, *The Resource War in 3-D: Dependency, Diplomacy, and Defense* (Pittsburgh: The World Affairs Council of Pittsburgh, 1980).
15. Morganthau, 114.
16. On the charge that American weapons tend to be excessively complex and costly, see James Fallows, *National Defense* (New York: Random House, 1981); and Richard G. Head (Colonel, USAF), "Technology and the Military Balance," *Foreign Affairs* 56 (April 1978): 544–563.
17. From a 1984 report of the European Management Forum; and *New York Times*, 14 February 1985, D-1.

18. Glenn R. Fong, "Export Dependence Versus the New Protectionism" (Ph.D. diss., Cornell University, 1982), 36; *Stuttgart Zeitung*, 22 October 1983, translated in *The German Tribune*, 13 November 1983; and *New York Times*, 15 January 1983, 29 February 1983, and 30 July 1985, D-2.

19. *New York Times*, 23 January 1985, A-1; 29 July 1986, A-1; and 9 January 1988 and U.S. Commerce Department statistics of November, 1987.

20. John Lukacs, *Outgrowing Democracy: A History of the United States in the Twentieth Century* (Garden City, NY: Doubleday, 1984), 65.

21. Christer Jönsson, "The Paradoxes of Superpower: Omnipotence or Impotence?" in Kjell Goldmann and Gunnar Sjöstedt, eds., *Power, Capabilities, Interdependence* (London: Sage, 1979), 76.

22. Ilse Spittelman, ed. of *Deutschland-Archiv*, quoted in *Deutsches Allgemeines Sonntagsblatt*, 15 July 1984, translated in *The German Tribune*, No. 1142, 22 July 1984, 3; and Z. K. Brzezinski, "The Soviet Union: World Power of a New Type," address to the annual meeting of The International Institute for Strategic Studies, 8 September 1983, 11 and 17.

23. U.S. Bureau of the Census, *Statistical Abstract of the United States, 1987* (Washington, DC: 1986), 325; and International Institute for Strategic Studies, *The Military Balance, 1986–87* (London: IISS, 1986), 19 and 36.

24. *Cincinnati Enquirer* (reprinted from the *Washington Post*), 23 July 1984.

25. Harry G. Summer, Jr. (Colonel, USA), *On Strategy: A Critical Analysis of the Vietnam War* (Novato, CA: Presidio Press, 1982), 13 and 17.

26. *New York Times*, 29 November 1981.

27. By the Federal Centers for Disease Control. *New York Times*, 11 November 1984, A14. More than fifty thousand Americans are murdered or commit suicide annually. The homicide rate for blacks is six times that for whites. *New York Times*, 12 February 1985, 7.

28. Michael Binyon, *Life in Russia* (New York: Pantheon, 1983), 55.

29. Morganthau, 128, 124 and 125.

30. *New York Times*, 8 November 1984, 19.

31. Robert M. MacIver, cited by Mostafa Rejai in his *Decline of Ideology* (Chicago: Aldine-Atherton, 1971), 5.

32. Lawrence T. Caldwell and Alexander Dallin, "United States Policy toward the Soviet Union: Intractable Issues," in Kenneth A. Oye, et al., *Eagle Entangled* (New York: Longman, 1979), 207.

33. Dimitry K. Simes, *New York Times*, 8 January 1984.

34. George Liska, *Russia and World Order* (Baltimore: Johns Hopkins, 1980), 117–118.

35. Alexander Dallin and Gail W. Lapidus, "Reagan and the Russians: United States Policy toward the Soviet Union and Eastern Europe," in Kenneth A. Oye et al., *Eagle Defiant: United States Foreign Policy in the 1980s* (Boston: Little, Brown, 1983), 198; and Dimitry Simes, "Take Small Steps toward Moscow," *New York Times*, 12 March 1984, A-19.

36. Morganthau, 129 and 135.

37. U.S. C.I.A., *Handbook of Economic Statistics*, cited in Philip Hanson, "Revising the Party Program," Radio Liberty Research, 8 May 1984, 2; and U.S. Bureau of the Census, *Statistical Abstract of the United States, 1984*, 884 (figures for 1980).

38. Interview with USSR Minister of Internal Affairs V. V. Fedorchuk, *Literaturnaya*

gazeta, 29 August 1984, 10. Translated in *Current Digest of the Soviet Press*, XXXVI, 34 (September 19, 1984), 2, 3, and 4.

39. *New York Times*, 6 June 1987, 37; 21 June 1985, D-2; and 7 October 1985, A-24, citing the American Catholic Bishop's pastoral letter on the economy.
40. Morganthau, 135.
41. David E. Kaiser, a book review, *The New Republic*, April 4, 1983, 33–34.
42. Henry A. Kissinger, *White House Years* (Boston: Little, Brown, 1979), 115.
43. Morganthau, 158.
44. Barbara Jelavich, *St. Petersburg and Moscow* (Bloomington: Indiana University Press, 1974), 457; and Arnold Horelick, "U.S.-Soviet Relations: The Return of Arms Control," *Foreign Affairs: America and the World, 1984*, 63, 3 (1985), 537.
45. Kenneth Maxwell, "A New Scramble for Africa?" in Erik P. Hoffmann and Frederic J. Fleron, Jr., eds., *The Conduct of Soviet Foreign Policy*, 2d ed. (New York: Aldine, 1980), 533.
46. Flora Lewis, "Dismal Diplomacy," *New York Times*, 2 October 1984, 31.

SELECT BIBLIOGRAPHY

Chaliand, Gerard, and Jean-Pierre Rageau. *Strategic Atlas: A Comparative Geopolitics of the World's Powers*. New York: Harper & Row, 1985.
Congressional Quarterly, Inc. *The Soviet Union*. 2d ed. Washington, DC: CQ, 1986.
*International Institute of Strategic Studies. *The Military Balance: 1987–1988*. London: I.I.S.S., 1987.
Krickus, Richard J. *The Superpowers in Crisis*. Elmsford, NY: Pergamon, 1987.
Medish, Vadim. *The Soviet Union*. 2d ed. Englewood Cliffs, NJ: Prentice-Hall, 1984.
* *Narodnoe Khoziaistvo SSSR v 1984 g.: Statisticheskii ezhegodnik* (The National Economy of the U.S.S.R. in 1984: A Statistical Annual). Moscow: Finances and Statistics, 1985.
Parker, W. H. *The Super-Powers: The United States and the Soviet Union Compared*. New York: Wiley, 1972.
*Scherer, John L., ed. *USSR: Facts and Figures Annual*. Vol. 10, 1986. Gulf Breeze, FL: Academic International Press, 1986.
*Sivard, Ruth L. *World Military and Social Expenditures: 1986*. 11th ed. Washington, DC: World Priorities, 1986.
*U.S. Bureau of the Census. *Statistical Abstract of the United States: 1987*. 107th ed. Washington, DC: 1986.

*Appear annually.

Chapter 4
Military Rivalry

> Whoever claims that force cannot suffice as an argument
> overlooks the character of politics, where the winner takes all.
> —Czeslaw Milosz

THE MILITARY AND SUPERPOWER POLITICS

(Please note: To facilitate discussion of this topic, a glossary appears at the end of the chapter.)

The pursuit of political values and goals may well involve military force, at least to impress and persuade, if not to intimidate and harm. Force can arise in the political struggle of gathering power and denying it to others. Since it is not possible for states to withdraw from politics they must, in order to survive, cope with the problems of force and war.

Despite the dangers of total nuclear warfare and its certain result—total destruction—the superpowers use their military forces for political ends. The USSR has used military forces to back up foreign policy goals more than 180 times between 1945 and 1979. Hints that force would be used have also been made. Khrushchev once said publicly that Britain could be destroyed with only six hydrogen bombs. The United States has deployed military units in support of its political objectives 215 times between 1946 and 1975. Implicit or explicit threats to use nuclear weapons were made nineteen times and the USSR itself was overtly threatened with nuclear attack four times, e.g., during the Cuban Missile crisis of 1962. American capabilities for active use of military force are being increased, as continued development of the Rapid Deployment Force as well as other special forces teams shows. The Soviets have created similar units.[1]

The United States and the Soviet Union have not yet come into direct combat, although in October 1962 in the Caribbean it appeared as if they would. In the Korean and Vietnam Wars, American forces fought armies well supplied by the Soviet Union. In Afghanistan the USSR fights guerrilla forces armed by the United States and its allies. The two superpowers' military forces are arrayed against each other and trained for total war. In this they serve the political purpose of intimidation. Occasionally, the intimidation becomes active, though usually stopping short of actual violence. During the Arab-Israeli War of 1973, the USSR requested that the United States intervene militarily in the Middle East along with Soviet forces to prevent the Israelis from destroying an Egyptian army. The USSR threatened to intervene militarily on its own if the United States refused. The United States did refuse and called an alert to show it was ready for war. The USSR decided to desist from intervention. But the United States did prevail upon Israel to agree to a cease-fire, thus saving the Egyptian army.

There have been instances of mutual active military intimidation. In late 1984 a United States task force with three aircraft carriers cruising off the Siberian coast touched off a vigorous Soviet reaction in which large numbers of Soviet aircraft began flying very close to the American carrier planes. Both sides were undergoing training for war and also playing a political game of matching all moves of the opponent in kind. Sometimes there is humor in the United States-Soviet military confrontation. In May 1984 a Soviet intelligence ship off the California coast picked up a U.S. Navy target drone aircraft that had landed on the water and began to steam away with its "prize." But, after U.S. Navy vessels got in its way, "negotiations" began and the drone was put back in the water and recovered by the U.S. Navy. A relationship of sorts has even begun between the two militaries. Officers of each country are sent to the other as "tourists" or "students." During the Carter administration, military lecturers were exchanged and American officers were allowed to watch Soviet winter maneuvers.[2] Although such contacts were at first discontinued by the Reagan administration they were revived in 1987.

Despite such attempts at creating a limited bridge between the super-powers' militaries, there is a permanent pattern of tension, threat, and counter-threat in United States-Soviet relations. For example, in August 1984, after President Reagan made a joke about bombing the USSR, a low-level military alert was ordered in the Soviet Far East. In 1982 Soviet spokesmen warned that, if the United States were to deploy new missiles in Europe, the USSR would put the United States under "equivalent risk." In 1983 a senior Pentagon official said that, if the USSR were to put nuclear missiles into Nicaragua, the United States would take measures similar to those used by President Kennedy during the Cuban missile crisis two decades earlier.[3] Superpower posturing often uses military images to make points.

Military power is a central fact of the superpowers' status and foreign policies. A superpower would quickly cease to be one if its military was seen as weak, disorganized, or incapable of fighting. Thus the superpowers' militaries are prepared for war almost anywhere in the world—and there is naturally a tendency to use them in war on occasion. American forces have been involved in two wars since the end of World War II—the Korean and Vietnamese—and Soviet forces have been in one—the war in Afghanistan. Soviet and American forces have also been used in situations of extreme tension or violence that cannot be called war. Soviet forces have put down rebellions against Communist rule in East Germany (1953), Hungary (1956), and in Czechoslovakia (1968). American forces have been sent into Lebanon more than once and fought for a few days in Grenada. Military units are continually used for symbolic and intimidational political purposes. This ranges from "showing the flag" by warships making port calls to military aircraft bringing food and disaster aid as well as movements of planes, ships, and units. For example, after Egypt seized the Suez Canal from Britain in 1956, the United States diverted a U.S. naval task force of fourteen ships from a scheduled European trip to a voyage through the Panama Canal, then a United States possession, in order to warn the Panamanians not to imitate Egypt. The 1987–88 American convoying of Kuwaiti ships in the Persian Gulf was a warning to Iran. The Soviets often fly large numbers of bombers right up to Norwegian airspace and even through Japanese airspace to make a point. Japan reported 285 such intrusions in 1982.

The European Confrontation

The main Soviet-American military rivalry is in central Europe, where two great military alliances, the North Atlantic Treaty Organization (NATO) and the Warsaw Treaty Organization (WTO), confront each other along a more-than-3,000-mile front from the north of Norway to eastern Turkey. Most United States forces stationed abroad are deployed in Europe, 354,000 of some 526,000 military personnel abroad, while the Soviet Union has 380,000 army personnel deployed in East Germany alone. Although the two alliances have about the same number of directly available military personnel in Europe, the WTO has a decided advantage in main battle tanks, artillery, infantry fighting vehicles, interceptor planes, and in forces nearby available for reinforcement.[4] This is indicated in Table 4.1.

Both alliances are prepared to fight on very short notice, although it is widely assumed that neither could carry out a surprise attack on the other and, therefore, each would have time to prepare for a war. A war in Europe is not likely, simply because it would be extremely destructive, even in its conventional phase. "Conventional" weapons are now much more deadly than in World War II. Another, more important, reason for the avoidance of war in Europe is that the conventional phase might well soon escalate to a level of regional nuclear-weapons use. This in turn would probably escalate to an all-out exchange of strategic nuclear weaponry from continent to continent that would destroy both superpowers as functioning societies. In other words, the NATO-WTO con-

TABLE 4.1. NATO—WARSAW PACT FORCE COMPARISON (FORCES IN PLACE IN EUROPE PLUS RAPIDLY DEPLOYABLE REINFORCEMENTS)

	NATO	WTO*
Military Personnel (all services)	2,600,000	4,000,000
Divisional Equivalents	88	115
Fighter-bombers	1,960	2,250
Main Battle Tanks	13,470	26,900
Anti-Tank Guided Weapon Launchers	12,340	18,400
Artillery/Mortars (tubes 100 mm and above)	11,000	19,900
Armored Personnel Carriers, Infantry Fight Vehicles and Other Armored vehicles	33,000	53,000
Attack Helicopters	560	1,135
Transport/Support Helicopters	1,960	1,180

* When fully reinforced, WTO forces remain larger in all categories except transport/support helicopters.
SOURCE: NATO Information Service, *NATO and the Warsaw Pact: Force Comparisons* (Brussels: NATO, 1984), Figure 2 on page 8. See also U.S. Department of State, *Atlas of NATO* (Washington, D.C.: GPO, 1985), 8.

frontation is a "doomsday machine" if allowed to move to war. Perhaps only "Grenada-sized" wars are safe for the superpowers.

Because of its deterrent value, the United States has refused to renounce "first use" of nuclear weapons, a long-term demand of the Soviet Union for a lower-scale military confrontation, although the United States has always said its "first use" would only be part of a defensive response to an attack from the East. The Soviet leaders seem to assume that NATO forces might be used against their system in East Central Europe, perhaps as a follow-up to an anti-Communist rebellion in the area. To make this unthinkable they deploy nuclear weapons to forward areas and provide their troops with tanks and vehicles that are resistant to nuclear fallout. The Soviets also believe the best defense is the capacity to go effectively on the offensive.

Yet the unlikelihood of war in Europe ought not to obscure the fact that the major geographical area of United States-Soviet competition is Europe, because of the area's importance, and that this competition uses military force as symbol and means. Soviet military power has undercut American power in Europe and undermined European belief in America's deterrent capabilities. As for the Soviets, the presence of American military power in Europe has been a major reason for the failure of revolution there.[5] Accordingly, the USSR strives to nullify or at least reduce the political usefulness of American military power in Europe and of NATO by developing a military force in Eastern Europe that seems overwhelming. In turn, the United States tries to undercut the political usefulness of Soviet military power by training for attacking the Soviet military in its rear. The same process of military action-reaction-action occurs elsewhere as well—the Middle East and Northeast Asia—but it is more active and dynamic in Europe.

The International Military-Political Context

The United States-Soviet military rivalry is related not only to direct concerns arising out of the superpower rivalry itself but also out of the international political context. This context is both fluid and heavily militarized. Even if the superpower rivalry did not exist, many of the new states deriving from the ending of European colonialism would be unstable. They are beset with the problems of "state-building," problems that took centuries for their former European rulers to solve. Often in new states militaries are the only groups with the cohesion and dynamism to govern. They seek military assistance abroad. This often has to come from the superpowers. In Africa, perhaps only Egypt and the Republic of South Africa are sufficiently developed to produce their own arms. This period of fluidity may last for decades, if not for a century or more. In every year since 1945 at least four wars were being fought, with 20 underway in 1986, almost all in the Third World. Half of the Third World countries are under military control. All of these fifty-seven military governments have carried out violence against the public. Since about 90 percent of the increase in world population will occur in the Third World, where military expenditures have increased greatly, the tensions of military rule there can only increase.[6]

Both the United States and the USSR are deeply involved in providing military aid to the Third World. This aid is in the form of grants (gifts) and sales of weapons and equipment and also involves the provision of instructors, advisers, training, and spare parts. A country's military agreement with another is important for its politics and economy. It is difficult to switch arms suppliers, though a few countries have done it, e.g., Egypt. Some countries try to avoid reliance on a superpower and, instead, deal with another major arms supplier, such as France or Sweden, but this can be costly and limiting.

During the period 1974–1978 the USSR exported $20.8 billion worth of arms while the United States exported $22.4 billion worth. This means they each provided one-third of total world arms exports during the period. The United States gave $20.8 billion of economic aid during the same period, but the USSR gave only $2.6 billion worth. Arms averaged nearly 15 percent of Soviet exports from 1968 to 1979, whereas the corresponding United States figure was 6.2 percent. By the early 1980s the USSR was the largest arms supplier to developing countries. Arms supplies and assistance currently may be the main instrument of Soviet policy in the Third World.[7]

Although the United States is certainly in the arms aid game at the same level as the USSR, the latter has certain advantages. First, the USSR, with an arms industry producing at a very high rate, can provide more weapons than can the United States and can deliver them faster and without red tape. Second, the USSR does not have to deal in money and is willing to accept goods in payment. Third, the USSR, lacking a pluralistic and open politics, does not have to contend with domestic opposition to arms deals, whereas the United States does. But, despite their efforts and limited successes, neither superpower has been able to "export" its political system through arms deals. Such aid also diminishes the power of the superpowers by increasing the military might of other states. Even today, some of these states could be defeated by a superpower only with some difficulty. Countries like Syria, Israel, and Cuba are real military powers, thanks heavily to arms from the superpowers.

United States-Soviet Military Spending and Power

There are two opposing fundamental facts about superpower military spending—it does not tell us a great deal about military matters as such, yet there are persons in politics who claim that such spending tells us all we need to know about one or another superpower's political nature, intentions, and military capabilities. Statistics on Soviet and American military spending were originally gathered by economists who wanted some indicator of what effect military spending was having on the economies of the superpowers. However, this information was seized upon by those who assumed it gave a measure of military power or effectiveness or used it for purposes of political argument.

The USSR spends at least 12–13 percent (some say 17–18 percent) of its gross national product on the military and the United States spends at most about 6–7 percent of its GNP, a little less than 30 percent of the federal budget. This is a smaller share of the GNP and budget than in the Eisenhower and Kennedy administrations. Since the American GNP is a third or so larger than the Soviet, Soviet military expenditures are not much larger than the American in monetary terms and, since American prices are much higher than Soviet, the USSR can get a great deal more for its expenditures (more "rumble for the ruble" versus less "bang for the buck").

Actual Soviet military expenditures are never publicized by the USSR. The Central Intelligence Agency's findings, though controversial, are the ones most often cited. Essentially, the CIA's analysts determine what each item in the Soviet military effort would cost in United States dollars. The possible margin of error is plus or minus 10–15 percent. This "building-block" methodology is considered by some to overstate the USSR defense effort relative to that of the United States.[8] It is extremely unlikely that general agreement will ever be reached. Table 4.2 gives an idea of the range of estimates.

TABLE 4.2. SOVIET DEFENSE SPENDING (IN BILLIONS OF RUBLES)

Source	1979	1981	1986	% Annual Growth Rate 1970–1980	% Annual Growth Rate 1982–1985
Official Soviet Budget	17.20	17.054	19.063	−0.4	
US CIA	59–75	70.75		3.7	
British Government	76–81	84.92	120.1	4.0	3–5%

SOURCE: IISS, *The Military Balance*, 1983–84, 13 and 1986–87, 33

TABLE. 4.3. UNITED STATES AND SOVIET DEFENSE SPENDING (IN BILLIONS OF UNITED STATES DOLLARS)

Source	United States	USSR
Central Intelligence Agency (1979-approx.)	115	170
World Priorities (1980); Reagan Administration OMB	114; 132.8	130
Defense Intelligence Agency (1981)	124	222
Committee on the Present Danger (1982)	180	235
U.S. ACDA (1984)	237	260
Reagan Administration OMB (1985-est.)	246.5	?
International Institute of Strategic Studies (1986)	286.7 (1985)	295 (1984)
Reagan Administration OMB (1988 fiscal year)	292.0	?

SOURCE: World Priorities, *WMSE, 1983*, p. 33; Committee on the Present Danger, *Can America Catch Up? The U.S.-Soviet Military Balance* (Washington, D.C.: CPD, 1983), p. 9; IISS, *The Military Balance, 1986–1987*, pp. 18 and 33; and US ACDA, *World Military Expenditures and Arms Transfers*, 1986, pp. 93 and 97. The Committee on the Present Danger uses DIA figures, whereas World Priorities uses CIA ruble figures but does not then convert them into dollars as does the CIA. The DIA figures given are from *The New York Times*, March 3, 1983, p. 5; and those for the CIA are from U.S. CIA, p. 6; the Reagan Administration OMB figures are in *The New York Times*, January 20, 1985, p. A18 and January 7, 1988, A-22.

The range of variation in estimates is indicated in Table 4.3 by citing the figures, this time in dollars, given by two American organizations of differing political orientations, World Priorities (WP) and the Committee on the present Danger (CPD) plus those given by the Defense Intelligence Agency.

Whatever the exact level of spending, the evidence is overwhelming that as a percentage of GNP, the Soviet Union (at 12–13 percent) consistently spends more on defense than the United States (at approximately 6 percent). From a smaller economic base than the American, the Kremlin maintains at least a quantitative edge in almost all indices of military power, from the number of men under arms to the number of strategic nuclear delivery vehicles.[9]

But several factors important for military power cannot be derived from spending figures: quality of weapons, equipment, and personnel; operational and war-fighting capabilities; morale; and cohesiveness and organization. For example, three-fourths of Soviet military personnel are short-term conscripts given little training beyond small-arms firing and close-order drill, whereas many United States military personnel serve for longer periods and receive intensive on-the-job training.[10] We also know that the Soviets spend very little on their personnel whereas the United States spends about one-third, if not more, of its military budget on personnel (since military retirement pay comes out of the military budget). Until recently, the Soviets put much of their effort into producing large quantities of weapons, but these weapons have not been equal in capability to comparable American weapons. Here we have a rivalry of numbers against technology. Although Soviet military expenditure has been growing since the late 1960s, but at a reduced rate of only 2 percent since 1976, only since the late 1970s have United States military expenditures begun to grow notably.[11] This American increase in spending resulted in a "very substantial"

Soviet increase in reaction after 1982.[12] All the results of these increases will not be available for several years, given the long "lead-times" necessary for the production of new military equipment (ten to twenty years in some cases).

An evaluation by an American military professional concludes that until 1980 the Soviet-American military equation had, in general, been going against the United States:

1. Numerical superiority increased only in fighters afloat and tactical airlift; the
2. United States lost ground elsewhere, except for four categories ... ICBMs, manpower, destroyers, carriers;
3. Reduced United States inferiority in three of those cases was caused by Soviet cutbacks, not added United States strength.[13]

Highlights of the post-1980 American military goals include: a 600-ship navy, a 16-division active-duty army, several very large nuclear-missile submarines, a Rapid Deployment Force for effective military intervention, the B-1 bomber and a newer "stealth" bomber, cruise-missiles (already deployed on some B-52 bombers and in Europe), other intermediate-range missiles, and new ships and aircraft for sealift and airlift. But buying military equipment does little for operational effectiveness. In 1987 "cannibalization" was still common in the American armed forces.

The USSR will try to keep ahead of the Americans. The Soviet military has acquired or is now acquiring: additional ICBM warheads, more intermediate-range missiles (the SS-20), new and quieter nuclear missile submarines, new ICBMs (the SS-19, SS-24 and SS-25), new army Operational Maneuver Groups to penetrate rear areas in war, additional warships (including a fourth small carrier with a full-size one under construction), better tank armor and cruise missiles. The USSR is maintaining its military procurement programs and improving quality in a modernization drive that should continue into the 1990s.[14]

Arms efforts of this scale are a burden for the superpowers' economies, particularly that of the less-developed Soviet Union. Is it intelligent to devote great resources to armed forces over time, particularly when technology pull necessitates continual discarding of equipment and weapons for ever more technologically complex, expensive, and difficult-to-maintain models? Buying arms today is like contracting for an insurance policy with an ever-rising premium. At the least, arms races take resources that could go to economic modernization and social welfare. Arms races may ultimately weaken an economy even if a few technological spinoffs do benefit it in particular places.[15] Gorbachev's acceptance of "reasonable sufficiency" and plans for economic reform as well as the shift in Congress' political makeup in 1986 and the American public's concern for the deficit may reduce both superpowers' rate of increase in military spending. Most respondents to an American poll of 1985 viewed the deficit as "very serious" and favor cuts in military spending.[16] It is not surprising that the two superpowers, at the Geneva summit meeting in January 1985, agreed to begin to negotiate controlling the arms race, with everything "on the table."

THE ISSUE OF WAR

Nuclear War: Fear and Uncertainty

During the early 1980s a fear that a war would break out between the superpowers was widespread in the United States, the Soviet Union, and Europe. The sources of this fear probably included: the Soviet invasion of Afghanistan and the concern that the USSR was heading for the Persian Gulf, the election of a United States president who publicly expressed strong anti-Soviet sentiments and had advocated attacking Soviet proxy forces, a violent anarchical conflict in Lebanon involving the intervention of forces supported by the United States and the USSR, the general realization that the United States was no longer militarily superior to the USSR, and the continued production of nuclear weapons and of new delivery systems for them. The lack of ratification of the SALT II arms control treaty and Secretary of State Haig's statement in 1981 of the United States' willingness to detonate a nuclear weapon as a warning to the USSR in a crisis may also have made war seem closer. Also, the United States was producing several new nuclear warheads per week in eight models and the Soviet Union was probably doing the same.

What had heretofore reassured many people in the West—nuclear weapons—now had an opposite effect. With superpower nuclear parity, the American nuclear guarantee lost much of its capacity for reassuring the Western public. The result was a mood of concerned fear. The general realization that the superpowers are mutually and completely vulnerable to each other in a "mutual-hostage relationship" was bound to have some psychological effect on the American public. And journalists' accounts suggest that fear also increased in the USSR. This was partly an effect, to be sure, of the Soviet press's emphasis on the anti-communism of the Reagan administration and its increases in the military budget.

This fear of a United States-Soviet war seems to have materialized in a new context—one of a United States government talking about nuclear war as an aspect of political strategy against the opposition of an organized disarmament movement. A nuclear "freeze" opposing the government's new political use of nuclear weaponry was gathering wide support. Perhaps one reason for the increased state of tension about war was the psychological effect of having waited so long for "the other shoe to drop," for the war that must, seemingly, follow from a permanent nuclear threat.

A growing body of popular-level literature about war between the superpowers has grown up. The novelists first dealt with a world after nuclear war decades ago in, for example, Aldous Huxley's *Ape and Essence* and Nevil

Shute's *On the Beach*. Perhaps the book that had the greatest impact was Jonathan Schell's *Fate of the Earth* with its claim that nuclear war would be followed by a "nuclear winter" lasting generations. Later research suggests this result is not inevitable although some studies of the Defense Department and the National Research Council accepted the theory.[17] Also effective was the TV film *The Day After*, shown in 1984. Top Soviet military men also viewed it, but it was not shown to the Soviet population. In addition, various films presented images of a post-nuclear world—*Mad Max* and its sequel *The Road Warrior* as well as *Bladerunner*. In a number of films produced during this period characters wander as outsiders through worlds they do not comprehend.[18] One conservative strategist and consultant to the Defense Department concludes a book: "The pieces are now on the board; the game [war] could begin at any time."[19]

While conservatives tend to see a nuclear war consciously begun by the Soviet Union, some liberals tend to see war as inherent in nuclear weapons themselves or in American government policies. The new American MX missile[a] becomes a major focus of this concern. The MX is decried, because of its accuracy, as a serious but vulnerable threat to Soviet intercontinental missiles, most of which are land-based. In a crisis the Soviets would supposedly be tempted to launch a "first strike" against the United States in order to protect their missiles.[20] An objection to a deliberate nuclear attack is that the attacking country would in effect inflict nuclear suicide on itself through the radioactivity and other environmental harm such an attack would produce.

The usual scenario of a nuclear war beginning accidentally involves a malfunctioning computer of the American radar system causing a United States president to launch a nuclear strike against the USSR, thinking he is responding to a Soviet nuclear attack. (This scenario is usually summed up with the phrase, "use 'em or lose 'em.") But the use of even a few nuclear weapons would kill millions of people and grievously impair the functioning of both superpowers. One United States survivable Trident submarine alone can launch 240 nuclear warheads, each one much more destructive than the two atomic bombs dropped on Japan in 1945. To "use 'em" still means to lose—in a "super" Chernobyl.[21]

Another war scenario is based on a possible "launch on warning" policy by the superpowers. Although this policy is not in effect, some writers have claimed that the deployment in Western Europe of new American intermediate-range (INF) missiles, which would strike the USSR six to eight minutes after launching, would drive the Soviets to rely on radar and computers alone for the decision to launch their missiles.[b] There are at least two strong obvious objections to this. One is risk. "Launch on warning" would make nuclear war

---

[a] MX or "missile experimental" is a highly accurate missile similar in size to the largest Soviet missiles. Although originally intended to be mobile and with its exact location concealed, political opposition forced it to be based in silos known to the Soviets.
[b] These INF missiles are now to be eliminated.

inevitable—because radar and computer errors are routine.[22] Another objection in the West to such a policy is that NATO never went to a "launch on warning" stance when the Soviets deployed comparable missiles. Still, we cannot say what would actually occur in any crisis involving the use of nuclear weapons because we have no experience with nuclear war. All scenarios are, therefore, guesswork.[23]

Since nuclear weapons will probably be with us for a long time, if not forever, the question naturally arises of how to deal with their psychological and political effects. In short, how are societies and individuals to handle fear? Even if no use of nuclear weapons in war is contemplated or possible, they are highly valued for prestige and "swagger" power.[24] Despite their limitations and danger and the fears they engender, nuclear weapons have had one profound peaceful effect. They have prevented war between the superpowers—so far. They can be likened to a very risky medicine that prevents death but also can cause death. Can a better war-preventative be found? The recent literature on the fear of nuclear war includes an important book by a physicist that exudes reason, compassion, and confidence—Freeman Dyson's *Weapons and Hope*.[25] Although Dyson says there is a basis to Schell's "nuclear winter" nightmare, he believes that even nuclear war would leave a "remnant population of survivors." In saying this, he echoes Einstein, who said that, even after atomic war, civilization would survive somewhere on earth. Dyson suggests that civilization's vast store of knowledge teaches us that humanity's business is "not tragedy but survival," and that we can find appropriate political forms for dealing with the nuclear threat.

However we deal with the nuclear problem, there was no way of avoiding it. Nuclear weapons were bound to be created. The English scientist-novelist C. P. Snow, writing in 1939, said of inventing a nuclear weapon: "If it is not made in America this year, it may be next year in Germany" (then under Hitler's control and embarking on world war).[26] Luck, of sorts, did attend their creation and subsequent use. Only two nuclear weapons have ever been used in war; and none for more than forty years. One reason for this restraint is that nuclear weapons are not normal weapons but power symbols and deterrents to war. Possibly they have established a limit to conflict between large states. It is even possible the bomb will bind people together in a common concern—avoiding its use—that has been lacking since the Middle Ages and their powerful religions. In this sense, the bomb is helping to create a new world common culture and thus decreasing the bases of conflict.

Conventional War

Although nuclear war is not what is called in Washingtonese a "viable option," what of so-called "conventional war"? But how conventional can conventional war be today? Are bacteriological and chemical agents to be a routine part of non-nuclear war? Similarly, although international agreements outlawed poison gas and dum-dum or expanding bullets used in World War I, they have not yet dealt with high-velocity and exploding bullets,[c] which have the same effect. Nor have napalm and anti-personnel munitions that spread razor-sharp "flechettes" over a large area been prohibited. Conventional war today is much more destructive of people than it was earlier, as events in Lebanon, Iran, Iraq, and Afghanistan show. In particular areas it can be as destructive of property and persons as can nuclear war, minus the long-lasting radiation. In fact, certain "conventional" bombing attacks of World War II killed more people than did the atomic bombs. Modern "totalistic" all-or-nothing ideologies such as nationalism shared by whole populations have increased the aims of war from the limited ones of taking territory and people to the annihilation of states, doctrines, and economics. As a result, the civilian can be in more danger than the soldier.[27]

The lion's share of the military budgets of the superpowers goes for preparation for conventional war. Nuclear weapons are, relatively speaking, not very expensive, taking only about 15 to 20 percent of the United States military budget. Conventional arms get high priority. The United States is developing a new rifle, the fourth since the Korean War. Chemical warfare equipment is standard for Soviet army units—as shown in Afghanistan in which, suggests a U.N. inquiry, the USSR has used it. The United States may develop a new nerve gas. New forms of biological warfare derived from genetic experiments may come to supplant chemical warfare.[28] The United States Army is the largest it has ever been in peacetime. The bigger Soviet army remains as large as usual.

There are various reasons for this general readiness for conventional war. Superpower status and rivalry seem to require a military capability ranging across the whole gamut of possible conflict, from dealing with terrorists to small-scale interventions to conventional wars to full-scale nuclear war. Moreover, "far from making conventional military capabilities obsolete . . . the nuclear stalemate . . . has reestablished a milieu in which conventional weapons can be employed . . . in certain circumstances."[29] Ironically, some of those who particularly fear nuclear war call for greater conventional military capability as a "firebreak" against a conflict automatically going nuclear. In addition, the superpowers are rich and can afford large conventional forces in order to deter each other at all levels. The superpowers also have a great deal to lose: the USSR in non-Russian territory and peoples, and the United States in foreign sources of raw materials and distant allies potentially coercible by the USSR. Recent American military thinking calls for greater emphasis on conventional arms in order to cope both with Soviet regional expansion and aggression by developing nations.[30]

The superpowers' status is to a real degree derived from the military capabilities they possess and their joint victory in World War II. How much

---

[c] The type bullet used in the attempt to assassinate President Reagan.

attention would the Soviet Union get in the world today if it had only a small or purely defensive military force? The United States, too, would be a lesser power with only a defensive force of the kind it had before World War II. Nevertheless there is no reason to expect a high rate of actual use of their military force by the superpowers. Neither sees many areas where its use is clearly called for and where success seems assured, and each has to exercise caution to avoid a general war. Both superpowers are limited, too, by the realization that war is a very chancy thing. The great Russian writer Tolstoy, who had seen war firsthand, correctly saw war as a desperate improvisation, in which all plans can come apart.

Wars between small nations, with the superpowers involved but at a distance, are still likely, but most future military violence will tend to be sporadic, clandestine, and not open and outright warfare.[31] A realistic view seems to be that in anarchical international life, military force and politics are connected. By itself, military power guarantees neither survival nor prosperity. But it is almost always the essential ingredient for both. Because resort to force is the ultimate trump card of all states, the seriousness of a state's intentions is conveyed fundamentally by its having a credible military posture. Without it, a state's diplomacy can lack effectiveness.[32]

George F. Kennan told student officers at the National War College in 1948: "You have no idea how much it contributes to the general politeness and pleasantness of diplomacy when you have a little quiet armed force in the background." He even thought of the basic concept of a rapid deployment force in advocating the use of "small, highly trained mobile forces, capable of acting swiftly in local situations to restore the balance of power."[33]

Both prudence and the residue of Bolshevism dictate to the Soviets that it is best to be so well-armed that the "die-hards" in the West do not win out and decide to "do in" the USSR. Capitalism is sometimes still presented as carrying "war within itself, like a cloud carries a storm," and accordingly the Soviet Union must defend itself by necessity.[34] In short, Soviet military power is always said to be acting defensively, even if it may seem to some to be carrying out aggression. Similarly, most people in the United States see the Soviet Union as at least a potential opponent, because the Soviet system is not a liberal democracy allowing private property and free enterprise and because it acts against American interests. Again, prudence and differing ideologies suggest a certain higher level of armament than would otherwise be acceptable. It is hard to believe the United States would be putting as much money and effort into its military today if the Soviet Union were not (1) politically so different, (2) opposed to the United States, and (3) so well armed.

MILITARY EXPERIENCE AND TRADITION

Both superpowers have utilized military means to expand over vast areas. Texas was added to the United States through war as were many of the non-Russian areas to the USSR. During the nineteenth century both systems were expanding—the Americans more spontaneously through a westward migration of farmers, but with the military very necessary in order to provide security for the settlers. In the Russian expansion, the military was in a more central role. The Caucasus, Central Asia, and the border areas along the rim of China were simply conquered by the Russian army. In both countries the military enjoys a high degree of mass popularity. However, Russia has long had a large army based on conscription, whereas the United States has had very small professional armies that were enlarged to a respectable size only at times of relatively rare national crisis. And even then, the army quickly shrank to near-insignificance at the end of the crisis.

The essential difference is that Russia was in near-permanent military crisis for centuries, whereas for the United States such crises were rare. Accordingly, a large army became a Russian tradition while in the United States the army remained a small instrument. Even in the 1820s the Russian army numbered about a million men. Another difference is that the Russian army, with its "harsh and often ruthless" discipline, was regarded as a "penal institution" in a lamentable state led by haughty incompetents, but still was a model for the rest of society and, indeed, one of the few respectable careers open to a person of the upper class.[35] Whatever Americans may think of their army, the above description does not fit.

It was much easier to establish an American national state than a Russian one. The Russians were trying to create a state while under Asian rule (the "Mongol yoke") for almost two centuries, while the Americans were able to free themselves from European rule rather quickly (1775 to 1781, only six years). The Americans were still very "English" in the 1770s and were fighting an "enemy" much like themselves in a rather "civilized" struggle where only political liberties were at stake for most. The Russians, on the other hand, were fighting a despotic people of a different culture and race through a series of frightful encounters where everything was at stake and no quarter was given. Even after the Mongols were off their backs, by 1400, the Russian state still had to contend with other military systems infringing on its territory—the Swedes, the Poles, the Prussians, the Turks, the Austrians and Hungarians, and even the remnants of the Mongol or Golden Horde. Any one of these forces might have destroyed the Russian state. Every spring a wall of men was fielded through conscription to ensure the maintenance of the state and of the Russian people and their way of life. "In the sixteenth and seventeenth centuries there was scarcely a year when Russians did not fight along their ... frontiers ... Military organization thus was a necessity, for without it Russian colonization, so essential to its economic survival, could not have been carried out."[36]

Naturally, defense became offense: foreign territory was taken and Russia was enlarged until it was the largest state in the world. But it still was not secure. Tradition had become ideology and Russia's expansionist tendencies aroused grave concern in Europe and elsewhere. As early as the 1600s, the philosopher Leibnitz was calling Russia "a tyranny worse than the Turkish" and "far too large a state." The image of Russia the warlike and aggressive was born. It has never died.

Over the centuries of armed struggle "the Russians, while still thinking of themselves as victims, had become a nation of warriors." An "obsession with military power and territorial expansion" served the needs of the economy for farmland and the needs of the monarch for land as payment for his servitors' support.[37] To what degree are the Russians still motivated in their military policy by a fear of attack or by the danger of retribution and the loss of power that they would suffer if the peoples they now control were to become independent?[38]

The coming to power of the Bolsheviks through the use of troops disloyal to the imperial regime continued the tradition of the standing army and the use of military force for political ends. A large new army was begun in late 1917 and, partly commanded by officers of the old army, it defeated the opposing conservative (White) armies and then re-incorporated areas that had broken away from Russia, some of them run by socialist governments. Some new territory such as Mongolia was also taken. The new state needed an army for defense against the anti-Bolshevik world, but it also found it useful in enlarging the sphere of Soviet power. This was especially true in 1945 and later in East Central Europe. Indeed, Bolshevism or Leninism is decidedly military-like in some of its assumptions, terminology, and tactics. Force and coercion are legitimate foreign policy tools if social life is a class war and capitalism is, by definition, a ruthless enemy doomed to extinction. The Red Army could be a radical socialist force that avoided the need Marx saw for a revolutionary working class.[39]

The American post-revolutionary system was secure. There was simply no need for a large standing army and none was ever brought into permanent existence, nor does one exist today, even after more than forty years of superpower status. The Americans decided to have a "well-regulated militia" on the Swiss example instead of a standing army.[40]

Yet a small army and a navy were created nevertheless—to protect the frontier from the Indians and commerce from pirates. The non-military ideal, not fully realizable, lived on in the American political culture. The small army "was engaged in almost continuous military action" against the Indians, but out of sight of the general population and without a draft or heavy expense. Despite the Civil War of 1861–1865, in general, "the American people went through the nineteenth century with a happy and harmless faith in an ineffective force which was protecting them from a nonexistent threat." The American army of 1895 numbered only 27,495 men. Accordingly, large sections of the American public have been uncomfortable with current relatively large military expenditures.

Around the turn of the century, such changes as industrialization, urbanization, internationalization of economic interests, the movement of

American interests and power onto the world scene, and the rise of Germany and Japan quickly led to a new American military arrangement. A General Staff was created. The National Guard was organized to provide a reserve for the Army, and the Navy was greatly expanded to become one of the world's three largest in 1907. Mobilization was the key and it was finally used in World War I and again in 1941 and 1950 and to some extent in the Vietnam War. By the 1950s the arrangement was changed in order to contain the Soviet Union. Now deterrence was based on a nuclear-armed strategic retaliatory force and a United States Army in Europe. These were supported by a carrier-dominated sea-control navy, a large Marine Corps and a worldwide network of military alliances. See Tables 4.4 and 4.5 for comparisons of the present military strengths of the United States and the USSR.

Military Thinking

Despite some overall similarities, there are strong specific differences between Soviet and American thinking about militaries and war. The Soviets eschew American-type concepts, such as controlled responses and restrained nuclear targeting and "dismiss much of Western strategic and limited-war theory as pretentious, pseudoscientific, and even metaphysical."[41] Given the Russo-Soviet experience of war in its full brutality and destructiveness, there can be no belief in limiting superpower war. The Americans, with a more restricted experience of war and with nonmilitary intellectuals giving military advice, are able to imagine all sorts of scenarios that Soviet military men would think unrealistic. To Americans, "the warrior's perspective has counted for little, perhaps because there is less and less connection between the military culture and the most influential parts of the civilized world." Two former American army officers maintain that the ethos of the business corporation has displaced traditional military values in the United States Army officers corps.[42] But in the USSR, since the military culture is both by tradition and necessity closely connected with political power and purpose, the Soviet military is the designated collective military theorist. Almost all Soviet military officers are members of the ruling Communist party, while a few are also on the Central Committee, an influential political body. All indications suggest that the Soviet officer corps' value system is very war-oriented and that it completely rejects the American "managerial" style.

To the Soviets, war is not limited by rules or amenable to "gaming" and other ploys and restraints fashioned by nonmilitary intellectuals. For a long time their military literature has stressed the traditional themes of surprise, shock, simultaneity, mass, momentum, superiority, and the feasibility of victory.[43] "In their view, a force capable of dominating events in war is more likely to ensure deterrence ... than is one ... that lacks those operational attributes." Although the Soviet leaders do not seem to have confidence in victory or to be planning a war, they appear to think that "a credible war-waging posture ... is something worth having in principle."[44]

TABLE 4.4. MILITARY FORCES IN BEING* (ALL FIGURES ARE REPRESENTATIVE AND APPROXIMATE.)

	United States	USSR
Total Armed Forces	2,143,955 (202,700 women) (no conscripts)	5,130,000 (no women) (perhaps 2,620,000 con- scripts)
Strategic Nuclear Forces		
Offensive Submarines	640 SLBM in 36 SSBN	983 SLBM in 77 SSBN
Long-range bombers	260	160
ICBMs	1,010	1,398
Nuclear warheads on above forces	about 2,125	about 6,420
Ground Forces		
Army	770,904 (76,000 women; no conscripts)	1,991,000 (1,400,000 conscripts)
Marine Corps	196,273 (9,700 women)	18,000
Army Equipment		
main battle tanks	14,296	53,000
armored fighting vehicles	23,772	62,000 (+ 20,000 reserves)
artillery		
guns and howitzers	5,450	29,000
mortars	7,400	11,100
	570,973	451,000
Navy	(48,000 women) (no conscripts)	(75 percent conscripts)
Naval Equipment		
Principal surface combatants,	222	269
e.g., aircraft carriers (large)	14 (3 on refit)	(1 under construction)
aircraft carriers (small)	—	5
battleships (with cruise missiles	3	—
cruisers	31 (3 on refit)	36
destroyers	68	61
frigates or other escorts	106	167
submarines	97	360
minor surface combatants	about 89	762
Air Force	605,805	453,000
combat aircraft	4,350	5,150
Strategic Nuclear Forces	(under airforce)	298,000

SOURCE: International Institute for Strategic Study, *The Military Balance 1986–87* (London: IISS, 1986). These figures can give only a very approximate idea of comparative Soviet and American military strength. It does not take into account such important variables as deployment, experience, will, quality, reserves, and societal support.

TABLE 4.5. THE TWO NUCLEAR ARSENALS

	United States	Soviet Union
Long-range nuclear forces (Range of more than 3,400 miles)	Land-and submarine-launched missiles 1,640 Warheads 7,900 Bombers 322 Bomber-delivered weapons 3,862	Land-and submarine launched missiles 2,346 Warheads 10,088 Bombers 160 Bomber-delivered weapons 940
Intermediate-range nuclear forces (Range of 600 to 3,400 miles)	Pershing 2's and ground-launched cruise missiles 332 Warheads 332	SS-20's and SS-4's 533 Warheads 1,435
Shorter-range nuclear forces (Range of 300 to 600 miles)	The U.S. controls the warheads on 72 Pershing 1A's in West Germany, but does not count them as part of its arsenal; the Soviet Union does.	Approximately 140 launchers for SS-23's and SS-12/22's. U.S. officials say each launcher has several single-warhead missiles.
Very-short-range nuclear forces (Range of less than 300 miles)	Missiles 700 Bombs on tactical aircraft 1,700 Artillery shells 1,650	There are no reliable figures for the Soviet Union in this category.

SOURCE: "On the Table: Two Nuclear Arsenals." Copyright © 1987 by The New York Times Company. Adapted by Permission.

DETERRENCE

This term can be defined as an effort to persuade an opponent not to take some action by convincing him that the costs and risks of doing so outweigh his possible gains.[45] This concept and the forces that support it are today at the center of the military aspect of the United States-Soviet relationship. Even though the superpowers' deterrents are different, both countries have made sure that an attack by one on the other would result in the attacker's destruction. In terms of deterrence, "destruction" means, in general that a superpower struck by another superpower's nuclear weapons, even those from a retaliatory strike alone, will no longer be able to function. Losses of all kinds—human, industrial, environmental, and agricultural—will be so severe as to make even emergency operations unlikely or at best fragmentary. Nuclear destruction is far more severe and generally incapacitating than was even the widespread damage caused in Germany by British and American "carpet bombing" during World

War II. Present-day nuclear bombs are much more powerful than the atomic bombs of 1945. Radiation, dangerous for decades and even longer, will render large areas uninhabitable and unusable. Deterrence in American thinking assumes nuclear war will bring "mutual assured destruction."

Supporting deterrence for both superpowers are a relatively large number of nuclear weapons on delivery systems in various basing modes with a significant number capable of being launched after even a nuclear attack has occurred. The United States has 13,873 nuclear warheads deployed, while the USSR has deployed 11,044.[46] Each country has more or less adopted a "triad" or triple basing mode for its nuclear weapons—land-based missiles in silos of reinforced concrete, submarine-based missiles launchable from under water, and bombers armed either with nuclear bombs or, recently, nuclear-tipped cruise-missiles. In the United States nuclear weapons are rather evenly distributed around the three "legs" of the triad, whereas the Soviets have put most of their strategic missiles in silos in the ground.

Deterrence is not a "defense" in the traditional sense. It does involve a threat that a certain action will trigger retaliation. This threat must be credible and sufficiently potent or there is no deterrence. The superpowers have not, so far, tried to make a nuclear attack on each other impossible or difficult. This would require the capability to destroy the attackers' nuclear weapons and delivery systems before they are launched or in flight. Acquiring such a capability would be a threatening act, since it would mean the abandonment of mutual assured destruction and seem a cover for an offensive stance. This capability was eliminated by the anti-ballistic missile treaty of 1972 or SALT I. The idea of a space-based defense, the Strategic Defense Initiative (SDI) raises the issue of replacing deterrence with defense. Here is how one scholar distinguishes between defense and deterrence.

> Defense is physical ... deterrence is psychological, useful before war breaks out. It keeps the enemy from moving in the first place ... once war has broken out ... defense must take over.... Today we invest great sums in weapons that are designed for deterrence only; they have no value at all for defense. This condition is unlike anything we have had in the past... [and] has come to be known as the *balance of terror*.[47]

The essence of deterrence is the old Middle Age hostage concept: "If you shoot at me, I'll kill your hostages." Each nation holds the population of the other hostage against the initiation of hostilities.[48] As Churchill put it, safety is made "the sturdy child of terror, and survival the twin brother of annihilation."

The Deterrence Debate

In recent years the American variety of nuclear deterrence has come under criticism. There is, first, the realistic criticism that deterrence does not necessarily deter. It is conceivable that a state's leaders may decide to accept the cost of launching a first strike on a nuclear power. This seems unlikely but it cannot be absolutely excluded. Deterrence, to work, has to exist in the mind of the opponent. He must accept the painful implications of deterrence—living within the limits set by *his* opponent. Will the United States and the Soviet Union always be led by rational persons who accept the unpleasant limitations of deterrence? What if an opponent's motivations and capabilities change drastically? Deterrence can fail and when it does it tends to fail in stages. At best, then, deterrence is a time-buying strategy and not a substitute for a creative approach that resolves the problem of conflict.[49] Deterrence without a freeze on weapons development has competition and growth of armaments built into it, a process that has the potential of undermining deterrence and the certainty of making it expensive and tension-ridden. This, particularly, is protested.

The Soviet leaders seem not to have accepted the fundamental assumptions underlying "American deterrence": the opponent is and will remain a rational being who will not attack because he is restrained by fear of a nuclear counter-attack. The Soviets seem to assume, instead, that deterrence can fail and that, accordingly, rationality and prudence dictate preparation to survive its failure. "Soviet doctrine has never accepted the principle of assured destruction as a guide to force planning.... nuclear war may be senseless, but someone might start it nevertheless..." Accordingly the Soviet Union must vigorously prepare with a sort of "war-fighting deterrence."[50] Soviet thinking about deterrence and its resulting procurements policy has undercut deterrence among both American liberals and conservatives. The former say it tempts war and total destruction while the latter say it allows the Soviets to become militarily more powerful than the United States and to use this power, at least politically, against American interests.

When the United States was, in effect, the world's only superpower, deterrence seemed a proper and an effective policy. But now that the Soviet Union has achieved military parity with the United States and has begun to exert its influence around the world deterrence no longer seems to some a sufficient policy for the United States.[51] Some critics of deterrence want the United States to adopt a war-fighting deterrence policy and a related war-fighting military doctrine, tactics, and capability. Only those, they say, can deter the more powerful Soviet Union from expanding its international influence further, under cover of its own "double deterrence" or war-fighting stance. Such a policy would require accurate and survivable weapons that could destroy Soviet governmental institutions and leaders as well as Soviet industry and population.[52]

This concept of what be might be called "hard deterrence" is opposed by the "minimal deterrence" proponents. They argue that war-fighting deterrence, if fully implemented, brings nuclear war closer. If both superpowers lack the full capability for waging nuclear war they have, it is said, one more reason for not starting one. But if they could wage such a war, they might decide, under the tension of a confrontation, to move to war to resolve the matter once and for all.

Here are two very different views of human psychology and great power game-playing. One, that of war-fighting deterrence, holds that only a strong and well-supported military stance avoids war, while that of minimal deterrence argues that a survivable small scale nuclear deterrent is sufficient to avoid war; that even the potential use of only a few nuclear weapons is too terrible for any power to risk. One view is pessimistic and operates on worst case assumptions while the other is optimistic and assumes rationality ultimately rules.

Proponents of minimal deterrence tend to hold that warfighting depends on being able to wage limited nuclear war, but neither the Soviet Union nor American allies are willing to allow the United States this freedom. And, if a nuclear war begins it is likely to escalate to total nuclear war—and total destruction. In addition, gathering the means for nuclear warfighting might itself result in nuclear war, since those means look like a first strike capability, something neither superpower wants the other to have. The argument proceeds:

> Thus, warfighting actually increases the likelihood of conflict through the proliferation of interests and instruments; it enhances opportunities for limited hostile action which may precipitate into a general conflict; it increases the likelihood of escalation...; and it increases the likelihood of an all-out war.... [53]

A similar concept of "finite deterrence" was put forth by Robert McNamara, a former secretary of Defense, who suggested that the United States need be able to do no more to the Soviet Union than to inflict "unacceptable damage" with fewer than 200 or so one megaton warheads. [54]

The objections to minimal deterrence are not insurmountable and may be only of a short-term nature. Yet, a minimal deterrent for the United States is out of the question until Soviet views change. "It takes two to tango." That is, unless the Soviet Union and the United States jointly adopt minimal deterrence, neither will adopt it. Such joint change in the superpowers' deterrent posture would require a rather long time period of successful and extraordinarily complex arms reduction negotiations and only a limited amount of proliferation of nuclear weapons among other states. This process has only just begun. Minimal deterrence will be acceptable to the superpowers only if it is sufficient to deter and, if necessary, strike back at, third powers who might use nuclear weapons against them. Possibly the superpowers will be forced to minimal deterrence by the frightening uncertainties and costs that nuclear warfighting has opened up. Why would the superpowers persist in living in a bottomless pit of fear, expense, and danger?

MILITARY SPENDING

Politicians have periodically called upon Americans to "bear any burden" in the defense of the country. Americans have responded by spending more on the military than any other people—now about 6.5 percent of the GNP. But it is politically difficult to continue this spending in a context of cuts in government spending and an anti-tax mood, high unemployment and a low-growth economy, lack of any major threatening international crisis and resurgence of traditional American dislike of foreign involvement.

President Carter began to increase defense expenditures by 3 percent a year in real terms. Later President Reagan was able, in his first term, to get public and congressional approval for a much larger defense budget. But by 1985 this scale of spending came under widespread criticism, even from other Republican office-holders. The military budget was then about $240 billion, 26.4 percent of the total budget or $968 per American.[55] Such a large budget could not escape scrutiny. Even before Reagan became President, "the U.S. military budget . . . is close to the gross national product of Canada, and is larger than the gross national product of all but eight countries in the world."[56] The Pentagon spends $28 million every hour.

The Soviet Union spends at least 12 percent of its GNP on defense. This is 50–80 percent more of the GNP than American military spending. The Soviet expenditure of this high percentage of key resources on the military prompts some Americans to support high United States defense outlays. Others argue that a large defense budget is economically debilitating and socially harmful. In reply, supporters of the budget, like a former Air Force Chief of Staff, respond that Americans spend more on recreation each year than on the air force, much more on gambling than the air force does on jet fuel and more on alcoholic beverages than on the air force.[57] Harold Brown, secretary of defense during the Carter administration, warned against an "alarmist" and "disruptive" response to high Soviet military outlays, but concluded that a failure to respond would be "imprudent, irresponsible and dangerous to American security."[58]

An argument for the present level of military expenditures is made by the Committee on the Present Danger, an association of prominent individuals concerned with the national defense and Soviet military power. The committee points out that more than 90 percent of Americans do not know that defense expenditures are less than 10 percent of the GNP. Hence, it suggests, any public mood favoring cutting the defense budget is based on incorrect assumptions. The committee deals with the issue of fairness by arguing:

> The defense program is not for the benefit of Secretary Weinberger, or even for the Pentagon, in the same way that the agriculture program is for the benefit of farmers or the student loan program is for students. The defense program is for the benefit of our generation and future generations of Americans.[59]

Somehow by 1985 a mood of "enough" toward military spending won out in American politics. The reasons are unclear, but the failure of the Soviet Union to win in Afghanistan, the publicizing of higher American military expenditures, and renewed arms control negotiations figured in producing a new public mood of greater security. In addition, presidents tend to become "lame ducks" in their second terms, and the forces opposed to a president try to capitalize on this phenomenon.

This anti-spending mood vis-à-vis defense did not arise overnight. President Reagan's increasing the defense budget was opposed by a wide range of critics from the beginning. Already by early 1982 it was reported that congressmen of both parties and specialists on military matters across the political spectrum were pointing out that the Reagan administration had not made a good case for a connection between Soviet military power and the need for additional military spending. They claimed the administration had not identified "the particular national interests that are jeopardized, devised a strategy to protect those interests or specified the forces and weapons needed to meet the threat." [60] Just because the Soviets spend a lot on defense does not necessarily mean the United States has to do the same. The USSR has greater military needs than the United States.

By 1983 the beginnings of the 1984 presidential campaign had brought wide publicity to the critical positions on defense spending and on military policies taken by several leading political figures. Senators Nunn and Glenn called for a sustained but slower growth in military spending and higher such spending by the allies. Senator Hart contended that the Reagan defense budget would result in an economic "debacle" and claimed that in a few years even large budgets would be unable to pay for the weapons ordered. He later added, "How much to spend is the wrong question. The right question is how to build an effective defense at a cost that won't bankrupt the country." [61] The dangers of the military budget for the economy also stem from part of it being "funny money," financed by a federal deficit and foreign investment that may later be withdrawn.

Former government officials also spoke out in the same vein, suggesting, for example, that large defense cuts are needed to help curb the deficit and bring long-term interest rates down in order to support a sustained economic recovery. A former Defense Department official said that since 77 percent of the defense budget is for conventional forces, a reduction of defense commitments around the world ("strategic disengagement") could save a full half of it. [62]

This argument was defeated at the level of presidential politics by Ronald Reagan's successful campaign for reelection. Yet the anti-defense budget position lives on within Congress and gathers strength with the public. Will it be successful? Time will tell. Once it is clear that much increased defense spending actually has been used only for starting up production, and not for the costs of some of the new weapons themselves, opposition to defense spending may well increase.

Are the Soviets willing to spend less on defense? Quite possibly. Their buildup to match the United States is basically completed, and additional military expenditures would unavoidably cut into Gorbachev's plans for economic revitalization.[63]

The U.S. Defense Industry

The Reagan military budget has been an enormous windfall for American firms specializing in weapons production. Contracts were generously awarded to them and their profits soared. This budget has no doubt provided jobs for many young engineers and technicians who might otherwise be unemployed and has brought a sort of prosperity to those parts of the country where the key plants of the defense industry are located, such as California, Texas, Connecticut, and Massachusetts.

The Defense Department payrolls totaled $53.3 billion in 1984[64] and the DOD bureaucracy was not able to ensure such large amounts were spent properly. Even spending the money was a problem. In 1981 a retired navy admiral asked a leading army general, in effect, "How will you ever spend all that money?" He replied with forced determination, "We will find a way." Three kinds of problems arose—excessive profits, poor quality products, and corruption itself.

Profits have been enormous for the American defense industry during the Reagan administration (see Table 4.6). The largest defense contractors enjoyed in 1984, on the average, a 25 percent return on equity, almost twice the average corporate return of 12.8 percent.

Criticism of this high rate of profit was unavoidable; with the Defense Department being blamed for overpayment, sloppy financial management, and the contractors criticized for excessive charges and disregard of the national

TABLE 4.6. PROFITS AT TEN LARGE MILITARY CONTRACTORS, AS OF JANUARY 1984

	Profits as Percent of Equity	1984 Profits (in millions)	Percent of Sales to US Government
Lockheed	42%	$572	85%
General Dynamics	30	382	86
Northrop	29	167	84
Martin Marietta	29	176	76
Boeing	26	787	42
Grumman	24	108	82
Rockwell International	21	496	63
Raytheon	18	340	49
Litton Industries	16	277	41
McDonnell Dougals	16	325	69

SOURCE: U.S. Census Bureau, 1984 annual reports, *New York Times*, April 9, 1985, D-1. Raytheon is the largest employer in Massachusetts.

interest and the taxpayer. In their defense, the contractors point out that weapons production is a risk-filled business. Profits may be low or nonexistent while they try to land a contract. Also, weapons production may cut off a firm from the civilian market and such a company deserves compensation.

Depending on ideology and inclination, critics have suggested various remedies. One is nationalization. Corporations doing mainly defense work are already, in effect, government industries. Lockheed sells 85 percent of its products to the federal government. Nationalization, it is argued, would lead to lower costs and greater stability in the defense industry. As it is now, a big defense contract requires drawing key employees away from other firms by offering higher salaries. A high-ranking Navy officer once said that any major Navy contract requires the same key 800 people. Nationalization would be an expensive step, since compensation would be required. Yet until World War II most American weapons were built, and built well, by government armories and shipyards.

Another solution suggested for excessive profits and high costs is the use of government plants to establish the true cost of an item—a form of "comparison shopping" for weapons. Of course there is an old standby—strict auditing of defense contractors and close inspection of their products. However, the DOD lacks the personnel for such close supervision, and defense firms exert political influence against the department or even hire away its key inspectors.

Another problem with the defense industry is the uneven quality of some of its products. For example, investigation revealed that it was common practice for microcircuit makers to falsely claim to have tested micro chips. Manufacturers have also substituted standard-quality chips for the better "Joint Army-Navy" or JAN chips required by defense contracts.[65] In contrast, the Soviets foster competition and give their military men the power to reject products not up to standard.

Some defense contractors act irresponsibly, and at times dishonestly, in billing the government. Admiral Hyman Rickover, often called "the father of the atomic submarine," said that "today the defense contractors have carte blanche. They can do anything they wish." He went on to say that several shipbuilders, when faced by cost overruns, recovered them plus the profit originally desired by successfully making greatly inflated claims against the Navy. "In evaluating these claims, I found numerous instances of apparent fraud," the admiral added.

The former manager of a division of the General Dynamics corporation, now living abroad in order to keep his personal freedom, has "freely admitted having inflated the estimated costs of General Dynamics shipbuilding work to obtain higher Government subsidies." By April 1985, forty-five of the nation's 100 largest defense producers were under criminal investigation and were facing a restructuring of their relationships with the government.[66]

Two other issues related to defense contractors are: the taxes they ought to pay and the scale and ethics of their political contributions. Defense contractors are legally able to defer payment of taxes. As a result, General Dynamics paid no taxes in 1984 despite pretax profits of $683.6 million. Indeed, it has paid no taxes since 1972. "The defense industry is awash in cash," one U.S. senator has said. The top twenty defense firms poured $3.6 million into political campaigns in 1984, mostly to congressional candidates who were supporters of increased defense spending and often were on committees that deal with military spending bills.[67] This pattern of contributions means that some politicians' campaign expenses are being paid for by tax monies.

Problems like these undercut public acceptance of defense spending—with a potential for a seriously disruptive effect on the American military and the foreign policy of the United States.[68]

Weapons and Weapons Technology

In the last decade a new generation of technology may have brought us to the threshold of "a true revolution in conventional warfare,"[69] e.g., Precision Guided Munitions (PGMs) and Remote Piloted Vehicles (RPV). This new technology has by now proceeded further and a revolution in strategic nuclear warfare is now also potentially possible, as the concept of the Strategic Defense Initiative (SDI) shows.

Several issues are thus raised. For example, what additional financial costs will this new technology add to defense budgets, what new educational and intelligence requirements are thus imposed on military personnel, what does this do to the military services organizationally, what new strategies are required for its use, what are its implications for the conduct of war and for the numbers of casualties and the kinds of injuries they will have? These questions have theoretical, practical, political, and moral implications.

Increasing reliance on technology by the United States is inherent in its weapons planning and procurement since it is politically unable to match the Soviet Union in either military personnel or quantity of weapons. Technology has therefore become the primary means by which the United States supports its policy of anti-Soviet deterrence.

The new weapons system that has elicited the most controversy and even fear is one that does not yet exist and may not exist for thirty years—the Strategic Defense Initiative (SDI). In fact, it may never exist, for a variety of reasons. It may not be technically feasible, as many specialists and scientists argue. It may be too expensive for the national well-being or for the maintenance of a large conventional military, still a fundamental requirement of American defense. Can one have thirteen or more large aircraft carriers and their support ships, and have SDI too? Will American politics allow SDI to be built, even if it proves feasible? The Soviets promise to "overload" it with missiles and warheads too numerous to handle and also to get "under" it by attacking from just off the American coasts. Offense has always tended to overwhelm defense. What sort of relationship will the United States have with the USSR if it also has SDI? Gorbachev, The Soviet General Secretary, has said that if the United States develops "space strike arms" the price could be "the scrapping of every prospect" for an end to the arms race.[70]

What SDI really promises is the further militarization of space. Would this enhance states' security or decrease it? Whatever it does, it will be a long time before the result is clear; this uncertainty is itself a producer of tensions and fears. Is it worth it?

The nature of SDI, as currently envisaged, is a "layered defense" of radars, sensors and laser or particle-beam weapons in orbit that could sense the launching of missiles early on and destroy some of them before they got into a position to discharge their warheads. In technical terms, SDI is intended to destroy missiles even in their "boost" phase, a goal the never built ABM system never had.

SDI would be an offensive or first strike, as well as a defensive system, one reason the Soviets are so concerned with it, since it would be able to destroy missiles in their silos, and indeed any target on or near the earth's surface. A purely defensive SDI would be one that could destroy only nuclear weapons that have been launched, something like a passive "force field" of science fiction.

President Reagan has defended SDI by saying, "But it isn't about war, it's about peace. It isn't about retaliation, it's about prevention. It isn't about fear, it's about hope. . . . By making missiles less effective, we make these weapons more negotiable. . . . the arms spiral will be a downward spiral, hopefully to the elimination of them." These are powerful and possibly politically effective words.[71] The opposition to SDI bases its position on several arguments: excessive cost and impracticality, destabilization of United States-Soviet relations, the end of arms control and an unlimited arms race. Opponents also contend that even if SDI is successful the Soviets could penetrate its defensive net anyway. The Union of Concerned Scientists has charged that SDI is "economically ruinous" because it will produce "deficits so large that the country could be ruined without a war."[72]

At present, however, SDI is only a *research program* to provide a future administration with the technical knowledge needed to determine whether to develop and deploy an advanced system of an SDI-type. The future of SDI will depend on the American political process, the actions of allies, the responses of the Soviet Union, and the outcome of arms control negotiations between the superpowers. The Soviets seem to have recognized that successful deployment is unlikely and accordingly have dropped their former unwillingness to negotiate with the United States on other weapons systems.

The dispute over SDI within American society is between people with diametrically opposed views of human nature, politics, and the capacity of science. It is not clear how they can reconcile their fundamental differences.

While SDI might be a way out of the nuclear dilemma, it also could encourage complacency, undercut effective military power, and isolate the United States from its allies and the key problems of the international arena.

SUMMARY

This discussion of military issues in United States politics is only a sampling of the problems being debated. Another question that must be explored concerns the comparative military quality of the superpowers. Because of the limited combat experience of the two nations since 1945 it is hard to make judgments about their militaries' combat capability. There is also debate on the necessity of reinstituting the draft, not only to provide a large reserve force and to increase the level of education and intelligence in the military, but to create a greater sense of unity in American society. Military service should be an obligation for *all* Americans, not just an economic necessity for the young unemployed, proponents argue. A related issue under discussion is "reforming the Pentagon." According to critics, strategic thinking, effective decisionmaking, and weapons procurement are hampered by the opposing interests of the individual services and by bureaucratic politics.

All of these matters impact on the larger issue of Soviet-American military rivalry. The key question we now face is whether a new Soviet leadership and a changed American political context will lead to an improved superpower relationship and a less intense military rivalry. Arms control will have a role in resolving this question.

REFERENCES

1. See Stephen S. Kaplan et al., *Soviet Armed Forces as a Political Instrument* (Washington, DC: Brookings, 1981); Barry M. Blechman and Stephen S. Kaplan, *Force without War* (Washington, DC: Brookings, 1978); *New York Times*, 11 December 1978, 6; 4 September 1979, 11; 20 September 1983, 1, 25; and *New York Times Book Review*, 28 June 1981, for a review by Adam Ulam of *Soviet Armed Forces*.
2. *New York Times*, 30 October 1977, 16; and 1 March 1978, 31.
3. *New York Times*, 13 October 1984, 3; and 19 April 1983; and Moscow Television, Domestic, 0826GMT, 27 March 1982, quoted in Radio Liberty Research 145/82, 31 March 1982, 1.
4. See International Institute for Strategic Studies (IISS), *The Military Balance, 1986–87* (London, 1986); and NATO, *Nato and the Warsaw Pact: Force Comparisons* (Brussels, 1984), 8.
5. Vernon V. Aspaturian, *U.S.-Soviet Global Rivalry and Western Europe*, Occasional Paper No. 179, Kennan Institute for Advanced Russian Studies, January 1984, 1, 17.

6. See Ruth Leger Sivard, *World Military and Social Expenditures, 1983 and 1986* (Washington, DC: World Priorities, 1983 and 1986).

7. U.S. ACDA, *World Military Expenditures and Arms Transfers, 1969–1978* (Washington, DC: GPO, 1980), Figures 12 and 17, 9 and 11; Joachim Krause, "Soviet Military Aid to the Third World," *Aussen Politik* (English ed.), vol. 34 (4/83): 393, 403, citing Stockholm International Peace Research Institute, *World Armaments and Disarmament—SIPRI Yearbook 1982*, 175ff; and Andrew J. Pierre, *The Global Politics of Arms Sales* (Princeton NJ: Princeton University Press, 1982).

8. Sivard, *WMSE*, 1983, 45; and IISS, *The Military Balance, 1983–84*, 13. For a critique of the CIA estimates, see Franklin D. Holzman, "Soviet Military Spending; Assessing the Numbers Game," *International Security* (Spring 1982): 78–101; his "Of Dollars and Rubles," *New York Times*, 26 October 1979, 31, and 9 March 1983, 23.

9. Coit D. Blacker, "Military Forces," in *After Brezhnev*, ed. Robert F. Byrnes (Bloomington: Indiana University Press, 1983), 139.

10. *WSME*, 1983, 45.

11. William J. Bishop and David S. Sorenson, "Superpower Defense Expenditures and Foreign Policy," in *Foreign Policy: USA/USSR*, ed. Charles W. Kegley, Jr., and Pat McGowan (Beverly Hills: Sage, 1982), 177–178; David Holloway, "Foreign and Defense Policy," in *Soviet Policy for the 1980s*, ed. Archie Brown and Michael Kaser (Bloomington: Indiana University Press, 1982), 43, 54; *New York Times*, 3 March 1983, 1.

12. William Zimmerman and Glenn Palmer, "Words and Deeds in Soviet Foreign Policy: The Case of Soviet Military Expenditures," *American Political Science Review* 77, 2 (June 1983): 365–366.

13. John M. Collins and Elizabeth Ann Severns, "Essentials of Net Assessment." Report No. 80–168S (Washington, DC: Congressional Research Service 1980), 18 (Summary of Graph 1, "Statistical Balance: January 1, 1980").

14. *The Military Balance, 1983–84*, 11–12 and *ibid*, 1986–87, 32 and 35–36.

15. See, for example, the works of the Columbia engineering professor Seymour Melman; Karl W. Ryavec, "Economic Reform: Prospects and Possibilities," in *Soviet Politics, Russia after Brezhnev*, ed. Joseph L. Nogee (New York: Praeger, 1985), 191; and *Christian Science Monitor*, 29 April 1985, 19. For an opposing view see *New York Times*, 16 August 1987, 31.

16. Most respondents to an American poll of 1985 viewed the deficit as "very serious" and favored cuts in military spending. *New York Times*, 5 May 1985, 32.

17. *New York Times*, 2 March 1985, A-l. The theory was first proposed in 1983 by a group of five scientists including Carl Sagan in a paper called the TTAPS study. Jonathan Schell, *The Fate of the Earth* (New York: Knopf 1982).

18. I am indebted to my colleague Jean Elshtain for some of this information. See also Janet Maslin's review of several films in *New York Times*, 4 March 1985. C-16 and Paul Brian's Op-Ed article on images of nuclear war in American popular culture in *New York Times*, 17 July 1985, A-23.

19. Edward N. Luttwak, *The Grand Strategy of the Soviet Union* (New York: St. Martin's Press, 1983), 116.

20. One book on the MX is: Herbert Scoville, Jr., *MX: Prescription for Disaster* (Cambridge, MA: The MIT Press, 1981).

21. See the Op-Ed article by I. F. Stone, *The New York Times*, 1 May 1987, A-35 and Albert Wohlstetter, "Between an Unfree World and None: Increasing Our Choices," *Foreign Affairs* (Summer 1985): 987.

22. See *The New York Times*, 3 May 1987, A-23 for some examples.

23. For some scenarios of nuclear war, see Arthur M. Cox, *Russian Roulette: The Superpower Game* (New York: Times Books, 1982), 3–28; and Ralph K. White, *Fearful Warriors: A Psychological Profile of U.S.-Soviet Relations* (New York: Free Press, 1984), 53–66. For differing views on avoiding nuclear war see Graham T. Allison, et al. eds., *Hawks, Doves and Owls: An Agenda for Avoiding Nuclear War* (New York: Norton, 1985).

24. Robert J. Art, "Nuclear Weapons and Military Power," in *International Politics: Anarchy, Force, Political Economy and Decision-Making*, ed. Robert J. Art and Robert Jervis (Boston: Little, Brown, 1985), 252, 253, and 257.

25. Freeman Dyson, *Weapons and Hope* (New York: Harper & Row, 1984), 297, 306–307, and 310.

26. An editorial in the English journal *Discovery*, partly reproduced in Bernard J. O'Keefe, *Nuclear Hostages* (Boston: Houghton Mifflin, 1983), 31–32. Einstein's famous letter to President Roosevelt on nuclear fission and the need for the United States to produce nuclear bombs is on pp. 36–37.

27. See the Epilogue of George F. Kennan's *The Fateful Alliance: France, Russia, and the Coming of the First World War* (New York: Pantheon, 1984). On technology in modern war, see David W. Ziegler, *War, Peace and International Politics*, 2d Ed. (Boston: Little, Brown, 1981), chs. 1 and 2; on the contrast between earlier and present-day wars, see Edmund Stillman and William Pfaff, *The Politics of Hysteria: The Sources of 20th Century Conflict* (New York: Harper & Row, 1964), 67.

28. See Jonathan B. Tucker, "Gene Wars," *Foreign Policy* no. 57 (Winter 1984–85), 58; *New York Times*, 5 December 1982 and 20 June 1985, A1.

29. Roger E. Kanet, "The Soviet Union as a Global Power," in *Soviet Foreign Policy in the 1980s*, ed. Roger E. Kanet, (New York: Praeger, 1982), 7.

30. *New York Times*, 11 January 1988, A-8.

31. On the restricted nature of future war, see, for example, Louis J. Halle, "Does War Have a Future?" *Foreign Affairs*, 52 (October 1973): 20–34; and Werner Levi, *The Coming End of War*, vol. 17 (Beverly Hills: Sage, 1981).

32. Art, 266.

33. Quoted in John Lewis Gaddis, *Strategies of Containment: A Critical Appraisal of Postwar National Security Policy* (New York: Oxford University Press, 1982), 39.

34. *Pravda*, 9 February 1981, 6.

35. Michael Florinsky, *Russia: A History and an Interpretation*, vol. 2 (New York: Macmillan, 1960), 738, 906–908, and 1321; and Edward Crankshaw, *The Shadow of the Winter Palace* (New York: Viking, 1976), 46 and 59.

36. Richard Pipes, *Russia Under the Old Regime* (New York: Scribner's, 1974), 20.

37. Dyson, 184; and Pipes, 118–119.

38. See the opposing letters of Igor I. Sikorsky, Jr. and Karl W. Ryavec in *The New York Times*, 14 July and 6 August 1981.

39. On the militarist tendencies of Leninist Marxism see Michael Voslensky, *Nomenklatura: The Soviet Ruling Class* (Garden City, N.Y.: Doubleday, 1984), 18–22.

40. Samuel P. Huntington, "Equilibrium and Disequilibrium in American Military

Policy," *Political Science Quarterly* LXXVI, 4 (December 1961), 485–486 and 489–490, 495, 499, and 501–502.

41. Rowan Kolkowicz, "Introduction: The Soviet Union—Elusive Adversary," *Soviet Union* 10, parts 2–3 (1983): 159, 176.

42. James Fallows, *National Defense* (New York: Random House, 1981), 181–182; Richard A. Gabriel and Paul L. Savage, *Crisis in Command* (New York: Hill and Wang, 1978), 20–21 and 137.

43. Benjamin S. Lambeth, "Contemporary Soviet Military Policy," *Soviet Union* 10, parts 2–3 (1983): 180.

44. Lambeth, 182–183 and 185–186; and a lecture by Condoleeza Rice at the Center for International Affairs, Harvard University, 17 March 1986.

45. Gordon Craig and Alexander George, "Deterrence," in *Force and Statecraft* (New York: Oxford University Press, 1983), 172.

46. *Christian Science Monitor*, 13 November 1987, 12, citing *The Military Balance, 1987–88*.

47. David W. Ziegler, *War, Peace, and International Politics*, 2d ed. (Boston: Little, Brown, 1981), 226–227.

48. O'Keefe, *Nuclear Hostages*, 223.

49. This brief outline of the problems of deterrence follows Craig and George, *Force and Statecraft*, ch. 13.

50. David Holloway, "Military Power and Purpose in Soviet Policy," *Daedalus* (Fall 1980): 20. See also his book, *The Soviet Union and the Arms Race*, 2d Ed. (New Haven: Yale University Press, 1984). This brief treatment of Soviet deterrence is based upon: Roman Kolkowicz, "Introduction: The Soviet Union—Elusive Adversary," and Lambeth, "Contemporary Soviet Military Policy," 153–176 and 177–200.

51. Kolkowicz, 164–165.

52. Colin S. Gray, "Warfighting for Deterrence," in Stephen J. Cimbala, ed., *National Security Strategy: Choices and Limits* (New York: Praeger, 1984), 195–196, 199, 209 and 211.

53. Vincent Ferraro and Kathleen Fitzgerald, "The End of a Strategic Era: a Proposal for a Policy of Minimal Deterrence," unpublished paper, Political Science Department, Mount Holyoke College, 22.

54. See Ziegler, *War, Peace, and International Politics*, 228–229.

55. U.S. ACDA, *World Military Expenditures . . . 1986* (Washington, DC: GPO, 1987), 97.

56. The Boston Study Group, *The Price of Defense: a New Strategy for Military Spending* (New York: Times Books, 1979), 279.

57. *New York Times*, 16 September 1981. The comparisons are based on data in the 1980 Statistical Abstract of the United States.

58. *New York Times*, 20 January 1981.

59. Committee on the Present Danger, *Defense and the Deficit* (Washington, DC, 1985), 5.

60. Richard Halloran, "Criticism Rises on Reagan's Plan For 5-Year Growth of the Military," *New York Times*, 22 March 1982, 1.

61. *New York Times*, 21 March 1983; 15 March 1983 and 18 November 1983.

62. Barry M. Blechman, "Do Guns Cut the Butter," and Earl C. Ravenal, "On Scaling

Down Defense Ambitions," *New York Times*, 16 January 1983 and 16 February 1984.

63. See Ryavec, "Economic Reform: Prospects and Possibilities."
64. *New York Times*, 10 March 1985, A-47, and 30 April 1985, D-17; and JFK School *Update* (May–June 1985): 3.
65. *New York Times*, 27 January 1985, F-1 and 8 and 16 April 1985, D1.
66. Rickover, Testimony to the Joint Economic Committee, 28 January 1982, *New York Times*, 22 March 1985, D-1 and 29 April 1985, D-1.
67. *New York Times*, 9 April 1985, D-12 and D-13.
68. See the five articles on the military spending debate in the *New York Times*, May 1985.
69. Dr. Malcolm Currie, former Director of Defense Research and Engineering in the U.S. Department of Defense, quoted in Phil Stanford, "The Automated Battlefield," *New York Times Magazine*, 23 February 1975, 12.
70. *New York Times*, 30 May 1985, 9.
71. *New York Times*, 30 May 1985, B-6, and 30 March 1985, 1; *Christian Science Monitor*, 13 March 1985, 16; U.S. Department of State, "The President's Strategic Defense Initiative," *gist* (March 1985).
72. The Union of Concerned Scientists, *The Fallacy of Star Wars* (New York: Vintage: 1984), 27.

SELECT GLOSSARY

ABM: antiballistic missile
ALCM: air-launched cruise missile
APC: armored personnel carrier
ASAT: antisatellite
ASW: antisubmarine warfare
AT: antitank
AWACS: Airborne Warning and Control System
BMEWS: Ballistic Missile Early Warning System
C³: command, control, and communications
C³CM: command, control, and communications countermeasures
CEP: circular error probable
CINCs: commanders in chief of the unified and specified commands
CTB: comprehensive test ban
CV: conventionally-powered aircraft carrier
CVN: nuclear-powered aircraft carrier
CW: chemical warfare
DEW: distant early warning
DOD: Department of Defense
DSCS: Defense Satellite Communications System
ECCM: electronic counter-countermeasures
ECM: electronic countermeasures
EMP: electromagnetic pulse
EW: electronic warfare

GLCM: ground-launched cruise missile
GPF: general purpose forces
ICBM: intercontinental ballistic missile
INF: intermediate-range nuclear forces
JCS: Joint Chiefs of Staff
LRINF: longer-range intermediate-range nuclear forces
MBFR: mutual and balanced force reductions
MILSTAR: communications satellite
MRLS: Mobile Rocket Launcher System
NATO: North Atlantic Treaty Organization
NBC: nuclear, biological, chemical
NCA: National Command Authorities
NMCC: National Military Command Center
NMCS: National Military Command System
NORAD: North American Aerospace Defense Command
NSNF: nonstrategic nuclear forces
PAVE PAWS: phased-array missile warning system
PLSS: Precision Location Strike System
RRF: Ready Reserve Force
SAC: Strategic Air Command
SAM: surface-to-air missile
SDI: Strategic Defense Initiative
SLBM: submarine-launched ballistic missile
SNDV: strategic nuclear delivery vehicles
SNF: short-range nuclear forces
SRINF: shorter-range intermediate-range nuclear forces
SSBN: nuclear-powered ballistic missile submarine
SSGN: nuclear-powered guided missile attack submarine
SSN: nuclear-powered attack submarine
START: Strategic Arms Reduction Talks
TOW: tube-launched, optically tracked, wire-guided missile
VSTOL: vertical short takeoff and landing
VTOL: vertical takeoff and landing
WTO: Warsaw Treaty Organization

SOURCE: The Organization of the Joint Chiefs of Staff, *Military Posture FY 1985* (Washington: US GPO, 1984)

SELECT BIBLIOGRAPHY

Some sources on the United States-Soviet military rivalry

Statistics

Collins, John M. *U.S.-Soviet Military Balance*: 1980–1985. Washington, DC: Pergamon-Brassey's, 1985.

*International Institute for Strategic Studies. *The Military Balance*. London.

NATO Information Service. *NATO and the Warsaw Pact: Force Comparisons*. Brussels: 1984.

*Sivard, Ruth L. *World Military and Social Expenditures*. Washington, DC: World Priorities.

*U.S. ACDA, *World Military Expenditures and Arms Transfers*. Washington, DC: GPO.

U.S. CIA, *Soviet and U.S. Defense Activities, 1970–79: A Dollar Cost Comparison*. Washington, DC: 1980.

*U.S. JCS, *United States Military Posture*. Washington, D.C.

*U.S. Secretary of Defense. Annual Report to the Congress. Washington, DC. It appears with a shorter *Executive Summary*.

Books and Pamphlets

Adams, Gordon. *The Politics of Defense Contracting*. New Brunswick, NJ: Transaction Books, 1982.

Allison, Graham T., et al. *Hawks, Doves, and Owls: an Agenda for Avoiding Nuclear War*. New York: Norton, 1985.

Berman, Robert P. and Baker, John C., *Soviet Strategic Forces: Requirements and Responses*. Washington, DC: Brookings, 1982.

Clausewitz, Carl von. *On War*. Edited and translated by Michael Howard and Peter Paret. Princeton, N.J.: Princeton University Press, 1976.

Cochran, Thomas B., et al. *Nuclear Weapons Databook*, vol. 1, *U.S. Nuclear Forces and Capabilities*. Cambridge, MA: Ballinger, 1984. Vol. 3 will deal with Soviet nuclear weapons.

Cockburn, Andrew. *The Threat: Inside the Soviet Military Machine*. New York: Vintage, 1984.

Collins, John M. and Bernard C. Victory. *U.S./Soviet Military Balance: Statistical Trends, 1977–1986*. Washington, DC: Congressional Research Service, 1987.

Craig, Gordon and Alexander George. *Force and Statecraft*. New York: Oxford University Press, 1983.

Dinerstein, H.S., *War and the Soviet Union*. New York: Praeger, 1980.

Dziak, John J., *Soviet Perceptions of Military Power*. New York: Crane, Russak, 1981.

Ehrlich, Paul, et al. *The Cold and the Dark: the World after Nuclear War*. New York: Norton, 1985.

Gabriel, Richard A. *Military Incompetence: Why the American Military Doesn't Win*. New York: Hill and Wang, 1985.

Gardner, John, et al. *Missile Defense in the 1990s*. Washington, DC: George C. Marshall Institute, 1987.

Gervasi, Tom. *The Myth of Soviet Military Supremacy*. New York: Harper and Row, 1986.

——. *Soviet Military Power*. Annotated and corrected. New York: Random House, 1988.

Ground Zero. *Nuclear War: What's in It for You?* New York: Pocket Books, 1982.

Hackett, John, et al. *The Third World War*. New York: Berkley, 1980.

Hart, Gary, with William S. Lind. *America Can Win: the Case for Military Reform*. Bethesda, MD: Adler and Adler, 1986.

Harvard Nuclear Study Group. *Living with Nuclear Weapons*. New York: Bantam, 1983.

Holloway, David. *The Soviet Union and the Arms Race*. 2d ed. New Haven: Yale University Press 1984.

Howard, Michael, ed. *The Theory and Practice of War*. Bloomington: Indiana University Press, 1975.

International Physicians for the Prevention of Nuclear War. *Last Aid: the Medical Dimensions of Nuclear War*. San Francisco: Freeman, 1982.

Jastrow, Robert. *How to Make Nuclear Weapons Obsolete*. Boston: Little, Brown, 1983.

——. *Why Strategic Superiority Matters*. New York: Orwell, 1983.

Jervis, Robert. *The Illogic of American Nuclear Strategy*. Ithaca, NY: Cornell University Press, 1985.

Kolkowitz, Roman and Mickiewicz, Ellen. *The Soviet Calculus of Nuclear War*. Lexington, MA: Lexington Books, 1986.

Larson, Joyce E. and Bodie, William C. *The Intelligent Layperson's Guide to "Star Wars."* New York: National Strategy Information Center, 1986.

Leckie, Robert. *The Wars of America*, Rev. ed. New York: Harper and Row, 1981.

Luttwak, Edward N. *The Grand Strategy of the Soviet Union*. New York: St. Martins Press, 1983.

——. *The Pentagon and the Art of War: the Question of Military Reform*. New York: Simon and Schuster, 1985.

Mandelbaum, Michael. *The Nuclear Future*. Ithaca, NY: Cornell University Press, 1983.

Military Publishing House. *Whence the Threat to Peace*. 4th ed. Moscow: Novosti Press Agency, 1987. This is the Soviet answer to the Pentagon publication *Soviet Military Power*.

Nye, Joseph S., Jr. *Nuclear Ethics*. New York: Free Press/Macmillan, 1986.

Parrott, Bruce. *The Soviet Union and Ballistic Missile Defense*. Boulder, CO: Westview Press, 1987.

Reichart, John F. and Sturm, Steven R., eds., *American Defense Policy*. 5th ed. Baltimore: Johns Hopkins University Press, 1982.

Schmid, Alex P. and Berends, Ellen. *Soviet Military Interventions since 1945*. New Brunswick, NJ: Transaction Books, 1985.

Scott, Harriet Fast and Scott, William F. *The Armed Forces of the USSR*. Boulder, CO: Westview Press, 1979.

Scoville, Herbert, Jr. MX: *Prescription for Disaster*. Cambridge, MA: MIT Press, 1981.

Snow, Donald M. *National Security: Enduring Problems of U.S. Defense Policy*. New York: St. Martins Press, 1987.

Soviet Acquisition of Militarily Significant Western Technology: an Update. Washington, DC: 1985.

Summers, Harry, G. Jr. *On Strategy: A Critical Analysis of the Vietnam War*. Novato, CA: Presidio, 1982.

Suvorov, Victor. *Inside the Soviet Army*. New York: Berkley, 1984 and Macmillan, 1983.

Union of Concerned Scientists. *The Fallacy of Star Wars*. New York: Vintage, 1984.

U.S. Department of State, *Atlas of NATO*. Washington, DC: GPO, 1985.

U.S. Department of Defense. *Soviet Military Power*: 1987. Washington, DC: GPO, 1987.

Van Cleave, William R. *Fortress USSR: The Soviet Strategic Defense Initiative and the U.S. Strategic Defense Response.* Stanford: Hoover Institution Press, 1986.

Wade, Nicholas. *A World Beyond Healing: The Prologue and Aftermath of Nuclear War.* New York: Norton, 1987.

Weigley, Russell F. *The American Way of War.* New York: Macmillan, 1973.

Chapter 5

Arms Control

Not even the most committed ideologue will be able to tell the difference between the ashes of capitalism and the ashes of communism.

John Kenneth Galbraith

What in the name of God is strategic superiority? What is the significance of it ... at these levels of numbers?

Henry Kissinger

I realized the importance of SALT, but it represented a search for an appropriate strategic balance ... rather than a genuine attempt to achieve nuclear disarmament.

Arkady N. Shevchenko

It is hard to see ... that arms control, as it has been pursued up to now, will lead to anything better than a regulated arms race....

David Holloway

Arms control apart, there is little else to give even symbolic, let alone concrete form to a marked reduction in tensions between Washington and Moscow.[1]

Robert W. Tucker

ARMS CONTROL V. DISARMAMENT

Arms control is a difficult and controversial undertaking. Its value is hotly contested by critics who claim it does not change the adversarial relationship between the United States and the Soviet Union. Getting rid of weapons, some of them argue, cannot eliminate the suspicions and conflict that brought the weapons into existence. Other critics charge that since arms control does not eliminate all weapons it is a meaningless process. But proponents of arms control see the issue differently. Since the superpowers' weapons may destroy them—and the rest of the world as well—one way to reduce this danger is to place strict limits on weapons and to encourage cooperation and parity between the superpowers.

Until recently, attempts at disarmament, or across-the-board reductions in armaments have been more noticeable than control of armaments, which usually involves both reductions *and* increases in arms. However, disarmament moves have usually failed, despite the fact that some international agreements were actually concluded.[2]

Arms control is a more realistic, though less satisfying, goal than disarmament. If nuclear weapons were eliminated they could be recreated, and the one state that had even a few might be in a position to dictate its own terms to all. Major disarmament is risky and complete nuclear disarmament could be a fantasy.[3] This does not mean arms control is easy to accept or implement. It has inherent problems.

Arms control has been defined well as: "all the forms of cooperation between potential enemies in the interest of reducing the likelihood of war, its scope and violence if it occurs, and the political and economic costs of being prepared for it." Arms control does not necessarily involve reduction of weapons or the prohibition of them but instead is concerned with establishing and maintaining trust and cooperation between potential enemies sufficient to reduce the dangers of war. It involves limiting testing, deployment and use of weapons, expanding the military information available, and both avoiding crises and making them more manageable. Stability and predictability are some of the goals of arms control.[4]

Problems of Arms Control
(Note that there is a glossary of SALT/START Acronyms at the end of this chapter.)

Those who prefer disarmament tend to be dissatisfied with arms control and may even see it as a betrayal of their ideals. "Disarmers" may see "arms controllers" as people with only limited concern for the several related issues "disarmers" consider central: war, killing, misuse of resources, militarism, etc. And, since "arms controllers" are often extremely knowledgeable about weapons and may do consulting for the military, "disarmers" may see them as having "sold out" to the forces favoring the use of force in politics. "Disarmers" see arms control measures as, at best, only a first step toward disarmament. A former director of a bureau of the United States Arms Control and Disarmament Agency (ACDA, pronounced "ak–da") has suggested that one reason for the Senate's failure to ratify the SALT II Treaty was the lack of support for it by disarmament advocates.[5]

Another difficulty facing arms control is that the thinking underlying it is closely related to military assumptions and the maintenance of deterrence, including mutual assured destruction. Some arms control supporters see arms control as an integral part of overall military and strategic thinking. Arms control may require additional weapons or even new weapons. This puts off or at least puzzles those who would rather proceed directly to reducing the danger of nuclear war. One specialist, now the ambassador to West Germany, writes of "a certain schizophrenia" that may result from considering the interrelationship between weapons and arms control and then makes a point typical of this mode of thinking: "new technologies may offer attractive solutions to the classical arms control goals of bolstering deterrence, minimizing damage if deterrence fails, and saving money." [6] In short, some arms control advocates see the arms race itself as a deterrent to the use of nuclear weapons.

New weapons technologies, however, are not welcomed by advocates of disarmament. One critic of arms control's linkage with weapons development says: "The arms control cure may in the end be worse than the nuclear weapons disease.... Nuclear arms agreements have not stopped the development of any weapons systems...." [7]

An arms controller could respond, "Yes, you are correct to a point. It is unrealistic to expect a government to eliminate a weapon in the 'pipeline' of research and development, prototype building, testing, mass-production, and deployment. Investment in a system creates interest groups supporting it. Don't ask for the politically impossible." Such a reply is inherently unsatisfactory and even angering to some. Yet arms control did prevent American anti-ballistic missiles from being deployed. It may still prevent them from being "re-born" as SDI. The arms controller might also respond, "Arms control has not always gone as we intended. Politics and technology moved faster than we could. But that is no reason to give up now. Let's try again. The main thing is to develop and introduce only those weapons systems that further arms control." As one very experienced Sovietologist puts it, "It does not make sense for us to introduce systems that are destabilizing, systems that will make us more trigger-sensitive." [8]

Dissatisfaction with arms control comes from the political left and center. However, the political right can also be suspicious of and opposed to arms control. Clear-cut military superiority is out of the question with arms control. Arms control emphasizes balance, parity, equality, and stability. This means living with the competitor in a state of permanent stand-off. It means too that each superpower can continue to try to expand its influence. Such a situation threatens the legitimacy of both systems for it means that neither Soviet "scientific socialism" nor the "American way of life" can win a clear victory. It means "waiting out" the other, not a pleasant prospect to those who would like to stop the other cold or try to "win."

Still another difficulty faced by arms control is its eventual goal of reducing weapons. One former director of ACDA has called arms control a kind of "unnatural act." In reacting to the insecurity arising from an opponent, people normally add, not reduce, weapons, defenses, etc. that can be expected to protect them. Relaxing their defenses would increase most peoples' feeling of insecurity. Even acquiring "overkill" may be emotionally satisfying to some—like buying excess insurance.

A more objective difficulty that has long plagued the arms control process is "technology creep" or "technology drive"—the devising of new weapons or improvements in weapons as part of routine laboratory work (R & D) without political controls. This then leads to requests by scientists, bureaucrats, and military men for funds to mass produce and deploy the new weapons. By that time the other side has begun doing the same thing in order to catch up, or is busily engaged in devising countermeasures. Arms control negotiations usually lag behind this technological-bureaucratic process, one that is highly politicized itself since the proponents of new weapons can usually find politicians to support them. As a result, "We and the Soviets are to some extent trapped by our military technology. Weapons developments . . . have themselves been responsible for some of the most alarming aspects of the present strategic situation." [9]

Technology, which cannot be controlled because even "nonmilitary" technology can have military applications, results in a high level of uncertainity and a continual fear that one side or the other will make a decisive breakthrough or at least a temporary but destabilizing leap forward. [10] Witness the furor caused by the mere idea of the SDI.

The main recent technological innovations that have disturbed strategic arms control and made it so contentious are MIRVs (Multiple Independently Targetable Reentry Vehicles, or a multi-warhead missile payload) and cruise missiles. Ironically, Soviet-American strategic arms control talks began only after MIRVs had been deployed by the United States Navy in the late 1960s. (The Poseidon, the replacement for Polaris, is a MIRVed missile.) The Soviets, earlier, had deployed Intercontinental Ballistic Missiles (ICBMs) before the Americans.

The cruise missile, too, is a product of new technologies. The destabilizing uncertainty here is the ease of hiding large numbers of cruise missiles almost anywhere. It they are loaded onto a ship under cover there is no easy way to know how many hundreds or possibly even thousands are on board. The missiles are less than 2 feet wide and about 20 feet long and can fly about 1,000 miles. Each battleship normally carries 32 but more could be on board.

These two weapons systems, MIRVs and cruise missiles, undercut arms control because they can, if they are proliferated, render a crucial requirement of arms control impossible to meet—the ability to know what weapons the opposition has. This is called verification and is a crucial requirement for predictability and stability.

Another problem of arms control is the powerful political and bureaucratic protection a weapons system acquires even before it is a fully deployed, operative system. This protection increases as development progresses. At first, a weapons system's supporters may be only a few military men and scientists. Next on the bandwagon are industrialists, stockholders, union leaders, politicians, and engineers. Then the weapon acquires a public constituency, including those who believe in "peace through strength" and those who are gaining jobs. And, once any money has been spent on a system it is hard to stop funding. A cessation of spending would affront the supporting interests and also lose the investment made. Even if the weapon has no clear military purpose its completion may be justified with the "bargaining chip" argument—it can supposedly be bartered away for a weapon of the opposition.

In order to prevent a weapon from coming into existence it is necessary to stop it early on, certainly no later than the R & D phase. Prototypes tempt mass production. The existence of a few handbuilt prototypes of the B-1 bomber facilitated mass production, even though the bomber's technology was already obsolescent. Accordingly, it is necessary for arms controllers to know about weapons in the early stages of their development. Partly for this reason ACDA is charged by law with determining the effects on arms control of weapons under development. However, this bureaucratic machinery requires a powerful political will favoring arms control expressed through the public, the Congress, and the presidency. This is not always present.

Limits of Arms Control
Even if arms control were able to overcome all these problems, it would still face inherent limits in reducing the danger of nuclear war and cutting armaments. The invention of nuclear weapons put humanity under a long-term threat that cannot be eliminated or even controlled perfectly in the short term. We exist in a new sort of "prisoners' dilemma" and even "chicken."[11] In addition, arms control assumes military force in order to operate.

> What we call 'arms control' is really an effort to take a long overdue step toward recognizing the role of military force in the modern world . . . . and that a main function of military force is to influence the behavior of other countries, not simply to spend itself in their destruction.[12]

In other words, arms control takes place within a context of military force. It tries to control this force but it alone cannot eliminate or even cut it drastically. Instead, arms control can be likened to careful but significant "sculpting" or shaping of the military context. Sometimes actual "whittling down" occurs but no more than this and not often. For one superpower to lose the capacity to destroy the other and several other powers would be to cease being a superpower, possible only in a reformed world. What arms control does, at best, is prevent this awesome capability from becoming destabilizing by heading off an unbridled arms race, fraught with unforeseeable developments, between the superpowers.[13] It cannot eliminate the potential use of armaments and the fundamental place of force in the international system. Accordingly, arms control must not be seen as a panacea for the problem of war. To do so is to be lulled into a false sense of security or to give up grappling with the danger of war. Perhaps arms control, because it deals with weaponry, rather than national intentions and outlooks, raises false hopes about war and peace. But "weapons do not cause war; they determine only its nature."[14]

Despite its successes, Soviet-American arms control has not stopped most weapons deployments. Although the superpowers concluded ten arms control agreements during the 1970s, in the same period the United States added 6,056 nuclear weapons aimed at the USSR while the latter added 3,903 strategic weapons aimed at the United States. And during the 1970s, while negotiating SALT, the Soviet Union spent much more than the United States on nuclear weaponry.[15] However, their joint move in 1987 toward eliminating intermediate-range nuclear weapons (INF) suggests that arms control may have a successful future.

No United States-Soviet arms control agreement can eliminate the danger of a Soviet-American conflict in a turbulent situation somewhere in the Third World where their interests clash. Here arms control can at best contribute to crisis resolution only indirectly by having built up a measure of mutual trust and a pattern of communication between the superpowers. Arms control can do nothing to constrain those interests in the world that would welcome a Soviet-American War.[16] Similarly, arms control does nothing to limit or control international terrorism, starvation in Africa, torture by dictatorships, and anti-democratic revolutions and coups—all matters that increasingly impinge on American power and politics to strong effect and may be among the major future problems of the world.

Most importantly, arms control cannot by itself eliminate the causes of the Soviet-American rivalry and the potential for armed confrontation. Nor can it alone change the sociopolitical nature of either the United States or the Soviet Union. Arms control without "trade control" will not significantly limit Soviet military technology. Arms control agreements will not by themselves move us along the road to a new détente. Arms control will have to be part of a larger, political "deconfrontational" process of talks, actions, and agreements in order to play its full role.[17]

> Arms control ... should be pursued without historical illusions regarding the impact of any agreement on the character of the Soviet system and its relationship with the West, for the long-term political rivalry will not be ended even by a comprehensive arms control arrangement.[18]

Ironically, successful arms control might well make clearer the funda-mentals of the United States-Soviet disagreement. Each wants to stake out an advantageous position for itself as a new world order takes shape around them and is determined that the other not get a better position. Arms control cannot do much to eliminate this competition for power and place.

Is Arms Control Necessary?

Arms control is pursued despite its many problems and limitations because of the overriding dictates of prudence. Without arms control the cost and potential instability of an arms race would be so great that the superpowers and their populations would be hostage not only, as now, to a potential disaster but to a nearly certain one. This is the philosophical and intellectual basis for arms control.

If we refuse to pursue arms control agreements we are making the arms race permanent, with possibly dire consequences. Forty years of "petrified peace" probably cannot last. To reduce the danger it is best to "pinch off small areas of competition" and sign concrete agreements as part of a series of small, continuous steps.[19]

Arms control, if pursued sincerely and intelligently, might create a more cooperative and less confrontational relationship between the superpowers. At the least, it could improve the mood and the atmosphere, both between them and, to a degree, in the world at large. But arms control, even at best, could not end the superpowers' antagonism and the rivalry. Arms control might also help produce a new climate within the superpowers; within the United States a sense that government and elites are again trying to protect citizens from a real danger and within the Soviet Union a feeling that the world outside is not thoroughly hostile. It is likely that some budgetary reallocations could be made from military expenditures to other purposes or at the least that taxes could be cut. But to cut spending a good portion of conventional forces would have to be reduced. This, however, is a worthwhile and indeed necessary goal that will take even more time.

A fundamental, unavoidable reason for pursuing arms control is that, given the dangers of not pursuing it, it is the central and necessary way to stabilize Soviet-American relations. Nothing else can substitute for it. "Arms control appears as the only variable in an otherwise unchanging conflict, and thus as the principal basis of hope" for its amelioration.[20] This inescapable fact puts arms control at the center of United States-Soviet relations. There has been a disinclination to face this fact among individuals in American politics reluctant to deal constructively with the Soviet Union because of the distaste with which they view that country. However, even among this group, once the limitations and requirements of actual policy-making are experienced, arms control or at least the appearance of it is seen as unavoidable. "As 1985 began, it was clear that arms control was not only back, but that it had resumed its place as the centerpiece of United States-Soviet relations."[21] The Soviets agree. Arbatov, the director of the USA Institute in Moscow, has said, "None of the spheres of Soviet-American relations is more important than arms control."[22] Although the Soviets sometimes use arms control as a ploy and for propaganda reasons, recent history shows they can take it seriously. In any event, they allow their relationship with the United States to improve only as arms control develops.

The crucial benefits of arms control to the United States are obvious if the potential Soviet military threat to the United States is considered. It is so serious that the United States Joint Chiefs of Staff have always favored arms control and, specifically, the SALT II Treaty. In 1985 they felt this way so strongly they split with the civilian secretary of defense on this matter, concluding that the United States would lose more than it might gain by renouncing the treaty. Such an action was one of President Reagan's options, and one that he did not then take. The "Chiefs" said that "lifting arms control would complicate military planning." The air force was concerned that renouncing arms control would remove the limits on nuclear warheads per Soviet missile and thus make vulnerable the single-warhead Mobile Midgetman missile planned for the 1990s. There was also a concern that all-out competition in nuclear weapons would drain away money for conventional forces. It might, for example, "sink" the navy's goal of a larger fleet.[23]

The United States military is concerned enough with the present scale of the Soviet military capability. But it, fortunately, is known, and measures can be planned to deal with it. However, an unbridled arms race, possibly brought about by the end of arms control, would produce a new, larger and only partially known problem. It would be very difficult to make plans concerning this unknown problem because its limits are also unknown. Such plans can become very expensive, given the military tendency to assume the "worst case" or worst possible outcome, whenever in doubt, and plan accordingly.

One American general, an adviser on nuclear arms policy to the White House and Congress, has said that "reciprocal violation" of SALT II makes no sense for the United States "because we have virtually no leverage" on Soviet missile buildups and accordingly the treaty "is in a sense a refuge for us."[24] Thus, the American military command favors arms control, and SALT in particular, in an overall sense.

The "worst case" results of no SALT II treaty were outlined well several yeas ago by Edmund Muskie when he was Secretary of State:

> Without the treaty, the Soviets can deploy 25% more strategic bombers and missiles...
>
> Without the treaty ... they will have several thousand more individual nuclear weapons.... Each of their heavy missiles[a] alone could carry 20–30 nulcear weapons instead of the 10 permitted under the treaty.
>
> Without the treaty, there is no prohibition on ... concealing ... strategic programs....
>
> Without the treaty, we would ... know less about more.[25]

---

[a] Note: Even the new American MX, ten of which were deployed as of early 1987, is not considered "heavy."

A secretary of state of a Republican administration has made a similar point. "The issue was not 'what situation [the agreement] perpetuates, but what situation it prevents.'"[26] In other words, even if one cannot make things better, they ought to be prevented from getting worse. Arms control tries to do this, albeit imperfectly.

SALT has prevented the arms race from going haywire. Significantly, the Soviets have not "breached" in any major way or "broken out" of the arms control agreements they have signed. This is a good sign that SALT is in their interests. In fact, the Soviets have dismantled about 458 operational missiles. This is more than 25 percent of the United States force numerically and about 30 percent in terms of throw-weight.[27] In the INF treaty signed in 1987 they have committed themselves, as has the United States, to destroy an entire class of weapons.

ARMS CONTROL IN UNITED STATES-SOVIET RELATIONS: A SHORT INTERPRETIVE HISTORY

Despite all the criticisms that have been leveled at arms control, it is nevertheless striking to note the arms control agreements that the two opposing superpowers have been able to work out. Clearly their competition is of a mixed variety, which includes cooperation in arms control as well.

Table 5.1's list of essentially ten agreements does not include several multilateral arms control and disarmament agreements for whose beginning the

TABLE 5.1. U.S.-USSR NUCLEAR ARMS CONTROL AGREEMENTS
(dates are of entering into force unless otherwise specified)

"Hot Line" Agreement (establishment of a direct Moscow-Washington communications link)—1963 (plus new agreement on improvements—1971 and agreement on further improvements, 1984)

Limited Test Ban Treaty—1963 (Britain also an original signatory)

Seabed Arms Control Treaty—signed 1971, in force 1972 (Britain also an original signatory)

"Accidents Measures" Agreement (agreement on measures to reduce the outbreak of nuclear war)—1971

ABM Treaty (SALT I) and *Interim Agreement on the Limitation of Strategic Offensive Arms* (two related agreements)—1972 (plus a new ABM protocol—1974), *ratified*

Prevention of Nuclear War Agreement—1973

Threshold Test Ban Treaty (limitation of underground tests)—signed 1974, *not ratified*

Tentative Arms Control Agreement (Vladivostok summit, 1974)

PNE Treaty (limitation of underground peaceful nuclear explosions)—signed 1976, *not ratified*

Strategic Arms Limitation Treaty (SALT II) (various related agreements)—signed 1979, *not ratified*[28]

INF Agreement—signed 1987 ratification to be debated by the U.S. Senate in early 1988.

START (Strategic Arms Reduction Talks) Agreement—under negotiation during 1988, possibly ready for signature at the Moscow summit in mid-1988, ratification to be debated by the Senate in late 1988. (If ratified, supersedes SALT II.)

United States and the Soviet Union were important or to which both have agreed. Among these are nuclear arms limitation agreements such as the Antarctic Treaty (ratified by the United States in 1960), the Outer Space Treaty (ratified in 1967), the Non-Proliferation Treaty (ratified 1969). Also to be noted are United States and Soviet adherence to: the 1925 Geneva Protocol for the prohibition of the use of poison gases and bacteriological means in war, the 1967 treaty prohibiting nuclear weapons in Latin America, the 1977 convention prohibiting hostile environmental modification, and the 1980 convention on the protection of nuclear material.

The Kennedy, Johnson, and Nixon Administrations: 1960–1972

Enormous amounts of time, negotiating effort, and political compromise went into the making of these agreements. During the Kennedy administration the process was facilitated by the mutual scare both powers experienced in the Cuban Missile Crisis of October 1962. The hot line agreement and the limited test ban treaty were soon concluded, in 1963. At last nuclear weapons pollution of the atmosphere had ended. But the agreements of the 1960s "did not limit weaponry.... They ruled out future possibilities in environments where neither side had any current intention of putting weapons.... They were, in a way, psychological precursors of SALT."[29]

Negotiations on limiting strategic arms might well have begun earlier had it not been for the escalation of American involvement in the fighting in Vietnam in 1965 and the Soviet invasion of Czechoslovakia in 1968. The assassination of President Kennedy in 1963 and the absorption of his successor, Johnson, in civil rights and other issues were also factors in the delay, although he and Soviet Premier Kosygin did have a brief meeting in the summer of 1967. It was not until 1969, the first year of the Nixon administration, that official SALT talks began. Even then, the SALT I agreement was not realized for almost three years.

There were several reasons why SALT I or the ABM treaty became possible. "There was a feeling in 1969 that a 'window' in time was approaching when the forces of the Soviets and Americans were sufficiently in phase and the psychology of the two leaderships was such that a nuclear arms control agreement might be feasible." American strategic forces had reached maturity; only qualitative improvements were now in the works. The Soviet strategic force would soon, in numbers, be equal to the American force targeted on the Soviet Union and could come to exceed it. The Soviets and the Americans were beginning to see that ABMs posed a "dangerous and destabilizing prospect" to them both.[30]

Mr. Nixon and his adviser Kissinger seemed to feel that after several years of an indecisive war in Southeast Asia the United States as a society and political system was unwilling to play the same anti-Soviet role it had earlier. Accordingly some new and reduced foreign policy stance was necessary to prevent a domestically forced abdication by America of its superpower role. In the Soviet Union the General Secretary, Brezhnev, though no reformer, did recognize that the USSR was now much more a superpower than it had been and that the United States was less a superpower. It had neither won in Vietnam nor prevented the USSR from reasserting its control over Czechoslovakia. He seemed to think it was now possible to get the United States to confirm the Soviet Union's new status through arms control and also use it to open the USSR to Western technology and grain through détente. That is, the Soviet Union might be able to grow in vitality and power through a new relationship with the West in which its American champion would finally accept, if only tacitly, the USSR as a growing power. This goal fitted in to a degree with Kissinger's grand aim: bringing the Soviet Union closer to the West by enveloping it in a network of ties it would find too useful to break and which would, it was hoped, come to "tame" the militarily expansionist side of the Soviet Union.

Specific reasons for SALT I are not hard to find. The Nixon administration realized that only by an arms limitation agreement might it "prevent the USSR from achieving numerical superiority in offensive ballistic missile launchers." American politics, with an unpopular war still going on, was not going to support a strategic rearmament program. MIRVs were introduced, yes, but this was not then a public issue. Soon the administration adopted the old Eisenhower doctrine of "sufficiency" and put aside the rhetoric of "superiority." New surveillance capabilities in space could insure against Soviet "breakout."[31]

The Soviets, too, had specific reasons for moving toward SALT. They did not want to face a race in ABMs with the technologically superior United States. This was essentially the same consideration that brought them back to strategic arms talks in 1985. They also wanted to slow down American MIRV deployments and to keep China and the United States from linking up. The Soviets are true pessimist-realists, always wary of the worst. The one big thing the Soviets wanted was "formal registration of strategic equality...." For them a SALT agreement would go far toward achieving this major goal.[32]

Even so, negotiations did not just pop into existence. One complicating factor here may have been Nixon's raising of "linkage," i.e., arms control only in conjunction with progress on other Soviet-American problems. But finally in November, 1969 the first official SALT talks began in Finland. And after a long "season of frustration" in negotiations of almost three years' duration, an ABM Treaty was signed at a Moscow summit meeting in May, 1972 and ratified by the United States Senate in the same year. The essence of the agreement was a halt to the development of ABM systems. Each country was to have only two limited ABM deployment areas, later cut to one, with no more than 100 interceptor missiles and 100 launchers per site and not to develop, test, or deploy qualitatively improved ABM technology.

SALT I has been criticized. It did not stop American or Soviet strategic weapons development. New systems as well as qualitative improvements eventually appeared. They cost money. But it did avoid more ABMs, something "neither side wanted but that each would have probably ended up building in the absence of an agreement." Still, there were plenty of problems left between the superpowers. The SALT I "interim freeze was no more than a negotiating moratorium," says one critic.[33]

Yet, despite its limitations, SALT I established a precedent of the superpowers negotiating successfully about strategic offensive arms. Even though it did not set permanent limits on offensive strategic arms and allowed their further production, it did slow down the pace of these processes and established some recognized base lines for existing systems.

Nevertheless, disagreement on the worth of SALT I persists. Some see it as an important achievement in reducing the risk of nuclear war. But, others point out, it allowed the USSR to keep a large advantage in certain strategic systems, it stopped United States strategic defense programs, letting the Soviets catch up in ABM technology, and it allowed them to concentrate on a rapid buildup of their ICBM force without fear of an American ABM system. This view conflicts directly with Kissinger's judgment: "After all, SALT I constrained no American program; it stopped several Soviet programs." With such disagreements it is no wonder SALT is controversial.[34]

After the conclusion of SALT I the Soviet-American arms control record becomes more mixed for several years. Agreements of some complexity and high potential value were negotiated and signed, but they were not all ratified, although they were nevertheless observed in the main by both sides. This pattern of observance without ratification was similar to the 1920s, when there were contacts between the two nations without formal diplomatic relations. It shows the limits of the American political system in carrying forward Soviet-American relations. Part of the system, the executive branch, including the military, may be able and willing to develop the superpower relationship through arms control while other parts of the system are able to stop progress, helped particularly by the constitutional requirement of a two-thirds vote in the Senate in order to ratify a treaty.

Two arms control agreements that were signed but remain unratified are: the Treaty on the Limitation of Underground Nuclear Weapons Tests of 1974 and the Peaceful Nuclear Explosions (PNE) Treaty of 1976. The former, also known as the Threshold Test Ban Treaty (TTBT), establishes a nuclear "threshold" by prohibiting underground tests exceeding 150 kilotons. Its ultimate purpose is to reduce first-strike capability by limiting confidence in new systems' reliability. The PNE treaty counters the derivation of weapons-related benefits prohibited by the TTBT treaty and specifies procedures for outside observers to monitor peaceful nuclear explosions.

By 1974 arms control was in political trouble in the United States. True, it would continue to develop for almost five more years at the government-to-government level and culminate in the SALT II Treaty of 1979. Certain elites, however, and the broader public, had begun to question Soviet-American arms control. In effect, it was losing some of the tacit public support it may have had and, perhaps more importantly, its opponents were acquiring better arguments and more public support.

SALT also suffered from being the product of those same administrations that had given the country Vietnam and Watergate. These events had set loose a great current of dissatisfaction with and anger at American institutions, their members and their products. There was also the corrosive effect of coming to arrangements with a Soviet Union that would not accept the status quo, open itself to the world, stop arming or treat its peoples decently. This came together to undercut the political worth of the 1974 summit meeting in Vladivostok, which established common limits on delivery vehicles, and the SALT effort as a whole. Progress in strategic arms control was further delayed by President Ford's failure to move to have the Vladivostok accord ratified because of lack of support within his administration.

The Carter Administration: 1977–1981

The Democratic administration of Jimmy Carter that came into office in January 1977 moved quickly to arrive at a new SALT agreement. The Carter administration began with an aura of apolitical freshness very appealing to an electorate that wanted a change from the politics of war, corruption, and power-jockeying that hung about the administrations of Nixon and Ford. Still, it went forward in its foreign policy without any resolution of the underlying sociopolitical problems of American politics apparent since the 1960s. This meant it had little leeway in arriving at a SALT II treaty.

Essentially, President Carter never chose between the two wings of his administration—the more liberal faction personified by Cyrus Vance, the secretary of state for most of the four-year period, and the more realist grouping best represented by Zbigniew Brzezinski, the President's national security adviser and initial "tutor" on international politics. The "liberals" tended to try for a new SALT treaty without making hard demands of the Soviets while the "realists," who also wanted a treaty, thought it necessary to get some modifications of Soviet foreign policy in the process. Either approach might have produced a SALT treaty if it had been followed carefully and consistently and had the president's unwaivering backing. This was not the case, however. The Carter administration seemed to be two separate administrations in its pronouncements and foreign policy moves; the media was always ready to magnify differences between Brzezinski and Vance into major conflicts and power struggles. This image of divisiveness did much to undercut the administration's political standing; it both annoyed the Soviets and tempted them to try for more than they could get in SALT.

President Carter, as a representative of the unavoidably variegated and fractious Democratic Party, would inevitably have had a problem of leadership, but he exacerbated it by not leading his administration into a clear policy toward the Soviet Union, and challenging the Soviet leadership directly by raising the issue of human rights in the USSR. Carter caused apparently sincere anger among the Soviet elite by meeting with a famous emigré dissident from the Soviet Union and by corresponding with the dissident physicist Sakharov.[35]

Jimmy Carter and his distinctive political style—populist, open and vocal—made the administration seem even more divided and also excessively idealistic for the world of international politics. His great foreign policy achievement was the Camp David Accords between Egypt and Israel, a worthy and important accomplishment still very popular in the United States. Unfortunately, however, he was unable to negotiate a new SALT treaty that the Senate and the country would accept. The reasons are not all to be found within his administration.

The Soviet Union continued to build up its military power during his four years in office, and this constant heaping of weapons upon weapons was threateningly apparent to the American public and its politicians and interest groups. During the 1970s, when the United States introduced no new strategic weapons system, the Soviet Union deployed at least two new types of missile submarines, several missile systems and a new bomber.[36] The Iranian hostage crisis, an event that frustrated and angered America, could have happened regardless of who was President. But it happened to Jimmy Carter and seriously undercut his domestic support. The economic recession did not help the administration either.

The Carter administration decided to try to renegotiate the Vladivostok formula the Soviets saw as a firm basis for agreement by pressing for deep cuts in nuclear weapons. In March 1977, a delegation headed by Secretary Vance went to Moscow with proposals to this effect and met with a stone wall of Soviet anger and refusal. Gromyko, the Soviet foreign minister, went on Soviet TV to lambaste the perfidious Americans. SALT had lost much momentum.

The new administration was quite out of touch with the realities of Soviet politics. Americans then in Moscow were in general agreement that the Vance mission would fail. The tone of contemptuous anger at the American move in the Soviet press at the time suggests strongly that the Soviet leadership had not found it politically easy to negotiate with the Americans. By asking abruptly for more and by also publicizing Soviet dissent, the Carter administration threw into doubt whatever complex deal on arms control had been made within the Soviet elite by the Vladivostok understanding. While thinking it was negotiating arms control with the Soviet Union, it was actually challenging its leaders and system.

Still, the March 1977 United States proposal for deep cuts in nuclear weapons was based on an understanding that the SALT ceilings were "too high and . . . make possible not only further weapons deployment but . . . also breed mutual insecurities"[37] as well as fostering political opposition to arms control from both left and right. President Carter wanted to reduce the total number of nuclear missiles to only several hundred and put United States-Soviet relations

on a "basis of reciprocity, mutual respect and benefit." Later Reagan was to
arrive at a similar position.

It was almost inevitable that the Soviets turned down the American arms
control proposal of March 1977. It called for a sharp turn downward in missilry
in a context of Soviet buildup and earlier American agreement to it. How was
arms control to go forward after this failure? The Carter administration was
publicly embarrassed and the Soviets were infuriated. Gromyko labeled the
March proposals a "cheap and shady maneuver." Any arms control agreement
that was now arrived at would look like an "ignominious retreat" in American
politics.[38] Accordingly, the road to SALT II was going to be hard slogging, and
valuable time needed for Senate ratification would be taken up by reassessment
and new negotiations. As Brzezinski outlines the post-1977 arms control
situation: "By the spring of 1978, United States-Soviet relations were stale-
mated. The SALT talks were at best creeping forward.... We were ...
increasingly portrayed as unable either to accommodate or to compete with the
Soviets."[39]

The administration reconsidered. Arms control negotiations were put on a
more realistic basis. The approach to human rights abuses in the Soviet Union
was lowered in intensity. American negotiating became calmer, the "public
drama associated with SALT" was thus reduced, various "backchannels" were
opened, congressmen were brought into the negotiations as advisers and Carter
cancelled the B-1 bomber project, though deciding to go ahead with the cruise
missile.[40]

Even so, SALT became "the most time-consuming issue of the Carter
administration, involving "a tedious process of negotiating" which "it was well-
nigh impossible to accelerate." It wound up as a "dizzyingly complicated affair"
akin to a Russian *matroshka* doll—a set of dolls "nested" inside one another.
Although it seemed close to being wrapped up in late December 1978, basic
agreement was reached only in May 1979 after a great deal of on-off, up-down
negotiations. Between January 1 and May 7, 1979 the secretary of state and the
Soviet ambassador met twenty-five times. All in all, six and a half years of three
administrations' time and effort had been involved. On May 7, 1979 at 3:15 P.M.
Secretary of State Vance reported: "Mr. President, the basic negotiations for
SALT have been completed."[41]

Not everything was clearly resolved. Certain issues remained. For Americans these included: Soviet advantages in throw weight, the encryption (coding)
of missile performance data, verification and supposed "Minuteman vulnerability." For Soviets problems lay in the development of a new American MX
missile and cruise missiles. SALT II had not eliminated strategic modernization.
This set of concerns was going to be important in preventing ratification of
SALT II.

Here are the main numbers of SALT II. A ceiling of 2,250 strategic delivery
vehicles of all types was set. The United States got a ceiling of 1,200 for the
MIRVed missile aggregate. The two sides split the difference on the MIRVed

ICBM subceiling and arrived at 820. Soviet concessions included the deployment of fewer MIRVs than Vladivostok had allowed while the Americans accepted the Soviet heavy missile force as it was.[42]

But the political context itself in 1979–80 was not one in which Americans were willing to come to easy agreement with foreign powers, much less a Soviet Union that had just begun a war to control a new area—Afghanistan.

SALT II was never ratified by the United States Senate. The Carter administration wound up with "neither détente nor SALT,"[43] and was defeated in its bid for a second term as well, passing into history under that embarrassing cloud of having meant well but not having realized its goals.

The Reagan Presidency Accepts Arms Control: 1981–1988

The Reagan administration was at first strongly against any new arms control arrangement. Its collective position on SALT was that it was a proverbial "one-way street"—all to the benefit of the Soviet Union. SALT was atmospherically antithetical to the new administration's goal of re-arming America, both militarily and emotionally. To it, SALT was weakening, and thus clearly incompatible with its views of itself, of America, of the Soviet Union and of the world at large. The Reagan administration had won the presidency on a platform with anti-Soviet, anti-SALT and rearmament planks. It intended to bring about a "new revolution" within the United States and its foreign policy. SALT had no place in these plans.

Later the administration realized that it needed SALT, or at least the appearance of it, in order to govern without too much difficulty and accordingly began to seem to move toward a new exercise in arms control, but under a new name—START (Strategic Arms Reduction Talks)—as part of the unavoidable politics of terminology. Still, many of its leading figures, including the president himself, were philosophically opposed to arms control as it had been practiced and would not move quickly or strongly. They were also sincerely opposed to the Soviet Union, its nature, and its policies, and they said so again and again in public.[41]

Reagan's anti-communism had the ring of sincerity, unlike Nixon's, which seemed opportunistic. And, whereas Nixon had much experience in foreign affairs and a good sense of the naturalness of contemporary world politics, Reagan had been a stay-at-home state-level politician, strongly oriented to a certain purely American way of thinking and acting and in a special American environment—California. Possibly the strongest and most often quoted statement of Reagan's about the Soviet Union was his characterization of it as an "evil empire" and "the focus of evil in the modern world." Significantly, later, when Reagan was trying to achieve an arms control agreement with the Soviet Union this speech was left out of the collection of key foreign policy statements of the Reagan administration issued by the State Department in May, 1984.

Progress in arms control was hesitant. Several groups on the far right of the Republican party mounted a public campaign to force the resignation of

Secretary of State Shultz after arms control negotiations began.[45] In addition, some leading conservative figures in the administration often made clear to the media their dislike of the Soviet Union and of arms control.

Talks on reducing intermediate-range nuclear forces in Europe began only in November 1981 while talks on limiting strategic arms did not begin until the middle of 1982. In both cases the administration entered negotiations unwillingly, having been "pushed to the bargaining table by political forces"—a combination of the activities of the new domestic network of nuclear freeze and disarmament groups and the actions of similar groups in Europe plus the importunings of Allied governments.[46]

A total refusal to negotiate on arms control was not politically feasible. It would have meant taking on an image of embattlement both domestically and in NATO, an image which itself would have weakened the administration. It was more intelligent, politically, to appear to negotiate. This is what the administration did. It put forth initial positions that were unacceptable to the Soviet Union and which were, therefore, unrealistic and could not serve as bases of agreement. The Soviets, on their part, were more willing to negotiate but were unrealistic too in thinking, apparently, that their new degree of military might and their activities in Eastern Europe and the Third World would not elicit real concern if not renewed opposition to them in both European and American politics.

The Intermediate Nuclear Force talks (INF) showed this pattern of mutual unrealism. The new acronym INF was introduced to replace the more contentious TNF or Theater Nuclear Force. The Europeans naturally did not like their countries designated a theater for war. Historically, the talks sprang from a NATO decision of 1979 to deploy new American intermediate-range missiles in western Europe as a counter to new Soviet mid-range missiles being deployed since 1977 (the SS-20) and at the same time to begin negotiations to limit such weapons. The new American missiles, not then in existence, were Pershing IIs and ground-launched cruise missiles (GLCMs). This was known as the "dual track" decision—deploy in response to Soviet deployments but negotiate at the same time. This approach reflected the new feeling, particularly in Europe, that additional nuclear weaponry, necessary as it may be for the sake of political credibility, does not bring additional security. The Soviets tried to use negotiations over the deployments to get the Europeans to cancel the American missile plans and become resigned to the Soviet missiles.

Many in the West, however, have never accepted the SS-20 as a defensive response to Soviet military needs. To them the SS-20 appears to be a weapon of intimidation, able to rain down nuclear destruction on Europe and Asia only several minutes after its launching from the Soviet Union.

When INF became a topic of negotiations, in November 1981, the Soviet and American positions were far apart. The United States' first proposal was the so-called "zero-zero" option—neither side would have any INF missiles, except for the short-range ones already in existence for many years. The Soviets rejected this outright, claiming that a balance in INF already existed, even before the new American missile deployments, because of the existence of American carrier-based and other nuclear-armed aircraft in the European theater. The Soviets proposed a freeze at their then existing level of SS-20s if the United States deployed no missiles in Europe. This position came to be known as the "half-zero" option, zero for NATO but an SS-20 force for the USSR.

The American side also insisted that global limits be imposed on the SS-20. Since it was a mobile system, it could be based anywhere in the USSR and targeted on, for example, China and Japan, friends of the United States. The Soviets refused to accept such global limits. They also insisted at first that they deserved a certain level of INF forces to counter British and French nuclear forces. This demand complicated matters and brought French and British pressure on the United States. They did not want an INF arrangement that would limit their independent nuclear capabilities or their sovereignty, or that would confirm the implicit Soviet demand that its own nuclear weaponry equal that of all the rest of the world combined. This allied position was accepted by the United States.

Continued negotiations did not produce a deal for years, until late 1987. For one thing, neither side could get what it most wanted. The United States demanded global ceilings and a French-British force level not swamped by Soviet deployments. The Soviets were against any Pershing IIs (medium-range ballistic missiles) in West Germany. In effect, both sides were negotiating not solely to come to an INF agreement but also to influence the course of politics in Western Europe. Both feared what an INF agreement might do to their overall power positions. Possibly the Soviets wanted more to pressure the West Germans into refusing Euromissiles than to seek an INF settlement with the United States. The American administration wanted to show through its own INF deployments that NATO was still functioning and that the West Germans particularly still had the nerve to stand up to the USSR politically. The Soviets were not to be allowed to "decouple" Europe from the United States.[47] This continuing superpower contention over Germany was crucial in their failing to agree on INF. Lastly, the international context became "bumpy." Brezhnev died in late 1982 and his successors, first Andropov and then Chernenko, were shortlived. The Korean airliner incident and the American invasion of Grenada in 1983 ended all moves toward a summit meeting.

When the German parliament approved the deployment of Pershing IIs on November 22, 1983 the Soviets terminated the INF negotiations immediately. They soon announced that talks could resume only if the American missiles were withdrawn and that they would put the United States under a threat similar to the one posed to the USSR by the Pershing IIs. It turned out that not Soviet threats, anti-Americanism, the peace movement, nor the increasing fear of war, all of which had contributed to huge anti-missile demonstrations and some violence, had changed the views of the majority of West Europeans. Governments favoring deployment were reelected. The Soviets had seriously miscalculated and excluded themselves from further INF negotiations until new, more favorable conditions might come into being and until they could work up a new approach.

The first Reagan administration also moved to Strategic Arms Limitations Talks, but not until June 1982. The administration decided that it had to begin strategic arms negotiations in order "to blunt the . . . freeze movement and . . . the growing opposition to the MX."[48] But no movement occurred because the central concerns of each side were not being dealt with: the U.S. concern with warheads and throw weight and the Soviet condition that START would have to include the cancellation of American INF deployments in Europe, since these weapons can reach the Soviet Union and thus are "strategic" in Soviet eyes.

START went nowhere during 1983. Complicating the negotiations was the struggle going on within the Reagan administration and between it and Congress and various interest groups. The administration claimed that progress was stalled because the Soviet side could not negotiate due to frequent leadership changes. The Soviets were tending to do no more than modify their former positions, and too slowly for the American pace of change.

The Reagan administration was unwilling to sign an arms control agreement until it had either regained military superiority or achieved a dynamic strategic equality. The Soviets were concerned with the future impact on their land-based ICBMs of the new American cruise missiles, MX and Trident IIs, and the new SDI. It is not surprising that the START talks were ended in December 1983, a month after the INF talks had been suspended.

With the "meat" of arms control no longer under discussion, the talks on Mutual and Balanced Force Reductions (MBFR) of troop levels in Europe were hung up and nothing came of suggestions for eliminating chemical weapons.

The fundamental worth of SALT II, signed in 1979 by President Carter and General Secretary Brezhnev in Vienna, was demonstrated by President Reagan's 1985 decision not to go for a large-scale "breakout" of SALT's limits on nuclear weaponry and to return to talks with the Soviets on arms control. It must have been personally painful and politically difficult for a president who had sincerely opposed SALT to have arrived at this decision. The Soviets too had to swallow a year's worth of their anti-American verbiage when they returned to arms control talks in early 1985.

On June 10, 1985 President Reagan announced he had decided to seek "an interim framework" or agreement of "truly mutual restraint" involving "real reductions in the size of existing nuclear arsenals." In this announcement Mr. Reagan stated:

> I have decided that the United States will continue to refrain from undercutting existing strategic arms agreements to the extent that the Soviet Union exercises comparable restraint and provided that the Soviet Union actively pursues arms

reduction agreements in the currently on-going nuclear and space talks in Geneva.[49]

He explained further the need to adopt "meaningful measures which improve security, stability and predictability," standard arms control concerns. Reagan said in 1985 that he had "no more important goal" in his second term than reducing and then eliminating nuclear weapons. But he cautioned that any arms control agreement must be "a good agreement—an agreement which meets the interests of both countries, which increases the security of our allies and which enhances international stability." This statement might have been intended both for public consumption and as a reply to Gorbachev, who had said, "There are no types of armaments that the USSR would not agree to see limited and eventually banned in agreement with other countries on a reciprocal basis."[50]

In addition, there is the guess that Ronald Reagan, having won a second term, wanted to establish as good a historical record for himself as possible and also help elect another Republican president to follow him, goals that require some amelioration of the superpower contention. This cannot be achieved without another arms control agreement. Another administration had decided to negotiate with the Soviet Union.

More specifically, negotiations were resumed because, on the Soviet side, it was clear that the Soviet pullout from arms control talks in 1983 had prevented neither deployment of new American INF missiles in Europe nor the beginning of SDI. The American side realized that although SALT II was imperfect, casting it aside would allow the Soviets to increase strategic forces faster than could the United States. The USSR had excess throw weight usable for many more warheads plus open missile assembly lines. Retaining SALT II gave at least some base lines for future reductions and kept alive the notion that negotiations had value. And, for both the United States and the Soviet Union, SALT had put some brakes on the arms race, by making each other's strategic force structure easier to predict. For the Soviets it was also apparent that any acceleration of Soviet military spending would have markedly deleterious effects on an already stagnating economy.[51]

Significantly, the Soviet leadership succession problem had finally been resolved with the accession of Gorbachev, a relatively young leader, in March 1985. This new general secretary was strongly oriented to economic reform and modernization as well as, of course, to consolidating his position—all goals that require a "breathing space" in Soviet foreign policy. The Soviets had to return to negotiations to get this respite from the United States. By mid-1985 then, the Soviets and Americans were no longer out-of-phase on arms control. As one very experienced specialist put it:

Deep U.S. dissatisfaction with modest strategic arms control agreements of the type we have known thus far, together with the Soviet Union's evident aversion to engaging in an unregulated competition in strategic defense, therefore provides both sides with powerful incentives for exploring a third alternative: an arms control regime that would avert the enormous costs, possible great risks and nerve-wracking uncertainties of an arms race in strategic defense in return for a long-term and more far-reaching agreement than ever before on strategic offensive weapons, notably including deep reductions or elimination of systems deemed particularly threatening by both sides.[52]

Time will reveal whether such a halcyon "third alternative" is realized. At the least, though, by 1985 arms control was again alive, although not yet clearly well. A START treaty was being approached through summit meetings and negotiations on INF.

Arms Control, 1985–1988

The year 1985 saw arms control negotiations begin but with much maneuvering and posturing by both parties, with several propagandistic plays to the gallery of world public opinion. Despite this game playing, which is better than no interaction at all, both sides seemed to be creeping forward toward a relationship more conducive to agreement, though without any new ideas for breakthroughs. Even a Reagan-Gorbachev summit meeting in November 1985 did not bring agreement.

Yet, by 1987 a new arms control situation existed. The summits of 1985 and 1986 had improved the political atmosphere, extensive discussions had been held by the superpowers during 1986 and some things had occurred for the first time that furthered arms control. At the 1986 summit, in Iceland, President Reagan had indicated to General Secretary Gorbachev that he would ask the Senate to ratify the TTB and PNE treaties. This he did in January 1987. Gorbachev agreed to "significant cuts," perhaps 50 percent, in the number of Soviet heavy ICBMs, a long-standing American demand.[53]

And although the USSR decided to renew nuclear testing it allowed a group of American scientists to monitor a test. This was a "first," as was Soviet publication of statistics on strategic arms using *Soviet*, not American figures. Some of the figures were a bit higher than previous American estimates. In addition, in 1987, the superpowers actually produced a minor arms control agreement. "Risk reduction centers" were set up in Washington and Moscow. By then the Soviets had accepted on-site inspection in order to verify an INF agreement and suggested that the superpowers conduct a nuclear test on each other's territories in order to improve verification techniques. By mid-year Gorbachev announced the Soviet Union would now accept a worldwide ban on medium-range and short-range missiles. Although the West German government and the outgoing NATO commander wanted to keep the German short-range missiles with American warheads in order to avoid losing options for opposing Soviet intimidation it was clear that the INF issue had never before been so close to resolution. It seemed an INF agreement was only a question of time and that a third Reagan-Gorbachev summit would then take place.

Many differences remained in arms control however. The two sides still disagreed on what is "strategic." The Soviets tend to count all nuclear systems capable of striking their territory. The United States counts only intercontinental systems. And, although, the Soviets have come to accept some SDI research they still are solidly against any deployment of SDI.[54] Without agreement on the SDI issue a new treaty on strategic arms is unlikely.

Still, the superpowers were closer together than in a decade or so. Each side's government seems to have parallel needs, each for different reasons. Mr. Gorbachev wants to get going on economic reform while Mr. Reagan wants a grand achievement in foreign policy. Both want the political benefits of success.

This unusual overlap of goals led in December 1987 to a Reagan-Gorbachev summit meeting in Washington at which a treaty eliminating all land-based medium-range missiles in Eurasia was signed. (The text was flown in from Geneva at the last minute.) This was a first in arms control. Not only was an entire category of nuclear weaponry to be eliminated, but on-site inspection of certain missile facilities and plants was to take place for a period of years. Agreement on the treaty was facilitated by Congress' limitations on the testing of SDI components and the reluctant decision of the West Germans to give up their older medium-ranges missiles with American warheads. Soviet SS-20s and American Pershing IIs and cruise missiles based in Europe were to be destroyed. President Reagan was able to appeal for broad public support for the treaty by saying "it is not just an arms control but an arms reduction agreement." The public seemed to agree. Sixty percent of Americans were in favor of the INF treaty. First Secretary Gorbachev had temporarily dropped his stipulation that SDI had to go before arms control could continue. Perhaps he had decided SDI was not going to work and, in any case, it would not be developed further once Reagan was no longer President.[55]

Despite the fact that signing the INF treaty is a real political achievement, its fate is unclear at this writing. Will it clear that "graveyard" of treaties, the Senate? Will its conservative foes in both superpowers manage to derail it? Will SDI again become a major obstacle?

ISSUES AND DEBATE

Arms control is an intensely politicized subject. It inevitably triggers basic emotions, particularly since it involves cooperative dealings with a well-armed opponent and rival. Many people are also disturbed that while negotiations drag on, the participants conduct business as usual—they do research on nuclear weapons and build prototypes, which they test, mass produce, and deploy as integral parts of their arsenals. It is no surprise then that arms control triggers debate and political struggle. Some of the issues and the debate surrounding them in contemporary American society are presented below.

Are Expectations for Arms Control Too High?

Despite the advantages of arms control it has come under criticism in recent years from both left and right as well as from the skeptics and doubting Thomases present in any society. Although we have stated some of the arguments of the left, including the "disarmers," we have not yet given the conservatives and the skeptics their due.

Some European writers suggest the problem with arms control is a fundamental one. One suggests that Western polities have not agreed on what sort and amount of military force or deterrence is required to maintain themselves at their current level of power and prosperity. "If there is no consensus on the requirements for nuclear strategic deterrence, there can be little on the purpose of strategic arms control." As a retired Royal Navy Commander puts it:

> It matters greatly whether we are facing an 'intentions' threat or a 'capabilities' threat. If we are facing an 'intentions' threat, then arms control negotiations are worse than useless, as Hitler taught us in the 1930s. But if the threat we face is one of 'capabilities,' then arms control and arms reductions are practical propositions.[56]

It is even possible that arms control quickens the arms race.

> *Negotiations* on arms control are détente-consuming, not détente-producing, since they highlight military asymmetries, generate concerns over military disadvantages, tempt linkages, and thus tend to increase rather than attenuate military and political distrust.[57]

Granted, arms control has not made the superpowers friends. But they were not friends even before they could harm each other with military force. Accordingly, even disarmament would not make them friends. Hence, the arms control–disarmament effort is not a basic part of the problems between them. Granted, too, that arms control has not reduced the superpowers' armaments overall. But these armaments exist not only to counter the other superpower but to buttress the two states' commanding positions in the world. If the superpowers were to disarm or "de-arm" conventionally what would China, Poland, Libya, Cuba, and other potential opponents do to their international interests? While it is true that the superpowers are very different ideologically and culturally, arms control assumes that difference and deals instead only with weapons systems. Much of arms control is technical and highly particularized. It can be pursued independently of political and cultural differences. Arms control has been overloaded by demands it cannot meet. Its limitations must be more widely recognized and accepted but its possibilities for reducing the threat of mutual nuclear war must be fully explored.

Can Agreements Be Verified?

American and Soviet arms control negotiators will never make an agreement whose provisions cannot be stringently and closely verified, i.e., proven, established by evidence. Yet the charge is continually made that the Soviets will "cheat" and get away with it. To be sure, this charge is sometimes merely a political ploy by those who do not want to accept arms control under any circumstances. If the verification of an arms control agreement can be called into doubt so is the agreement itself. The reason the charge is difficult to disprove is that since both sides commit minor violations, mostly technical in nature, there is always a limit to what can be established without a doubt about a secretive opponent's weapons and military capabilities. For example, it is probably not possible to know exactly how many nuclear warheads of a particular type the Soviet Union has. And, if the United States government has particular knowledge derived from espionage it does not want to compromise its sources.

The issue of verification is important because it can cause a fatal delay in the progress of a treaty through the Senate, as happened with the Salt II treaty. Verification becomes a political issue and a matter of debate because of the widely-held, though incorrect, view that verifiability is a question of black and white—that an arms control agreement either is verifiable simply, or else not at all. "Actually, verifiability is more nearly a question of shades of gray.... no agreed limitation on modern weapons can be verifiable with total certainty...."[58]

People with psychological makeups that cannot accept ambiguity will tend to demand absolute proof that the Soviets are adhering to an agreement—proof that can never be supplied. One analyst notes the existence of an extreme "school" of this sort, which he calls the "metaphysical" school of verification. Its watchword is, in effect, "We have never found anything the Soviets have successfully hidden." Another group troubled by verification problems are "legalists" who see any Soviet infraction of an arms control agreement as a breach of faith and a signal of larger problems.[59]

Those who accept its limitations consider verification as at most posing temporary and limited problems for arms control. They tend to hold that with technical capabilities supplemented by information derived through espionage no state can cheat in any militarily significant way without being found out, particularly since mutual surveillance by the superpowers is wide-ranging and continuous. It is also assumed that no general will use an untested weapon—the only kind of weapon whose capabilities might not be ascertainable. Thus, there are no important secrets in nuclear weaponry and significant violations of arms control agreements would be detected early and countered before the strategic balance was lost. Satellite photography from space can show the lines on parking lots and the numbers on license plates. The United States government can monitor closely: the numbers of missile launchers, bombers, submarines, the launch weight and throw weight of ICBMs, the number of reentry vehicles (RVs) released by missiles, and the characteristics of cruise missiles.[60]

Still, some politically important people seem to believe that sufficient verification is not possible. For example, Richard Perle, former assistant secretary of defense for international security affairs, has spoken of "unverifiable arms control agreements" and suggested they be replaced by a "classical resort to self-defense measures."[61] The Reagan administration, although not officially adopting such a view, has publicized various instances of possible Soviet noncompliance with arms control agreements. Ironically, even this action, taken partly because of pressure from right-wing supporters of the administration, shows that verification is adequate. The instances of noncompliance could not have been discovered otherwise. The big question is whether the specific violations that have been detected alter the strategic balance. Neither side has claimed this officially. At most, such charges are important for the politics of arms control, not arms control itself.

More openness on the part of the superpowers regarding the monitoring of strategic weaponry could relieve the negative pressure of verification issues on the arms control process. This may come about. Although historically the Soviet Union has been unenthusiastic to intrusive verification methods, in recent years it has acknowledged that more such methods are possible. The INF Treaty of 1987 includes a degree of on-site inspection unthinkable only a few years ago.

Linkage and Bargaining Chips: Help or Hindrance?

Two recurrent American practices impeding the progress of arms control have been the demand that any American agreement to arms control measures be "paid" for by change in Soviet international behavior unrelated to arms control and the tendency to build weapons to "bargain" with in arms control negotiations. While the reasoning behind these strategies has some logic to recommend it, the Soviets have never agreed to a deal openly involving linkage (the word itself is always rejected furiously) and bargaining chip weapons have rarely been bargained away. The elimination of INF missiles will be a first.

On linkage, the Soviets intimate that if their behavior in, say, the Third World, is to change, either conditions there will have to change first or the United States will have to do something pertinent on the spot. Actions in another context such as arms control negotiations can have no direct spin-off effect. Otherwise, the Soviet Union would be subject to a politics of pressure in America's interest, thus weakening the image and power of the USSR.

Even if, as they always do, the Soviets claim that linkage of arms control with other matters is impermissible they cannot avoid some of it if they allow any arms control progress to take place. "Linkage is not just a negotiating tactic but a condition of effective cooperation and a natural element in relations among political units that pursue multiple ends."[62]

Still, a leading Soviet foreign policy specialist, a member of the Central Committee, when asked if he believed in linkage replied, "not at all." He elaborated:

> "Well, no one can deny that all spheres of our relations with the United States are interconnected ... and that their improvement in one sphere creates ... a better overall climate....
>
> The big question, however, is not whether these interconnections exist, but what we do about them. Here one must have a clear sense of priorities. None of the spheres of Soviet-American relations is more important than arms control. Thus, if you really care about preventing war and stopping the arms race, how can you possibly put a brake on arms control on the grounds that the two sides are at odds over some local problem?... So what linkage does is ... work for a deterioration of relations in all spheres...."[63]

He has a point. But are the Soviet invasions of Afghanistan or Soviet troops in Syria only "local problems?" Many would say not. For example, the columnist George Will cites a Helsinki Watch report on Afghanistan where "the worst excesses of unbridled state-sanctioned violence against civilians" are occurring routinely and complains that this "has almost nothing to do with United States-Soviet relations" and that the "the arms-control process rests on certain illusions about the fundamental dynamic and aims of the Soviet regime."[64] Views such as these are widespread in American society. At the least, some people ask, "How can you make a good deal with a country that is killing people indiscriminately purely for some consideration of great power status?"

An alternative is manipulation of the USSR's desire for better relations and arms control with the West by an avowed and visible readiness on the part of the United States to defend its interests against the Soviet Union world-wide. In this way the Soviets would know linkage exists without it ever being made an explicit part of any Soviet-American agreement. It would, in effect, always exist in the background, in Soviet consciousness, but not in their open admission. Such a "strategic linkage" might, however, be difficult to sell in American domestic politics, where so many people see the United States-Soviet relationship as being either "good" or "bad" and not, as it often is, partly "good" and partly "bad." It might also limit progress in arms control if carried very far. The proper balance between arms control and other matters probably can never be worked out for long, if only because different United States-Soviet problems can be dealt with at different rates of speed and at different times. This question of linkage will therefore remain an issue.

Similarly there is disagreement on the value of bargaining chips in getting agreement in arms control. The academic specialists tend to be against them while some government officials argue in their favor. The essence of the "pro-chip" argument is that a danger carries more weight in negotiations than a non-danger and is therefore conducive to progress in negotiations. However, people may try to avoid danger by countering it with a comparable danger. In this way bargaining chips duplicate themselves in the adversary's back yard and become permanent fixtures of the superpowers' military capabilities.

The bargaining chip pattern is based on the belief that the Soviets have to be given an object to fear, say a new weapon, which they can eliminate only by making certain concessions in arms control, such as dropping one of *their* weapons. This approach might work if a new weapon of overriding power and significance could be constructed quickly. However, in the real world of weapons development, any new weapon in being has a long history of development during which it has been copied or matched by the other side. Accordingly, bargaining chip tactics do not work as intended. They only bring new systems into existence in the rival state. This has been true of: nuclear weapons, ICBMs, SLBMs, MIRVs, ASATs (though belatedly), INF and cruise missiles. It is likely to be true of SDI as well.

In the late 1960s MIRVs came to be seen as bargaining chips for the coming SALT I negotiations. There was little discussion then of the strain on arms control and American security posed by the multiplication of MIRVs. The present-day American bargaining chips are supposed to be the MX missile and possibly SDI.

Those opposed to the use of bargaining chips present several arguments. First, the "pro-chip" stance may be insincere, a mere political justification. That is, those who speak of bargaining chips really want to keep them, not bargain with them, but refuse to admit it. In any case, critics point out "as these programs advance, powerful domestic and bureaucratic constituencies will coalesce behind them.... The emphasis on developing 'bargaining chips,' therefore, may very well result in the deployment of weapons systems that would otherwise be avoided." Moreover, following a bargaining chip line limits weapons choices in the future.[65] Even an unwanted weapons system in existence cannot just be junked.

An eminent student of international relations says that "the U.S. should give up the game of bargaining chips. The tactic only feeds what is ... an important component of the arms race ... the 'action-reaction' phenomenon." He suggests that the United States should instead occasionally adopt temporary unilateral restraints on R & D and weapons deployment "and ask that they be reciprocated by comparable Soviet ones." This is safe, he says, because "nowhere is the Soviet Union so advanced that a temporary restraint on this side might lead to disaster...."[66]

The big bargaining chip question today is whether the SDI will become one. Even though it is still only an R & D program, it is the only weapons system the Soviets will consider a worthwhile trade for some of their brute throw weight. If the bargaining chip argument can be made to work with SDI in the special way it did for the ABM we might see a re-enactment of SALT I. In those negotiations both sides decided to forego a system that was just beginning to emerge, due to its high cost, inherent problems of development and dangers of destabilization.[67] If INF weapons are indeed discarded it may strengthen the "pro-chip" argument since the American INF was built with the negotiating position that it would be destroyed once the Soviet INF was destroyed.

There are a number of other issues inherent in the arms control process. "How much is enough?" is a perennial one. Others include: "How can modernization of nuclear weapons (a continual process) be reconciled with building new systems that are more secure, less threatening and less redundant?" "What is the best way to negotiate a politically acceptable and still significant nuclear arms control treaty with the Soviet Union?" "Is a freeze on nuclear weapons development an effective way of limiting the arms race and reducing nuclear weaponry?" These and other issues will not be put to rest for a long time.

SUMMARY

Since the United States-Soviet relationship is a competitive, suspicious, and unaccepting one, the two superpowers carry on their competition partly through arms control. Both try to use arms control to embarrass and weaken the other. Since the two have never taken each other's measure through war they must do it in other ways. Up to now however, "All arms control efforts have been within the 'talk-test-build' format. While talks drag on, both superpowers test and build new, more destructive systems far faster than they agree on measures to limit them."[68]

In order to break out of this nuclear rat race both sides will have to accept the idea of limiting the arms race and begin to work together to find practical ways to achieve those limits. This requires that they make a real effort to understand and accommodate each others' points of view. Moscow, for example, will have to see some virtue in American "rules of the game" such as balance of power, self-restraint, joint responsibility, and deterrence. Washington will have to accept the Soviet Union as an unwelcome but going concern, the Soviet reliance on land-based heavy ICBMs, at least for a time, and the tendency for it to try to improve its position in the world. Both will have to admit they are afraid of each other, are limited by each other's power, but that they can talk to and work with each other. To do this will require a new, more realistic leadership on both sides in order to control those who want to continue to pursue a politics of strength in a new world where the full use of strength would be disastrous to all. Neither is fully ready for this. Just as Americans have not taken into account the centrality, for the Soviets, of their "liberation" from strategic inferiority[69] the Soviets do not yet realize how willing the United States still is to compete with and limit the Soviet Union.

They can come to terms only by talking with each other, and arms control is unavoidably central in this. The SALT-START-INF discussions "have unquestionably increased the sensitivity to the other side's perspective in both capitals. While this sensitivity may not prevent conflicts of interest, it certainly contributes to a calmer analysis of those conflicts."[70] Indeed, "it may well be that the most important effect of the SALT process is not between the superpowers, but within them." During the SALT negotiations the Soviets became less secretive, providing some data on their weapons systems, and Soviet civilian and military authorities engaged in more dialog while American political elites began to accept some types of cooperation with the Soviet Union. What is taken for granted today was very difficult politically not so long ago.[71] For example, in 1982, at a conference on international affairs in Philadelphia, a Soviet delegate said it is "important" that top military men on both sides have discussions and even accepted deep cuts in principle "if the result is more security for both sides."[72]

To build on these possibilities for agreement requires that arms control be viewed in a brutally frank and realistic manner. Cynics and "disarmers" may not be capable of this, however. They lean toward insecurity and nuclear disaster, the former through an endless arms race and the latter by undercutting deterrence. Cynicism and negativism bring nuclear war closer while nuclear disarmament would make "conventional" war again possible. A leading historian asks, "Do we really want to make the world safe for conventional war—and if we did, how long would it take for war to become renuclearized?"[73]

Neither superpower is likely to abandon their common determination to maintain military "equivalence," mutual "assured destruction capabilities," and "equal security."[74] But, in pursuing these common goals, the United States and the Soviet Union have no sensible alternative other than to work together on that central issue of the superpowers' foreign policy: "how to relate defense to arms control, how to maintain ... strength while negotiating reciprocal limitations...."[75] This task makes the ancient puzzle of squaring the circle and Sysyphus' endless ordeal seem easy.

This chapter can close only in a tentative way, since the pursuit of security through arms and arms control is continuing. The rough shape of a potential deal is emerging—restraints on SDI in return for reductions in Soviet heavy ICBMs—then to the lowest levels of nuclear weaponry possible and eventually on to the central arms control issue and the one most difficult to resolve—the massive conventional military confrontation in Europe.[76] But the long walk to shaking hands over such a resolution has still not been traversed at this writing and it remains for the politicians to find their own unique way to that point.

REFERENCES

1. John Kenneth Galbraith, remarks on 8 June 1985 in Amherst, Massachusetts, *Daily Hampshire Gazette* (Northampton, MA), 10 June 1985, 15; Henry Kissinger, Moscow press conference, quoted in his *Years of Upheaval*, (Boston: Little, Brown, 1982), 1175; Arkady N. Shevchenko, *Breaking With Moscow* (New York: Knopf,

1985), 162 and 214; David Holloway, *The Soviet Union and the Arms Race*, 2d ed. (New Haven: Yale University Press, 1984), 180; and Robert W. Tucker, "Toward a New Detente," *New York Times Magazine,* 9 December 1984, 98.

2. For a brief history of disarmament agreements see: David W. Ziegler, *War, Peace, and International Politics*, 2d Ed. (Boston: Little, Brown, 1981), 249–267. See also Hedley Bull, "Disarmament and the International System," (a review of *The Arms Race*, by Philip Noel-Baker, 1958), *Australian Journal of Politics and History* 1 (May 1959) and various issues of the *Journal of Conflict Resolution*. For fuller discussion of, and a bibliography on, disarmament see J. David Singer, "Disarmament," *International Encyclopedia of the Social Sciences*, vol. 4, ed. D. L. Sills (New York: Macmillan & The Free Press, 1968), 192–202.

3. Bruce Russett, *The Prisoners of Insecurity: Nuclear Deterrence, the Arms Race, and Arms Control* (San Francisco: Freeman, 1983), 187–190.

4. Thomas C. Schelling and Morton H. Halperin, *Strategy and Arms Control* (New York: Twentieth Century Fund, 1961), 2, and Singer, 194–195.

5. Barry D. Blechman and Janne E. Nolan, "Reorganizing for More Effective Arms Negotiations," *Foreign Affairs*, 61, 5 (Summer 1983): 1157–1182.

6. Richard Burt, *New Weapons Technologies: Debate and Directions*, Adelphi Paper No. 126 (London: I.I.S.S., 1976), 31.

7. George Guttman, "Reason for Despair," *New York Times*, 30 December 1984, E-13.

8. Marshall D. Shulman, "What The Russians Really Want," *Harper's*, April 1984, 71.

9. Schelling and Halperin, 3.

10. *Ibid.*, 37.

11. Russett, 99–103 and 190.

12. Schelling and Halperin, 142–143.

13. Suggested by G. W. Rathjens and G. B. Kistiakowsky, "The Limitations of Strategic Arms," *Scientific American*, January 1970, in *The Conduct of Soviet Foreign Policy*, ed. E. Hoffmann and F. Fleron (Chicago: Aldine–Atherton, 1971), 391.

14. Ziegler, 247; Norman Graebner, "The Soviet-American Conflict: a Strange Phenomenon," *The Virginia Quarterly Review* 60, 4 (Fall 1984): 567.

15. Eugene J. Carroll, Jr., "Move Toward a Test Ban," *New York Times*, 5 January 1985, A-19; Alvin Z. Rubinstein, *Soviet Foreign Policy Since World War II* (Cambridge, MA: Winthrop, 1981), 184.

16. Arnold Horelick, "U.S.-Soviet Relations: The Return of Arms Control," *Foreign Affairs: America and the World, 1984*, 63, 3 (1985), 523. Horelick served as National Intelligence Officer for the USSR during the Carter administration.

17. Adam Ulam, quoted in *New York Times*, 10 January 1985, A-11.

18. Zbigniew K. Brzezinski, address to the 25th annual IISS conference, 8 September 1983, Ottawa.

19. Russett, 189; and Leslie Gelb, *Daily Hampshire Gazette*, (Northampton, MA), 13 October 1982.

20. Robert W. Tucker, "Toward a New Detente," *New York Times Magazine*, 9 December 1984, 99.

21. Horelick, 522. The term "centerpiece" for arms control has also been used by Robert W. Tucker, 98.

22. Georgi A. Arbatov and Willem Oltmans, *The Soviet Viewpoint* (New York: Dodd, Mead, 1983), 77.

23. *New York Times*, 5 June 1985, A-1 and A-10.

24. Brent Scowcroft, *New York Times*, 19 June 1985, D-28.
25. Edmund Muskie, "SALT and the Future of Arms Control," U.S. Department of State, *Current Policy*, No. 240, 16 October 1980, 1.
26. Henry A. Kissinger, *White House Years* (Boston: Little, Brown, 1979), 1245.
27. *Christian Science Monitor*, 11 June 1985.
28. U.S. ACDA, *Arms Control and Disarmament Agreements: Texts and Histories of Negotiations*, 1982 ed. (Washington, DC: GPO, 1982).
29. Gerard Smith, *Doubletalk: the Story of the First Strategic Arms Limitation Talks* (Garden City, NY: Doubleday, 1980), 18. Smith was the chief United States negotiator for SALT I, which produced the ABM Treaty in 1972.
30. Smith, 22 and 35; Henry A. Kissinger, *White House Years* (Boston: Little, Brown, 1979), 124.
31. *Ibid.*, 23, 24 and 30.
32. *Ibid.*, 31–35.
33. Kissinger, 1246; Richard J. Barnet, *The Giants* (New York: Simon and Schuster, 1977), 102; and Smith, 457.
34. Henry A. Kissinger, *Years of Upheaval* (Boston: Little, Brown, 1982), 268.
35. This judgment of Soviet elite reaction is based on experiences of the author at the USA Institute and elsewhere in the Soviet Union during the Spring of 1977.
36. See Chart I.E.1 in the FY 1985 Report to Congress of the Secretary of Defense, (Washington, DC: GPO, 1984), 49.
37. Zbigniew K. Brzezinski, *Power and Principle* (New York: Farrar, Straus, Giroux, 1983), 150.
38. Strobe Talbott, *Endgame: the Inside Story of SALT II* (New York: Harper and Row, 1979), 74, 78.
39. Brzezinski, 316. The discussion of SALT II here relies mainly on this memoir and Talbott's *Endgame*.
40. Talbott, 80, 83, 95, 105.
41. Brzezinski, 325, 170, 329, 331 and Talbott, 127 and 270.
42. Talbott, 130–131, and see U.S. Dept. of State, Special Report 46 (Revised) May 1979.
43. Brzezinski, 317.
44. Joseph L. Nogee, "Soviet Foreign Policy since Brezhnev," in *Soviet Politics: Russia After Brezhnev*, ed. Joseph L. Nogee (New York: Praeger, 1985), 227.
45. *New York Times*, 26 July 1985, A-3 and 28 July 1985, A-7.
46. Strobe Talbott, "Build-up and Breakdown," *Foreign Affairs: America and the World, 1983*, 61, 3, 605. For a more detailed presentation see Talbott's *Deadly Gambits: the Reagan Administration and the Stalemate in Nuclear Arms Control* (New York: Knopf, 1984).
47. Gerhard Wettig, "The Soviet Union and Arms Control," *Aussen Politik* (English ed.), Vol. 36 (1/85), p. 28.
48. Talbott, "Buildup and Breakdown," 604–605.
49. White House text, *New York Times*, 11 June 1985, A-10.
50. *Christian Science Monitor*, 11 June 1985, 1; Ronald Reagan statement in the *New York Times*, 11 June 1985, A-10, 20 January 1985, E23, 23 January 1985, A-1 and 16 December 1984, A-1.
51. Abraham S. Becker, "Sitting on Bayonets?: the Soviet Defense Burden and Moscow's Economic Dilemma," *Soviet Union* 10, parts 2–3 (1983), 308.

52. Horelick, 534.
53. See U.S. Department of State, *U.S. Arms Control Initiatives*, Special Report No. 160, January 1987; and Steven A. Hildreth, *Arms Control: Negotiations to Reduce Strategic Offensive Arms*, Congressional Research Service Issue Brief, 25 March 1987, 2.
54. Hildreth, 4.
55. *Christian Science Monitor*, 7 December 1987, 18; *New York Times*, 1 December 1987, B-24; President Reagan's address of 10 December 1987 in U.S. Department of State, *Current Policy*, No. 1032, 1; Elizabeth Drew, "Letter from Washington," *The New Yorker*, 11 January, 1988, 85–87.
56. Christoph Bertram, "Rethinking Arms Control," *Foreign Affairs*, (Winter 1980/81): 359; Michael MccGwire, "Dilemmas and Delusions of Deterrence," *World Policy Journal* I, 4 (Summer 1984): 765.
57. Bertram, 357.
58. U.S. ACDA, *Verification: The Critical Element of Arms Control* (Washington, DC, 1976), 21.
59. From a lecture by Professor Allen Krass of Hampshire College at the University of Massachusetts, 24 April 1985.
60. U.S. Department of State, *Verification of SALT II Agreement*, Special Report No. 56, August, 1979, 2–6.
61. An AP dispatch in *Daily Hampshire Gazette* Northampton, MA), 5 January 1985.
62. Lawrence T. Caldwell and William Diebold, Jr., *Soviet-American Relations in the 1980s*, (New York: McGraw-Hill, 1981), 291.
63. Arbatov and Oltmans, *The Soviet Viewpoint*, 77.
64. George Will, "True Soviets on View in Afghanistan," *Daily Hampshire Gazette* (Northampton, MA), 5 January 1984, 6.
65. Ted Greenwood and Michael L. Nacht, "The New Nuclear Debate: Sense or Nonsense?" *Foreign Affairs* (July 1974): 778.
66. Stanley Hoffmann, *Primacy or World Order* (New York: McGraw-Hill, 1978), 283–284.
67. My thanks to Bernard C. Victory for this scenario.
68. Eugene J. Carroll, "A Useful Nuclear Step by Moscow," *New York Times*, 7 August 1985, A-23.
69. Zbigniew Brzezinski, "Foreword," in Robbin F. Laird and Dale R. Herspring, *The Soviet Union and Strategic Arms* (Boulder, CO: Westview Press, 1984), xii.
70. Caldwell and Diebold, 133.
71. *Ibid.*, 98.
72. Valentin Bereshkov, author's notes. Bereshkov was Stalin's interpreter at Yalta and represented, I believe, Novosti Press in Washington in 1982.
73. Michael Howard in a review of Freeman Dyson's *Weapons and Hope, New York Times Book Review*, 8 April 1984, 7. Howard was Regius Professor of Modern History at Oxford and the author of *The Causes of War* and other works.
74. Laird and Herspring, 140–141 and 146–147.
75. Kissinger, *Years of Upheaval*, 274.
76. Robert Legvold, "Gorbachev's New Approach to Conventional Arms Control," *The Harriman Institute Forum*, 1, (1 January, 1988) and Kosta Tsipis, "If Arms Were Cut 50%," *New York Times*, 11 January 1988, A-19.

SALT/START ACRONYMS

ABM System: Anti-ballistic Missile System
ALCM: Air-Launched Cruise Missile
ASAT: Anti-Satellite Weapon
ASM: Air-to-Surface Missile
ASW: Anti-submarine Warfare
BMD System: Ballistic Missile Defense System
CEP: Circular Error Probable
ECM: Electronic Countermeasures
EMT: Equivalent Megatonnage
FBM: Fleet Ballistic Missile
FBS: Forward-Based System
FOBS: Fractional Orbital Bombardment System
GLCM: Ground-launched Cruise Missile
HSD: Hard Site Defense
ICBM: Intercontinental Ballistic Missile
INF: Intermediate-Range Nuclear Forces
IRBM: Intermediate-Range Ballistic Missile (see Ballistic Missile)
MaRV: Maneuvering Re-entry Vehicle (see Re-entry Vehicle)
MIRV: Multiple Independently Targetable Re-entry Vehicle
MLBM: Modern Large Ballistic Missile
MRBM: Medium-Range Ballistic Missile
MRV: Multiple Re-entry Vehicle
MSR: Missile Site Radar
PAR: Perimeter Acquisition Radar
PEN AIDS: Penetration Aids
RV: Re-entry Vehicle
SALT: Strategic Arms Limitation Talks
SAM: Surface-to-Air Missile
SLBM: Submarine-Launched Ballistic Missile
SLCM: Submarine-Launched Cruise Missile
SNDV: Strategic Nuclear Delivery Vehicle
SS: Diesel-Powered Attack Submarine
SSB: Diesel-Powered Ballistic Missile Submarine
SSBN: Nuclear-Powered Ballistic Missile Submarine
SSG: Diesel-Powered Cruise Missile Submarine
SSGN: Nuclear-Powered Cruise Missile Submarine
SSM: Surface-to-Surface Missile
SSN: Nuclear-Powered Attack Submarine
TEL: Transporter-Erector-Launcher
VP: Verification Panel

SOURCE: U.S. ACDA, *SALT LEXICON*, Rev. ed.

SELECT BIBLIOGRAPHY

I. Documents and Statistics

U.S. Arms Control and Disarmament Agency. *Arms Control and Disarmament Agreements: Texts and Histories of Negotiations*, 1982 edition. Washington, DC: GPO, 1982. (This is a revised edition of a publication originally issued in 1972.)
——. *Documents on Disarmament* (This is an annual publication issued since 1960.)
U.S. Congress, Senate. *The SALT II Treaty*. Washington, DC: GPO. 1979.

II. Books and Monographs

Blacker, Coit. *Reluctant Warriors: The United States, the Soviet Union and Arms Control*. San Francisco: Freeman, 1987.
Brzezinski, Zbigniew, ed., *Promise or Peril: the Strategic Defense Initiative*. Washington, DC.: Ethics and Public Policy Center, 1986.
Clarke, Duncan, L. *Politics of Arms Control: the Role and Effectiveness of the U.S. Arms Control and Disarmament Agency*. New York: The Free Press, 1979.
Clemens, Walter, C. *The Superpowers and Arms Control*. Lexington, MA: Lexington Books, 1973.
Cole, Paul M. and William J. Taylor, Jr. *The Nuclear Freeze Debate: Arms Control Issues for the 1980s*. Boulder, CO: Westview Press, 1983.
Krepon, Michael. *Strategic Stalemate: Nuclear Weapons and Arms Control in American Politics*. New York: St. Martin's Press, 1984.
Laird, Robbin F. and Dale R. Herspring. *The Soviet Union and Strategic Arms*. Boulder, CO: Westview Press, 1984.
Johansen, Robert C. *SALT II: Illusion and Reality*. New York: Institute for World Order, 1979.
Lineberry, William P., ed., *Arms Control*. New York: H. W. Wilson, 1979.
Mikheyev, Dmitry. *The Soviet Perspective on the Strategic Defense Initiative*. Washington, D.C.: Pergamon-Brassey's, 1987.
Miller, Steven E. *The Nuclear Weapons Freeze and Arms Control*. Cambridge, MA: Ballinger, 1984.
Myrdal, Alva. *The Game of Disarmament: How the United States and Russia Run the Arms Race*. New York: Pantheon Books, 1976.
National Academy of Sciences, Committee on International Security and Arms Control. *Nuclear Arms Control: Background and Issues*. Washington, DC: National Academy Press, 1985.
Newhouse, John. *Cold Dawn: The Story of SALT*. New York: Holt, Rinehart and Winston, 1973.
Neidle, Alan F., ed., *Nuclear Negotiations: Reassessing Arms Control Goals in U.S.-Soviet Relations*. Austin, TX: Lyndon B. Johnson School of Public Affairs, University of Texas at Austin, 1982.
Panofsky, W. K. H. *Arms Control and SALT II*. Seattle: University of Washington Press, 1979.

Parrott, Bruce. *The Soviet Union and Ballistic Missile Defense*. Boulder, CO: Westview Press, 1987.

Payne, Samuel B., Jr. *The Soviet Union and SALT*. Cambridge, MA: The MIT Press, 1980.

Russett, Bruce. *The Prisoners of Insecurity: Nuclear Deterrence, the Arms Race and Arms Control*. San Francisco: Freeman, 1983.

Schelling, Thomas C. and Halperin, Morton. *Strategy and Arms Control*. New York: Twentieth Century Fund, 1961.

Smith, Gerard. *Doubletalk: the Story of SALT II*. Garden City, NY: Doubleday, 1980.

Talbott, Strobe. *Deadly Gambits*. New York: Knopf, 1984.

——. *Endgame: The Inside Story of SALT II*. New York: Harper & Row, 1979.

U.S. Department of State. *Security and Arms Control: The Search for a More Stable Peace*. Washington, DC, 1983.

Chapter 6

Rivalry in the Third World

Like a siege, instability in the Third World has laid hold of
Soviet-American relations. . . .

Robert Legvold

. . . a world of powerful pygmies, staggering governments and
reckless, brawling fanatics. . . .

James Reston

Our situation today is quite dangerous, since so many people
spend so much time creating adversary situations.

Barbara Tuchman

And some foretell that the climactic struggle of the next era will
not be between East and West, but between the starving and
the industrialized nations—the South and the North!

Bernard A. Weisberger

The Third World does not exist. No two situations are alike.

Stanley Hoffmann

DEFINITIONS

The term "Third World" is a politicized one consciously devised to suggest that
a group of states exists apart from both the "first" world of liberal democratic
industrialized democracies and the "second" world of Marxist-Leninist states.
It also connotes a wide gap between industrialized and rather prosperous
northern Europe and the United States, and the less- or nonindustrialized and
former colonial countries. This originally French term (*tiers monde*), first stood
for the neutralists in the early period of the cold war and consciously used the

same archaic form *tiers*, as in the old term *tiers état*, or "Third Estate"—the commoners, the downtrodden, who have occasionally played a role in revolution. It came into American usage in the 1960s.[1]

The term has lacked precision. Some oil-producing countries have acquired wealth and influence but are considered Third World (e.g., Iran and Kuwait). Austria, Sweden, and Switzerland are neutral and nonaligned between the superpowers, yet they are not considered Third World countries—because they are industrialized and developed enough to export sophisticated finished products. Even if the term is taken to mean belonging to the almost one hundred nonaligned and nonindustrialized nations, there are serious political differences among them.

Some claim "third-worldness" is a psychological state—that of *dependencia*, inherent weakness, and constraint imposed by the more developed world. Most educated Colombians, for example, believe they are incapable of developing their own energy resources, yet some Third World countries, e.g., India, and China, seem to have great confidence in their abilities to manage their economic development by themselves.

Perhaps "the common theme among the Third World countries is the struggle for development"—as long as it is recognized that some are much further along the road than others. It should also be recognized that *poverty* in the Third World is much harsher than "*relative deprivation*" in the United States, where poverty is softened by features often lacking in the Third World, such as government food and financial aid, social security, hot and cold running water, and some meat in the diet. Many of the American poor are well off by Third World standards. But the governments of the Third World often lack the administrative structures or will to overcome poverty. The ruling elites, even if "socialist," can be more interested in developing national power, including military might, than in reducing the travails of their peoples.[2]

An urge toward development as a defining characteristic of the Third World is understandable, given that it enjoyed little economic development after 1400, about when the Western nations began "extraordinary growth." The drive for development has to deal all at once with a myriad of deeply entrenched interlocking problems: "growing population, inadequate food resources, unemployment of the rising white-collar class, social and personal maladjustments brought about by the rapid transition of a society which must jump from the feudal age...into the nuclear age."[3]

Yet some Third World countries have been able to achieve remarkable economic growth while areas of the "developed" world are falling into a "new Third World" situation of out-of-date industrial facilities and unemployment.

The Third World is also often characterized by an angry resentment of the "first world," born of past colonialism or military interventionism and envy of its wealth. These feelings, sometimes very deeply held, have tended to animate a stance of prickly independence and a "damn both your houses" attitude toward the superpowers.

It was a Third World because it rejected the notion of a world divided into two, a world in which only the United States and the USSR counted and everybody else had to declare for one or the other. It feared the ... superpowers. ... It distrusted their intentions ... and rejected their insistence that, in the one case in democratic capitalism and in the other in communism, they had discovered a way of life which others need do no more than copy. ... Above all they felt beholden neither to the United States nor to the USSR for their independence from European rule. ... [4]

Neither superpower has found it easy to operate in this changeable context of hostility and suspicion, where it is very difficult to define what "Third World" means. One scholar notes, it is "rarely clear" what key Third World countries are. Are they "political entities ... (i.e., states); ... evolving or inert economies; or ... haphazard or protean assortments of social, ethnic, tribal, or religious groupings?"[5] Is Iran mainly a state or a revolutionary movement?

The Third World is now several "worlds" existing at four or five different levels of economic, political, and societal coherence and capability, from so-called "international basket cases" and "micro-states" to wealthy countries or those with significant military power. Types of regime also vary widely. Is there a "fourth" or even a "fifth" world? The World Bank uses five categories (see Table 6.1): (1) very low-income countries with per capita yearly income below $250; (2) middle-income countries with per capita yearly income around $750 but still not well developed, e.g., Portugal; (3) the "surplus oil exporters" such as Kuwait; (4) the industrialized countries, mostly of northern Europe, North America, Japan, and Australasia; and (5) the "centrally planned economies" such as the USSR and China.[6] This is misleading, however, since some of the "middle income" states, despite the abject poverty in them, have rather modern sectors. India, for example, exports military jeeps to the Netherlands and West Germany. It produces military jets of Soviet type. It is the world's ninth industrial power and has the third largest trained labor force (after the United States and the USSR).[7] Very few places are living in a thoroughly traditional way now.

Despite the great variations within the Third World, the term remains in common use; although possibly the nonpejorative substitute, "less-developed

TABLE 6.1. WORLD BANK CATEGORIES OF STATES

Countries	GNP Per Capita (median values)	Number of Countries
Low-income	150	37
Middle-income	750	55
Industrialized	6,200	18
Surplus oil	6,310	6
Centrally planned	2,280	12

SOURCE: *The Economist*, February 3, 1979, 45.

countries" (LDC) is more frequently used. Other terms are: "developing countries," the "nonaligned," the "uncommitted," and the "non-Western world." Even the term "South" is used, although much of the Third World is in the northern hemisphere.

SIGNIFICANCE FOR THE SUPERPOWERS

Essentially, the Third World is significant for the superpowers because each thinks the other just might pull off a trick greatly to its disadvantage there. Even if this does not happen, it now and then looks to some as if it has. Government officials and the news media have claimed that events in the Congo, in Central America, in the Middle East, and in Southeast Asia were a total and important loss for now one and now the other superpower. Since the superpower competition is one of images and symbols as well as of military capabilities, these apparent losses and victories may have some meaning for the Soviet-American competition. At least there is a tendency for officials in both superpowers to think they do.

Still other observers say that, even if the superpowers are involved in the Third World, what is happening there is fundamentally independent of superpower politics. The Third World is going through, or trying to enter upon, that process of economic and political development the European peoples began after they emerged from the Dark Ages. The Europeans, however, traversed this historical period over several centuries. There was no way to hurry it. Things are different for the peoples of the Third World, however. The industrial world exists as a viable and copyable standard. With 60 percent of the population of the Third World under age twenty, there is enormous potential for violent impatience at slow progress. The big question is whether the Third World can arrive at suitable models of development and "telescope" the development process into a relatively short period, say, a century rather than centuries, and avoid becoming too entangled with superpower rivalry.

The development process could be shortened through superpower co-operation in coping with the Third World's problems. Rapid progress is possible. Although more people have died of hunger in the past several years than from all the wars and revolutions of the past 150 years, hunger as a fundamental problem has ended in thirty-five countries since 1945 and could be ended in most countries by the year 2000.[8]

But effective problem-solving may not occur in all parts of the Third World. In new states where diverse peoples find themselves under a government they had no voice in choosing, interethnic tensions and strife are almost inevitable. Each ethnic group tends, in a nationalistic postcolonial context, to want its own state. But there are not enough states to go around. Even Europe has "stateless" peoples, e.g., the Scots in Britain, the Basques in Spain, and the Slovenes in Yugoslavia. In the Middle East one ethnic group, the Kurds, is divided among five states. Interethnic conflicts can become international issues and may involve the superpowers. Both the United States and the USSR, at different times, have provided arms to the Kurds and both support different sides in the ongoing struggle between the Cambodians and the Vietnamese. In Ethiopia and Lebanon, wars stem fundamentally from interethnic differences, a source of much of the internal strife in sub-Saharan Africa as well. There can even be a people, or a fragment of it, with great power support (e.g., the Palestine Liberation Organization [PLO]) "adrift" on the world scene, seeking a state and a territory. This yearning and drive for their own states by large numbers of peoples produces great passions and violence and often puts into question the existence of present states. For example, will Pakistan survive the presence of the largest refugee population in the world, the Afghans?

Since many Third World states have disagreements with their neighbors over borders, water rights, and other issues, wars sometimes erupt between them and lead to the use of precious resources for the military. In early 1985 there were forty-one wars, rebellions, and uprisings taking place in the Third World. The United States was a major arms supplier to twenty of these states, while the Soviet Union had the same role for thirteen. Although some of these conflicts are presented as if they were confrontations between communism and democracy, most of them "involve complex combinations of economic, political, territorial, religious and ethnic factors..., not communism versus democracy."[9]

These wars are sometimes enormously destructive. High-technology and mass-destruction weapons are no longer the exclusive possessions of the major powers. Some Third World countries now have them, e.g., Syria, Iraq, Libya, and India. The list goes on.[10]

THE STAKES

These Third World wars can involve the United States. The "posture state-ment" of the Joint Chiefs of Staff may partially explain why.

> US interests are best pursued within a stable, peaceful international com-munity.... Conflicts anywhere in the world immediately affect the United States and its allies, and have the potential for global implications.[11]

Wars in the Third World may even merge with international terrorism into a long-term series of "rolling" wars of a new type, which threaten both Soviet and United States territory. A manufacturer of nuclear triggering devices says, "Simultaneous [nuclear] explosions in Moscow and Washington would be duck soup for a skilled, determined, well-organized terrorist group." A RAND Corporation study suggests that the face of future armed conflict is perhaps best exemplified by the war in Lebanon ... regular armies, guerrillas, private militias and terrorist gunmen ... openly assisted by or covertly sponsored by foreign states.... The distinction between war and peace will dissolve, and hostilities may be endless, with "peace" marked by continued confrontation and crisis.[12]

This wave of guerrilla-terrorist-new state conventional war tends to involve one or both superpowers and poses some danger of driving them into war between themselves. Former President Nixon rates the danger of superpower war stemming from Third World nuclear proliferation and escalation of local wars as second and third, respectively. He sees war by nuclear accident as most likely. President Mitterand of France has expressed greater pessimism. "I am convinced that the balance between the...industrialized nations and the others will be one of the causes...of world war."[13]

An eminent student of American-Soviet relations suggests the First World is potentially at the mercy of the Third. The Kuwaiti request for Soviet protection against Iran in 1987 was a form of successful blackmail of the United States, which then decided to offer its protection instead. Certainly, a small group of weak states is in a position, because of the West's "insatiable appetite" for oil, to affect the West's policies. Gaddis warns correctly that "one of our main concerns will need to be to avoid confusing the two kinds of threat we face—the Russians and the *nth* powers—and in particular not take action against one that could have the effect of bringing it into alignment with the other." (Emphasis in original.)[14]

Soviet-American competition in the Third World also revolves around American access to natural resources and the freedom of the seas and of trade. Foreign raw materials are not important to the Soviet Union with its nearly independent and resource-rich economy. Fear of losing sources of raw materials exacerbates American concern over Soviet naval intensions and capabilities and makes them seem offensive. As a colonel in the United States Marine Corps puts it, "We don't think the Soviet Union needs a large blue-water navy and we think that they are developing it to: (1) gain increased influence in the Third World and (2) strangle the United States by cutting it off from its friends and the resources its industries require."[15]

It is unlikely the Soviet Union would dare to cut off the United States from its indispensable sources of minerals and oil in the Third World. That would be a direct challenge that would risk war. Still, the problem is potentially so serious that Soviet naval capabilities and political influence in the Third World trigger very strong concerns, even fears, in Washington.

Instability in certain Third World resource bases creates the potential for another problem. For example, southern Africa is rich in raw materials indispensable to war industries—magnesium, chrome, titanium, lithium, gold, diamonds, etc. The West has insufficient sources of its own for some of these raw materials. A loss of African chrome would paralyze the American arms industry. A fighter jet's engine requires 1500 pounds of it.[16] Whatever ultimately happens in South Africa, domestic political turbulence or even turmoil there is assured in the short term.

The fear of a "resource war" has had some effect. President Reagan has appointed a "strategic minerals task force"; there is more talk of starting serious searches for alternative sources of supply of key raw materials and developing new production methods using substitute materials; and the Rapid Deployment Force for intervention in the Third World has been developed.[17]

The goal of securing foreign resources inevitably leads the United States to a concern for maintaining the freedom of the seas. The U.S. Maritime Administration lists thirty-one sealanes as essential for the free conduct of American foreign trade. Of these, twenty-three border on Third World territories. One out of every four or five American jobs is related to foreign trade. Keeping sea-lanes open requires either effective international cooperation or a large navy and either foreign bases or port rights. The need for foreign resources and bases makes areas almost unknown to the American public important to the United States. These areas may have governments not acceptable to most Americans, which exacerbates domestic criticism of American foreign policy. Accordingly, the maintenance of a strong American position on the world's sea-lanes is a problematic and occasionally a politically tense and difficult proposition.[18]

Some of this tension derives from American concern with the Soviet deployment of its new, large navy about the world. It now operates in all oceans and thereby can outflank almost all of the Eurasian-African rimlands. Although the Soviet Navy is not equal to the U.S. Navy in some key warfighting respects, such as attack carriers and sustainability at sea, it does not need to be equal in order to carry out its political missions of undercutting American interests and power. The founder of the new Soviet "super-navy" has pointed out its political efficacy. "The role of a navy is not limited to the execution of important missions in armed combat . . . it has always been a political weapon" because it can "exert pressure on potential enemies without the direct employment of weaponry."[19]

In their competition in the Third World, both superpowers have losses and gains. But the turbulent and political changeability of the Third World ensures that neither side is ever clearly winning or losing. Each country is trying to ensure that it retains a good, if not an advantageous, position in the world arena for the future. This superpower competition for power and place is one of the fundamental causes of Soviet-American antagonism at the present. As a majority of the specialists at a gathering on United States-Soviet competition in the Third World agreed: "The fact of competition between the United States and the Soviet Union in the Third World has had a profound effect not only on Third World countries themselves, but also on broader U.S.-USSR relations."[20] This effect will remain a significant one until either the Third World is able to exclude or limit superpower intrusions or until the superpowers change in nature or basic policy. At present, they are still too threatening to each other and the apparent chances for "success" in the Third World are too tempting for either to reduce its involvement there. Possibly "the Soviet Union is only beginning the truly imperial phase of its development."[21] Similarly, the United States, not having limited its demands for foreign raw materials, will continue to strive to maintain access to the Third World and to limit the Soviet advance.

Continuing disruption in the Third World may be to the Soviets' advantage. The Marxist base of the Soviet ideology has considered stability anathema. It posits constant change until final Communist worldwide victory. Such a destabilizing stance is a direct challenge, even an insult, to the Western commitment to the status quo, procedural change, and minimal violence.[22] However, as the Soviets are forced to protect existing Third World client-systems, they may become more accepting of stability.

RELATIVE EAST-WEST ATTRACTIVENESS

The Soviet model of rapid economic development has an appeal—limitation of mass consumption and the quick creation of an industrial base without mass protests. This may be attractive in places where the necessary natural resources exist. The Soviet model forcibly restrains opposition to the government—through security forces that penetrate society with an informer network. The USSR can also supply quantities of modern arms quickly to a government, possibly enabling it to survive a fight with neighboring states or opposing domestic groups. Economically, the USSR is willing to accept raw materials and goods as payment, minimizing the need for convertible currency.

In short, the USSR meets some of the needs of leaders who do not shrink from repression and central control as key means of rapid industrialization. Given the large number of new states, their problems, and the unpleasant memories of Western colonialism and imperialism, it is normal that some of them cleave to the Soviet Union. Most, however, will not, or will break away if they can. Marxism clashes with Third World nationalism and religious faith.

Many Third World leaders were educated in Western Europe and, although they are aware of the economic limitations of democracy, they know that democratic societies are more interesting and more dynamic and productive than Soviet-type systems. Similarly, Western economic aid, unlike Soviet, can allow a country "real money" with which to buy high-quality Western goods; the vast Western market is a powerful lure. Moreover, Western weapons, though more expensive and often complex, are usually better than Soviet weapons, although simpler Soviet weapons are well suited to Third World conditions. Egypt certainly was pleased to switch from Soviet to American weapons. Much of the cast-off Soviet gear wound up in Afghanistan, used against Soviet forces. The Libyans, rich in Soviet weaponry, lost abysmally to the Chadians with French and American support. Even Soviet sources admit that "credits and subsidies from capitalist countries make up 20% to 70% of the total aid given to socialist-oriented states." And, even though the Soviet Union gives free training in the USSR to 70–80,000 Third World citizens every year, the socialist states still lag behind the capitalist states in this effort. Consequently, "the latter generally have greater opportunities for an ideological impact on the developing countries."[23] In short, even socialist-oriented Third World countries can be strongly tied to capitalist countries.

Once a country achieves a certain level of development with Soviet aid, it tends to want to shift to Western aid, for only it can foster further development. (Soviet machinery is usually not up to world standards.) At any rate, although in the 1950s the USSR could seem a ray of pure, bright hope for the Third World, eventually the USSR found itself viewed as no better, and in some ways worse, than the Western powers.[24] Third World countries learned, for example, that the Soviet Union exploits them economically, though in new ways, such as reselling their products at lower-than-world-market prices, thereby undercutting their exports. At present, a number of African countries are transferring state-owned companies to the private sector in hopes of achieving economic growth.[25] Most Third World elites prefer to study in the vibrant and interesting West rather than in the restrictive and dull atmosphere of Soviet-bloc countries. This does not mean the West, too, is not often still seen negatively, as corrupt and exploitative.

THE LIMITS OF SUPERPOWER INFLUENCE

All this suggests there are definite limits to Soviet and American policy in the Third World. Despite mutual superpower self-confidence and even haughtiness, the cultures of the Third World are much older and given to self-pride and a sense of moral and cultural superiority over the upstart "superpowers." They are most unwilling to imitate either the United States or the USSR except in certain very specific ways that promise to enhance their national power and raise their standard of living.

A big question is: How much specific borrowing can be done successfully? Both Russia and the United States, despite their ideological and procedural differences, became superpowers on the basis of adaptations of Judeo-Christian ethics and culture. The moral-cultural basis is different in most of the Third World. The example of Japanese and other Asian countries' industrial success suggests that Western standards of living can be achieved on the basis of an updated Confucianism. In any case, the Soviet and American systems cannot be fully reproduced abroad. The Philippines, under American rule for almost fifty years, did not become a carbon copy of the United States. Nor have the countries of East Central Europe become fully Sovietized, even after forty-plus years. As Prince Bandar of Saudi Arabia has said, his country "wants to modernize, but not to Westernize.... Religious and cultural realities are more deeply rooted in history than secular development and military posturing can ever be." Foreign attitudes and policies toward the Middle East often "have little sense of what is deeply rooted, proven, and abiding in our part of the world,"[26] he says. This view applies, generally, to the entire Third World.

The superpowers' aims in the Third World are also limited by their inability to cope well with its complexities. Certainly, their "power" has little payoff there, where conflicts persist despite their "ministrations." The most the superpowers have been able to do there with their vast military power has been to neutralize each other.[27] They have not been able to defend their clients effectively. After the invasion of Grenada, its ambassador to Moscow lamented that the USSR decided that "every revolution must protect itself."[28] Similarly, the United States was unable to prevent the fall of the Shah of Iran even after the expenditure of billions of dollars to establish Iran as a pro-American "regional influential." Locally originated processes usually triumph over superpower intentions.

The Soviets have tended to overestimate what Third World revolutions can do for their interests, while the Americans have refused to see that such upheavals have been inevitable in many places. Instead of always producing Soviet allies, "political volatility and highly personalized domestic politics sometimes result in the fall of pro-Soviet leaders or in sudden shifts of alignment" away from the Soviet Union.[29] As for the Americans,

> The record—China, Cuba, Vietnam, Iran, Nicaragua—shows America—in its dread of Communism—frantically looking for an impossible "third force".... It also shows a deep reluctance to accept the idea that revolutions are, indeed, manmade hurricanes that Washington for all its might cannot stop or master once they begin to blow.[30]

Both the Soviets and the Americans are coming to recognize that the politics of many peoples of the world are still distinctive and independent of superpower wishes. The politics of states are really operating in different time frames and opposing cultural contexts.

This does not mean the United States and the Soviet Union will withdraw from the Third World. The Russians, one African guerrilla leader says, are "like elephants who come and go on the same track."[31] Although they can be stopped, they re-form and come forward again with single-minded purpose. The Americans, too, will "hang in there" because of their resource needs.

Methods of Influence

The primary inducements the superpowers use vis-à-vis the Third World are economic and military aid. In addition, each superpower supports its Third World allies diplomatically and each also attempts to influence the views of elites through propaganda and educational assistance. Finally, both superpowers display or apply their power and prestige in the Third World arena, occasionally in the form of military intervention, e.g., in Afghanistan and Grenada in a full-scale sense and in Ethiopia and Nicaragua in a more limited sense. Both are involved in "a conventional struggle for power centered in the Third World" similar to the earlier competitions of the European great powers.[32] The display of naval power to impress and intimidate is a striking example of this quasi-colonial aspect of the rivalry.

Economic Aid. A fundamental question is whether Soviet and American aid is an effective lever of political influence. Apparently not: The receiving countries are jealous of their sovereignty and always demand that aid be given "without strings." Furthermore, the superpowers are not the sole providers of aid to the Third World. Some of the other states providing aid and diplomatic assistance, such as Sweden, give much more in terms of percentage of the donor's GNP. The superpowers are not generous givers of economic aid. The United States ranks thirteenth among the seventeen major industrial powers in percentage of GNP devoted to development assistance. Its foreign aid program is less than 1.5 percent of the federal budget. Moreover, the United States gives most of its aid to only two countries—Egypt and Israel—much of it military aid not benefitting people in general.[33]

In terms of nonmilitary aid, the United States gives proportionately less of its wealth to poor countries than any other major non-Communist country. During 1981 and 1982 such aid averaged only 0.23 percent of its GNP although, because of the large size of the GNP, this aid was a very large amount in dollar terms, perhaps one-fifth of total Western aid. The Soviet Union does even less. At most, it gives 1.3 percent, compared with the American 1.5 percent, of its GNP in foreign aid. The United States has given far more in development assistance to the Third World than has the USSR. In thirty years the United States has given about $130 billion in foreign economic aid, while the Soviet Union during the quarter century 1954–1979 gave less than $10 billion.

Just as the United States gives most of its aid to a few countries, the USSR has its own favorites. Although it has economic cooperation agreements with seventy countries, about three-fourths of Soviet aid goes to only three countries: Cuba, Ethiopia, and Vietnam (including Laos and Cambodia, occupied by Vietnam). One-fourth of Cuba's GNP is made up of Soviet aid. Cuba may cost the USSR $12 million per day and Vietnam and Ethiopia $3–5 million per day. Others of its "special friends" have not enjoyed Soviet largesse. The Soviets have found that their economic capabilities and technological levels do not match their political aspirations. Moscow is simply unable to distribute large amounts of development assistance. Notably, foreign aid is not supported strongly by most Soviet citizens. Most Russians blame it for the shortages at home. For example, in 1977 Soviet friends of the author, when they asked their usual peasant supplier why she had no eggs, were told, "Brezhnev gave them all to foreigners." Moscow does little for disaster and famine relief in the Third

World.[34] Most of the food aid during the Ethiopian famine came from the West.

The Americans, too, have run up against definite limits in their aid efforts. A former United States Senator writes: "Experience demonstrates that, at best, American aid has had only a marginal influence...in promoting either stability or development, and almost no influence whatever on whether a country 'goes communist'".... [35]

American economic assistance has to be given with more realistic expectations. It may even feed anti-American revolutions when, for example, a ruling class uses it to enhance its own power or when it disrupts the traditional patterns of life. To serve long-term American interests, foreign aid ought to be given in accord with foreign ways and needs.

But, can more realistic aid policies also enhance the prospects for democracy in the Third World? If not, it will be hard to "sell" foreign aid to the American public. As it is, Congress did not produce a foreign-aid bill between 1981 and 1987; instead, aid has been kept up only through end-of-session "continuing resolutions." The Reagan administration began to think about fostering democracy abroad through open funding of democratic political parties, labor unions, and newspapers.[36] But such a policy could make democratic forces seem the stooges of outside interests and so might undercut their influence. The second Reagan administration has also cut support to the United Nations and the World Bank, increased United States control over direct aid, and doubled military assistance.

The Soviet Union is overextended because of its direct commitments to the war in Afghanistan and to high economic support of Cuba, Vietnam, and Ethiopia and because of its own increasingly serious economic problems and the onset of Gorbachev's reformist rule.[37] Accordingly, it will not offer much more economic assistance until, and unless, it successfully undergoes economic reform and also "solves," one way or another, the costly problems of Afghanistan and Eastern Europe.

Economic aid has neither made over parts of the world to the superpowers' likings nor enabled them to achieve clear strategic victories. It may, however, have denied clear fields of activity to the opposing superpower.

Military Aid. Security assistance is a major method used by the superpowers to influence the Third World. It has been defined as "many different types of military and military-related transfers...these include the transfer of military equipment, training, advice, personnel, services, and infrastructure support...." The assistance may be free or paid for in a variety of ways.[38]

Arms sales are an important part of security assistance. They are one of the most effective forms of foreign policy today. Says one authority, "Indeed, they may now be the prime instrument available to the Soviet Union, and a significant one for the United States, in their rivalry for the allegiance of much of the world."[39]

These arms have contributed to the increasing deadliness of war in the Third World and whether or not they cause wars, they may well make them easier to wage.

Thanks to Soviet-American rivalry, arms have been poured into these areas, so that Druse militiamen, Afghanistani tribal warriors, Central American Indians, Iraqis and Iranians, clothed in modern uniforms and ancient beliefs, make war with lethal new weapons produced in Czechoslovakia or California.[40]

Third World fighters no longer use obsolete weapons cast off by their former colonial masters. They are now often equipped with the very "latest thing" and are sometimes the first to use it in combat. Supersonic jet aircraft, long-range surface-to-air missiles, and the newest fighter planes are being sold to the Third World by the superpowers.[41] "Over three-quarters of the global arms trade now goes to the Third World."[42]

Some countries have received arms from both the superpowers. Yugoslavia, Egypt, Ethiopia, Somalia, and China are examples, as is Morocco. A Moroccan colonel fighting guerrillas has what he calls a "Russian-American marriage": a Soviet-built heavy machine gun mounted on an American armored personnel carrier.

Superpower motivations in giving large amounts of military aid are varied: improving their geopolitical position vis-à-vis one another, enhancing their force projection capability by acquiring base and overflight rights, establishing military surrogates, denying potential allies to one another, lowering the unit cost of weapons by enlarging the number produced, testing arms in local wars, creating employment at home, and supporting "front-line" allies in the superpower competition.

The ultimate goal of arms transfers is to gain leverage over the recipient countries' foreign-policy decisions. But this is rarely realized. "Influence and leverage are transitory phenomena: they can be lost even more quickly than they are acquired."[43] The Soviet Union supplied huge amounts of military aid to Indonesia and Egypt, but Soviet influence was eliminated suddenly in both countries. For almost thirty years, the United States gave most of its military assistance in Africa to one country—Ethiopia. But the government was overthrown by a military coup whose leaders later aligned with the USSR. Ironically, just as Soviet arms in Egypt wound up being used against the Soviets in Afghanistan, American arms sent to Ethiopia have been used against the pro-American government of El Salvador. Despite these "backfires" of security assistance, arms sales remain "attractive to policy makers who are in immediate need of instruments to help implement their strategies," i.e., they seem to offer short-term "fixes" to problems that trouble the superpowers.[44]

This mutual use of high levels of military aid exacerbates Soviet-American rivalry. A Soviet analyst views the Reagan administration as making "maximum use of broader arms exports as one of the main instruments of its rigid and militarized foreign policy line."[45] As if in reply, a West German journalist says, "Soviet military aid policy is...part of an expansive great power strategy based on the assumption that furtherance of Soviet-style socialism can only be achieved by expanding the power of the USSR and reducing the influence of the West."[46]

All the statistics available suggest the superpowers have had a huge arms trade with the Third World. By 1984 the USSR was the leading world exporter of arms to the Third World, with deliveries worth $8.6 billion compared with United States deliveries worth $4.8 billion. Whereas about 60 percent of United States arms exports go to the Third World, almost all Soviet arms exports do.[47] (See Table 6.2.)

The USSR leads in all categories. The biggest recipients of Soviet weapons are Cuba, Syria, Iraq, Libya, Vietnam, and India. The main recipients of Soviet military aid in Africa have been Algeria, Angola, Ethiopia, Guinea, Guinea Bissau, Libya, Mali, Mozambique, Nigeria, Somalia (now receiving United States arms aid), Tanzania, and Uganda, plus a few African liberation movements. The main recipients of United States military aid in 1984 were Israel, Egypt, Turkey, Pakistan, Greece, Spain, El Salvador, and the Republic of Korea. Most are Third World states. Three of these are in the Middle East. Egypt, the second biggest recipient of United States aid, has received 115 fighter planes, 460 tanks, and more than 1,400 armored personnel carriers, plus missiles and surveillance aircraft.[48]

Each superpower is maintaining regional military surrogates, which perform military roles they could not perform directly without making big

TABLE 6.2. SOVIET AND UNITED STATES ARMS DELIVERIES TO DEVELOPING COUNTRIES, 1979–1983, AS A PERCENT OF TOTAL ARMS DELIVERIES TO DEVELOPING COUNTRIES

Item	USSR	United States
Tanks	48	13
Antiair Artillery	39	3
Field Artillery	27	19
Armored Personnel Carriers	40	29
Major Surface Combatant Warships	24	19
Surface Combatant Warships	23	14
Submarines	21	0
Missile Attack Boats	46	0
Supersonic Combat Aircraft	56	14
Subsonic Combat Aircraft	33	31
Other Fixed-Wing Aircraft	17	5
Helicopters	50	9
Surface-to-Air Missiles	57	23

SOURCE: U.S. ACDA, *World Military Expenditures and Arms Transfers: 1985*, 31. For more recent statistics see the 1986 edition of this publication or Mark N. Kramer, "Soviet Arms Transfers to the Third World," *Problems of Communism*, XXXVI, 5 (September–October 1987), Table 3, p. 57

political waves. Cuba stabilizes certain leftist regimes in Africa by providing Soviet-trained combat-seasoned troops, thereby avoiding the possible superpower confrontation that would probably ensue if Soviet combat troops were deployed in Africa. Libya has supported certain anti-Western terrorism. Morocco and Pakistan might be considered American surrogates.

The superpowers occasionally involve themselves further in local conflicts such as the wars in Angola, Korea, Indo-China, Afghanistan, Ethiopia, Nicaragua, and El Salvador. This involvement can be either direct, through use of combat troops, or indirect, through provision of advisers, supplies, and weapons. Significantly, Soviet military aid has been decisive in several recent Third World crises, such as the Angolan Civil War of 1975–76 and in Ethiopia in 1977 where it was "vital in determining the outcome."[49]

Both countries are able to project their military power into the Third World, although the United States is still way ahead in numbers of foreign bases. The USSR has not been highly successful in getting full base rights abroad, except in East Central Europe and Mongolia. American military bases include: from the Philippines, Subic Bay, and Clark Field; through the Indian Ocean, Diego Garcia; to Cuba, Guantanamo Bay. The Soviet Union makes military use of certain airfields and anchorages in the Middle East, South East Asia, Africa, and Cuba. As yet, however, the USSR has no actual bases in the western hemisphere, and it is doubtful the United States would allow any to be established there.[50]

The future effects of superpower military aid and involvement are unlikely to be extremely rewarding for either side unless the world as a whole becomes violently unstable. Few new states will come into existence. Maintenance of ties rather than establishment of new ones will be both the goal and the result. Even this may be difficult, for new arms suppliers continue to appear and Soviet comparative advantage declines.[51] Both sides are coming to recognize that arms transfers and even a military presence do not guarantee influence or power. The Soviets "lost all" in Indonesia and Egypt, and the United States saw the same result in China and Iran. They may lose their respective "shirts" again, the Soviets in Angola and the Americans in the Philippines, where serious insurgencies exist.

Trade.   Trade, it is hoped, will incline a state to its trading partner's policies, perhaps even bring it into an alliance. Trade builds up a pattern of political expectations and understanding. It can be difficult, even painful and disruptive, for a state to change its trading partners.

In essence, Soviet trade with the Third World consists of exports of Soviet machinery, related equipment and arms, and imports of raw materials needed by the USSR such as crude oil, natural gas, food, and metallic ores. Only from India, its biggest Third World trade partner, does the USSR import significant amounts of machinery. It buys about 20 percent of India's exports. The USSR's major trade partners are in South Asia, North Africa, and the Middle East, with countries of Latin America increasing in importance and sub-Saharan or Black Africa being the least important.

Despite Soviet official statements to the contrary, "the most important factor motivating Soviet policy appear(s) to be the desire to expand hard currency exports, such as military equipment and petroleum products." A growing pragmatism and self-interest have been operative in Soviet trade with the Third World.[52]

In 1984 the USSR increased its exports to non-Communist developing countries by 3.8 percent, and its imports from them by 5 percent, achieving a trade surplus of about 3,400,000 rubles. After India, its next biggest partners were Argentina, Iraq, and Libya, with trade turnovers of about a billion rubles yearly in each case. Possibly 10 percent of Soviet hard-currency earnings come from Libya alone, as payments for arms. Soviet-Nicaraguan trade, negligible before 1980, has increased greatly, especially in the form of Soviet exports of oil, machinery, and arms.[53] The USSR decided to support Nicaragua because it is leftist, thus seeming to confirm Soviet ideological self-identification and also because the Sandinista government of Nicaragua is an embarrassment to the United States, the regional superpower. But recently Gorbachev has hinted he will reduce aid to Nicaragua.

The Soviet Union plans to increase trade with the Third World. The most notable change has been the marked rise in exports of military equipment, a source of big profits for Moscow. The Soviets realize that Third World countries can draw closer to the capitalist world. For example, in 1984 the African nation of Guinea, once following the Soviet economic pattern, began to emphasize foreign investment and private enterprise, even though many of its leaders attended Soviet universities.[54]

United States trade with the Third World is not determined mainly by government policy. Thousands of American firms are engaged in foreign trade in an open world market, much of it with less-developed countries. Particularly important in this trade are oil and raw materials such as key metals. The United States still has fundamental advantages over the Soviet Union in trade with the Third World. The United States can export food, for example, as well as a good share of the nonfood and nonfuel commodities the Third World imports.

The United States government can and does use trade for political ends. It can prohibit trade with a state, e.g., Libya. It can also offer or withhold Most Favored Nation (MFN) status. If granted to a country, this allows its products to enter the United States at the lowest customs duty applicable. Although the Department of Commerce works to facilitate American trade, the government, since it does not control firms, can have only a limited role in trade with the LDCs. The Soviet government can do more fine tuning of trade policy since it engages in actual foreign trade (there are no private firms in the USSR).

Educational Aid and Training.   Here is where the "struggle for hearts and minds" is waged—if there is such a struggle. Does study in one or the other superpowers or in English or Russian make a political difference in a less-developed country? It is probably too early to come to a conclusion. We should not expect that intellectuals can be effectively indoctrinated or even politically influenced by foreign study, particularly once they return to their own political environment. Some pro-Soviet leaders were educated in the West. Yet Tito, who had spent years in Moscow, kept Yugoslavia out of the Soviet camp.

But it could still make some difference for a superpower's influence in an LDC if many of its government bureaucrats and military officers had been educated in that superpower's universities. Access to key decision-makers might be facilitated. At least communication should be easier with knowledge of a superpower's language and its ways of doing things.

Whatever the political effects of providing education for Third World students, both the Soviet and American governments think the effort is worthwhile, with the Soviets probably training more nonaffluent foreign students than the United States. The USSR has even taken a lead in the number of students trained from Central America and the Caribbean, the "backyard" of the United States.[55]

The USSR may have spent over one billion dollars on scholarships for foreigners over the past twenty-five years. In 1978 over 20,000 black African students were studying in the USSR. There are an estimated 50,000 foreign students there, with 5,000 from 105 countries in one institution, Patrice Lumumba People's Friendship University in Moscow. The Soviets stress that such study is virtually free of charge and includes free lodgings and medical care as well as a monthly allowance.[56] Yet the results are sometimes negative. Soviet racism and aloofness, as well as student dissatisfaction with the course of study, have driven African students in Moscow to the American and other Western embassies in desperate but fruitless attempts to get out of the Soviet Union. Latin Americans may find it easier than Africans to study in the USSR, however.

Although the United States is open to foreign students, their need to meet entrance requirements and, above all, pay fees, has tended to ensure that most foreign students in the United States are from their country's elites. An American university chancellor reluctantly notes: "Heading a delegation to visit universities in India in 1980, I was ... gravely disappointed to discover how much more likely it was that a young Indian student would receive educational help from the Soviets than from us."[57] Similarly, an Ecuadorean teacher educated in the United States relates that many Ecuadoreans have taken up Soviet offers of a free education. A "formidable" number of Nicaraguans are to be trained in the USSR over the next five years. In 1982 37,000 Africans were studying in the USSR and Eastern Europe completely at those countries' expense, but only 3,000 Africans were studying in the United States under its government's sponsorship.[58]

In response to this pattern of rich students coming to the United States and poor students going to the Soviet Union, the United States government in 1986 began a $3.8 million program to bring poor, rural Central American students to the United States to study. The number will eventually reach 10,000 per year. Another approach is that of a consortium of Midwest state universities that is sending eighteen American professors to set up a college in Malaysia. It will provide two years of general higher education for 2,400 students who will later go to the United States for two years. There are also myriad private American educational programs for Third World students. A recent emphasis is on helping South African blacks obtain an education that will eventually help them govern. One very small college in the South is enrolling two new such students gratis every year.

Alliances and Diplomatic Networks.   Both superpowers have established networks of Third World alliances and both have had limited success and also much embarrassment and difficulty from them. Yet both the United States and the Soviet Union maintain their alliances with LDCs, perhaps for three reasons: to preserve their present power positions, to prevent each other from gaining further advantage, and to prepare to expand positions already achieved if the opportunity presents itself.

Since the USSR is a recent participant in this competition, the limit of its alliance achievement is still unclear. It is just possible that her present Third World allies are the last she will acquire. However, the Soviet Union does not and indeed cannot act as if this were so for reasons of both Marxist ideology and realpolitik.

Because the United States began to make alliances with states of the Third World during the 1950s, it got ahead in the game and also suffered some serious reversals, e.g., in China. At one time the USSR was ringed by American-centered alliance systems derived from former European colonial ties. Although NATO survives because of a definite mutuality of interests and a similarity of societies and politics, some of the alliances collapsed or never got off the ground. These American alliances with LDCs, unlike NATO, often existed more on paper than in the "hearts and minds" of the local populations, where nationalist forces opposed what looked like a new colonialism attempting to preserve traditional elitist rule.

The ten Third World states with which the Soviet Union has treaties of friendship and cooperation include: India (1971), Iraq (1972), Angola (1976), Mozambique (1977), Vietnam (1978), Ethiopia (1978), Afghanistan (1978), South Yemen (1979), Syria (1980), and Yemen (1984).

The common elements in most of these treaties are: duration of twenty years; mutual pledges of respect for territorial integrity, sovereignty, and noninterference; pledges of increased overall cooperation; vague promises of increased military cooperation; avoidance of antagonistic alliances; and consultation, including emergency consultation. Each treaty contains special provisions. For example, those with India and Vietnam are quasidefense pacts, for they are implicitly directed against Pakistan and China, respectively.[59]

Two of the Soviet Union's treaties of this type have been abrogated, with Egypt and Somalia, and one has lapsed, with China. Besides those Soviet losses there are the connections broken with Yugoslavia, Albania, the Congo, Guinea, Ghana, Algeria, Kenya, Indonesia, and Grenada. This last was broken by American military action. This shows the Soviet record in maintaining Third World alliances is quite mixed. No "breakaway" state has ever re-established close ties with the USSR.

The oldest Third World alliance system of the United States is the Organization of American States (1948), which has a mutual defense commitment undertaken in the Rio Treaty of 1947. More than twenty states are members. The United States also has bilateral defense treaties with South Korea and the Philippines as well as special political and defense relationships with Pakistan and Thailand. The United States also provides military aid to other countries, e.g., Israel and Egypt, the two countries which receive most American aid, and Jordan, Taiwan, and Rwanda in Africa. Arrangements such as these help give the United States the overflight and landing rights and base and port rights indispensable to maintaining superpower reach and clout around the globe.[60]

Despite the expanding military reach of the Soviet Union, the United States still operates in a favourable strategic environment in the Third World. Many of the Third World ties of Britain and France, made through colonialism, survive, especially in Africa. The British Commonwealth of more than forty member-states includes only two or three with close ties with the USSR. One of these is India, however. The French maintain all-round ties with most of the French-speaking states of Africa and occasionally assist them militarily, with the Foreign Legion or the Force d'Intervention, as in Chad against Libya in recent years. The plain fact is that the Soviet Union began its drive for a "place in the sun" very late and in a context dominated by the West.

Both superpowers face a more constrained environment in Third World alliances in the future. The American public and the Congress tend to be more knowledgeable and critical regarding such ties, whereas the Soviets are now a known quantity tarnished by previous failures and even betrayals. Both can expect to operate in a "buyers' market," with their "wares" being inspected more critically by Third World elites, which are now very experienced in foreign affairs. The Americans will face increasing difficulties in keeping some of the ties they have while the Soviets will tend to narrow and make more pragmatic their commitments to LDCs. This is suggested by the new program of the Communist Party of the Soviet Union, which states that the closest ties of the USSR with LDCs will be with those following "scientific socialism" (the Soviet model) but that "real grounds" also exist for cooperation with LDCs following the "capitalist path."[61] Possibly, if the USSR had never acquired its hold over East Central Europe, it would find its natural allies for some time among the often pseudoradical, modernizing, pretend-socialist military dictatorships of the Third World.

Soviet allies among the LDCs are not Soviet clones, however. Nationalism and self-interest are usually far more important than loyalty to the USSR. Soviet allies must not be treated simply as Soviet agents, or they will become even more dependent on the USSR. It does seem that "once radical movements consolidate their power and turn their attention to economic development, the West will become increasingly relevant and the Russians increasingly irrelevant to them."[62] This has been the case with China and Egypt, for example.

In any case, the USSR may well have gained two broad benefits from its Third World relationships: the projecting of Soviet power into regions not on its borders and much greater Soviet involvement in regional politics.[63] The task of the United States will be to maintain its alliances in the Third World and work as actively as possible with both non-Soviet and Soviet allies among the LDCs to keep the balance of forces as nearly favorable to its interests as possible. Trying periods, such as that with the Philippines in 1985 and 1986, will occur. But it is extremely unlikely that the Soviet Union can enlarge its Third World alliance network much, given the present cost of Cuba and Vietnam, the negative example of Afghanistan, an ally invaded by the USSR, and the Soviet need to institute a major economic reform at home and not acquire expensive new foreign burdens.

MAIN REGIONS OF SUPERPOWER RIVALRY

There are four main geographical areas of superpower rivalry in the Third World: Africa, Asia, Latin America, and the Middle East, in alphabetical order. It is a good idea to look at Soviet and American policy by area because American as well as "Soviet policy toward the Third World is highly differentiated by region, making uniform analysis difficult."[64] We might even decide the superpowers lack any coherent policies toward the Third World and are, instead, reacting to events or their perceptions of them and trying to stay or get ahead of their opponents as best they can.

Africa
The only places in Africa historically connected with the United States are Tripoli in the north, now Libya, where the United States once fought the Barbary pirates; and Liberia on the South Atlantic, where former American slaves once took control. There was almost no Russian connection with the continent until 1955, when the Soviet Union began to aid Egypt to counter British influence.

The American interest in Africa is fundamentally one of maintaining access to natural resources essential for its industry. This produces another interest—preventing a hostile power from controlling the trade routes to, from, and around Africa. The Soviet concern is much more a political one—to counter

Western influence in Africa, to demonstrate that Soviet practices are still pertinent to actual political situations, and to legitimate themselves as Marxists. Both superpowers play the game of influence competition and also seek military capabilities in Africa.

The main Soviet involvement in North Africa is with Libya, which buys, with hard currency, important to the Soviet economy, large amounts of Soviet arms, some of which it supplies to other Islamic countries, e.g., Iran. The Libyans get arms, Soviet military advisers, and at least the appearance of Soviet protection from the Americans and their ally Egypt. The Soviets get foreign exchange as well as an opponent through terrorism of Western-centered international norms of behavior. It may be a relationship between "two essentially incompatible partners."[65]

The United States has a major defense relationship with Egypt and has been taking an increasingly hard line against Libya because of its support of terrorist acts that have taken American lives. Significantly, North Africa contains no state, even Libya, that is an imitator of the USSR in sociopolitical principles and organization.

To the east, in the Horn of Africa, things are different. Here famine-stricken and conflict-ridden Ethiopia is led by a military government that has initiated changes intended to make the country similar to the USSR. Although of little inherent importance, the Horn is close to the Suez Canal, the Red Sea, the Persian Gulf, and the Indian Ocean. Accordingly, "both superpowers seem to have accepted it . . . as a region which their adversary cannot be permitted to dominate."[66]

The Horn has seen one of the most cynical shifts in Soviet and American foreign policy. Until the 1970s Ethiopia had a limited military relationship with the United States and Somalia, after 1969, came to have a significant one with the Soviet Union. But after a coup in Ethiopia cut the tie with the United States, and after a war began between Ethiopia and Somalia the USSR began large-scale aid to Ethiopia, the larger and more populous of the two countries. This aid, begun in late 1977, included a massive air- and sealift of arms as well as Cuban troops. Now Ethiopia began to gain in the war. The Soviet Union had accomplished something tangible. But there was a cost. Somalia expelled the Soviets, and the Americans eventually replaced them. Possibly, "the most significant development in the Afro/Soviet relationship is the likely gain of a committed ally in Ethiopia."[67] Ethiopia also signed a Friendship Treaty with the USSR in 1978 and has begun a Soviet-style reorganization of its society and government.

In northern sub-Saharan Africa neither the USSR nor the United States has an ally or an important area of competition any longer. When the Congo became independent in 1960, the Soviet Union became involved, but "its man," Patrice Lumumba, was killed and the opportunity was lost. Although the United States and the USSR supported opposing sides in the 1967 Nigerian civil war, with the Soviet-supported central government winning, Nigeria was too closely oriented to the West to become associated with the USSR. Other countries that seemed to be pro-Soviet at times, e.g., Guinea and Mali, changed their political course and the infamous Idi Amin of Uganda, whom the Soviets supported, lost power through defeat in war. In Ghana and elsewhere pro-Soviet leaders were overthrown in military coups, a common occurrence in Africa. Another problem the Soviets have had in central Africa is the presence of considerable French influence, aid, and even military power, as in Senegal, Gabon, and Chad, and some British influence as well, as in East Africa.[68] The field is much less open to Soviet penetration than in the past. The Soviets are a known quantity and African political elites are more experienced now. The Soviet Union no longer appears in Africa as a young suitor with a good line but as an aging roué with little new to say.

Partly because of the French presence, the United States has never tried for a major role in central Africa. It operates through normal diplomatic channels plus food and Peace Corps aid, although it has acquired some military rights in Kenya. The American private sector is involved as well, in the form of multinational firms and also universities and foundations, not to mention tourism. By 1980 private United States investment in Africa was about $6.5 billion dollars. This nongovernmental American role also manifests itself in the relationship between American black civil rights activists and African liberation movements, particularly in South Africa.[69]

It is in southern Africa that most of the sound and fury of superpower competition in Africa resounds. The Soviets and Cubans came upon the scene in the mid-1970s when the Portuguese, after a military coup at home, precipitously withdrew from their colonies of Angola and Mozambique, large and rich countries on opposite coasts of southern Africa. Although the United States government at the time leaned toward military counteraction, Congress did not allow it.

The USSR's presence in southern Africa, even though achieved partly through luck, is very important to it. Without its ties to Angola and Mozambique, it has only Libya and Ethiopia as allies in Africa. From Angola the Soviet Union can support the Namibian guerrillas, SWAPO (South-West African People's Organization), and black rebels of South Africa against apartheid and their leading organization, the African National Congress (ANC). But Soviet rewards have not been great and the gains are not firm.

The Soviet Union's connection with Angola and Mozambique has not led to Sovietization there or the creation of useful Soviet allies. Mozambique, a "Marxist-Leninist basket case" in the words of one U.S. Senator, is in very poor economic and political shape. Mozambique, plagued by a serious insurgency, had to sign a degrading agreement with South Africa in 1984.[70] The Reagan administration has aided Mozambique in a small way and has negotiated with Angola. The main source of Angolan foreign exchange is an American company, Gulf Oil, which operates a lucrative field there. Both Angola and Mozambique are finding that Soviet aid is not able to solve their problems. The

United States might even be able to eliminate the Soviet role there if it could persuade or pressure South Africa to stop attacking Angola and to withdraw from Namibia, something South Africa says it will agree to only if Cuban forces are withdrawn from Angola. Complicating things was the United States's decision in eary 1986 to aid the Angolan opposition forces led by Jonas Savimbi, UNITA, once supported by China, with missiles.[71]

Southern Africa is not a priority target of the Soviet Union, whose influence in the area may have peaked. The "Horn clearly has been of higher concern...." Moscow seems to assume southern Africa will be transformed through global developments and local struggles, not Soviet action. "In no case does the Soviet Union seem eager to assume the burden of the fight or to force a victory on behalf of its hosts."[72]

Current American perceptions of a Soviet threat to South Africa are a tribute to South African propaganda, to American concern about minerals, and to excessive American concerns about Soviet aims and capabilities. The United States can insure itself against mineral dependence on South Africa by developing alternative sources and by stockpiling. If the Soviets wanted to create difficulties for the West's industry, it would be much easier and quicker to do it in the Middle East. As a South African specialist herself puts it, "It seems unlikely . . . there are many people in the Kremlin who lie awake . . . wondering how to conquer South Africa . . . the short-term aim is in fact maximum influence with minimum expense." In fact, the Soviet Union and South Africa sometimes act in collusion, setting the prices of gold and diamonds and together "conduct a secretive and mutually beneficial partnership in international mineral markets."[73]

The problem for the United States in South Africa is how to encourage democratic political change but not help bring to power an anti-Western government.

There may be a new Soviet policy in Africa: (1) don't lose current struggles; (2) hang on elsewhere; (3) avoid getting involved in inter-African disputes; (4) do all possible to encourage African anger at the United States; (5) don't mess with European-African trade and aid; and (6) coexist with France, "the most important external actor in Africa." The results are not yet visible.[74]

The United States is not doing badly, but is vulnerable to charges of supporting apartheid. The United States will have to avoid further embarrassment by Libya and also continue to try to keep a good relationship with both Egypt and Israel, a difficult task over the long run. It would be best for the United States to settle in for an extended but low-key competition with the Soviets and adopt a long-term strategy that concentrates on the American strong suit—developmental assistance and political and cultural ties based on American-African common interests and mutual respect. Real African needs must come first in American policy. Success is possible. Particularly in recent years more African states have moved in the direction of the West and democracy than the USSR and Marxism.[75]

Latin America

This subcontinent, especially the Caribbean, has long been an area that has deferred to the United States. The governments and elites of Latin America have largely been unwilling until recently to act independently of their powerful northern neighbor. Many countries bordering the Soviet Union, however, e.g., Norway, Iran, Turkey, China, and Japan, do not follow Soviet wishes.

American investment and military potential combined with the limited foreign policy ambitions of Latin American leaders to grant the United States a special role in what is its strategic rear and psychopolitical weak point. But unlike Soviet direct military, political, and even cultural domination of East Central Europe, the "USSR's Latin America," the United States has exercised its superiority by "indirect means, usually an alliance with the native aristocracy and privileged governing class."[76] That the domination has been indirect is of little consolation to Latin Americans. It is the only foreign domination most of them know.

The United States fought a war with Mexico, thereby acquiring Texas, Colorado, Arizona, New Mexico, and California; facilitated a rebellion in Colombia that led to the creation of Panama and the Panama Canal; and often intervened militarily in various places in Central America and the Caribbean, e.g., Nicaragua, Haiti, Cuba, and the Dominican Republic. At one time the United States Navy had a permanent squadron off Brazil. The Navy still has a major base in Cuba. Many Latin Americans see this behavior as a pattern of Yankee or Gringo interventionism that has not yet ended and do not distinguish interventions of the United States government from those of American companies such as United Fruit, which at one time would "make and break" governments.

About 80 percent of United States exports to developing countries go to Latin America and the Caribbean is vitally important for the security of American trade, much of which uses the Mississippi, the Gulf, and the Caribbean. This is a vital fact of life for the U.S. Navy. Whatever happens in Central America, the United States will be footing an aid bill for certain countries there.

The Soviet Union came to have significant contact with Latin America even later than with Africa. Imperial Russia had done little in the region except sell weapons and was able to acquire only a modest presence there. By 1890 she had established diplomatic relations only with Mexico, Argentina, and Uruguay.[77] Until Castro's takeover in Cuba, Soviet policy had been inflexible, dogmatic, and a general failure even though a number of Communist parties came into existence in Latin America after 1917. Radical local nationalists were "far more inclined to opt for German Nazism or Italian facism than for Russian communism." From Stalin's death until 1960, Soviet interest in Latin America was "virtually nonexistent." Great distance, concerns closer to home, and the great power of the United States in the area made this natural. Accordingly, "for Moscow, Latin America has always been remote, geographically and psychologically." As late as 1982, "after" Cuba, Nicaragua, and El Salvador, Brezhnev expressed realism and caution by noting, "Vast stretches of ocean separate us from the Western hemisphere."[78] This brutal fact must haunt Fidel Castro and the Sandinistas, and was driven home in 1983 with the American invasion of Grenada.

It was the Cuban Revolution led by Fidel Castro that caught the Soviet Union's attention, but not immediately. Castro did not announce, "I am a Marxist," until early 1961, two years after he took power, though his brother Raul had done so earlier. Until then he seemed, and so the American press portrayed him, as an anti-authoritarian liberator in the Latin American tradition. At least four factors brought the Soviets to aid Cuba. First, the United States did not move effectively against Castro. Indeed, it offered him aid, even military jets. And then the CIA-arranged Bay of Pigs invasion of spring 1961 was not supported by regular forces and failed abysmally. The USSR realized that the United States was unwilling to depose Castro. Second, Castro's policies were radical, anti-business, anti-American, and anti-middle class. And he was in charge and ruthlessly so. The Soviets admire leaders who are in firm control. Third, by the early 1960s the Soviet Union had some experience in the Third World. Fourth, the West then seemed to be giving up its former power centers in the Third World. The long-held Soviet dream of a "revolutionary wave" coupled with the "decline of capitalism" seemed at hand. Cuba seemed another convenient—and safe—place for confirming the Soviet self-image of revolutionary Marxism and also for at least embarrassing, if not weakening, the USSR's chief rival—the United States.

Castro was not going to give the Soviet Union a compliant "new Bulgaria," however. Castro was and remains too independently powerful for the Soviets to have control. Castro and the Soviets have always had disagreements, some of them serious, and Castro has had a foreign policy of his own, including elements of which the Soviets disapprove. Cuba has been the Soviet Union's "France" or "Israel," irritatingly hard to control and with its own perspective.

A Soviet-Cuban partnership has emerged that, although very expensive to the USSR and dissatisfying and occasionally even galling to Castro, has served some of the fundamental interests of both. Cuba, with the USSR providing one-fourth of its GNP, is independent of the United States, though at the cost of economic backwardness, whatever social progress has been achieved. The Soviet Union has a tough, seasoned, and so far undefeated Cuban fighting force in Africa and a useful listening post and limited air and naval facilities in the Western hemisphere. In addition, Cuba serves as a good sponsor for Soviet policies in the Third World. "Castro's anti-imperialist credentials are impeccable, and the Latin-American character of Cuban society gives it credible ties beyond the Americas."[79] The Soviet Communist Party has heaped high honors on Castro. At the Soviet 27th Party Congress in 1986, Castro sat next to the leader of Poland, the largest Soviet client-state. Both Castro, a true revolutionary, and the Soviet Union, a great power, with each other's help, have found new worlds in which to operate.

Although United States governments find the Soviet-Cuban alliance irritating, they accept Cuba as it is, but warily watch it to ensure that the Soviet military presence there stays below a certain level. By Soviet-American agreement, no Soviet ballistic missile submarines may dock in Cuba, though a Soviet surface squadron calls twice a year. The main line the United States draws is against actual Cuban revolutionary activity or combat troops in Latin America. Military and other assistance to governments is frowned on but tolerated, as Cuban aid to Nicaragua shows.

While Cuba could not defeat a full-scale American invasion, its military strength and experience is formidable. Cuba receives about 55,000 tons of Soviet arms per year and has 160,000 active-duty military personnel backed up by 135,000 well-trained reservists and about 1,000 tanks and 200 jet fighters.[80] Cuba is one of those "powerful pygmies" created by revolutionary zeal and Soviet aid.

Since successful revolution with pro-Soviet tendencies has occurred in Latin America only in Cuba and Nicaragua—and twenty years apart, not a short interval—the Soviets' main line of advance is the conventional long-term one of diplomacy, trade, and, possibly greater acceptance of their presence. It may be the main success the Soviet Union achieves in the region. Whereas in 1960 the USSR had diplomatic relations with only five countries in the area, today it has them with sixteen countries. In addition, it has achieved a regularization of trade with Latin American countries, although the level is not high. Many more diplomats now know Spanish and have lived in the region and Soviet cultural exchanges and scholarships have expanded enormously. Still, only in Peru and Argentina do the Soviets have new economically significant relationships.[81]

The major irritant now in superpower rivalry in the region is political developments in Central America. Nicaragua and nearby El Salvador were more than ready for revolution because of exploitation by wealthy families, very limited development of governmental institutions such as schools and courts, serious overpopulation, scarcity of agricultural land, little economic development, and few natural resources. Although they existed at a semifeudal level, people there knew that life is much better elsewhere. The old way became intolerable and radicalism became politically pertinent. Once the United States stopped supporting the oppressive Somoza family dictatorship a raging radicalism emerged in Nicaragua. It took power in Nicaragua but has not yet been able to do so in El Salvador, where the United States is supporting a counterinsurgency war and a tenuous middle way in politics.

In Nicaragua a radical, partly Leninist group calling themselves Sandinistas, after Sandino, a revolutionary of the 1930s, took control in 1979 and adopted policies that are both radical and repressive. The liberal Carter administration, which had tolerated the revolution, was replaced by the conservative Reagan administration which refused to aid the new Nicaraguan government. To what degree the Reagan administration pushed the Sandinistas into the arms of the Soviets and to what degree the Sandinistas wanted to follow the Soviet pattern are issues still hotly debated. In any case, by now Nicaragua is a state with censorship, severe limitations on business and religion, radical social policies, and a large military heavily armed with Soviet weapons that is opposed by the United States both diplomatically and militarily by aid to its armed opponents, the "Contras," and to bordering states such as Honduras.

The Soviets and the Cubans had little to do with the success of the Sandinista armed revolution. The USSR had given "virtually no attention" to Nicaragua before 1979 and watched the uprising against Somoza with "no active involvement." Nevertheless, "the Soviets moved immediately to recognize the new government and to court it. . . ." The Sandinista victory spurred fresh Soviet discussion of armed struggle with most Soviet writers on Central America accepting it as inevitable and emphasizing the need to unify the Left.[82]

In 1981 the United States cut its economic aid to Nicaragua. In response, Moscow increased its aid and provided some weapons and military advisors. This support was "small, late and reluctant," but it extended superpower rivalry to Central America. Soviet tanks and helicopters arrived. The usual superpower "action-reaction" game was on. By 1984 the USSR was providing $300 million or more in aid per year, perhaps half of Nicaragua's aid from abroad. The rest came mostly from Latin America. By 1986 Soviet aid had doubled and included even more weapons, as well as most of Nicaragua's oil. However, by 1987 the Soviet Union and its East European allies were refusing to meet all of Nicaragua's economic needs.[83]

The significance of this aid is much debated. Some analysts say the Soviets are mainly playing a game of political symbolism and have no great ambitions in Central America, while others suggest Nicaragua is a Soviet-Cuban wedge in Central America and even all of Latin America.

The general Reagan administration goal is to make full consolidation of Sandinista rule as difficult as possible and inhibit the expansion of their influence. But it is likely that the Sandinistas will remain in power unless the United States takes direct military action against them. Although the United States could conquer Nicaragua in a few months, it is unlikely a clear alternative to the Sandinistas is available. The United States may have to live with a Soviet client and at most limit Nicaragua's foreign operations as best it can. This will be difficult. Certain groupings in American politics may well find it impossible to live with Nicaragua as it now is. Cuba, yes. It is an island, but Nicaragua is on the mainland. President Reagan has said unless democratization occurs in Nicaragua, the "only alternative" is a Contra victory.[84] The revelations of the Iran-Contra hearings before Congress in 1987 revealed the intensity of American conservatives' animosity toward the Sandinistas. Most Americans seem to agree there shall be no Soviet base in Nicaragua. Whether limited Sandinista participation in the peace plan of the other Central American countries will assuage American concerns is impossible to predict.

Latin America, particularly overpopulated Central America, is in a new and turbulent historical state. The United States no longer calls all the shots. Its "backyard" is not the place it once was, and never will be so again. This does not mean the region will be Sovietized. Although American influence throughout the region is on the wane, democracy seems to be spreading. In addition, Latin American governments are proud of their prerogatives and are not going to be greatly influenced by the new boy on the block. Latin American nationalism works more against Soviet policy than for it. The USSR's policies in Latin America are more the limited ones of great power competition than those backing up a vital interest at great cost. The Soviet Union will not risk open confrontation in a region where United States interests are much stronger and emotionally charged than are Soviet interests. After all, how many "Cubas" can the Soviet Union afford?

Still, eventually the United States will have to devise a well-rounded Latin American policy that minimizes the chances for additional anti-American revolutions and also turns Nicaragua and even Cuba away from the Soviet Union. This will only be possible through an acceptance of a degree of radicalism in Latin America. A "bottom line" will continue to exist—no Soviet bases or subversion—but negotiating with and even aiding radicals will be unavoidable.

The Middle East

The term "Middle East" is used here as a convenient name for the region from Egypt and Turkey in the west to Iran in the east, including states such as Israel, Syria, Iraq, Saudi Arabia, and several smaller ones around the Arabian Peninsula—places like Oman, the Yemens, and the United Arab Emirates, more than a dozen in all. This volatile and complex part of the world is of intense concern to both superpowers; however, they must be exceedingly careful in their involvement. The recent history of the region has seen several serious local wars with the potential of escalation. The brutal war between Iran and Iraq in the 1980s is an example. The United States' main concerns here are the maintenance of Israel, the flow of oil to the West, and keeping a position of influence. There are contradictions among these concerns.

The Soviet Union has a simpler, clearer major goal: holding on to a position of influence. It is not strongly committed to any one state in the region and it does not need foreign oil. However, since the USSR actually borders on the Middle East and overlaps culturally with it as the fifth largest Islamic country, it also, like the United States, has some rather emotion-laden concern for the region. As *Pravda* once put it, the Middle East "is an area that lies not across the Atlantic Ocean, but in proximity to Soviet frontiers...and it [the Soviet Union] is far from indifferent to the events that take place there."[85] The USSR must also impede American influence, side with Israel's opponents, and work to keep Islamic fundamentalism from moving into its territory. It also hopes to obtain a role in the management of regional affairs. It "invests" in the area in hopes of future gain.[86] With all this to do, the Soviet approach to the Middle East is as prone to trouble as is the American.

Soviet concern with the Middle East has a long background in Russian history. For centuries Russia was engaged in a struggle with the ruling Ottoman empire over good farmland, defensible borders, Slavic minorities, and access to the sea and world trade routes. Over time, Russia acquired much territory in the north of the region from the Ottoman empire and Iran. Twice Russia and Britain divided Iran into spheres of influence. The Russian Revolution cost Russia great territorial gains and access to the Mediterranean, promised her by Britain and France. But in 1955, through her arms deal with Egypt, the Soviet union was able to bypass the cold war barrier against her movement further into the region. "Thus, by 1960, . . . Russia was once again able to seek fulfillment on the oceans and toward the southern land mass of the Middle East. . . ."[87]

The Americans had little to do with the Middle East until the 1950s, when they tried to build an alliance system against the USSR involving Iraq and landed Marines in Lebanon in 1958 to support its then-Christian government. The big foreign actor in the region had been Britain. But after 1947 when the British decided they could no longer support the struggle against communism in Greece, the United States replaced Britain there and in Turkey as well. Thus the United States extended the policy of containment into the Middle East.[88] Soon President Truman, much to everyone's surprise, recognized the new state of Israel, reversing the position of the State Department. In effect, the United States took sides in one of the world's most bitter struggles. Although the United States did not aid Israel in its first war of survival with the Arabs and actually worked against it and its British and French allies in their 1956 attempt to get the Suez Canal away from Egypt, by the 1960s the United States had become Israel's major and almost sole foreign supporter.

By then the Soviets had changed sides in the Middle East. Although the Soviet Union had supported the establishment of Israel in 1948, Israel did not turn out to be the anti-Western radical state the Soviets had hoped it would be, and some Soviet Jews had shown enough interest in Israel to raise serious concerns among Soviet officials. The Arabs offered greater opportunities for Soviet foreign policy. But the USSR has always supported the right of Israel to exist. A leading associate of the fiery nationalistic Egyptian leader Nasser, who ruled at the time, says the Soviets were "sucked into the Middle East by events. It was not they who had started the great offensive but Egypt who had forced it upon them."[89] The USSR gave Egypt, Syria, and Iraq an enormous amount of weaponry, and by 1967 the Arabs may have thought they had superiority over Israel.

In mid-1967, after threatening moves by Egypt, Israel launched a surprise attack that destroyed the Arab air forces. The Soviets may have contributed to the beginning of the war by suggesting that Israel was about to attack

Syria. The Six-Day War ended with a clear Israeli victory. But the Americans persuaded Israel to stop its advance after the Soviets suggested they might take military action to prevent a total disaster from overcoming the Arabs.[90] The USSR now made another error. It broke relations with Israel and, since they have not been restored, it lost easy communication and possible influence with a major Middle East actor.

The 1967 war did not settle anything. It was followed by low-level fighting involving Soviet personnel during 1969 and 1970 and another Arab-Israeli War in 1973. By then Sadat, Nasser's successor in Egypt, had expelled Soviet advisors out of frustration with the limits of Soviet support. Again, after Israel was winning, the USSR suggested it might intervene, thus prompting the United States to go on partial alert, and, as in 1967, persuade Israel to cease its advance.

These years of conflict and tension revealed a complex interplay of Soviet-American-Israeli-Arab thought and action. The Soviets would not fight alongside the Arabs against the Israelis but would help them just enough to prevent defeat from becoming total. But it was clear only the United States, not the USSR, was able to restrain Israel—if only to a degree. It was not long before the United States became the leading superpower in the Middle East. Egypt and Israel came to a limited understanding through the efforts of Jimmy Carter, and Egypt became a major recipient of United States military and other aid.

In the past decade, the United States has enjoyed a better position than the Soviet Union in the region. However, "the very existence of the Arab-Israel dispute and the persisting enmity toward Israel . . . continue to facilitate a Soviet involvement."[91] The USSR has continued to make gains, but small ones. It has helped establish a fragile pro-Soviet state in South Yemen, sold arms to Kuwait, begun diplomatic relations with Oman and the United Arab Emirates, and even widened contacts with conservative Saudi Arabia and fundamentalist Iran. The Soviet Union has a place in the region, for "each Arab state wants to constrain Soviet activity in the Middle East but at the same time wants to use the Soviet Union for its own purposes."[92] Here we see again the "coercive power of the weak" at work as we did when tiny Kuwait was able to get American naval protection for its tankers in 1987.

By 1987–88 the Middle East situation had reached a sort of stalemate. Potentially destabilizing processes bubbled on. Egypt was troubled by Moslem fundamentalism. The Iran-Iraq war continued. Israel was entrenched in the Moslem West Bank, though facing violent resistance from local Arabs. Talks between Jordan and the PLO had broken down. Internecine warfare continued in Lebanon. Terrorism threatened United States citizens and interests, and President Reagan secretly negotiated arms transfers to Iran for the release of hostages. Several thousand Soviet air-defense personnel were encamped around Damascus, Syria. The United States Navy and Iran were playing a delicate game of chicken in the Persian Gulf. In short, all was unfortunately normal in a Middle East sort of way.

The achievement of peace between Israel and the Arabs involves risks for both sides. Any Israeli government is a coalition and can easily be forced to resign while any Arab ruler who advocates peace with Israel faces probable assassination or at least rebellion. A veteran American diplomat and Middle East specialist has noted that any politician of the region who came out in favor of peace with Israel was usually dead within two years. Soviet and American goals there keep the pot boiling and intensify superpower rivalry as well.

The Soviet strategy has been to try to unite the Arab states, along with "progressive" Arab organizations such as the Arab Communist parties and the PLO, into a large "anti-imperialist" front. United States-Soviet conflict in the region is inevitable. The superpowers have few common goals there, except preventing a general war that would involve themselves. Concern that working with the USSR would be seen as an abandonment of Israel has prevented United States governments from trying to work out a regional peace. The USSR is inhibited from working for peace with Israel and the United States because it fears loss of Arab support. For the Soviet Union, regional peace must yield permanent Soviet regional influence.

The political complexity and volatility of the Middle East will continue. Even if the Arab-Israeli conflict is resolved, the number of states and their changeable internal politics are enough to generate a level of conflict in this key area sufficient to keep the superpowers involved. A big question is whether the conflict level will rise and make the region dangerous to the superpowers themselves. Here Moslem fundamentalism, the Palestinian question, and nuclear weapons are major variables. Encouraging signs are the condemnation of terrorism by Gorbachev, his stress on reforming the Soviet economy, and Soviet willingness in early 1988 to support UN-sponsored action to bring the Iran-Iraq war to an end. There can be no Middle East settlement without Soviet consent.[93]

Asia

Asia as a whole cannot be categorized as part of the Third World. Some parts of it are quite highly developed in several ways. Japan is the best-known example.

Both superpowers have long had a presence in the region. The Soviet Union has been an East Asian power since 1689, when Imperial Russia gained territory by treaty with the Chinese empire, having occupied Chinese areas in Siberia and Manchuria. The Americans traded heavily with China even before their independence and later "opened" Japan to the outside world and established special privileges in China, acts backed by the threat of force.

Asia is not a dangerous region of United States-Soviet rivalry at the present time. This is ironic, for it was the American "loss" of China to communism in 1949 that precipitated the McCarthy period of nativistic emotional anti-communism with its blacklists of Hollywood figures and congressional investigations of "reds," real and imagined. This anti-communism led later to the Vietnam War. At present, however, communism in Asia is neither expansionist, except in Indo-China, nor firmly linked to Moscow. China, though still ruled undemocratically by a Communist party, has brought in thousands of foreign specialists from the West. Americans there are engaged in work as diverse as teaching English and studying aquaculture, and United States military planners no longer see China as a potential opponent.[94]

Accordingly, the politico-strategic picture in Asia is now more to the favor of the United States, particularly since Japan, booming economically, is a democracy closely tied to it. The regional balance is stable. The Soviet Union is not doing well politically in the area except in Vietnam and India. It is suspect in several other countries and is not important in Asia's trade. The Asian Communist states North Korea and Vietnam have severe economic difficulties. Afghanistan has been impossible for the USSR to pacify and a political liability besides, prompting Gorbachev to promise a Soviet military withdrawal. In Indonesia, communism was pushed out of the picture years ago with chilling violence. But the Communist insurgency in the Philippines shows no signs of ending. The only place in Asia where a relationship with the Soviet Union is sincerely welcomed is democratic non-Communist India, which receives massive military aid from the USSR. China, once closely tied to the USSR, has the measure of the Soviets. The Western and Japanese roles in China will continue to be greater than the Soviet unless forces leery of Western-style modernization win out in Chinese politics.

The United States-Chinese-Japanese "triangle" is the foundation of stability in East Asia and promises to last since both the Chinese and the Japanese reject close ties with the USSR. To Japanese, the Russians are "the least-admired foreigners" while Americans are the most admired. Japan and Russia have not had good relations during this century. A serious fishing dispute roils Soviet-Japanese relations as does Soviet improper occupation of four Japanese islands. Even years of a totally new and accommodating Soviet foreign policy could not establish good relations for the USSR with Japan or China, much of whose former territory is held by the USSR. There are, of course, limitations, though less serious ones, on better United States relations with China and Japan. The United States stands in the way of Chinese acquisition of Taiwan, most of whose inhabitants are not interested in Peking's calls for unification, and Japan does not buy many American products, thereby worsening the unfavorable balance of trade of the United States. Efforts are now being made to mitigate the Japanese-American trade dispute.

Being an Asian power by geographical fact, the USSR has strong concerns about its position, particularly because of the increasing economic, political, and military significance of Asia and the continuing American naval and air superiority in the Pacific. Moreover, Moscow finds that almost all states of the region are moving toward Western-style economic policies—decentralization, private enterprise, etc. Gorbachev's reforms are barely begun. Its "defensive imperialism" puts off states with which it needs better relations. It also lacks an attractive culture, quality goods, world-class technology, and the light touch in diplomacy. The main Soviet policy instrument, military power, has been counterproductive, driving most states away from the USSR.

The future in Asia is going to be different. At least three major powers of the region are going to take on much bigger roles there, and possibly further afield, than history has seen—China, India, and Japan. China has taken Tibet, maintained closer relations with North Korea than has the USSR, contended with Soviet-backed Vietnam, pressured the United States over Taiwan, and convinced the Soviets they ought to negotiate with it instead of attacking it. India is close to being the dominant state of South Asia and is trying to build a regional state system under its leadership. Although Pakistan has not accepted this, there is no power able to derail India's plans. Soon "the Indian navy will extend its reach over most of the Indian Ocean and might well acquire nuclear weaponry. Hostile Indian naval forces could complicate significantly American military activities there...."[95] India acquired a role in Sri Lankan internal affairs in 1987. However, India has grave inner weaknesses that may hobble her future. Japan is beginning to take an independent role in world politics and has chosen a good relationship with China over one with the USSR. Both superpowers are finding they have to operate within a more constraining framework in Asia.

ISSUES

There are several Third World issues affecting Soviet-American politics today. Here is a short sampling:

1. *Are the Soviets behind the instability and anti-Westernism of the Third World?*

William J. Casey, Reagan's first Director of the CIA, said, "Yes." Discussing insurgencies, he said:

> ... the Soviets go in and exploit the underlying social and economic discontents.... That gives them a base. They feed it with trained men and with arms. That drives away investment.... And as the economic discontent grows, more people go over to the insurgents' side.
>
> It's almost a no-lose proposition for the Soviets. They can stay in the background.[96]

Many would disagree. Ironically, one of those who does is a former Republican President, Richard Nixon: "While we should hold the Soviets accountable for the actions they take that are opposed to our interests, we should recognize that they are not responsible for all the troubles in the world."[97]

2. *Is it necessary for the United States to support undemocratic regimes?*

Many foreign affairs analysts in or close to government have argued that there is no choice; the world has to be dealt with as it is. True, probably only a third of the states in existence could be called democratic. Some go further and claim that many peoples are "not ready" for democracy. Others devise elaborate justifications for good relations with particular authoritarian regimes. South Africa is an example. One argument is that "authoritarian" (non-Communist) systems are capable of internal political change, whereas "totalitarian" (Communist) ones supposedly lack this quality. A long-time foreign correspondent writes, "After 40 years, I find myself still puzzled and pained about why my own country so often does not act as it talks and why many of my countrymen who demand freedom for themselves don't give much of a damn about it for others."[98] Possibly many Americans look down on "non-modern" peoples.

The costs of ignoring democratic aspirations have often been apparent. Undemocratic regimes do fall, leaving behind great internal animosity toward the United States. Look at Greece and Iran. More may fall—South Korea and Chile, for example. In 1986 the United States took a hand in facilitating the flights of dictators from Haiti and the Philippines. This was very popular in the United States, where "tin-horn dictators" have been decried and laughed at for decades. The Reagan administration holds that leftist dictatorships are the worst. True, they can get Soviet support and pose a national security problem for the United States. And different Americans see different regimes in varying lights. Leftist regimes tend to be able to hide their injustices well since they tend to have control of the media and are more "modern" in anti-democratic means and measures. Traditional authoritarianisms often seem not to understand how bad they look to Americans. Communists are more image-conscious.

The issue will remain a sore one for a long time. It took centuries for European states to evolve into democracies. Perhaps the underlying issue is: Do we have confidence in democracy?

3. *Should the United States intervene militarily in the Third World?*

This is a hot question, considering the aid given by the Reagan administration to anti-Soviet insurgencies in Afghanistan, Angola, and Cambodia. There is always a temptation to try to make general rules. The argument for is fundamentally that imperialism (whatever it calls itself) ought not to have it easy. The argument against is often stated with the slogan, "No more Vietnams," that is, an intervention might become an unpopular real war which weakens the United States.

The issue becomes even hotter now that there is a radical government receiving Soviet aid, including weapons, on the mainland of the western hemisphere—Nicaragua, which is repressing groups and institutions allowed to function freely in the United States—the press, churches, business, minorities.

Will Americans allow people to be shot down by Soviet weapons on the American *mainland*?

But even a conservative director of the CIA saw a problem with military intervention in Nicaragua. One, Latin American public opinion may well be automatically opposed. "It's the gringo problem: They don't want us down there." Two, "When we go down there, we play into the hands of Marxists to a degree; we give them a rallying point."[99]

Is not "containment" of Nicaragua enough? No, says an undersecretary of defense. "We know from experience that that doesn't work." A United States senator adds, "A Marxist government can't reform."

Other arguments for intervention include: breaking the seeming rule that going Communist is irreversible in order to raise the morale of non-Communist movements in the Third World, and to try to save people from a "brutal future."[100]

There are also those who favor military power as pressure, not use, and advocate combining it with regional power involvement (the Contadora process), and United States political and diplomatic measures, as well as propaganda and encouragement of democratic resistance within Nicaragua. The Contras are to be reformed—into "a full-fledged popular freedom movement."[101]

Many disagree with these positions. One argument against intervention made by a leading congressman is that Americans have no right to reform by force, like "God's avenging angels," governments with which they happen to disagree. A famous ex-senator points out that the use of force to "clean up" the world is a romantic, unrealistic enterprise doomed to failure.

The claims of national interest can also enter the dispute. A place unimportant to the United States does not suddenly become important once it becomes radicalized. And where will intervention end—with a world of "endless enemies?" This would leave the United States with a bigger problem than before intervention.

At the least, certain questions ought to be clarified to bipartisan satisfaction prior to intervention: What is to be achieved? What are our partners like? What do they expect of us? How far are we prepared to go? And, finally, what of the Soviets? Similar criteria have been included in six tests on intervention by Secretary of Defense Weinberger, e.g., forces should be committed only in a situation "vital to our national interest" in which victory is possible and American popular support is reasonably assured.[102]

The same issue exists for the Soviet Union. Although it is often stated that the Politburo can make decisions ignoring the considerations facing democratic governments, this is true only for small and short-term actions.

4. *Is a United States-Soviet "deal" or "code of conduct" in the Third World possible? (or: Is linkage feasible?)*

Some Americans want the Soviets to "lay off" in the Third World before agreeing to a deal on strategic weapons or to better relations in general. Others say, "Arms control is complicated enough without tying it to random developments in the Third World." The USSR has occasionally expressed a willingness to negotiate on specific Third World issues, such as the Persian Gulf and Afghanistan, as long as it is recognized that turbulence in the Third World is "inevitable" and that it will develop in a context of "continuing competition between the two world systems." This competition can, supposedly, be controlled by a "businesslike approach" by the superpowers.[103]

The objections to cooperation are partly ideological, partly strategic. Some believe that Soviet-American cooperation is a betrayal of American ideals and interests as well as those of the peoples of the Third World. Some feel such cooperation would only work to the advantage of the Soviets, who do not define their aid and involvement as intervention. In addition, a limitation of American involvement would undercut the status of the United States as a superpower as well as its ability to defend its access to natural resources and allies. Finally, it is argued that such cooperation is unrealistic and even naive. Great powers do not cooperate, it is said by those who use history as their guide. They struggle until one is defeated or gives up the contest.

SUMMARY

The Third World is generally considered important because it is a center of unpredictable change and of superpower competition, the outcome of which is still uncertain. A Mexican writer asks, is "the greatest change in this century" not the results of the struggle of the working class, but rather "the awakening of the great civilizations once colonized by the West?" At any rate, the developed world now has a close political and psychological relationship with the Third World: its problems become our problems.

The Third World, nevertheless, follows its own rules, needs, and inclinations, not those of the superpowers. Remember, most of these states have achieved freedom from colonialism and know what servitude is. Just as the United States' assumptions on proper socioeconomic political forms tend to be rejected, so do those of the Soviet Union. Forces in the Third World make it intractable to superpower control. Any approach to the Third World must be based on detailed understanding of local processes.[104]

The record of both superpowers in the Third World has been more one of frustration and failure than of success. The Soviets face major rebellions against governments they support, states that receive the Soviets' aid refuse to follow their advice, revolutions are not occurring, as Marx predicted, in industrializing countries, but only in the pre-industrial ones. Furthermore:

> All the revolutionary changes of the last two decades took place without Soviet involvement in the overthrow of the old regime—Cuba, Nicaragua, Iran, Afghanistan, Ethiopia, and the collapse of the Portuguese empire. Only in the case of Afghanistan, Angola and Guinea-Bissau had Moscow even had any previous direct contact with some of the new leaders.[105]

It is therefore not surprising that the USSR is now consolidating its positions in the Third World, downplaying support for leftist movements and regimes, and emphasizing ties with large non-radical Third World states as part of a normal great power competition with the United States.[106]

The Americans have had similar frustrations: they have been expelled from Iran, are continually tested by China over Taiwan, are bedeviled by terrorism, and are unable to resolve Middle East problems. African and Arab states almost always vote differently from the United States in the United Nations. Egypt, the second largest recipient of United States aid, opposed it 87 percent of the time in a recent year.[107] Many Americans refuse to face up to this Third World rejection and instead blame the Soviets for it. Anti-Soviet feeling in the United States rose sharply after the Iranian hostage incident and continues to be fueled by Libyan and Nicaraguan actions. However, instead of the United States seeing the USSR behind all the unpleasant occurrences in the Third World, it would be more rewarding to exert effective influence within the process of change itself. The end of the Marcos dictatorship in the Philippines is a good example of United States reinforcement of the current of change already underway.

Assuming present trends hold and recent history is a good guide, we can forecast that the Third World will develop further in accordance with its own beliefs and needs. It may "eventually build up regimes equally at variance with both Western and Soviet ways of life."[108] Just as colonialism went out of existence, so will superpower hegemony. However, although the drive for development has understandably been the priority in the Third World, the desire for democracy, pluralism, civil liberties, and respect for human rights is a powerful imperative. The drive for democracy is now widely evident—in places as far apart as Argentina, the Philippines, Haiti, South Korea, and South Africa. If democracy is a new stage in Third World Development, the United States may be able to further this trend. But whatever forces do take hold in the Third World, both the United States and the Soviet Union must learn to relate to it on its terms, not theirs.

REFERENCES

1. See *Safire's Political Dictionary* (New York: Random House, 1978), 723–724. For discussion of Soviet use of the term, see Daniel S. Papp, *Soviet Perceptions of the Developing World* (Lexington, MA: Lexington Books, 1985).
2. David W. Ziegler, *War, Peace and International Politics*, 2d ed. (Boston: Little, Brown, 1981), 384–385; Professor Harvey F. Kline, a specialist on Colombia; Walter S. Jones and Steven J. Rosen, *The Logic of International Relations*, 4th ed. (Boston: Little, Brown, 1982), 163.
3. Vera Micheles Dean, *The Nature of the Non-Western World* (New York: Mentor, 1957), 15 and 16.
4. David Calvocoressi, *World Politics since 1945*, 4th ed. (White Plains, NY: Longman, 1982), 94–95.
5. George Liska, *Russia & World Order* (Baltimore, MD: Johns Hopkins University Press, 1980), 95.

6. Bruce Russet and Harvey Starr, *World Politics* (San Francisco, CA: Freeman, 1981), 60–61.
7. *The German Tribune*, No. 1130, 29 April 1984, 7.
8. According to The Hunger Project, a charitable corporation.
9. Eugene J. Carroll, Admiral, USN, retired, from an AP report cited in *Daily Hampshire Gazette* (Northampton, MA), 19 March 1983, 8; and *New York Times*, 26 May 1985, E-5.
10. See Rodney W. Jones and Steven A. Hildreth, *Modern Weapons and Third World Powers* (Boulder, CO: Westview Press, 1985).
11. Organization of the Joint Chiefs of Staff, *United States Military Posture FY 1985* (Washington, DC: GPO, 1984), 1–2.
12. *New York Times*, 22 June 1985, A-28; and *RAND CHECKLIST*, No. 305 (November 1983), 2–3, citing Brian M. Jenkins, *New Modes of Conflict*, RAND publication R-3009—DNA, January 1983.
13. Richard Nixon, "Superpower Summitry," *Foreign Affairs* Vol. 60? (Fall 1985): 3; and Francois Mitterand in an interview, *New York Times*, 4 June 1981.
14. John Lewis Gaddis, "Containment: Its Past and Future," in *Neither Cold War nor Détente?* ed. Richard A. Melanson (Charlottesville: University of Virginia Press, 1982), 17 and 29; *New York Times*, 24 June 1987, A-7.
15. Personal communication, 1985.
16. Raymond Aron, "Ideology in Search of a Policy," *Foreign Affairs, America and the World*, 60, 3 (1981): 519; *Christian Science Monitor*, 10 March 1986, 23.
17. Congressman James D. Santini (D, Nevada), quoted in "Washington, Moscow, and the 'Resource War,'" Radio Liberty Research 433/80, 14 November 1980, 3; and Yuan-li Wu, *Raw Material Supply in a Multipolar World* (New York: National Strategy Information Center and Crane, Russak & Co., 1973), 46. See also Alfred E. Eckes, Jr., *The United States and the Global Struggle for Minerals* (Austin: University of Texas, 1979).
18. Arthur Gavshon, *Crisis in Africa* (New York: Penguin, 1981), 35; Dean, *The Nature of the Non-Western World*, 202–203.
19. Colin S. Gray, *The Geopolitics of the Nuclear Era* (New York: National Strategy Information Center and Crane, Russak, 1977), 65–66; and Norman Polmar, *Soviet Naval Power*, Rev. ed. (New York: National Strategy Information Center and Crane, Russak, 1974), 105 and 107, quoting Soviet Admiral Gorshkov.
20. "U.S.-Soviet Competition in the Third World" (a conference report) in *Strategy for Peace, 1984* (Muscatine, IA: Stanley Foundation, 1984), 22.
21. Robert Legvold, "The Super Rivals: Conflict in the Third World," *Foreign Affairs*, 57, 4 (Spring 1979): 757. Legvold attributes this view to Kissinger.
22. Elizabeth Pond, "Key Issue for Arms Talks—Maintaining Stability," *Christian Science Monitor*, 13 March 1985, 36.
23. Yu. S. Novopashin, "The Influence of Real Socialism on the World Revolutionary Process," *Voprosy filosofii* (Issues of History), 8 (August 1982); trans. in *Current Digest of the Soviet Press*, XXXV, 43 (23 November 1982), 11.
24. Dan C. Heldman, *The USSR and Africa* (New York: Praeger, 1981), 119.
25. For the example of re-exports of oil, see *The Economist*, 19 November 1983, 83–84. On privatization in Africa, see *New York Times*, 30 July 1987, D1. This process lends support to Richard Feinberg's thesis in his *Intemperate Zone* that, since most

Third World elites want to participate in the world economy controlled by the West, in the long term the Third World will gravitate to the West. I am indebted to my colleague M. J. Peterson for this reference.

26. Prince Bandar, Saudi Arabian ambassador to the United States, at Harvard University, 4 April 1984, quoted in JFK School *Update*, April 1984.

27. *Christian Science Monitor*, 11 April 1984, 1.

28. *New York Times*, 26 October 1983.

29. Carol R. Saivetz and Sylvia Woodby, *Soviet-Third World Relations* (Boulder, CO: Westview Press, 1985), 117.

30. Stanley Hoffmann, in a review of a book on the Iranian revolution, *New York Times Book Review*, 16 June 1985, 33.

31. Jonas Savimbi, leader of the National Union for the Total Liberation of Angola, *New York Times*, 9 October 1985, A-3.

32. Arno J. Meyer, "The Cold War Is Over," *Democracy* 2, 1 (January 1982): 32.

33. From an address by former Secretary of State Vance, *New York Times*, 6 June 1980.

34. Elizabeth Kridl Valkenier, *The Soviet Union and the Third World: An Economic Bind* (New York: Praeger, 1983), 147–148; Saivetz and Woodby, 136–137; and Jonathan Steele, *Soviet Power* (New York: Simon and Schuster, 1983), 173.

35. Frank Church (former U.S. Senator from Idaho), "Thoughts on the Limits to American Power," *New York Times*, 15 April 1984. Though made in 1972, these remarks are still applicable.

36. *New York Times*, 30 May 1982.

37. An update of a paragraph in Raymond L. Garthoff, *Détente and Confrontation* (Washington, DC: Brookings Institution, 1985), 1063.

38. Andrew K. Semmel, "Security Assistance: U.S. and Soviet Patterns," in *Foreign Policy USA/USSR*, ed. Charles W. Kegley, Jr., and Pat McGowan (Beverly Hills, CA: Sage, 1982), 268–269. Semmel has been an employee of the U.S. Defense Security Assistance Agency (DSAA).

39. Andrew J. Pierre, "The Global Politics of Arms Sales," in Daniel J. Kaufman et al., *U.S. National Security: A Framework for Analysis* (Lexington, MA: Heath, 1985), 401 and 402; reprinted from Pierre, *The Global Politics of Arms Sales* (Princeton, NJ: Princeton University Press, 1982).

40. Richard A. Weisberger, *Cold War, Cold Peace* (Boston: Houghton Mifflin, 1984), 315.

41. Pierre, 407; and William H. Lewis, "Emerging Choices for the Soviets in Third World Arms Transfer Policy," in U.S. ACDA, *World Military Expenditures and Arms Transfers: 1985* (Washington, DC: GPO, 1985), 33.

42. Pierre, 408.

43. Semmel, 269–270; and Pierre, 410–411.

44. Pierre, 412.

45. A review of A. I. Utkin, *The United States and Western Europe: The Arms Trade (International Political Implications)* (Moscow: Nauka, 1984), in *SShA* (USA), 4 (1985), trans. in JPRS-USA-85-007, 12 July 1985, 46–47.

46. Joachim Krause, "Soviet Military Aid to the Third World," *Aussen Politik* (English ed.), vol. 34 (April 1983): 397.

47. U.S. ACDA, 1985, 10 and 21.

48. U.S. Department of State, *Atlas of United States Foreign Relations* 2nd ed.,

(Washington, DC: GPO, 1985), 86; *Christian Science Monitor*, 23 May 1985, 18–19; *New York Times*, 15 October 1985, A-10.
49. Mark N. Katz, *The Third World in Soviet Military Thought* (Baltimore, MD: Johns Hopkins University Press, 1982), 140; Rajan Menon, "Military Power, Intervention, and Soviet Policy in the Third World," in *Soviet Foreign Policy in the 1980s*, ed. Roger E. Kanet, (New York: Praeger, 1982), 273; *Wall Street Journal*, 2 October 1985, 30.
50. U.S. Department of State, *Atlas of United States Foreign Relations*, 1985, 89 and 90; and *New York Times*, 25 October 1985, A-3.
51. U.S. Department of State, *Warsaw Pact Economic Aid to Non-Communist LDCs*, 1984 (Washington, DC: May 1986), 27–28.
52. Saivetz and Woodby, 146; Roger E. Kanet, "Soviet Policy toward the Developing World: The Role of Economic Assistance and Trade," in *The Soviet Union in the Third World*, ed. Robert H. Donaldson (Boulder, CO: Westview, Press, 1981), 348, 350, 352.
53. Source: British government statistics of November 1985; the statistics on Soviet-Libyan trade from Lisa Anderson, "Qadhafi and the Kremlin," *Problems of Communism* (September-October 1985): 37; and Moscow TASS, 1 April 1986.
54. Valkenier, *The Soviet Union and the Third World*, 24–26; *New York Times*, 23 April 1984.
55. *Washington Post*, 24 April 1983.
56. Ibid.; Edgar O'Ballance, *Tracks of the Bear* (Novato, CA: Presidio, 1982), 104; *The USSR and Developing Countries: Economic Cooperation* (Moscow: Progress Publishers, 1984), 127; *New York Times*, 16 June 1985, 22-B. See also Saivetz and Woodby, 143, 146.
57. E. K. Fretwell, Jr., Chancellor, University of North Carolina at Charlotte, Preface to *The United States and the Soviet Union: Confrontation or Cooperation in the 1980s?* (Charlotte: University of North Carolina Press, 1982), vi.
58. Representative Jim Wright of Texas, *New York Times*, 12 January 1986, A-13.
59. Robert Rand, Radio Liberty 377/80, 15 October 1980.
60. *Atlas of United States Foreign Relations*, 32, 83 and 85.
61. I am indebted to George Breslauer for his presentation, "Political Succession and Soviet Foreign Policy," at the national meeting of the American Association for the Advancement of Slavic Studies, Washington, DC, 2 November 1985; and to one by Mel Goodman at the Russian Research Center, 18 April 1986. And see also Francis Fukuyama, "Patterns of Soviet Third World Policy," *Problems of Communism*, XXXVI, 5 (September–October 1987) 8.
62. Pierre M. Gallois, "The Soviet Global Threat and the West," *Orbis* 25, 3 (Fall 1981): 651, 659, 661; Donald S. Zagoria, "Into the Breach: New Soviet Alliances in the Third World," *Foreign Affairs*, 57, 4 (Spring 1979): 736; Flora Lewis, "Marxism vs. Leninism," *New York Times*, 25 January 1985, A-27; and Zagoria, 740–741, 748, 749, 752.
63. Kenneth W. Dam, Deputy Secretary of State, address in Chicago, *Current Policy*, No. 525, 31 October 1983, 3.
64. "US-Soviet Competition in the Third World," in *Strategy for Peace*, 1984 (Muscatine, IA: Stanley Foundation, 1984), 16.
65. Colin Legum, "The Soviet Union's Encounter with Africa," in *The Soviet Impact*

in Africa, ed. R. Craig Nation and Mark V. Kauppi (Lexington, MA: Lexington Books, 1984), 25. See also Kenneth Maxwell, "A New Scramble for Africa?" Ch. 26 in *The Conduct of Soviet Foreign Policy*, ed. Erik P. Hoffmann and Frederick J. Fleron 2d ed. (New York: Aldine, 1980).

66. R. Craig Nation, "Soviet Engagement in Africa: Motives, Means and Prospects," in Nation and Kauppi, 36.

67. Marina Ottaway, "Superpower Competition and Regional Conflicts in the Horn of Africa," in Nation and Kauppi, 180; and Legum, 26.

68. *New York Times*, 15, 16, and 17 February 1986, 2. See Helen Kitchen, "Africa: Year of Ironies," *Foreign Affairs: America and the World 1985*, 64, 3, 579–580.

69. Gavshon, *Crisis in Africa*, 164 and 155.

70. *New York Times*, 8 April 1984; and *U.S. News & World Report*, 25 February 1985.

71. *New York Times*, 19 February 1986, A-1.

72. David E. Albright, *Soviet Policy in Southern Africa since Nkomati*, Occasional Paper, South African Institute of International Affairs, August 1985, 1; and Sam C. Nolutshungu, "Soviet Involvement in Southern Africa," *Annals*, AAPSS, 481 (September 1985), 141.

73. Kurt M. Campbell, "U.S. Depends Too Much on South African Minerals," *Boston Globe*, 2 October 1985; and "South Africa: The Soviets Are Not the Problem," *Washington Post*, 11 September 1985; Sara Pienaar, *Gorbachev's Appointment and Change in the USSR*, Occasional Paper, South African Institute of International Affairs, August 1985, 9 and 11. And see Campbell, *Soviet Policy towards South Africa* (New York: St. Martin's Press, 1986).

74. Seth Singleton, "Soviet Impact on Africa," presentation at the national meeting of the American Association for the Advancement of Slavic Studies, Washington, DC. 3 November 1985; and Kitchen, 576.

75. Partly based on a paper by Anthony Lake, "Hope and Realism about Africa," 5 November 1983. And see *New York Times*, 13 January 1988, A-2.

76. W. Raymond Duncan, "Soviet Power in Latin America: Success or Failure?" in Donaldson, ed., *The Soviet Union in the Third World*, 2; and John Spanier, *American Foreign Policy Since World War II*, 7th ed. (New York: Praeger, 1977), 196.

77. See Russell H. Bartley, *Imperial Russia and the Struggle for Latin American Independence, 1808–1828* (Austin: University of Texas Press, 1978), 77, 159.

78. James D. Theberge, *The Soviet Presence in Latin America* (New York: Crane, Russak, 1974), 1–3; Edmé Dominguez Reyes, "Soviet Relations with Central America, the Caribbean, and Members of the Contadora Group," *Annals*, AAPSS, vol. 481 (September 1985), 148; Steele, 224; and *Pravda*, 2 May 1982, quoted in Steele, 207.

79. Cole Blaisier, *The Giant's Rival* (University of Pittsburgh Press, 1983), 114; and *New York Times*, 15 February 1983.

80. Blaisier, 126; and U.S. Department of State, *Soviet Activities in Latin America and the Caribbean*, Current Policy No. 669, 28 February 1985, 2.

81. Howard J. Wiarda, "Soviet Policy in the Caribbean and Central America: Opportunities and Constraints," a paper presented at the Kennan Institute, Washington, D.C., on 2 March 1984, 9–11; and U.S. Department of State, *Soviet Activities*, 1 and 5.

82. Reyes, 149; Steele, 220; and Saivetz and Woodby, 111 and 112.

83. Steele, p. 200; Reyes, p. 150; Saivetz and Woodby, p. 87; *The Guardian,* 5 March 1981; *Wall Street Journal,* 3 July 1987, 13; and *New York Times,* 8 August 1987, A-1.

84. *New York Times,* 20 August 1986, A-1.

85. Quoted in Robert Rand, "The USSR: A Role in the Mideast Peace Progress?" Radio Liberty Research 205/83, 20 May 1983, 3. Date of *Pravda* not given.

86. Alvin Z. Rubinstein, *Soviet Policy since World War II,* 2nd ed., (Boston: Little, Brown, 1984), 213, 217.

87. Aaron S. Klieman, *Soviet Russia and the Middle East* (Baltimore, MD: Johns Hopkins University Press, 1970), 37.

88. Spanier, 42.

89. Mohammed Heikal, *Sphinx and Commissar: The Rise and Fall of Soviet Influence in the Arab World* (London: Collins, 1978), 278; quoted in Steele, 187.

90. Steele, 187–190; Saivetz and Woodby, 47.

91. Saivetz and Woodby, 97.

92. *Christian Science Monitor,* 18 February 1986, 40; Alvin Z. Rubinstein, "Soviet Policy in the Middle East: Perspectives from Three Capitals," in *The Soviet Union in the Third World,* ed. Robert H. Donaldson, (Boulder, CO: Westview Press, 1981), 155; and *New York Times,* 7 August 1987, A-3.

93. Seth P. Tillman, *The United States in the Middle East* (Bloomington: Indiana University Press, 1982), 269–270. And see Carol R. Saivetz, "Superpowers in the Middle East," *Problems of Communism,* XXXVI, 5 (September-October, 1987), 77–84.

94. Arthur W. Hummel, Jr., U.S. Ambassador to China, speaking to the Pacific and Asian Affairs Council, Waikiki, Hawaii, *New York Times,* 25 April 1982.

95. Selig S. Harrison, "Cut a Regional Deal," *Foreign Policy,* no. 62 (Spring 1986): 126–127.

96. Interview with William J. Casey, *U.S News & World Report,* 8 March 1982.

97. Richard M. Nixon, "Superpower Summitry," *Foreign Affairs,* 64, 1 (Fall 1985): 7.

98. A. M. Rosenthal, "Journalist among Tyrants," *New York Times Magazine,* 23 March 1986, 25.

99. Interview with William J. Casey.

100. Fred C. Iklé and Richard G. Lugar, *New York Times,* 5 June, A-8; and Joshua Muravchik, "Topple the Sandinistas," ibid., 3 March 1985, E-21.

101. See the full-page ad in *the New York Times,* 16 March 1986, E-26, by the group, friends of the Democratic Center in Central America.

102. *Christian Science Monitor,* 3 June 1985, 22; and *New York Times,* 29 November 1984, A-1.

103. See Henry Trofimenko, "The Third World and the U.S.-Soviet Competition: A Soviet View," *Foreign Affairs* 59, 5 (Summer 1981): 1040.

104. Katz, 167; Ferenc A. Vali, *Politics of the Indian Ocean Region and the Balances of Power* (New York: Free Press, 1976); Tony Smith, *New York Times,* 25 April 1982.

105. Steele, 167.

106. Francis Fukuyama, "Gorbachev and the Third World," *Foreign Affairs,* 64, 4 (Spring 1986), 725–726; Harry Gelman, "The Soviet Union in the Less Developed World," in Andrzej Korbonski and Francis Fukuyama, eds., *The Soviet Union and the Third World* (Ithaca, NY: Cornell, 1987), 302; and Fukuyama, "Soviet Strategy in the Third World," in ibid., 44–45.

107. *New York Times*, 17 June 1985, A-19.

108. W. W. Kulski, *The Soviet Union in World Affairs* (Syracuse University Press, 1973), 150.

SELECT BIBLIOGRAPHY

Clapham, Cristopher. *Third World Politics.* Madison: University of Wisconsin Press, 1985.

Crow, Ben, et al. *Third World Atlas.* Philadelphia: Open University Press, 1983.

Donaldson, Robert J., ed. *The Soviet Union in the Third World: Successes and Failures.* Boulder, CO: Westview Press, 1981.

Duncan, W. Raymond, ed. *Soviet Policy in the Third World.* Washington, DC: Pergamon Press, 1980.

Dunnigan, James F. and Austin Bay. *A Quick and Dirty Guide to War.* Updated ed. New York: Morrow, 1986.

Feinberg, Richard. *The Intemperate Zone: The Third World Challenge to U.S. Foreign Policy.* New York: Norton, 1983.

Feuchtwanger, E. J., and Peter Nailor. *The Soviet Union and the Third World.* New York: St. Martin's Press, 1981.

Freedman, Robert O. *Soviet Policy toward the Middle East since 1970.* New York: Praeger, 1975.

Fukuyama, Francis. *Military Aspects of the U.S.-Soviet Competition in the Third World.* Santa Monica, CA: Rand, 1986.

Gavshon, Arthur. *Crisis in Africa.* New York: Penguin, 1981.

Girling, John L. S. *America and the Third World.* London: Routledge & Kegan Paul, 1980.

Gurtov, Melvin and Ray Maghoori. *Roots of Failure: United States Policy in the Third World.* Westport, CT: Greenwood Press, 1984.

Halliday, Fred. *Soviet Policy in the Arc of Crisis.* Washington DC: Institute for Policy Studies, 1981.

Hammond, Thomas T. *Red Flag over Afghanistan.* Boulder, CO: Westview Press, 1984.

Hansen, Roger D. *U.S. Foreign Policy and the Third World: Agenda 1982.* New York: Praeger, 1982.

Harkavy, Robert E. and Stephanie G. Neumann, eds. *Arms Transfers in the Modern World.* New York: Praeger, 1979.

Heldman, Dan C. *The USSR and Africa.* New York: Praeger, 1981.

Hough, Jerry F. *The Struggle for the Third World: Soviet Debates and American Options.* Washington, DC: Brookings Institution, 1986.

Hosmer, Stephen T. and Thomas W. Wolfe. *Soviet Policy and Practice toward Third World Conflicts.* Lexington, MA: Lexington Books, 1983.

Jones, Rodney W. and Steven A. Hildreth. *Modern Weapons and Third World Powers.* Boulder, CO: Westview Press, 1985.

Katz, Mark N. *The Third World in Soviet Military Thought.* Baltimore, MD: Johns Hopkins University Press, 1982.

Korbonski, Andrzej and Francis Fukuyama, eds. *The Soviet Union and the Third World: The Last Three Decades.* Ithaca, NY: Cornell University Press, 1987.

Laqueur, Walter. *The Pattern of Soviet Conduct in the Third World.* New York: Praeger, 1983.

MacFarlane, S. Neil. *Superpower Rivalry and Third World Radicalism.* Baltimore, MD: Johns Hopkins University Press, 1985.

Marantz, Paul and Blema S. Steinberg, eds. *Superpower Involvement in the Middle East: Dynamics and Foreign Policy.* Boulder, CO: Westview Press, 1985.

Matheson, Neil. *The "Rules of the Game" of Superpower Military Intervention in the Third World: 1975–1980.* Washington, DC: University Press of America, 1983.

Menon, Rajan. *Soviet Power and the Third World.* New Haven, CT: Yale, 1986.

Nikiforov, A. V. *SShA i razvivayushchisya strany: Kritika Kontseptsii "vsaimozavisimosti"* (The USA and Developing Countries: A Critique of the Concept of "Interdependence"). Moscow: Nauka, 1984.

O'Ballance, Edgar. *Tracks of the Bear: Soviet Imprints in the Seventies.* Novato, CA: Presidio Press, 1982.

Ottaway, Marina. *Soviet and American Influence in the Horn of Africa.* New York: Praeger, 1982.

Papp, Daniel S. *Soviet Perceptions of the Developing World: The Ideological Basis.* Lexington, MA: Lexington Books, 1985.

Pierre, Andrew J. *The Global Politics of Arms Sales.* Princeton, NJ: Princeton University Press, 1982.

Porter, Bruce D. *The USSR in Third World Conflicts: Soviet Arms and Diplomacy in Local Wars, 1945–1980.* New York: Cambridge University Press, 1984.

Ra'anan, Uri, et al. *Third World Marxist-Leninist Regimes: Strengths, Vulnerabilities, and U.S. Policy.* Washington, DC: Pergamon-Brassey's, 1985.

Rothstein, Robert L. *The Third World and U.S. Foreign Policy: Cooperation and Conflict in the 1980s.* Boulder, CO: Westview Press, 1981.

Saivetz, Carol R. and Sylvia Woodby. *Soviet-Third World Relations.* Boulder, CO: Westview Press, 1985.

Sewell, John W., et al. *U.S. Foreign Policy and the Third World: Agenda 1985–86.* New Brunswick, NJ: Transaction Books, 1985.

Shulman, Marshall, ed. *East-West Tensions in the Third World.* New York: Norton, 1986.

Sivard, Ruth L. *World Military and Social Expenditures.* Washington, DC: World Priorities, 1986.

Steele, Jonathan. *Soviet Power: The Kremlin's Foreign Policy—Brezhnev to Andropov.* New York: Simon and Schuster, 1983. See particularly Part Two—"The Periphery."

Thompson, W. Scott and Andrew Walworth. *Fulcrum of Power: The Third World between Moscow and Washington.* New York: Crane, Russak, 1983.

Thompson, W. Scott, ed. *The Third World: Premises of U.S. Policy.* San Francisco, CA: ICS Press, 1983.

Tillman, Seth P. *The United States in the Middle East.* Bloomington: Indiana University Press, 1982.

U.S. Arms Control and Disarmament Agency. *World Military Expenditures and Arms Transfers 1986.* Washington, DC: GPO, 1987.

U.S. Department of State. *Atlas of United States Foreign Relations*, 2d ed. Washington, DC: GPO, 1985.

——. *Warsaw Pact Economic Aid to Non-Communist LDCs, 1984.* Washington, DC: May 1986.

The USSR and Developing Countries: Economic Cooperation. Moscow: Progress, 1984.

Valkenier, Elizabeth Kridl. *The Soviet Union and the Third World: An Economic Bind.* New York: Praeger, 1983.

Wessell, Nils H. and Joanne Gowa. *Ground Rules: Soviet and American Involvement in Regional Conflicts.* Philadelphia, PA: Foreign Policy Research Institute, 1982.

Whelan, Joseph J. *The Soviet Union in the Third World, 1980–1982: An Imperial Burden or Political Asset, and the Future?* Washington, DC: Congressional Research Service, 1985. (Report No. 85–112S)

Wiles, Peter, ed., *The New Communist Third World.* New York: St. Martin's Press, 1982.

Chapter 7

Trade, Technology Transfer, Cooperative Agreements, and Exchanges

---

> Technology transfer is one of the key issues which dominates our era. This issue will be crucial in rectifying the stupendous economic and even biological imbalances that fragment the modern world.
>
> *Jean-Francois Revel*

BASIC CONSIDERATIONS

There are those who believe that interchange—of minerals, commodities, and products, of techniques and technology, and of people themselves will improve the superpowers' relationship. It seems so obvious: countries that trade together and also show each other their unpolitical, cultural sides will get along. "Increased trade could draw the superpowers together," arms agreements and world peace would be facilitated, and the huge United States trade deficit would be reduced, it is claimed. A former president of France writes of the "pacifying value of trade."[1] It seems, ironically, that businessmen in large corporations and liberals, two groups usually with little in common politically, tend to agree on the presumed beneficial effects of trade on superpower conflict. But perhaps this theory is radically erroneous and only helps Westerners to convince themselves that trade avoids war. Unfortunately, "nothing has so far confirmed the theory."[2]

The confident view about the interconnection of trade and peace ignores some unpleasant facts. States that traded heavily with each other have gone to war nevertheless. Just before World War II, British-German trade was at a high level, and the night before Hitler invaded the USSR in 1941 trainloads of militarily important Soviet goods were still entering German territory. Second, interchange is limited by the Soviet and American governments. Technology is allowed into the USSR faster than it can be used, but foreign political practices are refused entry and foreign cultural patterns are severely filtered. The Soviet population is semi-isolated from the outside world. Westerners normally may go to only a limited number of Soviet cities and may not live in rural areas; most of the country is closed to visits by foreigners. The American government exercises "strict reciprocity" and limits travel by Soviets.

> To the Soviet leaders trade with the West is a means of opening up technological bottlenecks but certainly not of opening Soviet Society to wider East-West contacts. Indeed, ideological controls might even be tightened as trade with the West expands.[3]

Third, even if interchange occurs freely, it can breed resentment and be blocked by political "linkage." Look at the recent limitations on United States trade with Japan and Europe. Similarly, there have been Soviet voices suggesting that the Soviet Union reduce its imports and instead develop its own agriculture, machinery, and "hi-tech." Trade can lead to dependency, it is claimed. In 1981 then General Secretary Brezhnev complained about spending "large sums of money" on foreign equipment and technology which "we are fully able to make for ourselves...." A top government official expressed an opposing view, saying that hindering trade "inevitably inflicts damage" on Soviet research and development."[4] Gorbachev seems to want to facilitate East-West trade. But he may be forced to second thoughts. Soviet-American trade is similarly a political issue in the United States, where there is real concern that letting the Soviets buy large quantities of food and items of high technology will only strengthen them militarily and create more problems for the United States. Lenin's statement that capitalists will sell the Soviets "the rope" it can use to hang them with is often quoted.

Soviet trade with the United States will unavoidably be beneficial to Soviet military capabilities to some degree. Even a total break in United States-Soviet direct trade would not change this since the Soviets would acquire militarily significant products and technology from third parties or through subterfuges. Another fundamental fact of life about United States-Soviet trade is that neither superpower needs it in any absolute sense, although both would be inconvenienced to lose it, the Soviet Union more than the United States. This trade is very small for both countries. Only a few groups and industries in the United States see such trade as important for them: farmers who grow grain, especially corn; those who market grain or speculate in grain futures; computer and software manufacturers; makers of certain machine tools; and oilwell equipment producers. The Pepsi-Cola company has also found a market in the USSR. The chairman of the company is, naturally, a vigorous proponent of détente and superpower trade. The USSR may have chosen Pepsi over Coke as the favored foreign cola drink because of political ties between Pepsi's chairman and then-President Richard Nixon. Politics can be involved in almost any aspect of United States-Soviet trade.[5]

The relative insignficance of Soviet-American trade was evident even at its height in the 1970s. For the United States most of it consisted of grain exports and imports of certain raw materials. And Soviet foreign trade as a whole remains relatively small in relation to total Soviet economic activity, which is "heavily insulated from foreign transactions by the planning system, the separate domestic and foreign trade price structures and the inconvertibility of the ruble." The Soviet economy is still a semi-closed "administrative" economy, not decentralized and open to the world market like the American. Only about 4 percent of Soviet GNP derives from foreign trade and only about .5 percent of its GNP is spent on imports from the West. The Soviet Union's overall foreign trade fell by 5 percent in 1985.[6] This is true even though the Soviet Union operates almost 100 companies abroad, five in the United States, and that it has greatly expanded its foreign shipping, insurance, and banking operations in recent years.

The USSR's main Western trading partner in recent decades has been West Germany. In 1983 it accounted for 18.3 percent of the Soviet Union's trade with the West and 5.5 percent of its total trade. The order of the USSR's Western trading partners was: West Germany, Finland, Italy, France, Japan with the United States trailing last. Its main Communist trade partners were East Germany and Czechoslovakia. India is the major Third World trading partner of the USSR. In 1983 overall Soviet imports from the United States fell by 25 percent, and United States-Soviet trade that year had a total value of $2.34 billion, with much of this being American agricultural exports. This had not risen by 1987. Significantly, Sino-American trade rose to a record $7.7 billion in 1985, more than three times the level of Soviet-American trade, and was still increasing during 1986. Ironically, most of the increase in American exports to China is in manufactured goods, such as drill bits and high-technology products, items the Soviets want to get. United States trade with tiny Singapore is greater than its trade with the USSR.[7]

The simple fact is that the Soviet Union cannot offer much in trade that the United States really needs. It is not advanced enough to offer highly desirable manufactured goods and it lacks enough uncommitted oil to become a major supplier of the United States. Much of the USSR's oil and natural gas goes to Western and Eastern Europe. Similarly, the United States may not be the best possible grain supplier for the USSR. High American tariffs also inhibit trade with the Soviet Union. Soviet-American trade is more important politically than economically, and political considerations will be central to its future.

Needs and Reasons for Trade
Soviet and American trade needs are very different but potentially compatible. The Soviets want: high technology and particularly weapons-related tech-

nology; grain, mainly corn, as fodder for livestock and increasing meat production; and certain manufactured goods directly related to key areas of economic development, e.g., pipeline-laying equipment and special pumps. On the American side, although certain industries could make good profits from increased trade (computer manufacturers, for example), the American economy as a whole has no great need for Soviet products over those from other countries. Some American farmers have bought Soviet tractors because of their low price, set arbitrarily irrespective of actual cost, and the Soviets would like to market cars in the United States as they do in Canada.

Yet, because of free market competition in the United States, it is unlikely Soviet products, usually lacking high quality and attractiveness, would become favorites of many American consumers. It is still true that "American exports to the Soviet Union seem to be more important for them than they are to us."[8]

The increase of Soviet-American trade in the 1960s and 1970s was wrapped up with assumptions that détente, arms control, and trade went together. It seemed too that an international process of change was in motion and that the cold war rigidities were thawing fast. A general euphoric confidence that trade was a way to bring about a totally new Soviet-American relationship ruled in both Washington and Moscow. The doubts and reaction were still to come. It was a time of hope and a naive faith in which politicians rarely indulge. Perhaps the prospect of continued contention and its assumed nuclear dangers was too unpleasant to contemplate.

It was long forgotten—or not known—that United States-Soviet trade had been large previously, without producing a lasting improvement in relations. In 1930 Soviet imports from the United States totalled about $230 million, a big sum then, and 75 percent of this was machinery.[9] It was also forgotten that powerful American ethnic, religious, and union lobbies would oppose increased American-Soviet trade, as would the Department of Defense and the ideological right-wing.[10]

A major problem was that the Soviets and Americans had very different, and contradictory, hopes for the effects of increased trade. The Soviets seem to have seen trade primarily as a sign of acceptance by the United States of the USSR as it is and as a way to continue strengthening the USSR without risking economic reforms. The Americans harbored a belief that trade would prompt the Soviet Union to relax internally and become a more "ordinary" country, less militarized and less expansionist. Economic reforms in the USSR would have to involve decentralization of decision-making, prices set by a market and increased freedom of discussion and communication. This would limit the power and status of the ruling bureaucratic and political elites and also raise the danger of democratization like that in Czechoslovakia in 1968. "The discarding of reforms meant an increased emphasis on the acquisition of foreign technology" as well as more close involvement with the international economy and especially capitalism. Additional food, too, was to be provided through trade until Soviet agriculture could improve, again on the basis of technique, fertilizer, and machinery provided by foreign trade, and not by a return to private farming. The Soviets hoped that trade would eventually allow the USSR to export high-quality products and thus earn foreign exchange to buy the imports needed for further modernization.[11] The West was to be rendered less anti-Soviet through trade, perhaps even made dependent on its trade with the USSR. The Soviets were continually trying to sell Americans on the benefits of Soviet-American trade. For example, they claimed that increased East-West trade would make for higher employment, improved trade and payments balances, and generally greater economic buoyancy in capitalist countries.[12]

Other Soviet trade goals included acquisition of the technology for the qualitative military modernization required to match NATO, continued economic integration with Eastern Europe, and inhibition of American trade with China.[13] These goals still exist today.

The Nixon administration, for its part, wanted both to alleviate certain American economic problems and to begin the "domestication" of the Soviet Union in international life by giving it what was sometimes called "a vested interest in mutual restraint." Some even saw trade as "an important mechanism for promoting constructive change within the Soviet Union," or as loosening the "totalitarian corset." A higher Soviet living standard would lead to pluralistic reforms, it was thought. Arms control would flow from trade and help prevent nuclear war.

More and more people in the business community and in labor unions wanted increased trade with the USSR. Foreign firms were getting Soviet business, including big one-time sales like an automobile plant from Fiat of Italy. The war in Vietnam had produced high inflation rates. Farmers were having real difficulties. Perhaps the Soviet Union could buy their grain and also become an alternate energy source to OPEC and its embargoes and high-priced oil. Even the Soviet cheap labor force and absence of strikes was a consideration. "Thus, by the early 1970s, a deteriorating economy at home had served to convert the attitudes of a surprisingly large part of the business and union communities toward increased trade with the USSR."[14]

Politics and Trade: Recent History

A number of political factors carried the day against increased superpower trade. Fundamentally, the breakdown in trade relations stemmed from domestic political effects of the American failure in Vietnam and the increasing military capabilities and international presence of the Soviet Union at a time of American limitations and reduction of commitments abroad. The American political system as a whole was unwilling to reward the Soviet Union with equality and increased trade and other contacts at a time of American decline in power. Because of Vietnam and the Watergate scandal many Americans were in an anti-government mood and refused to allow the Nixon and Ford administrations to play the great-power game with the USSR; other, more conservative Americans refused to allow détente to develop through trade.

In this American political stew a variety of factors opposed to Soviet-American trade came together: the issues of human rights under communism, including treatment of dissidents and the emigration of Jews; the fears for national security resulting from the American failure in Vietnam; the OPEC oil embargo and greatly increased oil prices; Soviet movement into Africa; and the decline of the "imperial Presidency" and the rise of a Congress with many new and maverick members. When all this was combined with certain politicians' ambitions and the general unpopularity of the USSR in the United States a very heady political brew came into existence.

The Soviets were partly to blame. If they had reined in military spending, had not appeared with Cuban troops in three parts of Africa, had not been responsible for higher American bread prices and had relaxed domestic political controls, better Soviet-American trade might have survived. In the "great grain robbery" of 1972 the Soviet Union secretly cornered, at discount prices, one-quarter of the United States wheat crop—19 million tons—causing the market price of wheat and the price of a loaf of bread to double. It appears that certain United States government officials with ties to large grain dealers had allowed the "robbery" to occur. From then on the White House itself monitored grain sales. The "killings" the Soviets were making because of oil and gold price rises did not endear them to Americans either.[15]

By the end of the 1970s the political currents just described had stopped the rise in American-Soviet trade that had been developing since the late 1960s. (There had been hardly any direct trade during the cold war, when the United States directed economic warfare against the USSR.)[16] The key date for putting this trade on a new basis was 1969, also the year SALT began. A trade agreement was signed in 1972, the year of a summit meeting that granted the USSR nondiscriminatory tariff treatment with most favored nation status (MFN) for its goods entering the United States. The USSR agreed to pay most of its Lend-Lease debt.

Although United States-Soviet commercial relations expanded, politics ended this growth by 1976. Two highly political amendments to the 1974 Trade Act linked increased trade through greater American credits to freer Soviet emigration practices. However, once the arrangement became public the Soviets angrily said the deal was off, and also stopped making payments on their Lend-Lease debt.

The United States government made a major attempt to improve trade with the 1975 grain agreement, which promised to allow the Soviets to buy 8 million tons of grain every year.[17] Still, by 1977 Soviet-American trade was stagnating, with the volume of trade below $2.5 billion. Although this was ten times the 1972 level, most of it was in agricultural products and raw materials, with the Soviets now often taking orders for manufactured goods elsewhere. Some trade deals were still going forward, e.g., Corning's installation of a light bulb factory, but many American businessmen in Moscow were waiting to be called home and the really large deals were stalled. And, although trade for 1978 was a bit greater than for 1977, all the increase was in American agricultural exports, and trade in manufactured goods declined.

A big drop in total trade occurred in 1980 after the Soviet invasion of Afghanistan. The Carter administration embargoed additional grain exports to the Soviets (but allowed delivery of those already contracted for). It also completely suspended licenses for the export of high-technology items and oil and gas industry products. These actions produced some difficulties in the Soviet economy. Many animals that could not be fed had to be slaughtered early and smaller and less reliable pumps had to be used in a major gas pipeline.[18]

The Reagan administration suspended the grain embargo in 1981 and concentrated its efforts on limiting Soviet access to weapons-related high technology. Also during Reagan's years in office, businesses interested in trading with the USSR lobbied, with some success, for government facilitation of such trade. Domestic politics again dictated increased trade. Important businessmen called for "some kind of clarification on the transfer of technology" and complained that "the jobs are going to the Germans and Japanese, and we're losing out." In November 1982 American business executives at a conference on Soviet-American trade in Moscow attacked the restraints on trade with the USSR imposed by Presidents Carter and Reagan. In spite of such pressures, during 1983 the United States imported very little from the USSR and most of the $2 billion worth of Soviet imports from the United States was grain. Europe and Japan exported twenty times as much to the USSR that year. The level of Soviet-American trade was not much higher in 1984, despite the signing of a new grain pact in 1983 guaranteeing that supplies to the USSR would not be interrupted. American grain prices were appreciably higher than those of Argentina, now a major Soviet supplier.[19]

In 1985 the United States government decided to try to regain what it could of its former Soviet market and sent to Moscow the highest-level government delegation to travel there since 1979, but under constraints imposed by the Defense Department. The secretary of commerce found that no fundamental change in the trade relationship was possible without improvement in other aspects of the relationship.

United States-Soviet trade is still behind where it was in the 1970s and, more important, it now has limited chances for improvement because the trading context has changed. As noted, the Soviets are concerned about becoming dependent on the outside world, the United States has lost credibility as a trustworthy supplier (even though President Reagan has publicly promised not to restrict grain sales) and the Soviets simply do not now have the money for large foreign purchases, a factor exacerbated by the fall in oil prices in 1985 and 1986. An American banker was probably correct when he said, "Trade with the Soviet Union is history as far as American manufactured goods and big projects are concerned." In the 1986–1990 Soviet plan, the large contracts for plant and machinery are going to Japanese and European firms. Even in agricultural trade the United States is now only the USSR's supplier of last resort.[20]

TABLE 7.1. EXPORTS BETWEEN U.S. AND USSR, 1986
(in percentages of totals)

To USSR

soybeans	25.1
corn	22.5
fertilizers	20.9
other (including tracklaying tractors, special oils, and almonds)	31.5

To U.S.

gold bullion	25.6
ammonia	15.1
heavy fuel oils	13.5
urea	11.0
other (mainly special metals and furs)	34.8

In 1986 American exports to the USSR totalled only about $560 million while Soviet imports from the United States were only about $1.25 million (see Table 7.1). There was a bright side for the United States, however: It had a favorable trade balance with the Soviet Union. Trade may have been even less in 1987.

One reason for the unsatisfactory trading volume between the two nations is that their leaders disagree on the role of economics in political negotiations. Mr. Gorbachev has said he will not allow the United States to use trade to "interfere in our internal affairs" while American presidents have habitually cut back on United States-Soviet trade in response to Soviet actions unpopular to Americans. Thus the superpowers' very different cultures affect their economic relationship as well as their purely political one.[21]

TECHNOLOGY TRANSFER

Here is where the fur flies in the American domestic politics of superpower trade. As stated above, the Soviet military will unavoidably benefit from such trade. A computer sold to Aeroflot, the Soviet airline, to handle reservations and ticketing can also be used by the Soviet missile command for targeting. To keep the Soviet Union from getting militarily useful technology from the United States would require isolating the United States from the outside world, including its allies—a move that would defeat the decades-long American attempt to contain Soviet power. The only effective way to limit technology flow to the USSR is to establish controls, with allied help, over a limited number of key products and technologies. But even this is not "leakproof," and some other kinds of control suggested (e.g., over publication of research results) may limit American technological progress. One reason the United States is technologically ahead of the Soviet Union is because it is an open society allowing free communication. To become more like the Soviet Union would be self-defeating. Yet to ignore the issues that technology transfer poses for national security is both risky and politically impossible. Hence frustration and American domestic debate and conflict over this matter are inevitable.

Some definitions are in order. Technology denotes "knowledge or information of how to perform tasks, solve problems, or produce products or services." Its relationship to science is difficult to state. Perhaps technology "translates scientific relationships into 'practical use.'" Some technology is embodied in machines, but much of its exists only as information or knowledge. Technology transfer is a process whereby technology is "moved from one set of users to another"—"essentially a communication process." Technology is extraordinarily important for economic growth. Perhaps 40–50 percent of the American increase in output per capita between 1909 and 1949 was due to technological change. It is very important to an economy but it cannot be measured precisely. Hence controversy surrounds it, particularly when transfer of technology to the USSR is being discussed.[22]

Some Soviet technology is being acquired by the United States. The contribution, though small, of this "reverse technology transfer" is important in medicine, materials development, and nuclear physics. Soviet technology is reaching Western levels in certain machine tools, is even with that of the United States in aerodynamics and radar sensors, and may be ahead in lasers. In the past decade American firms have bought many licenses from the USSR, including ones for coal gasification and electromagnetic casting, magnetic impact bonding and flash butt welding. American railway rails are now welded with Soviet machines and even the SDI project has benefited from Soviet technology. The Soviet Union puts fewer restrictions on the export of its technology than does the United States.[23]

Technology transfer from the West is very important for the Soviet Union since it is trying to expand its power and influence. Although the significance of technology imports from the West must not be overstated, it has often been a key input into the integration of the Soviet and East European economies and the exploitation of new Soviet sources of natural resources. Indeed, the scientific and technological revolution has been called "one of the main sectors of the historic competition between capitalism and socialism...."[24]

Although Soviet economic and ideological gains derived from Western technology do not excite great concern in the United States, possible Soviet military gains do. The Department of Defense fears that the Soviets will adopt American technology—telecommunications, micro-electronics, automation and computers—for military uses such as more accurate missiles or better anti-submarine sensors. This view is echoed by Senator Sam Nunn, one of Congress' leading defense experts, who says that because of military applications of American technology by the Soviets, "Like a 'Catch-22,' we...end up competing against our own technology."[25] Since Americans tend to rely on high technology in weapons and equipment, not numbers of men, if the United

States' lead in technology were wiped out its national security situation would have seriously deteriorated.

The outflow of massive amounts of militarily significant technology from the United States to the USSR is a fact. It is not a scare story. The National Academy of Sciences found that there has been "substantial and serious" leakage of technology to the USSR, with a "significant portion" of it "damaging to national security." It accepted government assertions that Soviet technology acquisitions from the West have permitted the Soviet military to develop counter-measures to Western weapons, improve Soviet weapon performance, avoid hundreds of millions of dollars in R & D costs, and modernize critical sectors of Soviet military production.[26] American precision grinding machines for miniature ball bearings were used in developing the guidance system for the SS-18 missile. The recent covert export of Western machinery by a Japanese firm enabled the Soviets to build much quieter, and hence harder to detect, submarines.

The USSR will continue to try to acquire a broad range of American technologies for military purposes. Their highest priorities will be in micro-electronics, solid rocket fuel know-how, computer-aided aircraft design technology, and large-scale scientific computers.[27] A former chairman of the Joint Chiefs of Staff has claimed that as a result of this technology flow, "We now find the qualitative edge we once enjoyed dissipating at an alarming rate."[28]

There are knowledgeable voices arguing, however, that high-tech, although it improves Soviet weapons, is no cure-all for the serious problems of the Soviet economy as a whole. One economist notes: "The USSR is much too large a country, with too many industries and products, to be able to affect its growth and efficiency significantly through imports of technology."[29]

The Soviet economy is too centralized and old-fashioned to diffuse or apply all the technology acquired, and there is a limit to the amounts the USSR can either buy or steal. Some of the technology acquired, sometimes at great cost and effort, is simply not used. It remains a prestigious white elephant. The largest auto parts plant in the world, built with American help, is now running at one-third capacity but only through cannibalization of some of its expensive American machinery. No wonder Gorbachev wants a reformed economy.[30]

Only a revolutionary transformation plus a long-term overall link-up to the entire West might enable the Soviet economy to become efficient and fully modern. Again, this is too threatening to established interests to be begun soon. Even Gorbachev will not go so far. Still, Western technology has allowed substantial Soviet gains in certain sectors and the bridging of critical gaps.

Soviet Technology Acquisition: Legal and Illegal

The Soviet Union acquires foreign technology in a variety of ways, both open and covert, in a broad, long-term, and continous program of high priority. Parts of the Soviet foreign service as well as the two intelligence services, KGB and GRU, are technology acquisition bureaus. The effort and funds expended on technology transfer indicate it is very important to top people in the USSR. Gorbachev himself has publicly called for the rapid introduction of computers into Soviet high schools. Some of them may come from the United States since the Soviets have not mastered the semiconductor and disk-drive technologies required. They would probably be approved for export since the performance levels would be modest.

There are many open and legal ways in which the Soviets obtain United States technology. One big way is simply to buy unclassified studies of many American government agencies, including the DOD and NASA. One government official has called this a "massive giveaway program." The USSR also buys products that contain high technology and then subjects them to "reverse engineering" in order to acquire the technology embodied in them. The USSR buys some foreign licenses as well. Large-scale purchase of technical publications and books and their translation is routine. (NASA has translated comparable Soviet publications for years.) The author once accompanied a visiting Soviet electronics engineer on a visit to an American in his field. The Soviet engineer pointed out book after book that he had read in unauthorized Russian translation. Another open method of transfer is scholarly exchange. A Soviet scholar who spends a year in an American university laboratory takes away a great deal in his head. So do scholars from third countries who go from a stay in an American university or firm to a stay in the Soviet Union. The Soviets also derive quite a bit of American technology directly from third countries. American scientists who travel to the USSR probably also leave some valuable information there.

Soviet covert technology acquisition is quite well organized and sophisticated. "It involves illegal trade diversions utilizing dummy corporations in Liechtenstein and Switzerland, forged...and misappropriated documents and great amounts of cash." This illegal "trade" may meet many of the USSR's needs in micro-electronics. In 1979 10,000 of the Intel Corporation's most sophisticated semiconductors were stolen—for whom can only be guessed. Two persons working for the USSR established eleven companies in California as high-tech acquisition fronts during the 1970s. Internal Soviet documents acquired by French intelligence reveal that one Soviet agency spends about $1.4 billion per year for covert technology acquisition, thus obtaining 6–10,000 pieces of equipment and 10,000 documents annually, about one-fourth of them classified. By using pilfered documents on the United States F-18 fighter the USSR saved five years of development time and $55 million. A major American source is the civilian contractor.[31] The Soviets acquired a manual on a major American spy satellite from an employee of a civilian firm working for the CIA. Reputedly, the Soviets systematically use credit information to find people with access to sensitive high-tech who are in financial difficulties. In 1977 a Polish intelligence officer loaned money to such an individual working for an aircraft company and obtained details of the "quiet" radar for the as yet unbuilt Stealth bomber plus other key defense information.

The illegal shipment of high-tech equipment to the USSR and other countries, including Iran, has apparently become a "major, lucrative subsector" of the American electronics industry. Some people involved have earned $1 million or more a year. One high-tech international middleman shipped to the USSR falsely labeled equipment through two unrelated conduits: a phony freight forwarding company at Zurich airport and a Hong Kong import-export firm. The Soviets even tried to buy three banks in California in order to get information on the finances of companies and their executives. This is legal, and, though foiled by a CIA officer who noted a peculiar lending pattern by the Singapore branch of a Soviet bank, could be successful on another try. Perhaps it already is. Former CIA officers tried to obtain and divert to the USSR an American computer program used in electronic intelligence gathering.[32]

Clearly, the Soviets have learned how to manipulate the openness of American society, the poor security of many firms, and the problems and greed of some citizens. One wonders if the Soviets have not found interesting work for some of their former students trained in American business schools.

Controls

The United States, along with its NATO and other allies, has reimposed controls on technology transfer so as to at least inhibit Soviet acquisition of military and strategic technology and equipment. This is not easy in the face of the large-scale Soviet acquisition program, the difficulty of clearly identifying what ought to be or can be controlled, bureaucratic infighting within the American government, as well as differences between the U.S. government and its allies. Nevertheless, these new curbs have no doubt crimped, though not stopped, the flow of key technology to the Soviet Union. An important institution in the control process is the Coordinating Committee for Export Controls (COCOM), with fifteen member countries including Japan. COCOM determines what militarily relevant products and technologies should be controlled, reviews requests to ship doubtful items, and coordinates the administration of export control and its enforcement.[33]

The return to export controls stemmed from two or three interrelated factors: the attainment by the Soviet Union of military equality with the United States and the concerns this engendered, the entry of the Reagan administration, and "a massive public campaign stressing the spectacular cases" of technology leakage, which changed the Western political climate regarding exports to the East.[34]

Export control still faces problems and limitations, however. COCOM cannot limit exports and "re-exports" by non-members, the requirement of unanimity for its decisions limits its power, and there is fundamental philosophical disagreement between the Reagan administration and the other members.

A German specialist says the idea that tightened controls over technology might restore American military primacy is part of "some kind of nostalgia" and warns against "exercises in futility" and "self mutilating" actions. Too many controls will impede Western scientific cooperation and innovation, he adds. Becoming as restrictive as the Communists is only "importing the rope from the East." Risky inconsistency is noted, too, since China, still Communist-led, is allowed technology the Soviets are denied. One of the leading American proponents of increased controls, Richard Perle, a former assistant secretary of defense, admits that "despite its best efforts, the Pentagon has found it impossible to isolate precisely the Western 'component' in Soviet weaponry...." Europeans were particularly angered by the United States government's attempt to enforce controls on European companies. This raised the touchy questions of "extraterritorial reach," of American laws versus European sovereignty, and the loss of European businesses' professional secrets to Americans.[35] In the 1980s Europeans have said they would agree to stop the export of many more items if the United States would stop exporting grain to the USSR, something that is probably politically impossible for the Americans to do.

The United States has also imposed new restrictions of its own. They were begun by the Carter administration, when the White House began getting involved in the approval and denial of Soviet requests for technological export licenses. By 1981 the Reagan administration had Operation Exodus in effect, with the Customs Service focused on the issue. By 1984 twenty categories of know-how were prohibited from export to the Soviet Union.

The tightened controls over technology exports probably were well received by the public at large but produced some opposition from American business. The new export regulations for computers, for example, caused "widespread confusion" in the industry, and certain agencies instituted more restrictions than had been called for. Businessmen pointed out that export control would make American products less competitive, while labor leaders and elected officials complained about lost jobs. Universities and scholarly associations were concerned that research would be hampered.[36] What had seemed like a simple solution had many negative domestic ramifications.

Whatever is done, it must be recognized that "it will always be difficult to maintain fully effective control over flows out of an open society," that the United States does not have a monopoly on high technology, and that it is almost impossible that the transfer of technology would "immediately up-end the current military balance."[37] National power does not rest on a single factor. Besides, in the time it takes the USSR to assimilate and apply foreign technology the foreign source will have developed still better technology.

Thus it may be best to "focus controls on those situations (such as trade in technology that shortens military lead times) where a clear and present danger is demonstrable."[38]

A key part of any technology control and denial strategy is maintaining effective cooperation with all major sources in implementing it. This means with

Europe and Japan. The Reagan administration has done this to some degree, but it is not clear that it can maintain it. It wants to push further than the Europeans, who are justifiably skeptical that actual Soviet behavior can be altered and that controls can be equitably administered. Trade and cooperation among the countries of the West must not be sacrificed on the altar of technology denial. This outcome would damage the security of the U.S. and other democracies far more than any technology loss could. Perhaps the United States needs a new, fuller sense of what security is. Technology control is part, but not all, of security. Perhaps it would be wiser to do more to stay ahead and not worry too much about falling behind. A balance, a "golden mean" between control and innovation must be sought and maintained.[39] This will require more sustained cooperation between agencies of the American government than has often been the case, particularly between the Departments of Defense, Commerce, and State, as well as between these agencies and the intelligence community.

Sanctions

The matter of sanctions, or blanket denial of goods and know-how, merits brief discussion. Whereas controls only prohibit export of certain items within general categories, sanctions are meant to stop all items in a category from going to a particular country. Sanctions may include boycotts, blockades, embargoes, full or partial, as well as denial of credits or the blockage of assets. They seem to be a typically American response to Soviet actions Americans find particularly offensive. Possibly sanctions are grounded in a Puritanical tradition of cutting oneself off completely from an offender. Although sanctions have ostensibly been used to try to change Soviet behavior, in actuality they have been prompted by mass political attitudes in the United States demanding punishment of the Soviet Union. Sanctions are an attempt at shunning or banning an entire country. The only such attempt directed at Americans has been the OPEC oil embargo of 1973, a punishment of the United States for its support of Israel. There are five countries with which the United States now virtually bans trade: Cambodia, Cuba, Libya, North Korea, and Vietnam. China was once one of them. South Africa may become one.

Two outstanding recent examples of this method of limiting American-Soviet trade are the sanctions the United States imposed on the USSR after its invasion of Afghanistan in late 1979 and those put into effect after the Soviet-backed military coup in Poland in late 1981 that eliminated the Solidarity organization from Polish public life.

In 1979 the Carter administration imposed various sanctions on the USSR, including an embargo on 17 million tons of grain contracted for, the limitation of Soviet airline flights, the suspension of all validated export licenses to the USSR, and the boycott of the 1980 Olympic Games in Moscow. President Carter told Congress he felt it was his responsibility to make the Soviets realize they could not invade countries with impunity. "The Soviets had to suffer the consequences," he added.[40] It was the first direct Soviet military move outside their recognized sphere since 1945 and thus raised the question of whether additional such moves were in the offing. That Afghanistan had already been conceded, in effect, to the USSR in the 1950s was unknown or forgotten.

The next round of American sanctions against the USSR occurred after the Polish military coup, with the Reagan administration in office. Sanctions imposed on Poland included: banning shipments of agricultural products, ending Polish fishing in American waters and suspending landing rights of the Polish airline. Sanctions imposed on the USSR included ending Soviet landing rights completely, not renewing the cultural exchange agreement, suspending sales of oil and gas technology and the validation of export licenses for high technology, and, most important, banning the sale of equipment for the Soviet gas pipeline to Europe. But the Reagan administration was inconsistent; at the same time it imposed sanctions, it decided to sign a new grain agreement with the USSR.[41]

After the Soviets shot down the Korean Airlines plane in 1983, there were few possible sanctions left for the United States to impose. Another limitation of unilateral sanctions became apparent. Not only do they not change Soviet behavior, but the United States can run out of sanctions short of actual military action. Thus, two administrations had played their cards to no desired effect. Instead, Soviet-American trade plummeted, America's European allies were aggrieved by certain spinoffs of the sanctions, the United States had undercut its image as a superpower, and high-level Soviets including the general secretary were talking about limiting trade with the West. There is no evidence that sanctions made the Soviet Union hold back from anti-Western actions.

Despite its great power, the United States lacks the ability to change Soviet behavior through sanctions, even if they are total. This is partly because United States-Soviet trade is always too small for its disruption to cause real difficulties for the USSR. To be effective, sanctions must cause a failure of will within the government against which they are imposed. Instead, they usually stiffen that will and sour relations in general. It will be interesting to see what Western and United States sanctions do to the will of the South African government. None of the past American uses of economic sanctions have achieved significant foreign policy objectives.[42]

Future American attempts to use trade for political purposes should rely on hard bargaining rather than total sanctions. Limited sanctions might be useful, however, if they are imposed quickly in response to particular Soviet actions. A sharp response to a particular Soviet move tends to make the Kremlin cautious about repeating the move for a time. It is important to avoid appearing to lack determination. One specialist suggests that sanctions be made effective "only for a certain period of time, specified at the outset. . . ." A significant long-term avoidance of trade with the USSR, though it might slow down Soviet development, is unlikely to make it easier to deal with.[43]

COOPERATIVE AGREEMENTS AND
JOINT PROJECTS

The main impetus to this form of interaction was the 1972 Nixon trip to the Soviet Union. By 1974 at least eleven cooperative agreements had been signed by the two superpowers, creating some seventy joint projects between them. These included public health projects, environmental protection and energy programs, and artificial heart research. Although most have not developed as intended, one joint project has been rather spectacular—the joint docking in space of the American Apollo and Soviet Soyuz satellites in 1975.

Cooperative ventures were based on a feeling that détente, to develop, had to be as broad as possible and correspond with the wishes of both Soviet and American scientists to profit from each other's research. Fundamentally, since the entire world now faces some of the same problems and challenges, from pollution and other forms of environmental degradation to climatic changes and plant diseases, cooperation across ideological lines in dealing with these issues will facilitate their solution.

The cooperative agreements suffered from the same suspicions and attacks that undermined détente. But, despite the difficulties inherent in cooperation between the very different Soviet and American social systems, American working groups involved in these cooperative efforts reported benefits to American science ranging from "modest" to "a considerable amount of rethinking of technical approaches."[44] This does not mean that the Soviet participants cooperated easily, satisfactorily, or fully. They often did not. The National Academy of Sciences noted, for example, six-month delays in Soviet responses to correspondence and the apparent need of Soviet participants for face-to-face encounters with American participants for effective communication. In the joint work on space the Soviet side allowed American astronauts to see the Soyuz prior to liftoff "only under duress." But this was to be expected. The Russo-Soviet system, so secretive for centuries, cannot adopt new ways overnight.

Although the U.S. suspended most of the cooperative efforts after the Soviet invasion of Afghanistan, some have continued. For example, a joint study of arthritis among children was completed in 1985. A special Soviet satellite has been very useful in locating American planes downed in remote areas. In 1985 the National Academy of Sciences held a seminar, "Steps to Mars," at which the Soviet and American astronauts who met in space in 1975 were reunited and a joint mission to Mars was informally discussed. At about the same time, a congressional study concluded that valuable scientific gains could flow from renewed American-Soviet space cooperation, and without risk of technology loss for the United States.[45]

At their first summit meeting in Geneva in 1985, Reagan and Gorbachev approved a new agreement on joint work on environmental protection, including study of the effects of acid rain on forests and of the effects of pesticides on animals. The American negotiator of the accord said, "We have shown that two countries with very different political systems can, in fact, cooperate on a very important problem to achieve pragmatic results." In 1985 the 1972 accord on environmental influences on climate was extended for ten more years and the earlier agreement on agricultural cooperation was also resumed. The most interesting new cooperative effort is a private one, however. Small teams of Soviet and American scientists in both countries began to use seismometers to monitor nuclear test sites. The United States will gain valuable data on how the Soviet test site's geology transmits shock waves, enabling much more accurate monitoring in the future and perhaps ultimately allowing a new arms control agreement to be very well verified. Although the effort is officially private, it was facilitated by both governments.[46]

This shows what is possible in cooperation among the superpowers. Significantly, despite the harsh rhetoric and the global competition between them in the early 1980s, by mid-decade, and with a strongly anti-Communist president in office in the United States and a determined Soviet leader, the superpowers were again increasing their level of mutual cooperation.[47] The further development of this cooperation awaits a fundamental change in superpower relations that can probably be realized only through a new and mutually favorable strategic arms control agreement. We now come to a related sphere of cooperation—exchanges of persons.

Cultural Exchanges

This broad category of activities began in 1958 and has never stopped, although the numbers of people and groups involved have fluctuated in accordance with the overall superpower relationship. The exchanges have been called a barometer of United States-Soviet relations. Essentially, what is involved here are stays of one country's citizens in the other country, from short periods to a year or even more. The fundamental idea behind exchanges is the hope that international suspicions and hatreds can eventually be reduced and even transformed into friendly feelings by individuals, non-official persons who represent their countries' societies, not their governments or ideologies. The development of networks of personal contacts and of personal insights about the other people may at least begin to cut through the curtain of suspicion, fear and politicized perception that has beclouded United States-Soviet relations.

Or so it is hoped. But can the exchange of only a relatively few people, no matter how interesting, talented, well intentioned, friendly, and nonpolitical they may be, create a new and more positive relationship between superpowers with long-term divergent and conflicting interests? Or do exchanges serve only as shock absorbers for the inevitably bumpy and erratic course United States-Soviet relations must travel?[48] The fact that the cultural exchanges between the United States and the USSR have never ceased, even when formal agreements were not renewed, suggests that the exchanges are seen by both superpowers as useful ties that are not to be broken.

The content of these exchanges is diverse: performing artists, exhibits, scholars and students, public diplomacy, media, sport, and tourism.[49] Government officials, legislators, politicians, and military officers could be added to this list. For example, the United States Congress and the Supreme Soviet have exchanged delegations of members, and during the Carter administration even exchanges of groups of military officers took place.

Tourism between the superpowers has always been limited and one-sided. Until recently, only 100,000 Americans per year or fewer have been tourists in the USSR. Perhaps only one in every thirty Americans who go to Europe visits the USSR. Most of these Americans see only Moscow and Leningrad, not any of the non-Russian or rural areas of the country, and most cannot speak Russian. Only about a thousand Soviet citizens visit the United States each year. Most such "tourists" are really on *komandirovki* or official missions since ordinary Soviets lack both permission and currency for trips to *kapstrany* (capitalist countries). Probably any considerable expansion of Soviet-American tourism awaits a much calmer and more developed relationship overall as well as an unlikely relaxation of Soviet travel controls.

The exchanges could begin only after Stalin died in 1953. Official American attempts to establish exchanges during World War II produced no results. Finally in 1955, the year of an international meeting of heads of government, the Soviet Union invited a traveling American theater company to put on *Porgy and Bess* while a leading Soviet pianist and a violinist toured the United States. The next year several American scholars were allowed to do research in the USSR.

Government-to-government negotiations for a cultural exchange agreement began in 1957 and were concluded in 1958, with the signing of an agreement that was usually renewed every few years. After Afghanistan in 1979 the exchanges continued in reduced form without an agreement. Despite the sanctions imposed on the USSR, then Secretary of State Vance noted that "we have sought to avoid dismantling the framework of exchanges and cooperative activity developed with such great effort over the years." The Soviets, too, did not want to lose the scientific and other benefits of the exchanges.

Although the exchanges have always involved mainly private citizens and organizations on the American side, the Soviets insisted on a formal intergovernmental agreement. In this way, the Soviet penchant for formality was met and, more important, exchanges were made to imply equality between the superpowers, a long-term Soviet aim. Other objectives of the USSR in approving exchanges were: to gain access to American science and technology, to demonstrate its strides in modernization, to control and gain from the pent-up Soviet demand for foreign travel, and to acquire foreign currency. On the American side, both government and the universities wanted to learn more about the Soviet Union. Two generations of American specialists on Russia had never seen their object of study. The lead time for training a generation of Soviet specialists is about the same as for developing a generation of missiles. It is important not to become dependent on the Soviets for interpreters or to lose American credibility by having scholars who do not know the USSR first-hand.[50] At bottom, American policymakers wanted to reduce tensions and begin to influence Soviet society, in however small a way, by stimulating the free flow of information and ideas.[51]

Although fewer than a thousand people were exchanged annually during the early years by each side, real progress was made in achieving dialogue between professionals, laying ground rules and learning how to work with each other. Many American private organizations became involved in direct ex-changes of their own, including the YMCA, 4-H Clubs, bar associations, the U.S. Conference of Mayors, and librarians. Many exhibits and performing artists have toured the two countries, and some have been seen by millions on television.

The exchange for undergraduates is mostly "one-way." Although about 350 American students each year study Russian in the USSR under two programs, the Soviets have only begun to send undergraduates and secondary school students to study in the United States. There are two small Fulbright programs—an exchange of ten university lecturers and of five graduate students or young specialists in the fine arts. There are also exchanges between a limited number of American and Soviet academic institutions. The central scholarly exchange programs involve the exchange of about 180 American academics per year for visits of from one week to a year or two. Thirty-five of these are teachers of Russian, with an equal number of Soviet teachers of English coming to the United States. Between 1958 and 1983 about 1,700 Americans and the same number of Soviets were exchanged under these programs.[52] This is a very small number. The Chinese had more than 10,000 students in the United States in 1986.

Most Americans who go on the academic exchanges know Russian and have serious research projects. (The author went on the senior exchange in 1977.) These Americans must have great persistence, patience, and a sense of purpose for they must cope with great obstacles to, and even restrictions on, their work. But they are rewarded by the knowledge that comes from actually living inside the Soviet system, without the pleasant treatment and insulation with which the Soviets surround tourists and diplomats. When the author once told a retired Soviet colonel he had been in the USSR two months so far, he exclaimed, "You are now almost a Soviet!" The director of the main exchange program has said of these American scholars:

> They become sojourners in a land where the permanent struggle between cant and truth, between illusion and reality, brings them into daily collision with the most fundamental issues of values.... They return home with exquisitely heightened sensitivities to the contours of their own culture that few can experience who have not shared their journey.[53]

Alumni of this exchange have gained a realistic sense of how the Soviet Union functions—often with great bureaucratism and insensitivity—and of its many weaknesses as well as its strengths. Unfortunately, many American policy-makers have never been to the USSR and still see it in purely ideological and military terms that overemphasize its power.

We cannot know what effect life in America has had on the Soviet exchangees, who are no doubt selected on political as well as scholarly grounds. However, there must have been some effect. A Soviet chemist the author met by chance in the Lenin Library in Moscow bubbled over with happiness in describing his year spent at an American university—but he literally fled when someone else came within earshot. People like him come much closer to understanding the essence of America than the Soviet diplomats and KGB operatives in Washington and at the U.N.

The exchanges probably contribute, in a small way and over the long term, to a better United States-Soviet relationship. Still, the scholarly exchanges face real problems. American applicants are sometimes rejected by the Soviets because of their topics. Contemporary politics and economic processes are considered secret by the Soviets. Asymmetry is present here too. The Soviet side sends mainly scientists and engineers while most American exchangees are in Russian history, literature, or linguistics.

Problems such as these have occasionally resulted in calls by US politicians for a limitation on the exchanges until the Soviets become more open and forthcoming and for controls on access to military technology by Soviet scholars. Controls on the exchanges cut both ways. The president of the National Academy of Sciences says there are scientific fields in which Americans have a lot to learn from Soviet scientists. A Nobel Prize winner in physics at Stanford says that in condensed matter physics the Soviets are extremely strong and have been "very open."[54]

At present, exchanges between the superpowers, like their relations in general, are creeping back to a better state that could be dubbed "détente without détente." President Reagan called for "the broadest people-to-people exchanges in the history of American-Soviet relations," involving the yearly exchange of thousands of undergraduates and even children as well as increased athletic competition. "If we must compete, let it be on the playing fields and not on the battlefields," said the president.[55] At their first summit meeting Reagan and Gorbachev initiated six "people-to-people" exchange initiatives plus a new cultural accord. Soon a series of draft agreements were worked out and in mid-1986 it appeared that a new era of exchanges was about to blossom. The Cable News Network signed an agreement on exchange of journalists and programs, a "first"; and in the art world, Impressionist paintings from the USSR were temporarily exchanged for similar paintings from the National Gallery. But there were still limits. The list of 300 American books at the Moscow International Book Fair in 1985 might have been ideologically one-sided, with books by conservatives and neo-conservatives omitted—due partly to Soviet bans and partly to caution by the organizers, who did not want the whole list to be excluded by the Soviets.

It is too early to present a "balance sheet" of the exchanges in terms of the American national interest. Yet they have opened up a "second channel" of communication between the two superpowers' *societies* in addition to the discourse between governments. Also significant is that at least a few persons who know the other country firsthand are now in important positions in both governments. Moreover, American colleges and universities now have specialists in Russian affairs who know the country, at least to the degree possible given Soviet restrictions.

The Soviets may have gained more from the exchanges than have the Americans. Through them they have legitimated their regime to a degree and gained technological advantages. Yet, to do this, they have had to let some people out who are not political hacks. This may have a normalizing effect on Soviet life.

ISSUES AND DEBATE

There are no answers here. Everything relating to American-Soviet trade, cooperative agreements, and cultural exchanges is continually under debate in the United States. Here are a few of the issues.

Is United States-Soviet trade necessary or even beneficial to the United States?

Is such trade in the American national interest?

Those taking the "con" side can emphasize the low overall volume of such trade or its small share in GNP. Others would argue a bit differently, saying it is best not to encourage dependency on a partner that is ideologically opposed to the United States and what it stands for.

Those arguing "pro" would point out that some sectors of the American economy, such as grain farmers and computer, machine tool, and fertilizer manufacturers, really need Soviet business and that we ought not to sacrifice our economic interests to ideology or some sort of trade war. President Reagan's second secretary of commerce has said that America "shoots itself in the foot" by imposing export controls on East-West trade.

Does trade give the United States leverage over Soviet policies and, if it does, should it not be used?

This brings up sanctions and the "food weapon." Those who answer yes argue that the problems posed by the USSR are so vital for the United States that we must at least try to use trade as leverage, if not as a weapon. Since the USSR buys from us, it must need what it buys. Let us "put it to them" and get changes in their policy that reduce the differences and dangers between us. This is only prudent. Continued trade with no *quid pro quos* only strengthens the Soviet Union as it is—an opponent.

Those against using leverage claim that there is none. The Soviets can get along without our trade. They have done so in the past—and grown in power. Soviet-American trade barriers only result in economic costs for the United States—and perhaps social costs such as unemployment as well. The United States is unable to restrict trade effectively in any case. And are not such efforts at leverage only spurs to more conflict? Let trade continue, to heal disagreement or at least mute it, and begin the building of a structure of confidence between us.

Is trade between the superpowers immoral?

Those who agree point out that Soviet workers are grossly underpaid, without real unions and lack a meaningful vote as well. Moreover, prison labor is often used to construct plants and other infrastructure. This means Soviet products, and trade in them, are morally tainted and also underpriced. The Soviets engage in "dumping," to the detriment of our own workers.

Those who disagree might reply, "But if we don't trade with them, someone else will." Or, "Yes, they do things that are wrong, but they are most likely to respond to our human rights concerns if we are trading with them rather than trying to isolate them." Others advocate a step-by-step increase in trade in accordance with improvements that might occur in the Soviet human rights situation.

Can trade be conducted without undue technology loss?

Those who say no hold that the Soviet effort, open and covert, in technology acquisition is so massive and effective it cannot be countered except by stopping almost all trade in items of high technology content, e.g., computers. Even if the Soviets are "a few steps behind," they are still keeping up with us and in some ways are ahead, e.g., in numbers of weapons and in throw-weight. Look at what the Japanese have done with our technology.

Those who answer yes emphasize the inefficiency of the USSR in using foreign technology, the harm that broad and strict controls over technology transfer would do to American technological and industrial operations, and the need to control only technology of obvious military relevance, not all high technology or computers in general.

Do we have to pay the Soviets in order to trade with them?

Those opposed do not want to grant most-favored-nation status to the Soviets or lend them money at low interest rates. By doing so, they argue, we are giving them a break we ought to reserve only for friendly countries that operate on economic principles similar to ours. Also, why should we subsidize Soviet inefficiency and rigidity? If they want more trade with us, let them normalize their economy and government.

Others would argue that change to a freer arrangement in the USSR can come about only by giving the Soviets economic incentives to trade with us. Otherwise, they will trade with other Western countries that give them such incentives, and we lose business, or they will simply remain semi-independent economically and the whole world loses.

What is the benefit to us and our principles by allowing cultural exchanges? Some say the exchanges do not benefit the United States at all. They only serve the anti-American and anti-democratic interests of the USSR by facilitating its industrial espionage and propaganda and make it seem "friendly" when it is really as anti-American as ever. If we allow exchanges we must get back something worthwhile: human rights improvements and full reciprocity and access for our scholars and students. An exchange of paintings or even jazz groups does nothing to change the realities of superpower politics.

Others would say that only large-scale exchanges of people will begin to dispel suspicions bred during decades of mistrust. People-to-people contacts break the bonds imposed by purely political thinking. Most people do not "buy" ideology anyway; they only want reduced tensions and a chance of a better life secure from war. And exchanges benefit us, too. They give us the chance to get some of our values and even publications past the iron curtain, they facilitate a relaxation of the Soviet system and perhaps even begin its democratization.

SUMMARY

As this brief listing of issues suggests, Soviet-American trade and cultural exchanges will not face a smooth road. The American polity cannot, in contrast to the British or West German, easily accept trade and normal contacts with a country that routinely engages in violations of human rights as a necessary condition of its existence. West German-Soviet trade has been a major pillar of East-West trade.[56] The British tend to see trade as necessary to Britain's well-being and as separable from ideological considerations or preferences. Not so most Americans. In other words, American concern with trade with the Soviet Union is not a function of anti-communism or great power rivalry alone. It has specifically American cultural roots in active dislike of inhumane and undemocratic governments. Further, the United States is unlikely ever to have a "normal" economic relationship with the USSR since Soviet thinking about trade is based heavily on politico-military factors.[57] Soviet ideological aims, however unlikely of realization, are stated openly.

> Unquestionably, the socialist states' consistent course aimed at expanding equitable and mutually advantageous business ties with the capitalist countries ... makes an important contribution to increasing the influence of real socialism on these countries and on their revolutionary forces.[58]

Thus, Soviet-American trade is meant partly to "soften up" the United States and also, it is stated, get the Americans and the West to help finance Soviet-backed revolutionary systems, now getting 20–70 percent of their foreign aid from the West.

But the fundamental limitation on United States-Soviet trade is Soviet determination to remain free of dependency on foreigners. The Soviets may have little choice in any case: because of central planning, an inconvertible currency, and refusal to allow foreign investment they are unable to trade at appreciably higher levels. Trade may well increase, but only on a highly selective basis. To the extent the USSR itself and the countries of East Central Europe cannot meet the Soviets' economic needs there will be a tendency to look to the West.[59] But with the severe reduction in Soviet hard currency earnings brought about by the sharp fall in oil prices, "Soviet buying from the West is likely to be severely constrained," except for grain imports and selective purchases of machinery for high-priority re-equipping of existing plants.[60] Still, in 1987 the Soviets were discussing proposals for joint ventures with several large American companies. A real change is that part of such ventures' profits in foreign currency can be transferred out of the USSR by the American firms. The USSR is also trying to join GATT and other international trade organizations.[61]

The coming years will see both objections to trade between the two superpowers as well as calls for increasing it. Industries that stand to benefit and profit from it will press for it, as will those who see it as the best way "to develop common interests" that go well beyond trade itself. Those who want to stay well apart from the Soviet Union or who want to oppose it will point out the dangers of trade. Still others will emphasize the great gap between trade and the solution of historic conflicts between states. "Societies have needs which push them toward rapprochement, while states respond to national interests which push them toward separation."[62] Clearly, there are both costs and benefits to superpower trade. Perhaps the American goal should be to minimize these costs and maximize the benefits without threatening trade or superpower relations overall.

REFERENCES

1. Thomas H. Naylor, "For more trade with the Russians," *New York Times*, 17 December 1984, 23; James H. Giffen, reported in *Daily Hampshire Gazette* (Northampton, MA), 13 April 1985, 1. Naylor is a professor of Business Administration at Duke University and Giffen negotiated the 1976 contract for structural steel from Armco for the trade center in Moscow.
2. Raymond Aron, *The Committed Observer* (Chicago: Regnery Gateway, 1983), 230.
3. Zbigniew Brzezinski, "Trade and Ideology," *Newsweek*, 13 December 1971, 56. These words have held up well over the years.
4. *Pravda*, 24 February 1981, 5 and 27 March 1981, 2–3, quoted in Philip Hanson, "Foreign Economic Relations," in Archie Brown and Michael Kaser, *Soviet Policy for the 1980s* (Bloomington: Indiana University Press, 1982), 91, 92.
5. See Chapter 12, "The Pepsi Generation," in Joseph Finder, *Red Carpet* (New York: Holt, Rinehart and Winston, 1983); ibid., 207; *New York Times*, 11 November 1982.
6. Hanson, 67–68; Franklyn D. Holzman, *International Trade Under Communism*

(New York: Basic Books, 1976), 209; *New York Times*, 30 March 1986, A-13. Soviet sources have claimed foreign trade has a somewhat higher share in the GNP, e.g., S. Pomazanov "Business Cooperation Between the USSR and the West," *International Affairs* (Moscow), 3 (March 1979): 38.

7. British government statistics derived from the Soviet journal *Foreign Trade* no. 3, (1984); *New York Times*, 14 December 1984, A-3; 30 March 1986, A-13; 6 January 1986, D2; and 27 December 1984, D-14; and U.S. Department of Commerce, *Survey of Current Business* (February, 1987): 17.

8. Marshall Goldman, *Détente and Dollars* (New York: Basic Books, 1975), 4.

9. Ibid., 14, 17.

10. Angela E. Stent, "Technology Transfers in East-West Trade," *American Enterprise Institute Foreign Policy and Defense Review* 5, 2 (1985): 47.

11. Daniel Yergin, "Politics and Soviet-American Trade," *Foreign Affairs* 55, 3 (April 1977): 522 and 523.

12. S. Pomazanov, 42.

13. Hanson, 72 and Zigmunt Nagorski, Jr., *The Psychology of East-West Trade* (New York: Mason and Lipscomb, 1974), 203.

14. Hanson, 78; Brzezinski, "Trade and Ideology"; Jean-Francois Revel in Nagorski, x; Nagorski, xxiii and 195; Goldman, 72–75.

15. See Hanson on the windfall profits, 68–69; 161–66 of Richard J. Barnet, *The Giants*, (New York: Simon and Schuster, 1977); and Joseph Albright, "Some Deal," *New York Times Magazine*, 25 November 1973, 36ff.

16. Holzman, *International Trade Under Communism*, 125.

17. See Roger B. Porter, *The U.S.-USSR Grain Agreement* (New York: Cambridge University Press, 1984), Appendix D.

18. *New York Times*, 21 October 1977, D-1; Radio Liberty Research 86/79, 9 March 1979 and RL 381/80, 14 October 1980; Hanson, 77 and 79.

19. *New York Times*, 26 August 1983, A-1 and D-4 (text of agreement).

20. *New York Times*, 16 November 1982, D6; *The Economist*, 9 March 1985, 68; *U.S. News & World Report*, 7 February 1983, 41–42.

21. *U.S. News & World Report*, 7 February 1983; *New York Times*, 27 June 1985, A-3. For discussion of Soviet American cultural and other differences in their trade relationship see: Edward Beliaev, et al., "Understanding the Cultural Environment: U.S.-USSR Trade Negotiations," *California Management Review* 27, 2 (Winter 1985): 100–112; and U.S. CIA, *Soviet Strategy and Tactics in Economic and Commercial Negotiations With the United States* (Washington, DC: National Foreign Assessment Center, CIA June 1979). A West European businessman with many years experience dealing with the Soviets tells me this report is basically correct.

22. L.S. Eagleburger, *High Technology and American Foreign Policy*, (Washington, DC: AEI, 1985), 6; U.S. Congressional Research Service, Library of Congress, *Technology Transfer and Scientific Cooperation Between the United States and the Soviet Union: A Review* (Washington, DC: GPO, 1977), 57–60.

23. *U.S. News & World Report*, 17 January 1983, 56–57; *Wall Street Journal*, 21 March 1980, 1, 35; lecture, Kennan Institute, Washington, DC, 15 November 1985; and *New York Times*, 16 December 1986, C-1. I am indebted to Dr. Christine H. Teixeira for pointing out the importance of reverse technology transfer.

24. Holzman, 146–147; Hanson in Brown and Kaser, 1982, 72; B. Bessonov, "The Scientific and Technological Revolution and the Ideological Struggle," *International Affairs* (Moscow), 2 (1974): 65.
25. *New York Times*, 19 May 1985, E-5 and 23 February 1983.
26. *New York Times*, 1 October 1982, A-1 and A-11.
27. U.S. Government, *Soviet Acquisitions of Western Technology* (Washington, DC: GPO, 1982), 13–15.
28. John W. Vessey, Jr., (Gen. USA) "The Unrelenting Growth of Soviet Military Power," speech to the Economic Club of Chicago, 24 February 1983, in *Vital Speeches*, XLIX, 15 (15 May 1983): 457.
29. Holzman, 207
30. Source: an executive of the firm that supplied the machinery.
31. *New York Times*, 25 July 1983, Part Two of a three-part series on the KGB, 25 February 1981, A-15; and 19 September 1985.
32. *New York Times*, 5 October 1980, C-1; 4 February 1986, A-1 and 36; and 15 October 1981.
33. U.S. Department of State, "Controlling Transfer of Strategic Technology," *Gist*, April 1986.
34. Robert V. Roosa, et al, *East-West Trade at a Crossroads* (New York University Press, 1982), 80; Heinrich Vogel, "Technology for the East—the Tiresome Issue," *Aussen Politik* (English ed.), vol. 36, (February 1985): 123.
35. Vogel, 120–126. Perle's statement is from: Daniel Buchan, "Technology Transfer to the Soviet Bloc," *The Washington Quarterly* (Fall 1984): 132; *New York Times*, 23 January 1984, D-1 and 8.
36. *New York Times*, 8 February 1985, A-1 and D-3; 28 February 1984; 19 March 1984; D-1 and D-5; and 1 February 1982.
37. Roosa, 82; Nicholas Mavroules, "Denying Moscow High-Tech," *New York Times* 10 October 1983; Philip M. Boffey, "Assessing Technology Leaks," ibid. 2 January 1985, D-1 and 7.
38. Joseph S. Nye, Jr., "Can America Manage its Soviet Policy?" *Foreign Affairs*, 62, 4 (Spring 1984): 874.
39. These remarks are based upon: Roosa, 61; Stent, 51; William A. Root, "Trade Controls that Work," *Foreign Policy* 56 (Fall 1984): 61–80; Harold Brown, "Economic Policy and National Security," *Orbis* 26, 2 (Summer 1982): 386; and Vogel, 123 and 126.
40. Presidential Documents, vol. 16 (14 January 1980): 40–41. Cited in Raymond L. Garthoff, *Détente and Confrontation* (Washington, DC: Brookings Institution, 1985), 972. See also 952–953.
41. Garthoff, 1033–1034.
42. Robert Carswell, "Economic Sanctions and the Iranian Experience," *Foreign Affairs*, 60, 2 (Winter 1981–82): 260–264.
43. Garthoff, 970; and John G. Raley, "The Use of Economic Sanctions as a Political Weapon in U.S.-Soviet Relations," unpublished Ph.D. dissertation, Political Science, University of Massachusetts/Amherst, September 1986; and Bruce Parrott, "Conclusion," in *Trade, Technology, and Soviet-American Relations*, ed. Bruce Parrott (Bloomington: Indiana University Press, 1985), 362.
44. National Research Council, *Review of the U.S./USSR Agreement on Cooperation in*

the *Fields of Science and Technology* (Washington, DC; National Academy of Sciences, 1977), 5–8.
45. *New York Times*, 21 December 1984, A1; 17 July 1985, A9; and 18 July 1985, A-16.
46. *New York Times*, 13 December 1985, A-1 and 10; 10 February 1985, A27; 19 June 1985, A-8; and 6 July 1986, A-1 and 12.
47. A broad Soviet-American accord restoring scientific cooperation to a high level was signed in early 1988. See *New York Times*, 13 January 1988, A-1. See also U.S. Department of State, "U.S.-USSR Cooperative Scientific Exchanges," *Gist*, August 1987.
48. Dimitri Simes, lecture at Harvard University, 5 May 1986.
49. Yale Richmond, *Soviet-American Cultural Exchanges: Ripoff or Payoff?* (Washington, DC: Kennan Institute, 1984).
50. Kennan Institute, *U.S.-Soviet Exchanges* (Washington, DC: Wilson Center, 1985), 40, 42.
51. *Radio Liberty Research* 22/80, 11 January 1980; U.S. Department of State, *Far Horizons* 1, 4 (July 1968); letter of Secretary of State Cyrus Vance to J. K. Lombard, 6 March 1980; and Richmond, 3–6.
52. Richmond, 22–24.
53. Allen Kassof, "The American Scholar in the Soviet Union," *ACLS [American Council of Learned Societies] Newsletter*, XXXV, 3 and 4 (Summer-Fall 1984): 2.
54. *New York Times*, 4 May 1985, A-10, and 27 January 1981, C-3.
55. *New York Times*, 28 May 1986, Y-14; and 15 November 1985, A-1.
56. Jurgen Notzold, "Political Preconditions of East-West Economic Relations," *Aussen Politik* (English Ed.), vol. 36 January 1985: 50.
57. Gordon B. Smith, ed., *The Politics of East-West Trade* (Boulder, CO: Westview Press, 1984), 248.
58. Ya. S. Novopashin, "The Influence of Real Socialism on the World Revolutionary Process," *Voprosy filosofii* no. 8 (August 1982): 3–16. Abstracted in *Current Digest of the Soviet Process*, XXXV, 43 (23 November 1983): 10–11.
59. Bernt Conrad, *Die Welt*, 19 July 1984; translated in *The German Tribune*, 5 August 1984, 2; Holzman, 208.
60. Philip Hanson, "Prospects for Soviet-Western Trade in the Late 1980s," *Radio Liberty Research* RL 150/86, 9 April 1986. Hanson is referring to Gorbachev's speech of 11 June 1985 and Ryzhkov's Speech to the 27th Party Congress in 1986.
61. *New York Times*, 19 November 1987, D-2 and 20 January 1988, A-1 and D-28.
62. Yergin, 538; and Jean-Francois Revel, Introduction, Nagorski, xii.

SELECT BIBLIOGRAPHY

Bertsch, Gary K. and John R. McIntyre, eds. *National Security and Technology Transfer: The Strategic Dimensions of East-West Trade*. Boulder, CO: Westview Press, 1983.
Bornstein, Morris. *East-West Technology Transfer: the Transfer of Western Technology to the USSR*. Paris: OECD, 1985.
Brown, Lester R. *U.S. and Soviet Agriculture: The Shifting Balance of Power*. Washington, DC: Worldwatch Institute, 1982.
Byrnes, Robert F. *Soviet-American Academic Exchanges, 1958–1975*. Bloomington: Indiana University Press, 1976.

Carrick, R. J. *East-West Technology Transfer in Perspective*. Berkeley, CA: Institute of International Studies, University of California, 1979.

De Pauw, John W. *Soviet-American Trade Negotiations*. New York: Praeger, 1979.

Eagleburger, L. S. *High Technology and American Foreign Policy*. Washington, DC: American Enterprise Institute, 1985.

Finder, Joseph. *Red Carpet*. New York: Holt, Rinehart and Winston, 1983.

Gaer, Felice D. *Soviet-Ameican Scholarly Exchange: Should Learning and Politics Mix?* A Ford Foundation Reprint from *Vital Issues*, XXIX, 10 (June 1980).

Giffen, James Henry. *The Legal and Practical Aspects of Trade with the Soviet Union*. New York: Praeger, 1971.

Goldman, Marshall. *Détente and Dollars: Doing Business with the Soviets*. New York: Basic Books, 1975.

Gustafson, Thane. *Selling the Russians the Rope? Soviet Technology Policy and U.S. Export Controls*. Santa Monica, CA: The Rand Corporation, 1981.

Hamilton, Martha. *The Great American Grain Robbery and Other Stories*. Washington, DC: Agribusiness Accountability Project, 1972.

Hammer, Armand. *Hammer*. New York: Putnam's, 1987.

Hanson, Philip. *Trade & Technology in Soviet-Western Relations*. New York: Columbia University Press, 1981.

Hardt, John and George D. Holliday. *U.S.-Soviet Commercial Relations: The Interplay of Economics, Technology Transfer and Diplomacy*. Washington, DC: Committee on Foreign Affairs, United States House of Representatives, 1973.

Holzman, Franklyn D. *International Trade under Communism—Politics and Economics*. New York: Basic Books, 1976.

Jamgotch, Nish, ed. *Sectors of Mutual Benefit in U.S.-Soviet Relations*. Durham, NC: Duke University Press, 1985.

Kennan Institute for Advanced Russian Studies. *U.S.-Soviet Exchanges*. Washington, DC: Kennan Institute, 1985.

Kupferberg, Herbert. *The Raised Curtain*. New York: Twentieth Century Fund, 1977.

Levinson, Charles. *Vodka-Cola*. New York: Gordon and Cremonesi, 1978.

Melvern, Linda, David Hebditch and Nick Anning. *Techno-Bandits: How the Soviets Are Stealing America's High-Tech Future*. Boston: Houghton-Mifflin, 1985.

Nagorski, Zygmunt, Jr. *The Psychology of East-West Trade: Illusions and Opportunities*. New York: Mason & Lipscomb, 1974.

National Academy of Sciences. *Review of the US/USSR Agreement on Cooperation in the Fields of Science and Technology*. Washington, DC: 1977.

Parrott, Bruce, ed. *Trade, Technology, and Soviet-American Relations*. Bloomington: Indiana University Press, 1985.

Pisar, Samuel. *Coexistence and Commerce*. New York: McGraw-Hill, 1970.

Porter, Roger B. *The U.S.-USSR Grain Agreement*. New York: Cambridge University Press, 1984.

Raley, John G. "The Use of Economic Sanctions as a Political Weapon in U.S.-Soviet Relations." Unpublished Ph.D. dissertation, Political Science, University of Massachusetts/Amherst, 1986.

Richmond, Yale. *Soviet-American Cultural Exchanges: Ripoff or Payoff?* Washington, DC: Kennan Institute 1984.

Roosa, Robert V., Armin Gutowski and Michiya Matsukawa. *East-West Trade at a Crossroads*. New York: New York University Press, 1982.

Rosenblatt, Samuel M. *East-West Trade in Technology: A Purpose in Search of a Policy.* Washington, DC: International Economic Studies Institute, 1980.

Rositske, Harry. *Managing Moscow: Guns or Goods?* New York: Morrow, 1984.

Smith, Gordon. *Politics of East-West Trade.* Boulder, CO: Westview Press, 1984.

Sutton, A. C. *Western Technology and Soviet Economic Development.* 3 vols. Stanford, CA: Hoover Institution, 1969–1973.

U.S.CIA *Soviet Strategy and Tactics in Economic and Commercial Negotiations with the United States.* Washington, DC: National Foreign Assessment Center, CIA, 1979.

U.S. Congress, House Committee on Science and Technology. *Key Issues in U.S.-USSR Scientific Exchanges and Technology Transfer.* Washington, DC: GPO, 1979.

——, Subcommittee on International Finance and Monetary Policy. *East-West Trade and Technology Transfer.* Washington, DC: GPO, 1982.

——, Office of Technology Assessment. *Technology and East-West Trade.* Washington, DC: GPO, 1979.

——, *U.S-Soviet Cooperation in Space.* Washington, DC: GPO, 1985.

——, Senate, Permanent Subcommittee on Investigations. *Transfer of United States High Technology to the Soviet Union and Soviet Bloc Nations.* Washington, DC: GPO, 1982.

U.S Congressional Research Service, Library of Congress. *Technology Transfer and Scientific Cooperation between the United States and the Soviet Union: A Review.* Prepared for the Committee on International Relations. Washington, DC: GPO, 1977.

U.S. Government (operation EXODUS, originating agency anonymous). *Soviet Acquisition of Western Technology.* Washington, DC: GPO, April 1982.

Wilczynski, Josef. *The Economics and Politics of East-West Trade.* London: Macmillan, 1969.

Chapter 8

Contrasting Cultures, Domestic Politics, Public Opinion, and Diplomacy

> Never has there been a contest between two powers so fundamentally different.
>
> *Zbigniew Brzezinski*
>
> There cannot be many systems less well suited to deal with each other than the United States and the Soviet Union.
>
> *Henry Kissinger*
>
> I'll tell you why the Western Kreminologists are often wrong about Soviet foreign policy. They base their decisions too much on common sense.
>
> *Georgi Arbatov*
>
> The American believes that when there's a problem, there's always a solution.
>
> *Raymond Aron*
>
> ...in Russia, every difference of opinion carries in it the germ of a conspiracy.
>
> *Fitzroy Maclean*

CULTURE AND STYLE

Negotiations and interactions between rivals are always difficult, but they are especially troublesome and frustrating if the parties to the negotiations think differently, have different conceptions of normalcy, govern themselves and run their economies by opposing principles, and view each other as either enemies or untrustworthy and odd. This is just what we have in Soviet-American relations. To understand the origins of these differing thought patterns and opposing political and economic ideologies, we must explore the concept of national character, as determined by the culture of each of the superpowers. Culture may be defined as that complex of feelings and attitudes that the members of an ethnic group or national community share and act upon unthinkingly and automatically. It is a totality of "social usages" or ways of thinking and behaving that are rarely questioned from within a society. Once established, it has a powerful life of its own and has effects throughout social life—in work, in politics, and in technology. People can even be puppets of their cultures.[1] Not everyone in a nation, however, holds to that people's culture in the same way or to the same degree. There are always persons who are opposed to their own nation's culture, or to elements of it. This phenomenon is much more noticeable in the democratic United States than in the authoritarian Soviet Union, of course.

Political culture, or the common traditional and subjective orientations of people to politics, produces a distinctive political style for an entire society. A common political culture makes opposing political movements of a people similar in fundamental ways, even when their ideologies and goals are quite different. For example, in an established political system, two parties with very real differences on specific issues, such as taxation or the size of the military will usually share common attitudes toward key political values, the processes of politics, and the main governmental institutions. It is hard to find an American who wants to junk the United States Constitution or a Russian who is in favor of a small army. In other words, the mass of Americans and of Russians are each distinctive vis-à-vis the other in terms of the underlying political values that control, in an overall sense, the structure and operation of their countries' politics. Their political cultures differ strongly on such key political issues as: the place of the individual in politics, the scope and limits of governmental action, the nature of political authority, the problems posed by political dissidents, the security needs of the system, and others. The Americans seem the people of *glasnost* or openness, and Russians of secrecy.

This idea of cultural orientation to politics has been objected to on a number of grounds. It has been labeled racist, a myth, or vague. Its opponents, including Marxists, often claim class is more important for political behavior. Still others stress individual psychology as a major motivator in politics.

However, despite these problems and objections, it is generally recognized that one big underlying reason for the strained and oppositional nature of the Soviet-American relationship is the great difference in cultures of the American and Russian peoples as they carry over into their contacts and rivalry. Obviously, such differences trouble or alarm each other's peoples and leaders. Otherwise it might be possible for the Soviet-American rivalry to be handled coolly as a classic great power competition. Instead, it often becomes a moral issue for the Americans and a security issue for the Russians, with much emotionalism thrown in. It is no surprise then that throughout writings on

United States-Soviet relations there are often comments—sometimes critical, angry, or even despairing—on the problems caused for those relations by differences between the way Russians and Americans think, look at things, and act.

George F. Kennan has spoken of "the permanent environmental factors of the Soviet-American relationship"—differing traditions and customs, differing ways of looking at things, and differences in the ways the two peoples see themselves and each other.[2] These factors are cultural in origin.

Certainly, Khrushchev and Nixon, the Soviet and American leaders who tried to ignore American and Russian cultural differences and facilitate superpower agreement, came to grief. The Americans considered human rights issues too important to ignore, while Russians abhorred the reductions in the military and other basic changes Khrushchev was making, changes that Gorbachev is again attempting.

History lays a burden of experience on a people that is passed on from one generation to another. Russia went through a harsh revolution. Yet while it underwent outward industrial transformation, old concerns and patterns of behavior were reinforced. The Russian sense of uniqueness and the fear of outsiders were given support by Stalin's building of "socialism in one country." The old Russian tradition of a nation in arms was continued. Many thousands of Tsarist officers and bureaucrats were kept on by the revolutionary regime and old procedures and even laws were copied. "The new, revolutionary institutions carried the signs of an ancient heritage."[3] Once institutions were carried over, the thinking characteristic of them was given a new lease on life. In addition, the ethnic and geographical base of the Soviet Union remains about the same as it was before the revolution.

The people of the United States, too, have long considered themselves unique and their country as a special place to be kept apart from the corrupting influences of other philosophies and political systems. George Washington's warning in his Second Farewell Address is the standard political expression of this attitude applied to foreign policy. "Avoid foreign entanglements," he advised Americans. The American people have not been comfortable with their status as a superpower or with their ties to foreign countries. They remain culturally distinctive in politics and their ideological and political differences are minor in content and effect compared with those of many other peoples. This cultural continuity in politics and foreign policy has lasted despite the extraordinary physical transformation of the United States since 1945—suburbanization, shopping malls, the sexual revolution, the move to the Sun Belt, the appearance of feminism, the youth culture, the drug scene, omnipresent violent crime, and new protest movements centered on environmental and nuclear freeze issues.

The Russians and Americans share a few similarities in their political cultures—a feeling of superiority to foreigners, especially Europeans, a suspicion of foreign ways and thinking, a respect for technology, and a future orientation. This has never been sufficient for lasting cooperation, however, despite at least one attempt, by Franklin Roosevelt, to achieve some agreement with Stalin by stressing Russia's and America's common suspiciousness of the British. "The dominant culture of neither the Soviet Union nor the United States has much understanding of, and probably has strong prejudice against, the political and economic systems of the other."[4]

American Cultural Origins

The origins of the American distinctiveness in political culture probably lie in the predominance among the first English settlers of members of various religious sects that developed out of the Protestant Reformation. The Puritans and Quakers would be the most obvious examples. Political dissidents were common among them as well. Although the idea that conscience, grace, and individualism ought to be central to Christianity is a very old idea, its adherents had always been dubbed heretics and were repressed or even physically exterminated until a few European political systems came to allow such people a degree of toleration. But not until they came to North America were they able to become politically dominant in a territory where the institutions of the state and the army could be kept weak. Moreover, only in North America was it possible to construct an un-European social and political system with non-conformist Protestantism at its core. "Neither King nor Court nor Church could stretch over the ocean to the wild continent" where "the freedom of the wilderness whetted their appetites for more freedoms," says Theodore H. White.[5] With such origins, the United States has never been a thoroughly secular state. It is "a moral and ethical society without a state religion." Its public schools have long taught "a kind of generalized Protestantism as a form of 'character building.'" As Catholics and Jews, as well as antireligious people, became more numerous, a feeling that might be called "the spirituality of the Republic" partly replaced religion. But religion is still very important in American politics and has recently fostered a powerful reassertion of traditional moral values and conservative politics, showing that religion and politics are still organically linked in the United States as they were in the 1600s.[6] Three recent presidential candidates have theology educations: Jesse Jackson, Gary Hart, and Pat Robertson, and one, Paul Simon, is the son of a clergyman.

The religious basis of American culture combined with the almost unique historical experience of long-term physical isolation from unbeatable enemies. All of America's past opponents either went away, were conquered, or were defeated on their home ground, while the United States remained secure from attack. Accordingly, American culture refuses to accept either having opponents as a normal part of international life or the permanency of international rivalry. The leading Sovietologist Jerry Hough notes:

> The American elite and the American public have gained little of the perspective on international relations that is acquired in a long history of

involvement with countries that are equals. They have never really accepted that conflict in international relations is inevitable, that other countries' pursuit of their interests is normal and should not lead to moral outrage.[7]

It is not surprising, then, that "it is difficult for Americans to think of relations with the Soviet Union as a long-term process to be managed indefinitely rather than as a near-term problem to be 'solved.'"[8] One writer even says that Americans are still in thrall to a dangerous myth—"deliverance from evil"— instead of accepting serious conflict between persons and societies as natural.[9]

On top of a unique past there is a unique present. In brief, many Americans live too well and in too "American" a way—in comparison with most of the world's people—to have an easy understanding of life or foreign affairs elsewhere. The United States is unique in having almost half its people living in suburbs that are far from their places of work, in homes that they own on properties that are enormous by standards elsewhere.[10] Many Americans are wealthy but do not know it since they use American standards for comparison. In effect, the American middle class lives like an aristocracy of some Third World countries. Home equity accounts for a staggering 41 percent of the net worth of Americans, and 26.2 percent of white households have a median net worth exceeding $100,000.[11] Refuge-like suburban life may intensify American idealism and divorce from international realities as well as fear of socialism. No wonder Americans tend to have difficulty understanding the tumult in the world and why American dependence on foreign raw materials drives the United States to take conservative positions abroad and oppose the Soviet Union so strongly.[12] Clearly, any American government must protect the excessively high American standard-of-living or be in serious trouble at home. This also drives American suspicion of the Soviet Union since its ideology and policies put pressure on American private enterprise and capitalism.

All this worldly success and isolation from the rest of the world tend to give Americans great confidence in themselves and their country's power—even allowing them to think of war "more lightly than other people, discussing the options with a cheerful optimism and an abstract bloodthirstiness not found elsewhere, and entertaining theories of complete and lasting solutions." A former undersecretary of state cites a combination of "an undiscriminating commitment to physical violence" as an easy solution for problems plus "a compulsion to operate alone," like a cowboy, as distinguishing features of the popular American approach to foreign policy. It is as if Rambo were playing Trivial Pursuit, forgetting that the world of the TV news is indeed real for other people.[13]

In actual fact, however, these violent tendencies are rarely applied full force by the American government, which is constrained by social forces based on the milder side of American culture. Nevertheless, American political culture is extremely dualistic, both isolationistic and interventionist, for example, and not conducive to supporting a long-term stable foreign policy. For one thing, although the United States government often "brandishes" military force through deployments of one sort and another, it rarely uses that force in war itself. This sort of behavior suggests a big split or dualism in American political culture and society, and one that puzzles and worrries both friends and foes of the United States.

A number of specific American cultural features are continually cited as affecting United States foreign policy, including policy toward the Soviet Union. An "engineering approach" to politics, the feeling that any problem can be solved, is a reflection of the pragmatic way the United States has been developed. The American predilection for compromise is a reflection of long-standing domestic political practice in keeping together a large and multi-ethnic society. But a failure of compromise in foreign policy often results in an isolationistic rejection of the other party. The cold war is an example. In many other political systems, compromise is seen as a sign of weakness or lack of principle.

Legalism is another feature of American political culture. The search for a legalized and orderly world order has been a major theme of American foreign policy in this century. But in relations with the USSR, it is often charged, Americans are too prone to agree to deals that cannot last since for the Soviets agreements are merely temporary expedients, not permanent "laws" of inter-relations. Even Ronald Reagan, who was able to avoid giving in to legalistic proclivities during his first term, eventually began searching for an arms control agreement with the USSR in order to justify his administration in terms of basic American cultural feelings.

Another American cultural feature bedeviling United States-Soviet relations is the American unwillingness to accept people not from our main "source" civilizations—the British Isles, Germany, and Scandinavia. This old American prejudice may still live in an anti-Russian feeling underlying anti-communism.

Lastly, there is the pure dynamism and volatility of American culture. What is not an issue for years suddenly becomes a central problem in Soviet-American relations, e.g., the desire of many Jews to emigrate from the USSR. American culture, though continuous in its fundamentals, is extremely change-able in its political specifics. Accordingly, the United States often looks perfidious or at least undependable to the Soviets. "Why keep bringing up new issues and reopening agreements already made," they say. Americans would reply, in effect, "We cannot really get along until you are like us." "Too much to ask," the Soviets would answer.

Russian Cultural Origins

In turning to Russian political culture, we are aware that Russians are less than half the population of the Soviet Union. A leading specialist on Soviet society notes that "from a statistical viewpoint, I consider it [the USSR] as fifteen different countries" and that there is no "average Russian."[14] True, but the

Russian people is socially and politically dominant in the USSR and certain Russian cultural tendencies still operate powerfully on both the style and content of Soviet policies. Gorbachev, despite his apparent newness of style, is of Russian peasant background from an area of Russia with little contact with the West historically and might be best seen not as a "new" type but as a typical Russian who happens to have confidence and determination. In any case, he will have to operate mainly through Russians. He is the first Soviet leader since Stalin to praise "the great Russian people" as "an inspiring example" for what are, by implication, the lesser peoples of the USSR.

The Mongol and Byzantine sources of the Russian state resulted in an autocratic central government that was extraordinarily powerful vis-à-vis other potential domestic political forces. Neither the church nor the nobility could permanently limit the Russian monarch, the Tsar. Merchants and cities in Russia lacked the independent status they had in Europe. The peasantry remained enslaved and subject to sale by their masters until 1861. In addition, no revolt ever succeeded until 1917 and because of the Mongol conquest Russia missed passing through two of the cardinal events of the West—the Renaissance and the Reformation. There was no independent sphere. The Tsar upheld autocracy, orthodoxy, and Russian nationalism until history passed him by in 1917.

By the late seventeenth century, Russia had become a large multiethnic empire with an established tradition of expansion by conquest, and the military and civil bureaucracy to facilitate it. Russians tended to strongly support this imperial expansion and rule. Even many of Russia's great writers, men like Pushkin, Tolstoy, and Dostoevsky, who were at times opposed to aspects of the system, took part in Russia's conquests or supported them sincerely. Eventually, an "imperial consciousness" became part of Russian culture and may have grown into a "drive for global preeminence" despite continual protestations of peacefulness and expressions of insecurity, apparently sincere, by many Russians who, like people everywhere, tend to compartmentalize their thinking.[15]

It is ironic that the overthrow of Tsarism gave a new lease on life to many age-old traits of Russian political culture. They must have been deeply imbedded in many people's minds. Marxism did bring change, but its result was more that of a new attitudinal layer sandwiched in among the old layers of culture than a thoroughly victorious force. The Russian population, whatever its fascination with the blue jeans, video cassettes, and other elements of Western pop culture, is still very traditionally Russian in terms of political assumptions and values. The Russian population is still one that, by and large, accepts extremely centralized, arbitrary, and bureaucratized rule as normal and perhaps even necessary to avoid disorder, the fear of which seems to be very strong among Russians. The belief that Russia has a unique and special role in the world apparently also remains.[16]

Although Marxism is officially sponsored, it is a Russianized version also "rooted in the historical experience of centuries of absolutism" and may not be important for what Russians actually think.[17] Possibly "Marxism has been ritualized and incorporated as one element of an authoritarian political culture, the most potent ingredient of which is Russian statist nationalism...."[18] One long-term Western correspondent says that, "of all the ideas and beliefs and forces of allegiance that crisscross through Soviet society, patriotism is the most pervasive and the most powerful."[19] Even the word *Soviet*, with its revolutionary connotations, is now roughly equivalent to the old term *Rossiisky* or "Russia-wide." Marxism and Russian authoritarian, expansionist nationalism have merged.

There are a number of specific features of Russo-Soviet political culture that affect United States-Soviet relations, and Soviet foreign policy generally. Many seem of ancient origin, although some may have been affected by the Soviet regime and its Marxist ideology. First, there is that typically Soviet complex of insecurity, secretiveness, suspiciousness, and "demandingness." This cluster of attitudes and behavior first became a Soviet-American problem during World War II. What is at the core here is not clear. An American corporation executive with experience negotiating deals in more than fifty countries says that the Russians are the "most insecure people in the world"— and try to cover it up and compensate for it by keeping their demands high and being secretive about their goals.[20] One reason for the insecurity may be the fear of disorder and revolution of a multiethnic system held together ultimately by force. If Soviet political processes ever took a democratic course, the whole edifice would be put under severe strains and might collapse. In his excellent book on Soviet society, *The Russians*, Hedrick Smith presents an interesting diagram drawn by a Russian scientist picturing the almost-stark Russian fear of political freedom. In effect, politics is presented there as a very shallow bowl out of which the rolling "ball" of free politics would inevitably flip to disaster. Perhaps this explains what one British counter-espionage official calls "typically Russian paranoia about conspiracy and treachery."[21] Hence, suspicion and secretiveness are necessary to forestall disaster. These traits may be understandable, but they are very annoying, if not an affront, to Americans, who tend to think that free politics will work out well for everyone.

Another difficulty in the superpower relationship is Russian political quiescence and acceptance of authority, at least on the surface. It is difficult for Americans to feel safe with a rival that lacks a political opposition and the normal free flow of politics and apparently is not yearning for them either. Although the powerful Soviet control system of informers, security police, and repressive laws is usually seen as explaining Soviet political passivity, there may be a deeper, cultural answer—a general pattern of leaving politics to those trained for it and of believing Russia is always right. Many of the dissidents in the USSR have been non-Russian.

None of the foreign military interventions of recent decades—Hungary, Czechoslovakia, or Afghanistan—has produced any protest movement or even a mass protest attitude like that sparked in the United States by the Vietnam

War. After all, Russia was built by conscious military expansion, not by small groups of settlers who later called for military aid in securing their new property. Accordingly, Russians seem to be generally in agreement on the acceptability of using military force to maintain their position in the world. This cultural predilection naturally concerns Amercians. As a Polish ex-Communist once said to me, "The Russians refuse to negotiate with any people once it is inside the empire, although they are perfectly willing to negotiate with people who are still outside." Americans have been much less willing to rule foreigners, as shown by the withdrawals from the Philippines, areas of the Caribbean, Central America, and the interior of Mexico; although the Mexican border area, Puerto Rico, and Hawaii have been retained.[22]

Still, the acceptability of conquest by Russians is mitigated by a general fear of war and a strong aversion to taking risks. However, fear of war is used by the Soviet leadership to justify high military expenditures and to encourage a fear and suspicion of foreigners, especially the Americans. Gorbachev once told a crowd that "not everyone abroad wants peace. . . . They fear that we will be successful in our peaceful intentions. They fear this! And accordingly they want to drag us into an arms race."[23] The difference between the American and Russian fears of war is one of the main asymmetries between the mass psychologies of the two peoples. For the Russians, the fear of war is still a living fear; while for the Americans, it is an abstract or intellectual concern. Soviet leaders themselves may fear war can be close. But it is very unlikely that the Soviet elite would initiate a war with the United States. A high-level Soviet defector writes: "Nuclear war could only be a last resort, to be initiated solely if the Soviets were fully convinced that the very existence of the nation was at stake, and if there appeared to be no alternative."[24] The touchiness and bluster the Soviets display on war is also an annoyance to some Americans. No one enjoys being told continually he is a warmonger. Yet, the general American lack of fear of war makes the United States appear risk-oriented and, hence, dangerous to Russians, who tend to be risk-averse and slow moving. Former West German Chancellor Schmidt has commented on the cautiousness of the Russians: "They feel their way . . . and as a result are dismayed and confused by the United States, its rapid political changes, attitudes and strategies."[25] It will be fascinating to see if Gorbachev makes Russia more flexible and open to the clash of ideas.

Despite their tendencies to caution and slowness in action, Russians may feel they can outlast the frivolous and faddish Americans. As a top Soviet foreign affairs specialist puts it, "We may have a smaller gross national product than the United States but we can stand greater hardship."[26] This sort of attitude is itself a problem. Not endurance but creative overcoming of one's own cultural limitations is required for better foreign relations today. Unfortunately, the Soviet leaders still have little understanding of how their thinking and actions can contribute to anti-Soviet feelings or heightened suspicions in the United States. For example, in explaining the shooting down of a civilian airliner and the invasion of Afghanistan, the Soviet leaders not only did not accept responsibility or apologize but also spoke and acted as if other countries would have done the same thing and as if the world outside is just like their world. Even Gorbachev, who has occasionally allowed himself to be questioned by foreigners on Soviet policy, has replied in self-assured but sometimes limited and self-serving ways.[27] He once suggested to a group of congressmen that the United States could solve its race problems by setting up separate states for blacks and other minorities. A black congressman said he found the remark "somewhat offensive." Another congressman said the suggestion highlighted the difference between the American emphasis on individualism and the Russian tendency to "think of people as classes."[28]

How is it possible for the American and Russian cultures, both rather successful in certain ways, to come to terms? Not easily, it is clear, particularly when both cultures have an imperial-like tendency to intervene, one way or another, on a global basis. In the United States, for example, "both ends of the political spectrum employ ... imperial arguments."[29] Whereas the Right wants to intervene in Central America, the liberals and the Left favor intervention in South Africa. Many Russians, too, seem to want to remake the world. This is an old Russian tendency. At any rate, America has run up against an adversary with "a fundamentally different view of politics: a view with a longer historical span and greater psychological depth, one of an old civilization that may have been updated, but was not uprooted...."[30]

Similarly, the Soviets, too, confront a very different culture. Ironically, they both fear the United States and need its products and acceptance, yet they do not understand it and consequently—to their great disappointment and annoyance—have been unable to find a basis for a profitable lasting coexistence.

Both America and Russia face a painful problem: to get along with one another each people would have to give up some of its most cherished ways of thinking and acting and become more like the other. Since neither can do this, any coexistence between them will have to be shallow and cannot involve fundamental agreement except perhaps in a limited way in a few common aspects of both cultures. (See Table 8.1.) Soviet-American relations require for their effective management leaders on both sides who can accept the frictions and problems arising out of cultural differences and yet not let them get out-of-hand or exaggerate them.

DOMESTIC POLITICS

Aspects of the superpowers' domestic politics hinder the improvement of their relationship and occasionally even worsen it. This is easier to see in American politics than Soviet as the US system is more open to examination, allows itself to be criticized, and is decentralized in foreign policy making.

TABLE 8.1. CONTRASTING AMERICAN AND RUSSIAN CULTURAL TENDENCIES

Cultural Tendency	United States	USSR
Standard for decisions	Legalism	Politics
Goals	Short range	Long range
Popular expectations of government	Justice	Fairness
Conflict	Abnormal	Normal
Leading societal principle	Individualism	Collectivism
State of society	Dynamic and volatile	Stable and even rigid
Organization of government	Decentralized	Highly centralized
Pace of societal change	Rapid	Slow
Sentimentality and idealism	High	Low
View of the individual's effect on government	Some	None
View of problems as solvable	High	Low

Since it is so easy to find evidence of pettiness, narrowness of interest, and outright error in American politics, some analysts have tended to lay most or even all of the blame for the problems of superpower relations on the more open and democratic American system. It is in the nature of Washington politics that it "leaks from the top" right into the media. Once, when the author asked a State Department official a question, he replied, "Our view on that is appearing in _____'s column in the *Post* on Thursday."

The nature of Soviet politics is itself a problem for superpower relations. Since decisions there are made behind the scenes and without the participation of many groups in society, the Soviet political process takes on a sinister appearance, which encourages belief that its purposes are the worst possible for American interests. "Why are they so secretive if they are not planning all-out to nail us?" Americans might ask, particularly those who are most inclined by ideology, psychology, or personal interest to be anti-Soviet. This general position came to dominate in Washington after the election of 1980. In effect, the Soviet invasion of Afghanistan helped elect Ronald Reagan.

The secretiveness of Soviet politics is an amalgam of Russian tradition, Leninist ideology, Stalin's actions, and the convenience of the chief politicians. The Soviets are just not going to let us see much of their political process. A Soviet Arms control negotiator once told his American counterpart, "We know so much about how you make decisions. Americans are talking about this and writing about this all the time.... But you know little of how we make decisions and we are not going to tell you. Because we do know, we have some chance of influencing your decisions. Because you don't know, your chances of influencing ours are limited and we intend to keep it that way."[31]

Soviet political principles and practices violate the fundamental political assumptions and beliefs of most Western political groupings. But this does not necessarily mean that Soviet politics harbors single-minded ideologues effectively using their every waking moment to bring about the West's destruction. Instead, most Soviet leaders are men with very specialized engineering degrees who are wrapped up in maintaining the highly bureaucratized and inefficient industrial system they inherited. No doubt they would like to expand this system's power and its size but that is extra—the primary job is to keep it going pretty much as it is or, as Gorbachev suggests, improve its operation. This includes not allowing freedom of expression or the other democratic freedoms. Granting such rights would transform the political system into a type with which the leaders have no experience and which they probably could neither control nor keep focused on industrial and military production, the main economic goals. Even Gorbachev's "openness" is a limited one.

This view of the Soviet leaders as primarily managers, albeit dictatorial and inefficient ones, is not widely accepted in the United States. But we do know that, despite great differences in ideology, civil rights, leaders, and political process, the United States and the USSR both have governments that try to regulate internal conflict, set general goals, maximize the national interest and conduct foreign policy, including relations with each other. In short, both have governments, and all governments have similarities, if only because they all are led by politicians and are trying to make and implement policy while coping with disagreement.

Quite possibly, the "inner politics" of the superpowers' governments are primary in determining their present and future relationship.[32] What one country can do in foreign affairs and even domestically is determined heavily by the domestic politics of the other and by how that politics is perceived in the other superpower. A special pattern of action-interaction-counteraction exists. In effect, the whole range of American domestic policy, from welfare to pollution controls, is affected by Soviet domestic policy, at least to a degree. Similarly, what the Soviets are willing to do on one or another domestic matter depends somewhat on what the Americans are doing. This interconnection is pushed to extremes by those who are extremely fearful of the other power, and those who feel threatened by an improvement in the superpower relationship. In the USSR the groups particularly threatened are the propagandists and the security police, while in the United States the corresponding groups would be defense industry employees and the Defense Department. Some in both militaries would be threatened as well, as would true ideologues on both sides. Those in the high-prestige inner circle of "national security" in government would tend to lose from improved superpower relations.

The problem is greater in the USSR because government there is much stronger and considerably larger and not open to public pressures. Brezhnev, who died in 1982, struck a deal of sorts with those opposed to a better relationship with the United States by giving "the apparatus of orthodoxy and control ... a free hand to tighten the lines of ideological vigilance at home...."[33] This was not a solution, however, for the crackdown created a renewed anti-Soviet backlash in the United States centering on the American concern for human rights and civil liberties. Americans had unrealistically assumed peaceful coexistence would produce a less repressive Soviet Union.

Soviet expansionism, which had come to be a necessity for Soviet domestic politics—one way of legitimizing the system and giving mass deprivation a public purpose—seemed to many Americans to be an attack on both American ideals and assumptions regarding the conditions for a better relationship. "Stable and beneficial relations cannot be reconciled with the pursuit of expansionism, and an unrelenting buildup of military power. . . . Détente is not divisible," it turned out. Renewed Soviet expansionism would "preclude the restoration of even a semblance of détente even on arms control questions where compromise is possible. . . ."[34]

Similarly, the Soviet maintenance of severe restrictions on, and punishment for, even mild dissent undercut détente. No matter that, as always in Russia, "deviation was seen as tantamount to social treason . . . one was either a subject of holy Moscow or a foreigner and, by definition, an enemy."[35] That this viewpoint is still with us is clear from the remarks on emigration made by Arbatov: "When somebody leaves our country and goes to the West, it means that he or she is rejecting the whole set of social values and ideals of the Soviet people. . . ."[36]

Dissent can now be expressed in the Soviet Union, though at a heavy cost. For example, although the Stalinist law restricting freedom of speech still is on the books, it may be interpreted "much more narrowly" and, although repression of dissidents continues, it has become "a bit less severe." But relaxation is too little or even insignificant in American eyes. There are still "certain fundamentals that Soviet citizens cannot explicitly criticize in the media" and there remain "tight controls on the form or tone of what may be said."[37] This is still true despite the minor relaxation of controls by Gorbachev.

The Human Rights Issue

In the 1970s American politics magnified the human rights issue into a general stumbling block to any improvement in United States-Soviet relations. Both liberals and conservatives who favored an active United States role abroad "seized upon the human rights theme as the perfect reproach" to the Nixon-Kissinger approach to the Soviet Union. Indeed, human rights in the USSR is an old superpower issue. In 1933 President Roosevelt raised it with the Soviet ambassador, who replied that his government would not alter its domestic policies for foreign rewards. In the late 1970s the Carter administration made human rights a major part of its foreign policy, and not only vis-à-vis the Soviet Union. The human rights issue was now one of American domestic politics. It enabled the administration "to rally support from liberal Democrats, conservative Republicans, and Jewish groups in both parties." However, pushing human rights in the USSR was an attack on "the Soviet elite as a whole" who may have wondered if it was part of some new attempt to destabilize the Soviet system.

In response, the Soviets mounted a massive human rights campaign of their own directed against the United States. Soviet media emphasized the difficulties of Native Americans and blacks, especially some of their activists in prison.

Also, the Soviets stressed American unemployment and racism to counter American emphasis on Soviet limitations on civil rights, political participation, and emigration.[38] Apparently sincere outrage was expressed to the author by Soviet foreign policy specialists in 1977, just after President Carter had met with a leading dissident who had been released. The Soviet elite seems to see dissidents as criminals. Ironically, in the 1970s the Soviet government responded to a degree to American human rights concerns by releasing some prisoners from jail and allowing them and some others to emigrate. But it would not formalize the practice or allow the Americans to call the shots.[39] Unfortunately, the Carter administration's form of human rights policy worsened Soviet-American relations and made arms control more difficult because it demanded too much too fast and poisoned the tone of the relationship.[40]

The Reagan administration came to office in 1981 determined to push the Soviets even harder on human rights but to not criticize the anti-Communist allies of the United States that also violated human rights. Professor Jeane Kirkpatrick, appointed the United States permanent representative at the United Nations, had argued that criticizing pro-American "authoritarian" regimes undercut the central struggle with the "totalitarian" and anti-American USSR.[41]

The Soviet Union signed the Helsinki accords in 1975, whereby it seemed to promise certain human rights in exchange for the apparent recognition of its enlarged territories in Europe. This raised in legalistic American politics a belief that a new international legal agreement had been entered into by the USSR and that performance in the American legal sense by the Soviet Union could be demanded and obtained.[42] However, the Helsinki Final Act is neither a treaty nor a legally binding agreement although it does carry "considerable moral weight because it was signed at the highest government level."[43]

The final section or "basket three" of Helsinki has been the main point of contention since it promises family reunification and the right to emigrate, among other rights. A small group of American congressmen who met with Gorbachev stressed the need for the USSR to observe the Helsinki accords strictly. Otherwise, they said, Congress would tend to be skeptical about the value of entering into other agreements with the USSR. It was a message that did not go down well.[44]

A great deal of debating sound and fury on Helsinki and human rights has been issued by both superpowers at the various follow-up conferences. The vocal and strong American government approach to human rights has not induced a liberalization inside the USSR. It may even have resulted in a stricter internal climate. Dissidents have not been treated more lightly nor has Jewish emigration increased. Whereas more than fifty thousand Soviet Jews were allowed to leave in 1979, only about a thousand had been able to emigrate during 1985 while 1986 and 1987 were not much better. Soviet intransigence and pride were evident in the response Gorbachev made to British politicians on the issue: "You govern your society and leave us to govern ours. . . . I could quote a few facts about human rights in the United Kingdom. . . . You persecute entire communities and nationalities. Again, you have got 2.3 million unemployed."[45]

Although the United States approach has not been productive, it is difficult to change it. As Secretary of State Shultz has said: "Throughout our own history, we have always believed that freedom is the birthright of all peoples and that we could not be true to ourselves or our principles unless we stood for freedom and democracy not only for ourselves but for others."[46]

Nevertheless, by late 1985 President Reagan had muted American emphasis on human rights in the USSR. A few days after his first summit meeting with Gorbachev, he told the Cabinet that there would be no more public pressure on Moscow on the subject. Apparently, former President Nixon had advised Reagan that a less-combative stance would be more likely to produce results. In February 1986 a leading Soviet dissident, Anatoly Shcharansky, was released from prison and even allowed to emigrate, and in March the president refused to meet with the wife of the most famous Soviet dissident still in the USSR, Andrei Sakharov.[47] A decision had been made not to do as President Carter had done in early 1977. Another American administration had moved, or been moved, toward the center in its Soviet policy.

What is the best American strategy on the Soviet human rights issue? The Soviet leadership will have to recognize the issue has real meaning in the West, while the American government will have to develop a human rights position that fits naturally into its overall Soviet strategy and also stands a fair chance of achieving results. "Ethics and power must be harnessed together and purpose balanced by capacity."[48] Some general guidelines for American policy might include: keep raising the issue with the Soviets, but quietly; publicize the facts but not in the President's speeches; never concede anything on human rights to the USSR; never urge Americans to say or do less on human rights. Public pressure allows quiet diplomacy to work, says Shcharansky.

Stumbling Blocks in U.S. Politics

Just as human rights issues stand in the way of good relations between the two superpowers, there are certain permanent features of American domestic politics that have the same negative effects. These include delays in decision making and consensus building caused by constitutional fragmentation and geographical dispersion of power, the influence on foreign policy of short-term political appointees, and frequent elections, which upsets the continuity of the superpower relationship and allows that relationship to be used against the incumbent administration. These factors, as well as the ability of any determined interest group to affect US foreign policy result in an ever-changing and even incoherent policy toward the Soviet Union.

Another impediment to good relations is the profound difference in the nature and experience of the political elites. The large United States elite tends toward lawyers who serve in Washington temporarily as a result of elections, while the Soviets have a small elite that is trained in engineering and has a long pattern of service in the party or state bureaucracies.[49] Elections can be heavily dependent on circumstance and the public mood and can produce presidents and staffs lacking in foreign policy experience or even experience in the federal government. This has been true of both the Carter and Reagan administrations. The Soviet bureaucratic "ladder of success" usually produces leaders thoroughly committed to established Soviet points-of-view and goals who are well experienced in their central government's practices.

Moreover, the United States-Soviet political relationship is bound to be negatively affected by the class, ideological, historical, and structural differences between American and Soviet domestic politics. For example, people of business and property dominate American political life, while the USSR is dominated by ex-peasants, Gorbachev included, and ex-workers with long experience in the Communist Party bureaucracy or *apparat*. Naturally, the ideological language and symbols of the two systems are very different, and the Soviet Union has only one centralized political party, while the United States has two factionalized parties.[50] This factionalization has severely limited progress on arms control during the Reagan administration. Its top members have been in "passionate disagreement" on the usefulness of arms control treaties, and at least one top member of the administration has said publicly he is against a new arms control agreement.[51]

The lack of a foreign policy consensus and the influence on general political moods of independent politicians and interest groups with access to the media make for a volatile political environment for American policy toward the Soviet Union. The public mood of neo-isolationism that followed the Vietnam War allowed the USSR to expand its influence into Africa and was itself followed by a harsh reactive mood of anti-Sovietism after the invasion of Afghanistan. Things have come full circle in only half a decade.[52] Electoral politics also has its role. During the 1984 election the Reagan campaign ran a memorable TV ad showing a bear stalking in a forest and with a voice that said, "Isn't it smart to be as strong as the bear...?" At the end the ad showed a man with a rifle. The tag line was "President Reagan. Prepared for Peace."

Perhaps the Soviets have an edge on the Americans. Because of their stronger sense of history, Brzezinski says, "the Russians realize that their competition with America is historically protracted. As a result, they are less susceptible to being influenced by every superficial shift in the nuances of the rivalry, and they are more adept at manipulating the atmospherics of the competition...."[53] Still, despite Soviet steadiness in the rivalry, their attempts to influence American domestic politics have had little effect, though Gorbachev may have some successes.

The bottom line is that the nature of the Soviet Union and its deeds, not Soviet propaganda or diplomacy, have the primary effect on American public opinion. The moods of the American public on the USSR are not aberrant behavior; they result from Soviet actions that are correctly perceived as opposed to American principles or interests and from recognition that the Soviet system represents values largely rejected in the United States. These American moods can change greatly, partly in accordance with Soviet behavior. If Soviet statements are to be believed, American domestic politics is seen as a powerful, often unpredictable and illogical, and commonly frustrating force. Soviet Americanists today even push Marxist materialist explanations to the side and recognize that "the psychological mood in the United States with regard to Soviet-American relations . . . is unstable and prone to fluctuation. . . ." [54] But even such semirealistic writers tend to blame the unique American historical experience and "right-wingers" for this situation instead of recognizing the partial responsibility of the USSR for it. In recent years the Reagan administration and its apparent attempt to achieve military superiority over the USSR has been a special Soviet concern. To the Soviets, Reagan appears both more ambitious and more dangerous than did former United States presidents. [55]

Soviet Domestic Politics

What now of Soviet domestic politics and United States-Soviet relations? First, there are the basic political features Americans tend to react against. To put them most simply: the Soviet Union is ruled by a bureaucratic-like political elite of a few hundred thousand persons, mostly Russian men, known as the *apparat* (management) of the Communist Party, the only political party allowed, which exercises control of varying degrees over all matters of significance, from promotions in the military, through the running of factories, to family policy. The main means used to exercise control are: (1) required inclusion (cooptation) of most persons with positions of responsibility into the centrally directed and disciplined Communist Party; (2) supervision over administration and social groupings by party members; (3) filling of key positions throughout society only by party approval; and (4) the presence of important party members on all leading governmental and other bodies. The top party bodies, the Politburo and the Secretariat of overlapping membership, control key appointments throughout the party *apparat*; do not allow open disagreement in the party, much less another political party; maintain close control of the media and exercise pre-publication censorship of all publications; and maintain a large security police that utilizes a nationwide network of informers and operates in an extraconstitutional manner. This political machinery is masked by an elaborate facade of a governmental arrangement with a liberal constitution and elected parliaments (soviets) that make laws. However, there is no mechanism whereby the constitution can be made to apply. The courts, also controlled by the party, never deal with constitutional issues. Most of the rules and regulations are issued by government agencies without soviet (legislative) approval and there is usually no choice of candidates on the ballots; the official candidates for the legislatures are always elected (except sometimes at the village level). The men at the top of this powerful political edifice are able, in effect, to manufacture support for themselves and dominate both decisions and policies. [56] It is hard to find a political arrangement more at variance with American ideals and practice. Even the American big-city machines of the past did not have such a degree of control.

These great powers of the party *apparat* do not make it all-powerful, however. The Soviet Union is not a full-fledged totalitarianism, although its leaders clearly have totalitarian aspirations and tendencies. The Soviet system has some mass support, at least among Russians, and is extraordinarily powerful but somehow is still unable to achieve a stronger position abroad or an efficient economy or administration domestically. The party faces a general listlessness and economic ineffectiveness even though it has effectively avoided large, organized opposition.

Furthermore, neither Russian culture nor Leninism allow internal voices of criticism and self-limitation to have a public role. The possible factionalization of the party between forces of orthodoxy and modernization or between conservatism and reformism[57] does not meet the American wish for a definite built-in political limitation on Soviet militarism and expansionism. Soviet politics seem medieval and inherently an affront and possibly also a threat to American political principles.

Many Americans are also affronted by some Soviet foreign policy methods—the extensive use of spying, the continual disagreeable din of anti-American propaganda, and the offensive, persistent charges of American intent to attack and invade the Soviet Union, as well as military and other aid to states with virulently anti-American positions and intents such as Libya.

The nature of the Soviet political elite also stimulates American anti-Sovietism. Though Americans tend to accept a class structure based on merit, they are offended by one based on the elitist enforced subservience of an entire population. The Soviet party *apparat* is a patently dictatorial ruling class, albeit one with a theoretical rationalization for its dominance—Leninism, an elitist Marxism. But Americans have always regarded formal ideologies as facade, trickery, or self-justification. A belief system that puts down individualism is unacceptable to them. Moreover, the Soviet elite between Khrushchev and Gorbachev (1964–1985) seemed to be living in the past and isolated from the latest currents of thought and action. Indeed, it may not have been able to understand the Americans and seemingly thought they would accept the Soviet Union as it is in return for the peace and profit promised by détente Soviet-style. This misunderstanding of American politics is illustrated by the remark of a Politburo member to a Democratic senator who was trying to point out that some members of his party might vote against SALT II even if President Carter favored it. "But can't you discipline them?" the Politburo member asked.[58]

As we have seen, the harsh Soviet treatment of dissidents, even nonviolent ones, by the Soviet government has been especially troubling to Americans. In the USSR anyone who publicly acts or speaks in a way that is different from offical policy is an "other-thinking one"—a dissident and, hence, an opposition-ist. The regime will not accept even support and pro-regime statements from its subjects unless they are within official guidelines and part of an officially controlled body's approved actions. The punishment of relatives and incarceration of dissidents in mental hospitals may be the measures most repulsive to Americans. The refusal to allow people to leave the country is also repugnant to American values. Thousands freely emigrate from the United States every year. Soviet political trials have political effects in the United States. One American congressman who had been supporting SALT II said, in reaction to the trial of two prominent dissidents, that he could not imagine "a SALT treaty . . . with a nation that terrorizes its own people."[59] Although the Soviet Union is "nowhere near the top of the world list" in violation of human rights, its controls are "analogous to the suppression of dissent by Christian churches in the Middle Ages"—medieval in scope and style.[60]

With the accession of Gorbachev as general secretary in 1985, a new ruling generation with little involvement in Stalinism and apparently devoted to domestic modernization and reform came to fill the top positions in the USSR. Gorbachev himself seems relatively pragmatic and deeply concerned with the rigidities and incipient backwardness of the Soviet Union and determined both to get the country moving again and to change its image in the West. Accordingly, he has allowed a limited freedom of expression. He seems to be putting priority on domestic development over foreign expansionism, although he cannot, in order to survive and maintain his support, give up any Soviet gains in foreign affairs. Americans have tended to welcome his policies. It will be interesting to see if domestic politics in both superpowers now allows some progress to be made in the Soviet-American relationship.

PERCEPTIONS—AN OVERVIEW

How Soviets and Americans think about each other will affect and even determine their policies toward one another. Unfortunately, the images people have of the other country can be either mere inventions or distortions resulting from fears, irrational concerns, or, sometimes, reflections of self-images. "The Russians are just like us" is a common example. "The Americans must want military power for anti-Soviet activity" is another such image, but from the Soviet perspective. People in both superpowers have erroneously seen the other country as a new Nazi Germany, a phantom image out of their past. Such thinking in extremes easily leads to violent swings and "flip-flops" of rhetoric and policy.

Exaggeration and oversimplification are common in the superpowers' views of each other, particularly since politicians engage in the manipulation of people's attitudes. The classic example may have been Winston Churchill's eloquent "iron curtain" speech in Fulton, Missouri, in 1946. Yuri Andropov's 1983 letter to a Maine schoolgirl emphasizing the Soviet Union's peaceful intentions was also a form of personalized image-changing directed at the

American public. "What a nice man—writing to that girl" was the desired reaction. Once created, perceptions and misperceptions cannot easily be uncreated.

Leaders and Leaderships

Leading politicians in both systems have the ability to affect their people's perceptions of each other. Doing this is one of the functions of leadership. "The way in which leaders of nation-states view each other ... is of fundamental importance in determining what happens in relations among states."[61] Realistically, however, it is difficult to identify the actual images leading politicians have of the other superpower. All politicians are dissemblers to a degree, for one thing, and Soviet leaders rarely speak openly as individuals. Mostly they enunciate the carefully considered policies of the Politburo in the special language of Soviet Marxism. Yet we must begin with some reasonable assumptions based on what we know about the views held by Soviet and American leaders.

Neither country has been run by people with open hatred for the other side. Even Ronald Reagan's anti-Sovietism has been one more of distaste and contempt than hatred. Conversely, no Soviet leader has made destruction of the United States a public goal. Yet clearly both sets of leaders have, since the beginnings of the cold war, been more than willing to engage in an open and somewhat colorful verbal competition with their opposite numbers. Khrushchev (1957–1964) did the most along this line—perhaps even more than the Soviet elite wanted, for he was removed partly for his excessively risky and embarrassing competition with the Americans in the Berlin and Cuban crises of 1961–62. The game-playing over the imagery of arms control between President Reagan and General Secretary Gorbachev is only a recent example. More such jockeying is likely between the two leaderships for some time. Indeed, the two political systems now require that their respective leaders be capable of standing up to the other superpower. And certainly no one expressing friendship for the opposing superpower can be a leader at this time. Even if antagonism is absent in particular leaders, other influential people on both sides may foster enmity and divisiveness between the two countries.

Only among some American Presidents before Truman have there been favorable images of Russia. Woodrow Wilson welcomed the Russian Revolution of 1917 and called the Russians "democratic at heart" and "generous." Herbert Hoover saw the new Soviet Union as a "murderous tyranny" under "Bolshevik murderers." Franklin Roosevelt, although he tended to ignore potential sources of conflict with the USSR, called it "a dictatorship as absolute as any...." Harry Truman saw the USSR as "trying to expand the boundaries of their world, whenever and wherever they can," putting the United States to "a long hard test of strength and stamina...." Dwight Eisenhower saw the USSR purposely stalking the United States as "Communism's final and greatest victim-to-be" but also, interestingly, saw Soviet policy as frightened by "demons of its own invention" and a "self-induced hysteria," thus suggesting that Soviet aggressiveness was not permanent and was somehow "curable." He also spoke of the Russian "hunger for peace." John F. Kennedy may have been the first American President to speak of a reconciliation between superpowers. He warned that "no government or social system is so evil that its people must be considered as lacking in virtue" and spoke of the common interests of the superpowers: "So let us not be blind to our differences, but let us also direct attention to our common interests and to the means by which those differences can be resolved."[62]

It is no secret that Ronald Reagan is deeply and sincerely opposed to the Soviet system. A leading American political analyst says one of Reagan's four core beliefs is "Stand up to the Communists." President Reagan's most memorable statement about the Soviet Union is that calling it "the focus of evil in the modern world. . . ." He has made a number of other equally pointed and disapproving comments about the Soviet Union. Yet, by 1985 he was sounding, at least now and then, a bit like Presidents Eisenhower and Kennedy. In September 1985, for example, he said that the two superpowers could prevent a world war and that "we're going to try to find a way to deal practically with them."[63]

Naturally, Mr. Reagan's anti-Sovietism had much support within the top echelons of his administration. In March 1987 Secretary of Defense Weinberger spoke very firmly about the USSR before a Senate committee. Since the United States was, he said, faced with becoming "second in military power to the Soviet Union," it must follow a "strategy of countervailing" power, which may require the use of military force to defend American vital interests. Elsewhere, he said the Soviet Union still seeks "world domination—it's just that simple."[64]

Statements such as these by top-level officials of the Reagan administration seem to have the ring of sincerity. In general, the USSR is seen as a "brutal regime" with a "propensity to use military force." Robert McFarlane, once the National Security Adviser, said even incremental improvements in United States-Soviet relations would require a fundamental change in Soviet official thinking.[65] George Shultz, Reagan's second secretary of state, was more inclined to see Soviet-American relations as amenable to improvement but nevertheless expressed a no-nonsense position on the subject.

> . . . our policy begins with the clear recognition that the Soviet Union is and will remain a global superpower . . . our policy, unlike some versions of détente, assumes that the Soviet Union is more likely to be deterred by our actions . . . than by a delicate web of interdependence.[66]

How does Mr. Reagan's opposite number, Secretary General Gorbachev, feel about the United States, his main foreign policy problem? We cannot know for sure, but we can at least look at what he has said in private to leading American officials. When Gorbachev met with Shultz and McFarlane in late

1985, Gorbachev presented to them a view of the United States that was a mirror image of Reagan's depiction of the USSR as an "evil empire." More than that, he seemed to believe what he said—that the United States was a corrupt society controlled by exploiting capitalists which had opposed the USSR throughout its history and remained its implacable foe. At other times, however, he has expressed only exasperation with the United States, as when commenting on the inability of its government to keep secret the proceedings of confidential meetings. At the 27th Party Congress in early 1986, he publicly presented, at first glance, the standard *Pravda* view of the United States as a greedy imperialism, but also wove in strands that may indicate he has a more complex and even realistic view of the rival superpower. Although Gorbachev was sharp in his criticism of the United States, he directed his criticism at the "right wing of the U.S. monopoly bourgeoisie" rather than at the entire bourgeoisie. And in his later speech calling for a ban on nuclear tests, he appealed to the "wisdom and dignity" of the Americans and refrained from anti-American statements. This was good politics, of course, and some would call it propaganda, yet it suggests Gorbachev is somewhat discriminating in his views of the United States. He also seems to have a differentiated view of international politics, having said that today both competition and interdependence exist between the two world systems of capitalism and socialism and that the "genuine national interests" of the United States are *not* those of its "military-industrial complex."[67] The passage of time will allow a clearer idea of Gorbachev's views on the United States to emerge.

It is undeniably difficult for Soviet analysts to "read" American politics well. Their own practices and assumptions can get in their way. For example, Soviet commentators initially welcomed Reagan's presidency, thinking that he would be like Nixon, long on rhetoric but in favor of realistic negotiations. The Soviets often seem not to be able to understand or accept the existence of some of the fundamental features of the American political system—the relative autonomy of law, the inherent limitations on American politicians' power, the lack of a central or ultimate control mechanism in the governmental structure, and the naturalness of the system's fluidity and volatility. Instead, they seek to identify either Marxist-recognized "forces" or political puppet-masters who must be "in charge." Some professional Americanists know better, but we have no evidence their more realistic and varied views are also the views of the political leadership or are even ever conveyed to them.[68]

A top-level Soviet diplomat, once a protégé of Gromyko, the former Soviet foreign minister, says that the Kremlin leaders cannot "comprehend fully the mechanism of the U.S. political system."

> There is little grasp of the relationship of American congressmen to their constituencies, the real role of public opinion and that worst bugaboo, freedom of information, which they see as a threat to security. The idealism of the American Revolution, carried over into both domestic and foreign policy more than two hundred years later, is perceived by the Soviets as a crippling naïveté.

A leading American analyst seems to agree:

> The Soviets have an extraordinary penchant for misapplying the conspiratorial norms that govern their political process in their attempts at understanding ours. A dramatic example is the persistent suspicion ... that Watergate was a plot against Richard Nixon by the enemies of détente....[69]

This suggests that vestiges of Marxism remain to influence the Soviet elite's thinking about the "capitalist" United States as well as, possibly, a bitter envy at being unable to either catch up to or overawe the Americans. An emigré sociologist from the USSR suggests that this envy "has turned into something even more bitter and even malicious...." Soviet spokesmen have frequently hurled invective at the Reagan administration or expressed a hopelessness in ever coming to acceptable terms with it. A former Soviet ambassador said that the United States under Reagan was trying to destabilize the Soviet Union. In 1983 a leading American journalist found a great deal of "outright hostility" toward the United States among Soviet officials, with some even suggesting it ought to be treated "like Albania," that is, ignored—a view not uncommon about the USSR in the United States. A top party functionary called Reagan administration policy "more militarist and reactionary than that of any postwar Washington administration." *Pravda* once described Reagan as "a Roman Caesar" and a candidate for "world dictator."[70]

Still, Soviet spokesmen always claim that the Soviet Union wants to improve relations with the United States. Mikhail Gorbachev has tried to implement this line but, given the elite's very strong anti-American and anti-Reagan sentiments, his progress has been difficult. One positive sign is that Soviet propaganda is always pro-peace, never pro-war. This may alleviate the fears of the Soviet people, who know that a superpower agreement would enable them to live better and breathe easier. Recently, official Soviet views on capitalism have been modified. It is no longer seen as inevitably aggressive and militaristic, which suggests a degree of official Soviet hope for a better relationship with the United States. But what about ordinary citizens? What do the Soviet and American publics think of each other's governments and their policies?

Public Opinion

In the United States, public opinion polls are common and ordinary people are not afraid to express their views on political issues. Although the Soviets also conduct public opinion polling, little of it is overtly political and deceptive answers are common. Thus, we are forced to fall back on anecdotal and other "soft" sources for the Soviet public's view of the United States.

How the peoples of two countries look at each other goes a long way toward determining the nature of their relationship, and even whether they have a relationship at all. Soviet actions often trigger unfavorable visceral responses in the American body politic. Americans sometimes wonder why the Soviets put up with their system at all. It is likely, however, that Americans are more negatively inclined toward the Soviet government and Soviet life in general, with its shortages and heavy-handed bureaucratic tendencies than toward the Russian people themselves, whom they hardly know. Similarly, American actions and the American way of life can be puzzling or repellent to ordinary Soviets. While Russians probably admire Americans and their relative wealth and efficiency, they are mystified by the workings of U.S. government as they do not understand democratic principles and processes. The Soviet public is probably also repelled by some of the facts of life in a capitalist economy— unemployment, the need to pay for higher education, and the need to find a job. (In the USSR one can expect to be assigned a job.)

It is usually assumed that Americans tend to be anti-Soviet because they are anti-Communist. This is generally incorrect. Americans overall have differing views of different Communist countries; some, like China today, are viewed rather favorably; others, including the Soviet Union are not. Something other than Communist ideology in the USSR makes Americans anti-Soviet. Probably the central elements in this are Soviet military power and global ambition. Soviets have some fears of the United States, but not because it is capitalist. Rather, the possibilities that the United States will back some future militaristic Germany or China or achieve military superiority through a technological breakthrough excite deep fears among Russians, as does the concern that the Americans, who have not had a war on their own territory recently, may be willing to risk war.

The history of American views of Russia has been one of antipathy and rejection, except just after Tsarism fell in 1917. Then a democracy was unrealistically expected for Russia. In 1941 the American public tended to dismiss the Soviet Union "as an undependable and somehow negligible factor in world affairs. . . . hostile disillusionment toward the Soviet Union had chilled down to tepid indifference. Soviet Russia was trying to play both ends against the middle and to hell with it. It was too weak to resist Germany anyway. Turn its picture to the wall." [71]

During World War II, Americans tended to view Russia favorably, only to have their hopes dashed by the Stalinization of Eastern Europe after the war. As early as May 1946, 58 percent of Americans believed that the Soviet Union wanted to rule the world (up to 78 percent a year later) and 36 percent believed that members of any Communist organization in the United States should be killed or imprisoned. In August of 1946 a Gallup poll revealed that 80 percent of Americans believed Soviet spies were active in the United States. [72] A long, tense cold war followed until tiny blossoms of apparent internal relaxation and renewed Soviet-American cooperation appeared in the last year of President Kennedy's life. During the détente period, Americans again came to harbor great expectations of liberalization in Soviet society. But these were also dashed—this time by the Soviet reimposition of strict controls.

Poll results indicate that the Soviet system can be massively unpopular in the United States and that Reaganism's popular base was partly in place years before Reagan was elected. "After 1975, the mass public began to feel insecure about Soviet military strength and adventurism, and public opinion began to drift to the right," supporting increased defense budgets and later Ronald Reagan out of basically defensive impulses, not aggressiveness or interventionism. By 1982, a large majority of the American people, 84 percent, saw the Soviet Union as a threat to the United States, while fully 49 percent saw it as an outright enemy, with 69 percent believing it would not hesitate to use nuclear weapons against the United States in certain cases.[73]

By 1982–83 the American public was tending toward noninternationalist inclinations and began to want conciliation with the Soviets. A *Los Angeles Times* poll of March 1982 revealed that 59 percent wanted to "be more conciliatory" versus 54 percent who wanted to "get together" with Russia. By April 1983 a *New York Times* poll found that, although Americans felt by about three-to-two that the Soviet threat was growing, by an even bigger margin of two-to-one they felt that the American arms buildup would only cause a greater increase in Soviet arms. By almost three-to-one the public felt the best American policy was a mutual freeze on nuclear weapons, not a United States military buildup. Apparently, the high point of American support for higher military spending was in 1980, when Ronald Reagan was elected President. The public's support for Reagan's SDI project was very high in 1983: 67 percent in favor and 25 percent against, reflecting American defensive instincts and faith in technology.

In 1984, although more than 60 percent of Americans thought the Soviets were expansionist and only understood force, almost all, 96 percent, felt that "picking a fight with the Soviet Union is too dangerous in a nuclear world." The same poll showed how misinformed Americans are. Only 10 percent knew that both the United States and the USSR had signed the SALT II treaty. Yet American public opinion on the USSR changes greatly in response to events. In 1983, because of the Soviet shooting down of a plane with more than fifty Americans on board, the number of persons who called ABC News favoring "strong action" against the Soviet Union almost doubled. By late 1986 almost half of the American public, 45 percent, was for "toughness" in dealing with the Russians while about the same percentage, 44 percent, was for "reducing tensions."[74]

With this sort of split and swing in public opinion, it is no wonder United States policy toward the Soviet Union is itself bifurcated, tending both to military power and to negotiation. It is also not surprising that American military power is so rarely used in war; there is very little support for that. It is instead seen mainly as a defense or "insurance policy." Ronald Reagan's calling SDI, with its offensive capabilities, a "shield" fits in very well with this popular mentality.

The Soviet public's view of the United States during the 1920s and 1930s is unknown. But it may well have been favorable since the U.S. had supplied the country with food during the post-revolutionary famine, and Stalin did not criticize America during the Great Purges of the 1930s. In fact, he had used it as an ideal in his slogan, "To build a second America." Not until after World War II, with its severe weakening of Russia's former opponents and the beginning of American "containment" of the USSR did the United States become a major target of Soviet propaganda. Ordinary Russians though, never regarded the United States as a definite enemy of the Soviet Union until after President Reagan's severe denunciations of the USSR. He seems to have frightened the average Soviet citizen as no former American president ever has.

Apparently, the combination of anti-Soviet actions taken by the Carter and Reagan administrations, including the American boycott of the Moscow Olympics and military aid to the Afghans, has (combined with official anti-American propaganda in response to these actions), produced a real anxiety among Soviet workers and peasants, many of whom blame their troubles, even crop failures and shortages of consumer goods, on the United States and President Reagan. One former Soviet soldier says Soviets are inclined to believe what they are told about aggressive American intentions toward the Soviet Union because Soviet television shows American weaponry, but very little of the Soviet military build-up. Once an absolute hush fell over a Soviet movie theater audience when the newsreel showed American carriers and other military maneuvers. The film was preceded by a short anti-American talk by a young woman, an "agitator," whose talk the audience applauded.[75]

But, despite this present tendency toward anti-Americanism by Russians, there is still among them a reservoir of respect, envy, and admiration of the United States and the material side of the American way of life, especially its productivity and its wealth of consumer goods. After seeing again and again examples of ordinary Russians' respect, even veneration, for the power, efficiency, and productivity of the United States, some observers may feel the Americans have already won. An American economist has noted that Russians rejected the notion of copying Japan in their managerial practices because "they felt much closer to the Americans." There is strong pro-American sentiment among some non-Russian Soviets, especially the three non-Slavic peoples on the Baltic Sea—the Estonians, Latvians, and Lithuanians. They have been close to the West culturally and often have relatives in the States. However, among Russians, any appreciation of American liberal democracy exists mainly among the educated, although not widely so even there. Russian history and culture have been authoritarian and collectivistic. Accordingly, America's showy individualism and public airing of disputes look anarchistic to most Russians. There are reports that many Soviets sometimes see the United States as a country about to fall apart.[76] No doubt Ronald Reagan has scotched this view, but he has not provided one Russians prefer.

Unfortunately, we now lack, and probably will continue to lack, sufficient believable poll data on Soviet attitudes toward the United States. All we know, or think we know, is that the Soviet public admires Americans and their economic achievements but is puzzled by American moods, politics, and policies and is concerned that certain actions of the United States government may threaten or bring about a general war. Soviet polls of the early 1980s on reactions to media coverage of international affairs found that relations with the United States were seen as important by 82 percent, a larger percentage than for any other country, and that the United States was seen as having the second highest standard of living among foreign countries. However, it was also seen as having the second worst record on human rights.[77] It is difficult to guess from this what the overall Soviet public's view of the United States is. It is fascinating to speculate on whether Soviet public opinion is pushing Gorbachev to an arrangement with the United States. Possibly Gorbachev is faced with a distinct Soviet public opinion ascertained through unpublished polls and KGB and local party organs' reports.

Propaganda and Espionage

Both countries engage in propaganda to sway public opinion. They try to reach each other's citizens with short-wave radio broadcasts. Each likewise tries to influence citizens of third countries against the other superpower. Both also spy on one another. Much of this attempt to learn the secrets of the other side is really research—detailed, specific, and determined research in open sources by members of the CIA and KGB who are doing what is essentially scholarship, although with governmental and military needs in mind.

The conduct of active measures and disinformation has always been a small part of the two countries' efforts vis-à-vis each other despite what the media and the very active "industry" of spy novels suggest. Fiction is usually more exciting than fact. And although some citizens of the superpowers are opposed to such means, they are usually accepted as unavoidable by government officials. The extent to which terrorism is aided or directed by the superpowers' spy agencies is still a controversial question.[78]

Although we cannot learn all the details of the superpowers' espionage operations against each other, considerable facts are known about past actions, partly because of defections and failures on both sides. During the late 1940s and in the 1950s, the CIA put native agents into the USSR and the Communist states of Eastern Europe.[79] The United States has had agents within the Soviet Foreign Ministry, military intelligence, and possibly the KGB. It has certainly been able to debrief hundreds, if not thousands, of knowledgeable defectors from the USSR and has even been able to listen in on Soviet leaders' radio-telephone conversations. Rumor has it that in the 1950s the United States had about one thousand Soviet citizens on the CIA payroll. The CIA also attempts to convince and to entrap Soviet officials to work for it. Although human intelligence (HUMINT) is still important, "the most important source of technical intelligence gathered by the United States is that collected by photographic and electronic reconnaissance satellites." Before satellites, ships and planes were used.[80]

The Soviet Union has an advantage over the United States in carrying out intelligence operations. The United States is an open society in which even Soviet diplomats, despite FBI surveillance, are able to spy. Soviet covert operatives, "illegals," both Soviet and American, are even freer to operate. The case of Colonel Abel, who lived in Brooklyn under the cover of an artist and who actually broadcast information to the USSR, is the most well-known. He was eventually exchanged for Francis Gary Powers, the pilot of the CIA U-2 spy plane shot down in the USSR in 1960. The Soviets are able to "buy" agents from among Americans with access to secrets who either are in financial difficulty or who are willing to sell out their country for momey. Entrapment of Americans in the Soviet Union is also pursued. And, of course, Soviet reconnaissance satellites are as present in the skies as are the American ones. In addition, flights of the USSR's airline, Aeroflot, have purposely gone off course a number of times, flying over United States Air Force bases and naval shipyards. Soviet ships, ostensibly fishing vessels, regularly monitor test firings of American missiles and conduct surveillance of American naval stations as well as monitor American radio and telephone conversations. Soviet diplomatic missions in the United States also engage in such activities.[81] In any case, although mutual espionage by the superpowers produces anger and annoyance on both sides, without it they would trust each other even less.

DIPLOMACY AND NEGOTIATIONS

Diplomacy has been defined as the management of international relations by negotiation. In reality though, diplomacy is often war by other means. This is particularly true now that war has been excluded from the American-Soviet competition. Negotiations and diplomacy, indeed, the relationship itself, becomes the main field of superpower contest and contention. The two giants often use the form and language of diplomacy not to reach conciliation and agreement but as a way to embarrass and show each other up.

The summit meetings between Reagan and Gorbachev could not produce agreement. They were contests or "matches" as much as they were negotiating sessions. Both Reagan and Gorbachev feared the summits would be made a trap for them. Given the suspicions arising from the conflictful nature of the Soviet-American relationship, any negotiations between the two powers will inevitably be hedged round with wariness and permeated with contention.

It has long been said that states have no permanent friends and that an ambassador is sent abroad to lie and spy for his country. But at the same time, diplomacy, limited and imperfect and troublesome as it may be, is "an essential element in any reasonable relation between ... nation and nation."[82]

Diplomacy, whether seen broadly as the entire complex of making and carrying out foreign policy or narrowly as a technical process of communicating and negotiating between governments, is required to obtain other states' consent to realizing one's own state's national interests. Such consent is achieved by a mixture of persuasion, pressure, bargaining, and compromise operating through an orderly procedure toward an agreement. If the agreement is fully formalized, it may exist on paper as a signed treaty.[83]

With the large-scale entry of revolutionary Russia and the egalitarian United States into diplomacy some significant changes occurred. Public opinion and propaganda came to have a role in foreign policy. The Americans began to push public diplomacy after World War I as an attempt to rid the world of the secret diplomacy that was blamed for that war. And, although diplomacy has long involved a bit of low-key espionage, the Soviets seem to have made it a major function, with about one-third of their embassy staffs being KGB operatives. Recently diplomacy has come to provide cover for deadly "active measures"—bombings, assassinations, and other terrorist acts—some of which may have been supported by the USSR and its sister states, e.g., Bulgaria and Czechoslovakia. Diplomacy has long been based on the threat of force, but this use of anonymous, deadly violence to further states' ends is new and signifies, among other things, that the traditional core of diplomacy is under severe strain. It may be more dangerous to be a diplomat than a soldier these days. Certainly, the former is an easier target.

Still, traditional diplomacy has extremely valuable functions and is necessary in order to resolve or at least ameliorate differences between states and prevent conflict from running wild and possibly developing into actual war. Good diplomacy has the virtues of "quick adaptation to new situations, clever use of psychological opening, retreat and advance as the situation may require, persuasion, the *quid pro quo* of bargaining, and the like."[84]

The general tasks of diplomacy are: (1) to determine one's own objectives in the light of the power actually supporting them, (2) to assess other nations' objectives and the power actually behind them, (3) to determine the extent to which these different objectives are compatible, and (4) to employ the means suited to realize objectives. More specific functions of diplomacy in action are: (1) protection of a state's interests and its citizens abroad, (2) representing a state abroad, (3) observation and reporting, and (4) negotiation.[85] It aims at "the striking of compromises by parties with differing perspectives and clashing interests."[86] This is often very difficult. But only through negotiations can someone's actual intentions be determined. Official positions can be mere pretense, which negotiations can refine into actual bargaining positions and eventual agreement. In any case, it is safer to be on speaking terms than not with those with whom you disagree.

Entering negotiations is often politically difficult, particularly for a democracy. The Soviet Union, on the other hand, has a domestic control system which allows its government to negotiate secretly, at least from its own population. The most notable example is Stalin's secret and very rapid conclusion of an agreement with Hitler's Germany dividing up Poland and East Central Europe. The United States usually has to negotiate inside the "goldfish bowl" of media and public attention; witness, for example, President Reagan's "secret" negotiations of 1985–86 with Iran for the release of American hostages in Lebanon. They became public and an embarrassment for the administration. Another American limitation is the need of government to negotiate with the domestic interest groups and government agencies that demand a say. A former Secretary of State has said that he had to spend at least half his time on the domestic politicking for a policy before he could even begin to talk to foreigners.[87] Government agencies can have their own negotiating positions. As one pro-arms control scientist has said, "Negotiating with the Soviets, who worries about that? It's negotiations with the White House and the Pentagon that are the first concern."[88]

Certain kinds of negotiations can be very popular with Americans. These particularly include negotiations aimed at peace in which the United States appears as an "honest broker"—the Camp David talks between Egypt and Israel chaired by President Carter being the best recent example. Americans tend to prefer a strong, assertive foreign policy, but one oriented toward solutions and eventual peace, not bellicosity and conflict.[89] Negotiations with the Soviet Union do not fit into this category as they tend to involve weaponry and areas of contention and remind people of the possibility of war. In addition, United States-Soviet negotiations always raise false hopes among some Americans and serious disquiet among others. Not only that, there seems to be a fear among the public that the United States will inevitably be tricked by the Soviets, whom some feel are too unsavory to talk to at all. Only a decided change in Soviet policy toward Afghanistan and Poland plus significant arms reductions might make the USSR a more acceptable negotiating partner in the eyes of many Americans. But all this would have to be negotiated, and so here we have something like a "Catch-22." Unfortunately, it is easier for the Soviets and the Americans, like two people sharing the same apartment but unwilling to forge a lasting commitment, to try to go on as they have—negotiating fitfully "around the edges" but never tying a serious "knot."

Negotiating with the USSR is unpleasant for some Americans, yet necessary to produce a better world. It is important, for one thing, not to isolate the USSR from the West, for then that nuclear superpower would fall back upon its "despotic traditions, resentments and anxieties.... Its first victims would be what we profess to care about in foreign affairs—human rights, Eastern Europeans and a safe world." A failure to negotiate is also to throw away two major opportunities—(1) a deal with a new Soviet government driven to reduce superpower tensions and arms costs by a strong desire to revitalize Soviet society and the economy and (2) a limit to a new and fantastically expensive round in the arms race that could last for decades.[90]

By now, the United States and the Soviet Union have been negotiating with each other for more than half a century. Negotiations have limited the superpower competition and have resulted in many agreements in the military, economic, political, and cultural spheres, notably SALT I and II. But diplomacy can affect the relationship "only marginally," says a former American foreign service officer who specialized in United States-Soviet relations.[91] The superpower relationship is competitive, and most of the agreements concluded have affected only a fraction of American and Soviet military programs and foreign policy behaviors. Yet past negotiations have had an important role in reducing the intensity and unpredictability of United States-Soviet rivalry. Though this is not the best outcome imaginable, it is an improvement over the full-blown cold war of the past. More development of the relationship is possible. A recent Soviet general secretary said that "it is difficult ... to comprehend the logic of those who say that tension is inevitable in relations with the USSR...." He went on to call for "honest, businesslike negotiations" on national security issues conducted on the basis of "equality and identical security."[92] Many Americans tend to agree, while others find the concept of "equality" troubling.

Diplomatic Representation

The Soviet Union has three sets of diplomatic representatives in the United States—at the embassy in Washington, at a consulate in San Francisco, and at the United Nations in New York City. Technically, the latter is not in the United States at all and is formally made up of three delegations—Soviet, Ukrainian, and Belo-Russian. The United States has diplomats in two Soviet cities—an embassy in Moscow, the capital, and a consulate in Leningrad. There are about one hundred diplomats at each embassy and about eighteen at each consulate.

This scale of diplomatic representation is extremely limited. Both countries want and could use more consulates on each other's territory. But security concerns and politics stand in the way. The FBI argues that it cannot keep adequate track of what KGB operatives under diplomatic cover are doing now, particularly since other Communist embassies also engage in espionage. The Soviets are not certain they want American diplomats and associated CIA operatives in non-Russian areas of the Soviet Union. The United States would like to have consulates in Soviet Central Asia and in the Baltic republics—areas with considerable anti-Russian sentiment, as the 1986 riots in Kazakhstan show. And, of course, the issue of reciprocity cannot be avoided. For every additional consulate one superpower is granted, the other wants one in return. Perhaps an increased level of trade and an improved climate in superpower relations would allow more diplomatic representation. But this would require that espionage be reduced and feelings of insecurity enhanced on both sides.

Both superpowers have developed a cadre of diplomats who specialize in the other superpower. One of the original four Americans so trained, George F. Kennan, was the originator of the containment doctrine in the late 1940s and also a prolific writer on Soviet history and Soviet and American foreign policy. Another Soviet specialist, Jack Matlock, was on the staff of the National Security Council during part of the Reagan Administration and was then appointed ambassador to the USSR by President Reagan. Anatoly Dobrynin, Soviet ambassador in Washington for more than twenty years, became one of Gorbachev's top advisers. At last a Soviet leader has a close adviser with really significant experience in the United States.

Nevertheless, American diplomats experienced in Soviet affairs can be ignored by the policy makers. Also, the many United States government agencies that deal with the USSR have sometimes done so without any co-ordination, much less communication. Every major institution in Washington can come up with its own Soviet policy. Even within the State Department, there can be little communication between the Soviet desk, the researchers on the USSR, and the policy planning staff. Under President Reagan the State Department's Soviet expertise was brought into play only late, and within strong constraints. A key meeting on Soviet policy early in the Reagan administration included no one with any Soviet experience.[93]

In terms of formal diplomatic structure, the USSR gives more prominence to relations with the United States than the United States gives to its ties with the USSR. Whereas the Soviet Foreign Ministry has a department for the United States alone, in the U.S. Department of State relations with the Soviet Union are the responsibility of a Soviet desk within the Bureau of European and Canadian Affairs. It has periodically been suggested that United States-Soviet relations be upgraded in organizational terms, possibly by creating a bureau for Soviet-Communist affairs and a joint presidential-congressional commission for them.

But even without an upgrading, the superpowers' diplomats are either negotiating or talking to each other in a large variety of forums. Besides embassy contacts in capital cities, there are the various sets of arms negoti-ations, as well as talks on navies, nuclear energy, and other topics.

Public Diplomacy by Governments.   Formal talks are not the only way in which the governments of the superpowers communicate or conduct diplomacy with each other. Both these states have never fully accepted the traditional European model of diplomacy, a model that centers on elites, experts, formal negotiations, and secrecy and that derives from the behavior and attitudes of aristocracy. Americans have long tended to see diplomats as "cookie-pushers" who could be dispensed with if only leaders and representatives of ordinary people could talk face-to-face. The early Soviet hopes for a new diplomacy were epitomized by Trotsky, promising in 1917 that he would "close up" the Tsar's Ministry of Foreign Affairs, and by the Bolsheviks' use of radio and other forms of propaganda to foment revolution. With such anti-traditionalist attitudes, both superpowers tend to use so-called public diplomacy, or attempts to obtain public support for policy directly from citizens of other countries. Both superpowers make enormous and very expensive efforts to influence each other's publics. Soviet censorship and jamming of American broadcasts cannot completely exclude them, while the Soviet leadership, particularly the vigorous and very confident General Secretary Gorbachev, find the American media will take their messages to the American people. (Few Americans have shortwave receivers or are inclined, it seems, to listen much to Soviet broadcasts to them.) Both Soviet and American leaders have even been able, occasionally, to address the other country's citizens directly on their own domestic television. Brezhnev did so while in the United States in 1973, Nixon in the USSR in 1972, and Reagan and Gorbachev in New Year's messages in 1986. This may eventually become routine, even while much remains in dispute between the superpowers.

Some of this public diplomacy is either pure propaganda or attempts to embarrass or weaken the other side. It can build up such a head of steam as to block chances of any agreement. At such times there are calls for both sides to end their "grandstanding" and return to traditional secret contacts. For example, in early 1986 Secretary of State Shultz said, "We're not going anywhere" until both sides stop conducting their diplomacy in public. "We will get somewhere . . . when we're able to have some discussions that are relatively quiet and direct," he added. Sometimes the superpowers go to TV and the press even before the diplomatic negotiators hear each other's statements. "This isn't diplomacy at all; it's plain old pitchmanship," one commentator writes.[94] Public diplomacy can be a way of avoiding formal diplomacy, usually still the only route to agreements that bind governments.

Nongovernmental Negotiations. An almost uncountable number of American individuals, groups, foundations, and businesses are involved in this activity. A common argument against such contacts is that Americans are largely unable to get behind the official facade of government-controlled organizations in the USSR. Those in favor of informal negotiations hold that putting a wide range of Americans' views to the Soviet government is a way of breathing some realism and flexibility into the Soviet system. Talking with a country as diverse as the United States cannot be accomplished effectively through one, formal channel. Eventually, the Soviet will have to decentralize their contacts.

The range of such American "talking contacts" with the USSR is extraordinarily broad, from Trout Unlimited, a conservation organization fostering fishing exchanges, to the National Academy of Sciences, to Turner Broadcasting Corporation, which sponsored the "Goodwill Games" in Moscow in 1986. The National Academy of Sciences pledged to use all its channels with the Soviet scientific community to press for the release of Sakharov, the Soviet physicist who had been placed in internal exile in 1980. He was eventually released. The Academy had shown its willingness to suspend all contacts with Soviet scientists. Such United States-Soviet nongovernmental contacts are integral aspects of the superpower negotiating process, although it is difficult to specify their exact role.

Academic contacts and discussions are common. For example, every year a Soviet-American dialogue between academics takes place at Dartmouth College with funding from the Kettering and Rockefeller Foundations. Meetings such as these are held in hopes of improving mutual comprehension of attitudes, intentions, and policies.[95] It can be a long and uncomfortable process. Once a Soviet delegation arrived at an American campus to view its reportedly automated library. The director embarrassedly told them the reported marvels had never been implemented. But the Soviets refused to believe him and were convinced they were being denied access for political reasons. Similarly, many an American delegation has found it hard to believe what it is told in the Soviet Union. In 1984 and in 1985 the Kennedy School of Government and the U.S.A. Institute, a Soviet research organization, held joint conferences on crisis prevention attended by scholars from both countries. The idea behind the project was to clarify and define American and Soviet interests in various geographical regions in order to help avoid crises. The Carter Center at Emory University held a meeting in Atlanta in 1985 on international security and arms control with top-level participants from the superpowers and the Federal Republic of Germany, France, and China.

There are a number of travel-study seminars that give American faculty and students the chance to engage in discussions with groups of Soviet citizens. For a number of years an American group called The Citizens Exchange Council has been sponsoring such tours of the Soviet Union for any persons willing to pay travel costs. Travel by ordinary Americans to the USSR is particularly important when neither the President, nor three-quarters of the House of Representatives, nor half the Senate have ever been to the USSR. Very few of the Soviet leaders have ever been to the United States. Perhaps if enough Americans voice their own views directly to Soviet citizens it will get through to the Soviet leaders that there is a definite authenticity and depth to Americans' desire for peace and their concerns about certain practices of the Soviet Union.

Perhaps the most ambitious citizen-to-citizen project so far has been the "sister cities" plan, the attempt to get the residents of hundreds of American and Soviet cities to think of themselves as paired with people in a city in the other superpower. It is hoped that, after an initial exchange of materials about their cities, delegations of residents will exchange visits and that eventually a regular pattern of correspondence and travel will emerge and a mass feeling of friendship between the peoples will develop. Just possibly the project may aid in opening up many Soviet cities, now closed to foreigners, to visitors from the West.

All this is well-intentioned, say critics of citizen diplomacy, but how can two peoples communicate when they have so little in common politically? If the conversations are on innocuous topics, there will be no communication of the essence of contentious, democratic America. Important advice on citizen diplomacy comes from a famous ex-Soviet dissident, Natan Sharansky (formerly Anatoly Shcharansky). He emphasizes that Americans should insist on contacts with all of the people they want to see, not just those approved by the Soviet government. The Soviets can be made to change their behavior if enough time and effort are made. Also, we should demand that the Soviets be forthright and forthcoming in these contacts. Americans must not play games and deceive themselves in their contacts with Soviets.

Government-to-Government Negotiations. During most of the Reagan administration there was little serious negotiation with the Soviets. However, President Reagan was a president almost uniquely strong domestically to negotiate successfully with the USSR and gradually he began to move in that direction, though not smoothly and perhaps not willingly. Eventually, therefore, Reagan and Gorbachev were able to get beyond diplomatic grandstanding and posturing to actual negotiations on concrete texts, notably the medium-range missile agreement.

> There is a recurring Soviet pattern in superpower diplomacy: First, the new Administration would be greeted with a generous offer to talk, meet, and to settle "outstanding differences." Then, there would be a display of pique over a hesitant or negative response. Then would come a Soviet decision point: either to launch more aggressive testing or to shift to a posture of more genuine accommodation.[96]

The Americans, too, have a pattern—one of continually raising the ante and demanding more than the Soviets are willing to give at any point. Finally, in 1987 the Soviets, no doubt on the basis of a personal decision by Gorbachev, broke their pattern. They stopped insisting on three matters: limitation of SDI, counting the British and French nuclear deterrents, and avoiding on-site inspection—at least in order to wrap up the deal on medium-range missiles.

Negotiations with the Soviet Union cannot eliminate the fundamental antagonism in the superpower relationship, but they can allow some reduction of tensions connected with certain key issues—regional conflicts, weaponry, and trade. It is essential, however, that any United States government negotiating with the Soviets have a definite position or clear goals and be prepared to endure a difficult and trying negotiating process over a long period of time.

It is too early to tell if, under Gorbachev, Soviet negotiating is becoming uniformly speedy. The current willingness of the USSR to move rapidly on some issues may not last. Above all, no American President can afford to be too experimental in negotiations with the Soviets. A failure in foreign policy can be irretrievable and have serious negative effects for decades. Accordingly, the Soviets cannot be given "freebies" in hopes they will reciprocate. Why should the Soviets give anything away to someone who is already weakening his negotiating position?

One reassuring fact is that the superpowers have maintained diplomatic contacts and discussions even during times of tension. And, even when big matters cannot be negotiated, these contacts can be kept up and the superpowers can talk broadly about mutual concerns. Such discussions can eventually result in a better understanding of interests and a better basis for agreements. An interesting suggestion for laying the basis for more fruitful negotiations with the USSR is to hold top-level regular meetings, perhaps even summit meetings, on both specific and technical matters and on issues of crucial importance to the two countries.[97] As Gorbachev has said: "The situation must be improved. . . . It is time to begin somewhere, to get moving."[98]

Whatever agreements the United States and the USSR make, their negotiations will often still be difficult. As a veteran United States negotiator has put it, "Negotiating with the Soviets is a little like putting coins in a broken vending machine. Just talking to it won't do any good." The Soviets might make their own statement of frustration with the United States. Perhaps— "You push a boulder up to the summit, and the Americans switch to a new set of issues." It is very difficult for many Americans to accept that "we cannot negotiate a position of superiority over the Soviet Union. We can only negotiate a position of equality."[99] But many Americans do not think the Soviets will be content with equality.

The lack of trust between the superpowers is only one indicator of the many cultural differences that plague their diplomacy. Americans live in a private-enterprise "bargaining society" and tend to see diplomacy as a process in which mutual concessions and compromise produce a lasting result beneficial to both sides. Russians come out of a state-centered society in which the elite wins most of the benefits. There is no requirement that concessions granted by one side be matched by concessions from the other side. Another cultural difference is the tendency of the Soviets to start with broad declarations of principle, while the Americans tend to begin with specific matters, even details. The Soviets are fully capable of holding to a position that blocks progress for long periods and then suddenly giving it up and wanting rapid progress. This tends to be offensive to Americans, while Soviets may be put off by American tendencies to talk about matters that appear extraneous to the Soviets: civil rights, for example. The Soviets can complain that raising such matters is asking something that negotiation cannot give. American politicians tend to think that they can charm or talk Soviet politicians into agreement, failing to realize that Soviet politics is not a matter of winning elections.

Still, despite American-Soviet cultural differences, negotiations on a number of matters have been brought to conclusion. And, despite the tenaciousness and firmness with which they begin negotiations, Soviets can eventually compromise. It seems, "once they start adjusting, they always seem to be in a great hurry to wrap things up. . . . A skillful negotiator can extract Soviet concessions."[100] For example, Brezhnev, who seemed like a model of patience and even stolidness, became very eager for agreements with Nixon.

It is necessary to distinguish between Soviet strategy, long-term goals, and special negotiating tactics and style, on the one hand, and the "flexibility, pragmatism, and even opportunism" of Soviet negotiations when and if they decide to go for a closure of negotiations and an agreement. Significantly, a leading, rather conservative, scholar of the Soviet Union admits: "Whenever they are interested in a settlement, Communist diplomats act in a traditional manner, efficiently and undeterred by difficulties."[101]

A big question, then, is how to get the Soviets to the "end game" of a negotiation. A primary initial requirement is to enter only into negotiations the Soviets can reasonably be expected to conclude. Good knowledge of the Soviet system and its needs and problems is important. The context and timing of negotiations must be favorable as well; both international politics and Soviet and American domestic politics must allow a reasonable chance of attaining an agreement. It is essential to decide beforehand what one wants and what one will not give up. Now patience and good negotiating style carefully honed to deal with the Soviets must be brought to bear. Informal discussions between formal sessions are also useful. Informal probing and exchanges played a key role in concluding the SALT agreements.[102]

The fact that some United States-Soviet negotiations have been successfully concluded does not mean that superpower negotiations are not a special sort of problem. Remember, in negotiations with the Americans, the Soviets are dealing with the most powerful "significant other" who also epitomizes for them the non-Soviet world's opposition to the USSR and its goals and possible expansion. In such a situation, why should the Soviet negotiator be all sweetness, light, and clarity?

A former United States ambassador to Moscow has said that negotiating with the Russians is somewhat "unpleasant" since they "antagonize you . . . when they start out; they try to put you on the defensive right away." A contemporary commentator notes that "the Soviet Union is a sluggish, hidebound, suspicious partner in negotiations."[103] A United States negotiator of academic exchanges says the Soviets always take a position that would be very costly to the United States side if taken seriously, e.g., "We cannot pay for it; you will have to do it." Several American negotiators, in both the government and private enterprise, have said that the American negotiator must be prepared to walk away in order to break an impasse. One very successful American negotiator for a large corporation says he has occasionally slammed shut his briefcase and left the table only to find himself telephoned and invited back to the negotiations as if nothing had happened.

How much of the special nature of Soviet negotiating style remains? Some changes have occurred as the Soviet elite have come to lead a more relaxed life and to learn more about the outside world. Soviet diplomats are now more professional and their approaches more polished and businesslike, while specialists have greater input into negotiations. Still, certain Soviet characteristics remain. One in particular is worth noting—the tendency to force the other side to take the initiative and offer proposals.[104] The Soviet negotiator can act like a silent judge—letting the other side try to come up with ways of moving the negotiations forward. This is sound as pure tactics go, but it cannot produce goodwill. No wonder so many American negotiators are "turned off" by dealing with the Soviets.

Americans, too, seem to have a particular kind of diplomacy that creates special difficulties in dealing with the Soviets. Henry Kissinger has noted that American habits of democratic consultation lead to a cult of foreign policy-making by committees, which cannot work well in dealing with a long-term foreign political challenge reflecting a very different history and values. This "rule by committee" still exists. One American former negotiator says that, despite the fact that Soviet diplomats have less routine interdepartmental contact with each other than do Americans, they "always seemed on a longer leash than ours to probe and talk about virtually any related topic. Our negotiators were invariably held more tightly to scripts hammered out by every agency with any conceivable interest in the subject." Problems may be inherent in American diplomacy. Some diplomats cite the absence of discipline in Congress. A United States ambassador mentions failure to reconcile conflicting views, staking out positions that are later scrapped, and sending confusing signals. One of the United States negotiators of SALT I sees the greatest problem of the American side as the "absence of consensus" on goals resulting from the burden of "continual negotiating and maneuvering among various elements within the American government."[105] Some of this may be "fixable" and some not. An avoidable problem is not having amateurs making Soviet policy. Under Reagan most of the real makers of policy toward the USSR were people who had not studied the country, had not been there, and did not speak Russian.[106]

SUMMITS AND SUMMITRY

The high point of United States-Soviet negotiations is the summit meeting between an American president and a Soviet general secretary. Table 8.2 offers a summary of them. To some, however, it is a low and dangerous point to be avoided. Seasoned diplomats and experienced scholars of foreign affairs tend to see summits as pernicious exercises in make-believe and self-delusion. Many think only experienced and specialist negotiators working in their own way at their own pace can bring about good and lasting agreements. Summits involve generalist and sometimes, in the American case, amateurish politicians working under electoral pressures. It may have been President Lyndon Johnson who said that every American president who has met with a Soviet leader has lost his shirt. Yet, summits are unavoidable. As the diplomat who led the American negotiating team in SALT I says, "The real bargaining must be done by the political leaders who are on top of all the angles," including especially the purely political ones.[107] It is only they, after all, who may be able to persuade their countries' bureaucrats, military men, and other leaders to accept and implement Soviet-American agreements. Moreover, in the American case, the president must also persuade the population, or key parts of it, to accept such agreements.

TABLE 8.2. UNITED STATES-SOVIET SUMMIT MEETINGS

World War II

1943—Tehran (Iran)
1945—Yalta (USSR)
1945—Potsdam (defeated Germany)
(All included the British Prime Minister as well.)

Postwar

July 1955, Geneva
Eisenhower, Bulganin, and Khrushchev
Main topics: Aerial surveillance, East-West relations, German reunification

September 1959, Camp David
Eisenhower and Khrushchev
Main topics: Disarmament, cultural and scientific exchanges

May 1960, Paris (aborted)
Eisenhower and Khrushchev
Main topics: Berlin, disarmament, East-West relations
(Cut short because of U-2 spy plane incident)

June 1961, Vienna
Kennedy and Khrushchev
Main topics: Nuclear test ban treaty, Laos, Berlin

June 1967, Glassboro, New Jersey
Johnson and Kosygin (Kosygin was not party leader but only head of government)
Main topics: Middle East, Vietnam War, nuclear arms

May 1972, Moscow
Nixon and Brezhnev
Main topics: SALT and ABM treaty

June 1973, Washington, DC
Nixon and Brezhnev
Main topics: SALT, trade, exchanges, research on agriculture and nuclear energy, transportation, and oceanography.

June and July 1974, Moscow and Yalta
Nixon and Brezhnev
Main topics: Treaty banning underground nuclear testing, ten-year economic pact

November 1974, Vladivostok
Ford and Brezhnev
Main topic: SALT treaty

August 1975, Helsinki
Ford and Brezhnev
Main topics: European security, SALT treaty

June 1979, Vienna
Carter and Brezhnev
Main topic: Signing of SALT II treaty

November 1985, Geneva
Reagan and Gorbachev
Main topics: Nuclear arms reduction, exchanges   (*continued*)

TABLE 8.2. (Continued)

Postwar

October 1986, Reykjavik, Iceland
Reagan and Gorbachev
Main topics: Nuclear arms reduction and SDI

December 1987, Washington, DC
Reagan and Gorbachev
Main topics: Signing of INF treaty, human rights, regional issues

May 1988, Moscow
Reagan and Gorbachev
Main topics: Human rights, regional issues, trade, signing of minor control agreements

The standard thinking on summits is that they must be "carefully prepared" beforehand by the diplomats and the top leaders' political advisers in order to result in the formal political conclusion of agreements worked out in advance. This expresses the long-standing view of the nineteenth-century British foreign minister that one never goes to a meeting without knowing its outcome beforehand. It is usually held that a summit that fails to produce concrete results would set back relations. In any case, a surprise at a summit meeting, as at Reykjavik in 1986, when the Soviet leader suggested the elimination of all nuclear weapons and the President agreed in principle, sends shock waves through both domestic and international politics which take a long time to control.

Certainly, the history of United States-Soviet summits does not induce optimism about their positive effects. Even "well-prepared summits" have not been shining successes. Possibly, the Nixon-Brezhnev summits of the early 1970s might have been a long-term success if the Watergate scandal had not resulted in Nixon's resignation. The other type of summit has been the "let's get to know each other" summit. The worst of these was the Vienna summit of 1961 between newly elected President Kennedy and the veteran of Stalinist politics, Khrushchev. The meeting, occurring after the failed American-sponsored Bay of Pigs landing in Cuba, seemed to have convinced the Soviet leader he could make gains at American expense. The Soviet introduction of offensive missiles into Cuba followed, a ploy that was defeated only by adroit American maneuvering coupled with the threat of war.

Despite the risks inherent in such summits, it is often suggested they become routine. For example, during the Carter administration, Brzezinski, the national security adviser, suggested, with Carter's approval, that "both sides adopt the practice of holding regular, informal annual discussion meetings not tied to specific agreements." Brzezinski "felt that such meetings would provide the basis for more serious discussion of contentious issues, without generating public expectation of wide-ranging agreement."[108] This may not be a bad idea if public expectations are kept down and if neither side surprises the other or gives in to new ideas uncritically.

Nixon and Kissinger have said that the informal meetings at the Nixon-Brezhnev summits were the best use of the leaders' time.[109] These, however, were well-prepared summits attended by experienced political professionals on both sides. Brezhnev once said that "summit meetings . . . are the most useful for a better understanding of each other's positions and intentions and for adopting serious political decisions" as well as making it possible to "untie knots and to make decisions that signify further progress." (Brezhnev was in five summit meetings with three American Presidents.)

Former President Nixon has said that annual summit meetings are essential to develop "rules of engagement" that could prevent the superpowers' profound differences from causing armed conflict. The first priority of such summits ought to be, he says, not arms control but "potential flash points" of wars. He adds that scheduled summit meetings inhibit antagonistic acts and, if they are at all successful, they are very useful tools for getting both countries' bureaucracies moving. Of course, "it is far better to have no agreement at all than to negotiate a bad one." A former government official says that the more often summits are held the easier it will be to avoid negative political effects.[110]

A continual problem of summits is their tendency to become both media events and prisoners of excessive public expectation, particularly in the United States. However, summitry fits in well with American cultural predilections for "getting along" by putting differences aside through compromise in a sort of international bipartisanship. The public effect of a superpower summit can be like "that of a large whisky: a warm glow, a relaxed feeling, a tendency to put the slippers on . . . there's no need to worry." If this mood is shattered, political trouble inevitably follows. "Summit meetings . . . do create high expectations; and . . . the spirit of Geneva or Camp David fades quickly, and the harsher, quarrelsome relationship is restored."[111]

Governments, publics, and political systems are more than extensions or props of their leaders; they are political "beings" in their own right, with interests and goals, and cannot be brought into agreement through a few hours spent in front of a fireplace.

In November 1985 the first United States-Soviet summit in six years took place at Geneva between President Reagan, then in his second term, and the new Soviet General Secretary Gorbachev, twenty years the American's junior. Reagan first proposed the summit in March when Gorbachev came to power and later said he wanted to deal practically with him and would meet him more than halfway. The Politburo declared it was ready for improved relations with the West. Although the killing of a United States officer by a Soviet sentry in East Germany set back the move toward the summit, progress was revived. The road to the summit was helped along by Western European governments and even the United States industrialist Armand Hammer, well-connected in the

USSR. Preparatory talks were held by the diplomats in Helsinki, Moscow, and elsewhere and the outlines of an agenda emerged by August. The Soviet ambassador identified three groups of questions: international security, regional conflicts, and United States-Soviet relations. American officials added a fourth category: human rights. Reagan's spokesman said the President's approach to Gorbachev would be serious, related to the issues, nonhostile, and future-oriented. Still, the immediate pre-summit meetings were rocky. One United States official said Gorbachev used a "bare-knuckled," tough lawyer manner in meeting with Secretary of State Shultz, who admitted just before the summit that United States-Soviet differences on major issues had not been narrowed. Gorbachev had learned there would be no compromise on SDI. Although the summit was "well-prepared," its prospects were not bright.

The results were meager. No breakthrough occurred on arms control though joint commitments were made to try to proceed toward real reductions in strategic weaponry and an agreement on medium-range missiles. Some broadening of cultural exchanges was worked out. Reagan and Gorbachev spent five hours in one-on-one discussion. The President claimed a "fresh start" had been made and that, although there was no meeting of minds on fundamentals, the two sides understood each other better. The big unresolved issue that limited progress was the American unwillingness to limit SDI.

But, since both sides still wanted an agreement or at least the appearance of one, another summit was inevitable. The year 1986 was one of American congressional elections. A summit or even the promise of one would tend to improve Republicans' chances. The administration also wanted to talk to the Soviets on arms control and other issues that limit United States-Soviet relations, such as Jewish emigration and Soviet activities in Afghanistan. The Soviet leader needed a new "détente" that would reduce the pressure on the USSR to maintain its military might at such an expensive level and would also allow the start of a significant economic revitalization of the country. Still, United States policies worked against a summit almost as much as for it. The United States continued to test nuclear weapons and thus ignored the Soviet moratorium on tests. American warships sailed to within six miles of the Soviet Black Sea coast. A large reduction in Soviet representation at the United Nations was ordered. Libya was attacked. The Soviets, for their part, continued to fight in Afghanistan and to aid the Sandinistas in Nicaragua.

"Vigorous and pointed" preparations for this second Reagan-Gorbachev meeting in Reykjavik, Iceland were underway by June 1986, despite the surface deterioration of United States-Soviet relations. The Soviets seemed to have decided they did not need a total elimination of SDI research, that they could allow additional verification, and that talks on chemical weapons might go forward. The Americans were also willing to proceed as long as the summit dealt with more than the single issue of arms control. Before he left for Reykjavik, Reagan said the agenda was "a broad-based" one. A spokesman for Gorbachev said that he would "do all in his power to bring about reasonable compromises" and that the agenda was "flexible."[112]

What happened at Reykjavik is not fully clear. Yet more than enough became known to cause great consternation in defense and conservative circles in the United States. The two leaders went beyond their agenda and their "handlers" and actually discussed eliminating all ballistic missiles and even all nuclear weapons. "Utopia," exclaimed a liberal columnist. America's allies were stunned. What about British, French, and Chinese missiles, many asked. A French wit suggested that politicians should not be allowed to negotiate alone. Although both sides were in agreement on a 50 percent cut in all strategic missile warheads and a global limit of one hundred warheads on medium-range missiles, the meeting broke up without an arms-control agreement and with no date set for another summit. Soviet agreement apparently depended on an American concession on SDI. Gorbachev had insisted that there be no testing and development whatsoever and that research be confined to the laboratory.[113]

President Reagan defended his breaking off of the talks rather than compromise on SDI, claiming that it "is what brought the Soviets back to arms control talks" in the first place. He emphasized his readiness to continue to deal with Gorbachev. The State Department stated that "SDI ... remains the best insurance policy that any future arms reduction agreements will be implemented and adhered to by the Soviets." The secretary of state argued that Reykjavik was a success in that it qualitatively shifted the terms of United States-Soviet debate, "for the first time" raising a "genuine possibility of substantial *reductions* in Soviet and American nuclear arms."[114]

The general secretary accused the United States government of deliberately misrepresenting the outcome of the Reykjavik summit, of "whitewashing the destructive position of the U.S. administration, which came to the meeting unprepared ... with the old baggage." He asked why the United States would need to keep SDI if there were no missiles for it to defend against. He also reiterated that "the President did ... consent to the elimination of all ... strategic offensive arms" at Reykjavik and criticized him for lacking the will to make a "turn in history" when United States and Soviet positions had been closer than ever before. But Gorbachev added: "Let us not panic. This is not the end of contact with the United States."[115]

At best, each side had confused the other. Both leaders went beyond the terms of reference prepared by their diplomats and advisers. Summitry had again gone awry and produced disagreement and criticism, as well as dashed hopes. But the American public supported the President's refusal to compromise on SDI, 66 percent to 21 percent. (This was about the same as in a poll three years earlier: 67 to 25 percent.) Interestingly, only two Americans in five had ever thought summits would lead to agreements and almost half felt they would fail.[116]

The American military and some congressmen were shocked by the President's offers. The joint chiefs of staff made clear they had never advocated scrapping all strategic nuclear weapons. Senator Sam Nunn deplored the negative effects on United States retaliatory capability and NATO conventional nuclear defense since under the President's proposals the USSR would have kept its air defenses and its large conventional forces. Nunn said he was "relieved" at the failure of Reykjavik since the President's proposals had "not been thought through" and closed by saying United States arms-control goals have to be refashioned and interlinked with the needs and capabilities of NATO; the nuclear force levels of Britain, France, and China; and United States strategic nuclear forces.[117] NATO governments were also shocked. They could now see that NATO's doctrine of nuclear deterrence was in effect challenged and perhaps undercut by Reagan's offer at Iceland.

It is certainly odd that the American team had not been prepared for an attack on SDI by Gorbachev. Everyone, it seems, except the administration knew it had to come. Again an American politician thought he could make a summit go all his way. But Gorbachev, for his part, should have known Mr. Reagan was personally committed to SDI and should have offered a big deal that did not include SDI. Could he have sold this to his associates, however?

Many liberal Americans criticized the President for not having concluded a deal. This was the chance of a lifetime in United States-Soviet relations, they argued. There were charges that agreement was not reached because it would have led to significant cuts by Congress in the military budget and, of course, in the SDI program. Other liberals, however, suggested that the President was heading, in his own way, toward a new and very far-reaching arms-control agreement that liberals ought to support.[118]

Whatever the perspective, the Iceland summit ended with an icy mood between the superpowers in an atmosphere of some turbulence and lack of clarity. To be fair, even if the summit had resulted in an agreement, fundamental American and Soviet interests would still have been in conflict. No summit conference, or even a series of them, can eliminate that conflict. Still, it is gratifying that overly ambitious goals, inadequate preparation, surprising one's negotiating partner, and mutual propagandistic recriminations could only delay the superpowers' mutual search for improved relations.[119] By the spring of 1987, in expert-level negotiations on medium-range missiles, the superpowers had made real progress toward an arms-control agreement in this major area of weaponry. This made possible a summit of a higher order—in Washington by the fall of 1987. Here was signed the INF treaty eliminating medium-range missiles in Eurasia (covered in Chapter 5).

STRATEGY

This topic has been discussed so far only implicitly or in terms of the conduct of diplomacy. But strategy—the art of overall direction—deserves separate consideration. To develop a strategy, statesmen and leaders must recognize the problem, have a clear vision of the outcome desired, and also be able to implement the strategy successfully. These are difficult conditions to meet in a changing, open, and pluralistic society like the United States, especially with respect to a powerful nation that excites feelings of apprehension, rejection, and suspicion among many Americans. Yet a general strategy is possible for the United States vis-à-vis the Soviet Union. The United States is really a rather stable sociopolitical system in which change is more a matter of style and of frequent shifts about a rather broad center than of deep or radical deviations from the center. Even Ronald Reagan has not been able to institutionalize his views as the dominant perspective in the body politic. Moreover, he has given mainly lip service to the views of the small but vocal right wing as he moves toward accommodation with the Soviet Union.

It is extremely unlikely that future presidents will come to Washington with anything like Mr. Reagan's anti-establishment, activist anti-Sovietism. Ronald Reagan is unique. American governments to come will probably not adopt radical foreign policies, either of the Left or the Right. The continual debate, openness, and pluralism of a political system in which power is divided between president, Congress, and key elites and interest groups will prevent the adoption of foreign policies of narrow concept, limited support, or clearly dangerous implications. This suggests some stability and coherence will exist in future American policy toward the Soviet Union. This policy will unavoidably be surrounded by debate and disagreement, but any sound and fury are likely to have little permanent effect on overall governmental strategy toward the USSR. The American public and its elites have seen many faults in several of the "gimmick policies" of the past thirty years and accordingly are unlikely to tolerate another such "non-strategic" policy for the foreseeable future. Americans are going to have to live within a conflict, though a lessening one, with the Soviet Union and make the best of it. Hence, the inescapable drift toward strategy. Just coping is not good enough. Any strategy will have to bring results—reduced tension with the USSR; little or no further expansion of Soviet-controlled territory; and reduced drain of military expenditures.

Are such results realizable? Yes, they are. Both the international context and the internal situation of the Soviet Union are no longer conducive to Soviet expansion. This is a fact that the Soviet elite has had to accept. The prime Soviet concern is no longer with expansion but with reforming its society, coping with the problems of modernizing. Reform is now the Soviet Union's one and painful option. Just tackling this, in Gorbachev's own words, "will take generations." It is extremely doubtful reform can take place with a Stalinist stance of secretiveness, opposition to everything foreign, and expansionism. But, the conservative will ask, can we live with a reformed and thereby strengthened Soviet Union? Yes. First, we will have no choice. Second, a reformed Soviet Union will be a very different system. It will be much more westernized than it is now; and it will be much more closely intertwined with the outside world, including the United States. It will not be able to return to Stalinism or even full anti-Westernism. Among the various American options for Soviet policy, a realisitic acceptance of a mix of confrontation and cooperation is both unavoidable and the best strategy possible, at least for some time. But in the future the confrontation should be decreased and the cooperation increased, although not automatically. Linkage will have to operate, though there is no need to use the term as a challenge to the Soviets. Soviet military intervention in areas vital to the United States will have to be met by American counteraction.[120] The Soviet Union now needs the West in order to compete effectively with it. It must remain close to the West, both to exert some influence and to get those periodic infusions of grain and high technology that its own economy cannot provide until it fully westernizes. The course toward the future is beset with irony and contradiction.

Conventional victory over the Soviet Union is no longer possible. The Soviet Union is now too strong to be defeated with its conquerors still existing as functioning societies. The only victory possible is through a policy of successfully managed confrontational cooperation or competitive coexistence. Such a policy is, however, exceedingly difficult to defend in American politics, among both liberals and conservatives, although the American working class could accept it. Ironically, it is in effect the very policy the Reagan administration has had to adopt, though unwillingly and not openly, in its last years. The post-Reagan period in American politics promises to be a realistic and constructive one. For one thing, we now know so much about the Soviet Union that it is no longer the riddle, puzzle, and enigma Winston Churchill once declared it to be. This makes it possible to have some adequate level of public understanding of the USSR that precludes panic, alarm, and unreasoning hatred or fear of it and allows a coherent and long-term American strategy toward it. However, "The United States has to learn to live with a level of security considerably lower than that we enjoyed in the past"[121] and to recognize that no American strategy can by itself bring about a liberalized or easy-to-get-along-with Soviet Union. "The Bear Doesn't Dance to Our Tune."[122] This does not mean the Soviet Union will not change, even in the direction of liberalization. That result, however, is far off if it comes at all.[123] Perhaps a "normal dictatorship" with some "islands of separateness" or additional refuges from state demands is the most change possible in the near term. This kind of change now seems in the works if Gorbachev remains in power. The American public's acceptance of the inherent limits of a Soviet strategy is difficult but is realizable if the Soviet Union does not embark on new military expansions. Such a self-limitation seems to be occurring now, after the failure and embarrassment of Afghanistan and the need for retrenchment abroad in order to engage in economic reform.

Part of an American strategy must include communication and negotiation with the USSR, and in as many ways as possible. But this communication must not be pure challenge and propaganda. It must include calm, open and realistic attempts to mitigate problems in the relationship, such as armaments and their rate of increase. The Soviets would be receptive to such an approach. As former ambassador Dobrynin puts it, "The best way to ease the present tension is by chipping away at the edges of disagreement, reaching accord on comparatively minor issues and creating an atmosphere in which it would be easier to tackle the bigger questions." But he advises against trying to move fast for, given the differences between Americans and Russians, haste could cause friction and undo what has been achieved.[124] What is most negotiable should be negotiated first, e.g., trade. Arms control ought not always be first, though progress here is necessary.[125] Democratic aspirations need not be forgotten. They can remain as ultimate standards for an improved relationship.

Another requirement for an effective Soviet strategy is that the United States maintain a military balance of power with the Soviet Union but that this not become a fetish. American power is not fundamentally military but rests upon its economic capacity, its relative lack of serious societal divisions, and its natural and long-standing friendly relationships with many other countries. These countries, together with the United States, constitute a permanent and unbreachable barrier to Soviet "success." To throw away or diminish the vast power already on America's side would be the worst folly and the only way the Soviet Union could ever achieve world preeminence.

SUMMARY

This chapter has ranged over a number of topics related to the superpower relationship: the tensions stemming from the profound differences in American and Russian cultures and political systems, the difficulties arising from opposing and sometimes distorted perceptions, the challenge and promise of negotiations, and the problem of strategy. The associated questions and issues can be resolved only through the progress of the American-Soviet relationship over the years ahead.

There is no way for the cultural attributes of a people to change except over very long periods of time. Domestic political systems, too, are very slow to change but perceptions are more easily adjusted, particularly through increases in knowledge and expansion of contacts. We have seen that there are fundamental problems in the American view of the Soviet Union. Liberals tend to see the Soviet Union as a country emerging into normality from the effects of Stalinism and deprivation. Conservatives tend to see it as a vast military monster oriented only to internal control and foreign expansionism. Both views are exaggerated. The Soviet population will probably not be able to perceive the United States accurately either, until it has ready access to more and better information about the outside world. The pressures of the need for reform may bring about a more open Soviet Union over the next few decades.

The negotiating process is the easiest to improve. Both governments now have almost half a century of experience in dealing with each other. We have seen that the superpowers are fated to negotiate. However, negotiations are a means, not an end, and negotiations with a rival that has a different cultural background and political system are not going to be easy. Yet they can be fruitful. Diplomacy in United States-Soviet relations needs to accomplish a great deal in five broad areas: arms control, regional issues, human rights, trade, and exchanges. Through a combination of realism, confidence, and a drive for success, as well as avoidance of fruitless strategies, the superpowers will learn to accept the limitations of their relationship, avoid unnecessary antagonisms and move toward future improvements. As the dean of American specialists on the Soviet Union writes: "You *can* conclude useful agreements with the Soviet side, and they *will* respect them—on condition, however, that the terms be clear and specific, not general; that as little as possible be left to interpretation; that questions of motivation, and particularly professions of noble principle, be left aside...." and that the United States "show a serious and continued interest in their observance." [126]

REFERENCES

1. See the discussion under Culture and Culturology in the *International Encyclopedia of the Social Sciences* (New York: Macmillan, 1968); and Raymond A. Bauer, "The Psycho-Cultural Approach to Soviet Studies," *World Politics* VII, 1 (October 1954), 119–132. Bauer reviews books by Margaret Mead and Dinko Tomasic on Russian culture.
2. From a speech in November 1983. See *Harper's*, April 1984, 9.
3. Thomas B. Larson, *Soviet-American Rivalry* (New York: Norton, 1978), 29. For specific examples of continuity in administration, see T. H. Rigby, *Lenin's Government* (New York: Cambridge University Press, 1979), 40, 51, and 230–238.
4. Lawrence T. Caldwell and William Diebold, Jr., (untitled) in *Eagle Entangled: U.S. Foreign Policy in a Complex World*, ed. Kenneth A. Oye et al. (New York and London: Longman, 1979) 207.
5. "The American Idea," *New York Times Magazine*, 6 July 1986, 13.
6. See Paul Johnson, "The Almost-Chosen People," *The Wilson Quarterly* (Winter 1985), 84, 87, 89.
7. My letter in *The Atlantic* (April 1984), 12; Jerry F. Hough, *The Struggle for the Third World* (Washington, DC: Brookings, 1986), 286.
8. Joseph S. Nye, Jr., "Can America Manage Its Soviet Policy?" *Foreign Affairs*, 62, 4 (Spring 1984): 863, 867.
9. Mona Harrington, *The Dream of Deliverance in American Politics* (New York: Knopf, 1986).
10. Kenneth T. Jackson, *Crabgrass Frontier* (New York: Oxford University Press 1986).
11. *New York Times,* 19 July 1986, 46.
12. See Sanford J. Ungar, *Estrangement: America and the World* (New York: Oxford University Press, 1985).
13. William Pfaff, "Reflections: Splendid Little Wars," *The New Yorker*, 13 January 1986, 54–55; George W. Ball, "Reagan's Ramboism...," *Christian Science Monitor*, 28 April 1986, 18.
14. Murray Feshbach, quoted in Leslie H. Gelb, "What We Really Know about Russia," *New York Times Magazine*, 28 October 1984, 76.

15. Zbigniew Brzezinski, *Game Plan* (Boston, MA: Atlantic Monthly Press, 1986), 20–21. Brzezinski also cites some of the work of Richard Pipes.
16. Suggested by Frederick C. Barghoorn and Thomas F. Remington, *Politics in the USSR*, 3d ed. (Boston, MA: Little, Brown, 1986), 12–15 and 44.
17. Stephen White, *Political Culture and Soviet Politics* (London: Macmillan, 1979), 21. Quoted in Barghoorn and Remington, 34.
18. Barghoorn and Remington, 59–60.
19. David Shipler, *Russia* (New York: Times Books, 1983), 278.
20. This American businessman sold the Soviets the largest auto-parts plant of its kind in the world.
21. Peter Wright, *Spycatcher* (New York: Viking, 1987), 260.
22. On the USSR as a colonial empire, see Hugh Seton-Watson, *The New Imperialism*, 2d Ed. (Totowa, NJ: Rowman and Littlefield, 1971).
23. *Pravda*, 30 July 1986, 1. Gorbachev was speaking to workers in Khabarovsk.
24. Georgi A. Arbatov and Willem Oltmans, *The Soviet Viewpoint* (New York: Dodd, Mead, 1983), xvi–xvii; *New York Times*, 9 August 1986, A1. The quotation is from Arkady N. Shevchenko, *Breaking with Moscow* (New York: Knopf, 1985), 369.
25. *New York Times*, 27 November, 1981, A-3.
26. Arbatov and Oltmans, 40.
27. See the article by Serge Schmemann in the *New York Times*, 14 September 1983; and on Gorbachev, see Zhores A. Medvedev, *Gorbachev* (New York: Norton, 1986), 125, 228, 237.
28. *New York Times*, 18 April 1987, A-5.
29. Brzezinski, 23.
30. George Liska, *Russia and World Order* (Baltimore, MD: Johns Hopkins University Press, 1980), 117–118.
31. Leslie H. Gelb, "What We Really Know about Russia," *New York Times Magazine*, 28 October 1984, 67.
32. Marshall D. Shulman, "Toward a Western Philosophy of Coexistence," *Foreign Affairs* 52, 1 (October 1973), 40.
33. Shulman, 48.
34. Seweryn Bialer, *The Soviet Paradox* (New York: Knopf, 1986), 331–332.
35. Marc Raeff, *Understanding Imperial Russia*, trans. by Arthur Goldhammer (New York: Columbia University Press, 1984), 14.
36. *Komsomolskaya pravda*, 27 May 1983, quoted in Julia Wishnevsky, "The Curtain Falls on Jewish Emigration," RL 232/83, 15 June 1983, 4.
37. Jerry F. Hough, *How the Soviet Union Is Governed* (Cambridge, MA: Harvard University Press, 1979), 280, 286, 291.
38. The Soviet propaganda campaign continues. For example, *Pravda* published an article on a Native American in prison that was a mirror image of American articles on imprisoned Soviet dissidents. *Pravda*, 14 June 1984, 5.
39. See various contributions in *The Making of America's Soviet Policy*, ed. Joseph S. Nye, Jr. (New Haven, CT: Yale University Press 1984), especially pp. 17, 163, 199, 281, and 315–316.
40. Kenneth W. Thompson, "Human Rights and Soviet-American Relations," in *Neither Cold War nor Detente?* ed. Richard A. Melanson (Charlottesville: University of Virginia, 1982), 137–138.

41. See her article in *Commentary*, November 1979, 34–45.
42. See the letter by Burton Caine, a Professor of Law, in the *New York Times*, 3 October 1985, A-26.
43. U.S. Department of State, "Helsinki Final Act: Tenth Anniversary," *Gist* (July 1985): 1.
44. *The Christian Science Monitor*, 15 April 1985, 10.
45. An AP dispatch, *Daily Hampshire Gazette* (Northampton, MA), 19 December 1984, 2.
46. Address to the Commonwealth Club of San Francisco, 22 February 1985, in the *New York Times*, 23 February 1985, 4.
47. Tamar Jacoby, "The Reagan Turnaround in Human Rights," *Foreign Affairs* (Summer 1986): 1083.
48. Karl E. Birnbaum, "Human Rights and East-West Relations," *Foreign Affairs* 55, 4 (July 1977): 796; and Thompson, 149.
49. Zbigniew Brzezinski and Samuel P. Huntington, *Political Power: USA/USSR* (New York: Viking, 1964). See especially "Cincinnatus and the Apparatchik," 150–173.
50. See Larson, pp. 86–91.
51. *New York Times*, 24 July 1986, B-8.
52. On the lack of consensus, see Ole R. Holsti and James N. Rosenau, *American Leadership in World Affairs: Vietnam and the Breakdown of Consensus* (Boston: Allen & Unwin, 1984).
53. Zbigniew Brzezinski, "Moving from Standoff to an Interim Accord," *New York Times*, 29 January 1984, E-19.
54. N. N. Popov, "The U.S. Psychological Climate and Soviet-American Relations," *SShA* (USA), 10 (October 1985), trans. in US JPRS-USA-85-013, 30 December 1985, 29 and 40.
55. Bialer, 312 and 319.
56. Karl W. Ryavec, "Nikita Khrushchev and Soviet Politics," in *Government and Leaders*, ed. Edward Feit, (Boston, MA: Houghton Mifflin, 1978), 291.
57. Marshall D. Shulman, "Overview of U.S.-Soviet Relations," U.S. Department of State *Statement*, 26 October 1977, 7; and Stephen F. Cohen, "The Friends and Foes of Change: Soviet Reformism and Conservatism," in Cohen, *Rethinking the Soviet Experience* (New York: Oxford University Press, 1985), 128–157.
58. *Washington Post*, 19 November 1978.
59. Don Riegle (D), Michigan, quoted in the *Washington Post*, 12 July, 1978, A-1 and A-13.
60. P. H. Juviler, *Revolutionary Law and Order* (New York: Free Press, 1976), 106; and David Lane, *State and Politics in the USSR* (New York: New York University, 1985), 295.
61. A. L. George, "The 'Operational Code': A Neglected Approach to the Study of Political Leaders and Decision Making," *International Studies Quarterly* 13, 2 (June 1969): 190, quoted in Karen A. Mingst, "National Images in International Relations," *Coexistence* 21 (1984): 176. Short works on United States-Soviet perceptions include: Alexander Dallin, "The United States in the Soviet Perspective" *Adelphi Papers*, No. 141 (London: IISS, 1979); Richard K. Herrmann, "Analyzing Soviet Images of the United States," *Journal of Conflict Resolution*, 29, 4 (December 1985), 665–697; Daniel S. Papp, "Soviet Perceptions of the American

Political Milieu," *Parameters*, X, 2 (June 1980), 69–78; Karl W. Ryavec, "Six Soviet Books on the American Political System," *Slavic Review*, 30, 2 (June 1971), 366–377.

62. These quotations are drawn from selections in Eugene Anschel, ed., *The American Image of Russia: 1775–1917* (New York: Ungar, 1974), 30–32 and 177; Benson Lee Grayson, ed., *The American Image of Russia: 1917–1977* (New York: Ungar, 1978), 44, 47–48, 152, 219, 225, 212, 214; and Peter G. Filene, ed., *American Views of Soviet Russia* (Homewood, IL: Dorsey, 1968), 282, 387, and 388.

63. Kevin Phillips, quoted in the *New York Times*, 18 March 1986, A-1; White House press release of the President's speech of 16 September 1985, 5.

64. U.S. Department of Defense press release of 4 March 1981; and *The Boston Globe*, 11 April 1984, 3. Such views were sincerely and deeply held, according to persons who had talked with the Secretary, e.g., Leslie Gelb, a discussion at Five Colleges, Inc., Amherst, MA, 12 October 1982.

65. *New York Times*, 4 September, 1983, and 22 August 1985, A-1.

66. U.S. Department of State press release, *New York Times*, 16 June 1983, A-5.

67. *New York Times*, 2 October 1985, A-16; and 19 August 1986, A-12; Archie Brown, "Change in the Soviet Union," *Foreign Affairs* (Summer 1986): 1061–1062; *Boston Globe*, 23 March 1986, 24; and M. S. Gorbachev, "Politichesky doklad . . .," *Kommunist* 4 (1986): 54–55.

68. On Soviet Americanists, see Morton Schwartz, *Soviet Perceptions of the United States* (Berkeley: University of California Press, 1980).

69. Arkady Shevchenko, *Breaking with Moscow* (New York: Knopf, 1985), 280; Strobe Talbott, *The Russians and Reagan* (New York: Vintage, 1984), 14–15; and see Bialer (1986), 357.

70. Vladimir Shlapentokh, *Christian Science Monitor*, 8 April 1986, 21; *New York Times*, 5 July 1982; *Literaturnaya gazeta*, 29 September 1982; and *Pravda*, 20 June 1982.

71. "Soviet Industry," *Fortune* XXIV (July 1941): 61, quoted in Raymond H. Dawson, *The Decision to Aid Russia, 1941* (Chapel Hill: The University of North Carolina Press, 1959), 42.

72. George H. Gallup, *Gallup Polls: 1935–1970*, 3 vols. (New York: Random House, 1972), passim.

73. William Schneider, "Public Opinion," in *The Making of America's Soviet Policy*, ed. Joseph S. Nye, Jr., 23 and 24; National Opinion Research Center poll, 1982 (NORC 82), 66 and 71; and Jamie Kalven, "A Talk with Louis Harris," *The Bulletin of the Atomic Scientists* (August/September 1982), 4.

74. A *Los Angeles Times*/Cable News Network poll of 14–18 March 1982, cited in William Schneider, "Conservation, Not Interventionism; Trends in Foreign Policy Opinion, 1974–1982," in *Eagle Defiant: United States Foreign Policy in the 1980s*, ed. Kenneth A. Oye et al. (Boston: Little, Brown, 1983), Table 2–3, 60; *New York Times*/CBS News poll, *New York Times*, 15 April 1985, A-1 and A-13; a NORC 1982 poll, ibid., 24 April 1983, A-24; a Public Agenda Foundation/Center for Foreign Policy Development of Brown University poll, ibid., 7 October 1984, A-21; an ABC News telephone poll, September 2–3, 1983; a *New York Times*/CBS News poll, 28 September–1 October 1986, ibid., 9 October 1986, A-10.

75. *U.S. News & World Report*, 24 September 1984, 32; and personal experience in USSR.

76. Blair A. Ruble and Mark H. Teeter, "Notes from Moscow and Leningrad: December 1981," *Russia* 4 (1981).
77. See RL 223/83 of 8 June 1983.
78. For an overview of Soviet espionage and active measures, see Chapter 5 in Richard F. Starr, *USSR: Foreign Policies after Détente* (Stanford, CA: Hoover, 1985).
79. Thomas Powers, *The Man Who Kept the Secrets: Richard Helms and the CIA* (New York: Knopf, 1979), 39–40; and Jeffrey T. Richelson, *The U.S. Intelligence Community* (Cambridge, MA: Ballinger, 1985), 179.
80. *Newsweek*, 31 July 1978, 31, and 21 July 1980, 69–70; *U.S. News & World Report*, 31 March 1975, 16–17; and Victor Marchetti and John D. Marks, *The CIA and the Cult of Intelligence* (New York: Knopf, 1974), 206 and 207.
81. Jeffrey T. Richelson, *Sword and Shield* (Cambridge, MA: Ballinger, 1986), 96, 99, 102–103, and 107.
82. Sir Harold Nicolson, *Diplomacy*, 3d Ed (London: Oxford University Press, 1969), 4. This fine little book, first published in 1939, remains useful.
83. See Jonathan Frankel, *International Relations*, 2d ed. (New York: Oxford University Press, 1969), 99–101.
84. Hans J. Morganthau, *Politics among Nations*, 4th ed. (New York: Knopf, 1967), 530.
85. Ibid., 519; Frankel, 99.
86. Robert J. Art, "Nuclear Weapons and Military Power," in *International Politics*, 2d ed. Art and Jarvis (Boston: Little, Brown, 1985), 266.
87. From a speech by Dean Rusk in the *New York Times*, 11 February 1984.
88. *New York Times*, 30 August 1983.
89. Ibid., 1 April 1985, A-6, based on poll results.
90. Stephen F. Cohen, *Sovieticus* (New York: Norton, 1985), 120; W. Averell Harriman, "Let's Negotiate with Andropov," *New York Times*, 2 January 1983; Walter J. Stoessel, quoted in ibid., 17 November 1983, A-9. Harriman and Stoessel have both served as American ambassadors to Moscow.
91. Thomas B. Larson, *Soviet-American Rivalry* (New York: Norton, 1978), 9.
92. K. V. Chernenko, *Pravda*, 12 November 1984, in *CDSP* XXXVI, 45 (5 December 1984): 21.
93. Source: A former State Department official.
94. *New York Times*, 31 March 1986, A1; and Flora Lewis, ibid., 3 April 1986, A-27.
95. See, for example, Philip D. Stewart, *Dartmouth XII: A Soviet-American Dialogue* (n.p.: Kettering Foundation, 1982).
96. William C. Hyland, "U.S.-Soviet Relations: The Long Road Back," *Foreign Affairs, America and the World: 1981*, 60 (1982): 527–528. Hyland was the deputy director of the NSC staff from 1975 to 1977.
97. Senator Howard H. Baker at Dartmouth College, *New York Times*, 11 June 1984; Roger Fisher, "Big-Power Interests," ibid., 26 September 1981; F. Stephen Larrabee, "Start Rehabilitating Relations with Soviet," ibid., 15 February 1984; Dimitri K. Simes, "Take Small Steps toward Moscow," ibid., 12 November 1984. Baker became President Reagan's Chief-of-Staff in March 1987.
98. *Pravda*, 21 May 1986, 1, trans. in *CDSP* XXXVIII, 20 (18 June 1986), 28.
99. Quoted in Arthur M. Cox, *Russian Roulette: the Superpower Game* (New York: Times Books, 1982), 201.

100. Helmut Sonnenfeldt, "Soviet Negotiating Concept and Style," in *A Game for High Stakes*, ed. Leon Sloss and M. Scott Davis (Cambridge, MA: Ballinger, 1986), 25.
101. Hannes Adomeit, "Negotiating, Soviet Style," *Problems of Communism* XXXI, 4 (July–August 1982): 60; and Richard Pipes, "Some Operational Principles of Soviet Foreign Policy," U.S. Congress, Senate Subcommittee on National Security and International Operations (Washington, DC: GPO, 1972), 1.
102. Raymond L. Garthoff, "Negotiating with the Russians: Some Lessons from SALT," *International Security* 1, 4 (Spring 1977): 18.
103. Jacob Beam, quoted in Adomeit, 62; Strobe Talbott, "Buildup and Breakdown," *Foreign Affairs: America and the World: 1983*, 62, 3 (1984), 612. ,
104. Adomeit, p. 61; see also U.S. Congress, House, *Soviet Diplomacy and Negotiating Behavior* (Washington, DC: GPO, 1979), 521–525.
105. Henry Kissinger, "Reflections on American Diplomacy," *Foreign Affairs*, 35, 1 (October 1956); Leslie H. Gelb, "What We Really Know about Russia," 56; Alexander Haig, *New York Times*, 2 April 1984; Richard Burt, ibid., 21 March 1980, A-8; and Garthoff, "Negotiating with the Russians," 19.
106. *New York Times*, 12 March 1984, and 30 August 1986.
107. Gerard C. Smith, *New York Times*, 24 September 1985.
108. Zbigniew K. Brzezinski, *Power and Principle* (New York: Farrar, Strauss, Giroux, 1983), 165–166.
109. Gordon R. Weihmiller and Dusko Doder, *U.S.-Soviet Summits* (Lanham, MD: University Press of America, 1986), 105.
110. Brezhnev's interview to the German newspaper *Vorwarts*, printed in TASS, 2 May 1978, and quoted in RL 219/82, 26 May 1982, 1; Richard Nixon, "Superpower Summitry," *Foreign Affairs*, 64, 1 (Fall 1985): 1, 9, 10; and Richard N. Haass, *Christian Science Monitor*, 21 April 1986, 14.
111. "Double Summit, Please," *The Economist*, 4 October 1986, 15; John Newhouse, "The Diplomatic Round: Summiteering," *New Yorker*, 8 September 1986, 42.
112. *Sunday Times* (London), 25 May 1986, p. 22; *New York Times*, 7 October 1986, A-13, and 10 October 1986, A-12.
113. *New York Times*, 13 October 1986, A-9, 24 October 1986, A-1 and A-14, and 26 October 1986, A-1; U.S. Department of State, "The Rejkjavik Meeting," *Gist* (December 1986); and, for an outline of the experts' discussions, see Paul H. Nitze, "The Nuclear and Space Negotiations," U.S. Department of State, *Current Policy*, no. 910 (February 1987): 2–4.
114. *New York Times*, 14 October 1986, A-1; U.S. Department of State, public reply of 3 December 1986, to a letter from this writer; George Shultz, "Rejkjavik: A Watershed in U.S.-Soviet Relations," U.S. Department of State, *Current Policy* no. 883 (November 1986): 1.
115. *New York Times*, 13 October 1986, A-9, 14 October 1986, A-13, and 23 October 1986, A-12.
116. A Cable News Network poll reported by AP, *Daily Hampshire Gazette* (Northampton, MA), 20 October 1986, 2; *New York Times*/CBS polls, *New York Times*, 16 October 1986, A-11.
117. *New York Times*, 25 October 1986, A5; *Congressional Record—Senate*, 17 October 1986, S 16575-S 16577. See also Nunn's remarks on TV quoted in Elizabeth Drew, "Letter from Washington," *New Yorker*, 27 October 1986, 131–132.

118. See the Op-Ed articles by Anthony Lewis, Arthur Macy Cox, Anthony Lake, *New York Times*, 16 October 1986, A-31, 6 November 1986, A-35, and 23 March 1987, A-19.

119. See the articles by Dimitri K. Simes and James Reston in the *New York Times*, 26 October 1986, E-23, and 29 October 1986, A-27; and Michael Mandelbaum and Strobe Talbott, "Rejkjavik and Beyond," *Foreign Affairs* 65, 2 (Winter 1986/87); 215–235.

120. Seweryn Bialer, *The Soviet Paradox* (New York: Knopf, 1986), 369, 370, 373. See also Hoffmann, "Contain Moscow: Cooperate Too."

121. Seweryn Bialer, "Mutually Accepting Nuclear Parity," *New York Times*, 7 July 1983.

122. The title of an article by Seweryn Bialer and Joan Afferika. A short version is in the *New York Times*, 12 December 1982, E-19.

123. Karl W. Ryavec, "The CPSU, Institutions and the Political System," in *Soviet Society and the Communist Party*, ed. Ryavec (Amherst, MA: University of Massachusetts Press, 1978), vii-xviii.

124. Madeleine G. Kalb, "The Dobrynin Factor," *New York Times Magazine*, 13 May 1983, 92.

125. George F. Kennan, "Reducing Tensions," *New York Times*, 15 January 1984; Averill Harriman, ibid., 27 July 1986, A-23; *Soviet Leadership: Changes and Challenges*, a Stanley Foundation conference report, 1985, 15.

126. George F. Kennan, "Reflections: Breaking the Spell," *New Yorker*, 3 October 1983, 53.

SELECT BIBLIOGRAPHY

Culture and Society

Berdyaev, Nicholas. *The Origin of Russian Communism*. Ann Arbor: University of Michigan, 1960.

——. *The Russian Idea*. Westport, CT: Greenwood, 1979.

Billington, James H. *The Icon and the Axe: An Interpretive History of Russian Culture*. New York: Random House, 1966.

Binyon, Michael. *Life in Russia*. New York: Pantheon, 1983.

Boorstin, Daniel J. *The Genius of American Politics*. Chicago: University of Chicago Press, 1958.

de Tocqueville, Alexis. *Democracy in America*, a classic in many editions.

Lee, Andrea. *Russian Journal*. New York: Vintage, 1984.

Lerner, Max. *America as a Civilization*. New York: Simon and Schuster, 1957.

Masaryk, Thomas G. *The Spirit of Russia: Studies in History, Literature, and Philosophy*, 2d Ed. Translated by Edward Cedar Paul and W. R. and Z. Lee. London: G. Allen, 1955.

Nikolayev, Vladimir. *The Americans: As Seen by a Soviet Writer*. Translated by Dudley Hagen. Moscow: Progress, 1984.

Pond, Elizabeth. *From the Yaroslavsky Station: Russia Perceived*. New York: Universe, 1981.

Shipler, David. *Russia: Broken Idols, Broken Dreams*. New York: Times Books, 1983.

Smith, Hedrick. *The Russians*. New York: Quadrangle, 1976.
Stoessinger, John G. *Nations in Darkness: China, Russia and America*. New York: Random House, 1971.
Szamuely, Tibor. *The Russian Tradition*. New York: McGraw-Hill, 1975.

Domestic Politics and Foreign Policy

Bialer, S., ed. *The Domestic context of Soviet Foreign Policy*. Boulder, CO: Westview Press, 1981.
——. *The Soviet Paradox: External Expansion, Internal Decline*. New York: Knopf, 1986.
Brzezinski, Z. K., and S. P. Huntington. *Political Power: USA/USSR*. New York: Viking, 1964.
Caldwell, L. T., and W. Diebold. *Soviet-American Relations in the 1980s: Superpower Politics and East-West Trade*. New York: McGraw-Hill, 1981.
Gorbachev, Mikhail. *Perestroika: New Thinking for Our Country and the World*. New York: Harper & Row, 1987.
Medvedev, Zhores. *Gorbachev*. New York: Norton, 1986.
Nye, Joseph S., Jr., ed. *The Making of America's Soviet Policy*. New Haven, CT: Yale University Press, 1984.
Rosenau, J. N. *The Domestic Sources of Foreign Policy*. New York: Free Press, 1967.
Schwartz, Morton. *The Foreign Policy of the USSR: Domestic Factors*. Encino, CA: Dickenson, 1975.
Wallace, W. *Foreign Policy and the Political Process*. London: Macmillan, 1971.
Yanov, Alexander. *Détente after Brezhnev: The Domestic Roots of Soviet Foreign Policy*. Berkeley: Institute of International Studies, University of California, 1977.

Perceptions
Anschel, Eugene, ed. *The American Image of Russia, 1775-1917*. New York: Ungar, 1974.
Aspin, Les, and Jack F. Kemp. *Realities of Soviet Power: Two Views*. Washington, DC: American Enterprise Institute, 1978.
Barghoorn, Frederick C. *The Soviet Image of the United States: A Study in Distortion*. New York: Harcourt, Brace, 1950.
Bialer, Seweryn. *Stalin's Successors: Leadership, Stability and Change in the Soviet Union*. New York: Cambridge University Press, 1980.
Boulding, Kenneth E. *The Image*. Ann Arbor, MI: University of Michigan Press, 1961.
Filene, Peter G., ed. *American Views of Soviet Russia, 1917-1965*. Homewood, IL: Dorsey, 1968.
Gilbert, Stephen P. *Soviet Images of America*. New York: Crane, Russak, 1977.
Grayson, Benson Lee, ed. *The American Image of Russia, 1917-1977*. New York: Ungar, 1978.
Halperin, Jonathan J., and Robert D. English, eds. *The Other Side: How Americans and Soviets Perceive Each Other*. New Brunswick, NJ: Transaction, 1982.
Jervis, Robert. *Perception and Misperception in International Politics*. Princeton, NJ: Princeton University Press, 1976.
Lenczowski, John. *Soviet Perceptions of U.S. Foreign Policy*. Ithaca, NY: Cornell University Press, 1982.
Lockwood, Jonathan S. *The Soviet View of U.S. Strategic Doctrine*. New Brunswick, NJ: Transaction, 1983.

Malcolm, Neil. *Soviet Political Scientists and American Politics.* New York: St. Martin's, 1984.

Mandelbaum, Michael, and Strobe Talbott. *Reagan and Gorbachev.* New York: Vintage, 1987.

Pranger, Robert J. *Six U.S. Perceptions of Soviet Foreign Policy Intentions.* Washington, DC: AEI, 1979.

Rapoport, Anatol. *The Big Two: Soviet-American Perceptions of Foreign Policy.* New York: Pegasus, 1971.

Schwartz, Morton. *Soviet Perceptions of the United States.* Berkeley, University of California Press, 1978.

Solzhenitsyn, Alexander I. *The Mortal Danger: How Misconceptions about Russia Imperil America,* 2d ed. Translated by Michael Nicholson and Alexis Klimoff. New York: Harper & Row, 1981.

Talbott, Strobe. *The Russians and Reagan.* New York: Vintage, 1984.

U.S. Congress (Senate) Committee on Foreign Relations. *Perceptions: Relations between the United States and the Soviet Union.* Washington, DC: GPO, 1978.

U.S. International Communication Agency. *Soviet Elites: World View and Perceptions of the U.S.* Prepared by Gregory Guroff and Steven Grant. Washington, DC: 1981. (Research Report R-18-81.)

Van Oudenaren, John. *U.S. Leadership Perceptions of the Soviet Problem since 1945.* Santa Monica, CA: Rand, 1982. (R-2843-NA in the Rand Publication Series.)

Welch, William. *American Images of Soviet Foreign Policy.* New Haven, CT: Yale University Press, 1970.

Zimmerman, William. *Soviet Perspectives on International Relations: 1956–1967.* Princeton, NJ: Princeton University Press, 1969.

Ties, Diplomacy, and Negotiations

Amercian Enterprise Institute. *Dealing with the Soviet Union,* Washington, DC: AEI, 1985.

Brement, Marshall. *Organizing Ourselves to Deal with the Soviets,* Santa Monica, CA: Rand, 1978.

Brzezinski, Zbigniew. *Power and Principle: Memoirs of the National Security Adviser, 1977–1981.* New York: Farrar-Strauss-Giroux, 1983.

Carlson, Don and Craig Comstock, eds. *Keeping the Peace when It Matters Too Much to Be Left to Politicians.* New York: Tarcher/St. Martin's, 1986.

Feltham, R. G. *Diplomatic Handbook.* White Plains, NY: Longman, 1970.

Garthoff, Raymond L. *Détente and Confrontation: American-Soviet Relations from Nixon to Reagan.* Washington, DC: Brookings, 1985.

Iklé, Fred C. *How Nations Negotiate.* New York: Harper & Row, 1964.

——. *International Negotiation: American Shortcomings in Negotiating with Communist Powers.* Washington, DC: GPO, 1970.

Jamgotch, Nish, Jr., ed. *Sectors of Mutual Benefit in U.S.-Soviet Negotiations.* Durham, NC: Duke University Press, 1985.

Jönsson, Christer. *Soviet Bargaining Behavior: The Nuclear Test Ban Case.* New York: Columbia University Press, 1979.

Kennan, George F. *Memoirs (1925–1950).* Boston: Little, Brown, 1967.

Kissinger, Henry. *White House Years.* Boston: Little, Brown, 1979.

——. *Years of Upheaval.* Boston: Little, Brown, 1982.

Krickus, Richard J. *The Superpowers in Crisis: Implications of Domestic Discord.* Elmsford, NY: Pergamon, 1987.

Mandelbaum, Michael, and Strobe Talbott. *Reagan and Gorbachev.* New York: Vintage, 1987.

Pipes, Richard. *International Negotiation: Some Operational Principles of Soviet Foreign Policy.* Washington, DC: GPO, 1972.

Sloss, Leon, and M. Scott Davis. *A Game for High Stakes: Lessons Learned in Negotiating with the Soviet Union.* Cambridge, MA: Ballinger, 1986.

Starr, Richard, F., ed. *Public Diplomacy: USA Versus USSR.* Stanford, CA: Hoover, 1986.

Steigman, Andrew L. *The Foreign Service of the United States.* Boulder, CO: Westview Press, 1985.

Talbott, Strobe. *The Russians and Reagan.* New York: Vintage, 1984.

U.S. Advisory Commission on Public Diplomacy. *1986 Report.* Washington, DC: GPO, 1986.

U.S. Department of State. *Atlas of United States Foreign Relations.* Washington, DC: GPO, 1985. (An annual publication.)

———. *Realism, Strength, Negotiation: Key Foreign Policy Statements of the Reagan Administration.* Washington, DC: GPO, 1984.

U.S. Congress. House. *Soviet Diplomacy and Negotiating Behavior: Emerging New Context for U.S. Diplomacy.* Washington, DC: GPO, 1979. (Reprinted in 1983 by Westview Press, Boulder, CO.)

U.S. Congress. Senate. Subcommittee on National Security and Government Operations, *The Soviet Approach to Negotiation: Selected Writings,* Washington, DC: GPO, 1969.

Warner, Gale and Michael Shuman. *Citizen Diplomats.* New York: Continuum, 1987.

Weihmiller, Gordon R., and Dusko Doder. *U.S.-Soviet Summits: An Account of East-West Diplomacy at the Top, 1955–1985.* Lanham, MD: University Press of America, 1986.

Propaganda, Espionage, and Active Measures

Bamford, James. *The Puzzle Palace.* Boston, MA: Houghton-Mifflin, 1982.

Barron, John. *The KGB Today: The Hidden Hand.* New York: Reader's Digest, 1983.

Bittman, Ladislav. *The KGB and Soviet Disinformation: An Insider's View.* Elmsford, NY: Pergamon, 1985.

Breckinridge, Scott D. *The CIA and the U.S. Intelligence System.* Boulder, CO: Westview Press, 1986.

Carson, William R., and Robert T. Crowley. *The New KGB: Engine of Soviet Power.* New York: Morrow, 1985.

Cline, Ray. *The CIA: Reality vs. Myth.* Washington, DC: Acropolis, 1981.

Cline, Ray S., and Yonah Alexander. *Terrorism: The Soviet Connection.* New York: Crane Russak, 1984.

Crowley, Robert T., and William R. Corson. *The New KGB: Engine of Soviet Power.* New York: Morrow, 1985.

Dulles, Allen. *The Craft of Intelligence.* New York: Harper-Row, 1963. (Reprinted in 1985 by Westview Press, Boulder, CO.)

Freemantle, Brian. *KGB: Inside the World's Largest Intelligence Network*. New York: Holt, Rinehart and Winston, 1984.

Kirkpatrick, Lyman B., Jr. *The U.S. Intelligence Community*. New York: Hill and Wang, 1973.

Lamphere, Robert J., and Tom Schactman. *The FBI-KGB War*. New York: Berkeley, 1986.

Marchetti, Victor, and John D. Marks. *The CIA and the Cult of Intelligence*. New York: Knopf, 1974.

Martin, David C. *Wilderness of Mirrors*. New York: Ballantine, 1981.

Myagkov, Aleksei. *Inside the KGB*. New York: Ballantine, 1976.

Prados, John. *The Soviet Estimate: U.S. Intelligence Analysis and Russian Military Strength*. New York: Dial, 1982.

Richelson, Jeffrey T. *Sword and Shield: The Soviet Intelligence and Security Apparatus*. Cambridge, MA: Ballinger, 1986.

——. *The U.S. Intelligence Community*. Cambridge, MA: Ballinger, 1985.

Rocca, Raymond G., and John J. Dziak. *Bibliography on Soviet Intelligence and Security Services*. Boulder, CO: Westview Press, 1985.

Rositzke, Harry. *The CIA's Secret Operations*. New York: Reader's Digest, 1977.

——. *The KGB: The Eyes of Russia*. New York: Doubleday, 1981.

Sakharov, Vladimir with Umberto Tosi. *High Treason*. New York: Ballantine, 1987.

Schultz, Richard H., and Roy Godson. *Dezinformatsia: Active Measures in Soviet Strategy*. Washington, DC: Pergamon-Brassey's, 1984.

Shevchenko, Arkady N. *Breaking with Moscow*. New York: Knopf, 1985.

Sterling, Claire. *The Terror Network*. New York: Holt, Rinehart and Winston, 1981.

Turner, Stansfield. *Secrecy and Democracy: The CIA in Transition*. Boston: Houghton Mifflin, 1985.

Tyson, James L. *U.S. International Broadcasting and National Security*. New York: Ramapo Press, 1983.

Yakovlev, Nikolai. *CIA: Target USSR*, Moscow: Progress, 1980.

Strategy

Bialer, Seweryn. *The Soviet Paradox: External Expansion, Internal Decline*. New York: Knopf, 1986.

Brzezinski, Zbigniew. *Game Plan: A Geostrategic Framework for the Conduct of the U.S.-Soviet Context*. Boston: Atlantic Monthly Press, 1986.

——. *Power and Principle: Memoirs of the National Security Adviser, 1977–1981*. New York: Farrar-Strauss-Giroux, 1983.

George, Alexander L., ed. *Managing U.S-Soviet Rivalry: Problems of Crisis Prevention*. Boulder, CO: Westview Press, 1983.

Hoffmann, Stanley. *Primacy or World Order: American Foreign Policy since the Cold War*. New York: McGraw-Hill, 1978.

Horelick, Arnold L., ed. *U.S.-Soviet Relations: The Next Phase*, Ithaca, NY: Cornell University Press, 1986.

Kissinger, Henry. *White House Years*. Boston: Little, Brown, 1979.

——. *Years of Upheaval*. Boston: Little, Brown, 1982.

Liska, George. *Russia and World Order: Strategic Choices and the Laws of Power*. Baltimore: Johns Hopkins University Press, 1980.

Leonhard, Wolfgang. *The Kremlin and the West: a Realistic Approach.* New York: Norton, 1986.

Nye, Joseph S., Jr., ed. *The Making of America's Soviet Policy.* New Haven, CT: Yale University Press, 1984.

Ulam, Adam B. *Expansion and Coexistence: Soviet Foreign Policy*, 1917–73 ed. New York: Praeger, 1974.

Conclusion

Toward the Future: Limits and Possibilities

This book has emphasized the most important topics of superpower relations. Although there are many significant issues yet to be resolved, it appears in early 1988 that Soviet-American relations are creeping back to a better state that could be called "quiet détente." The reasons for this are largely inadvertent and do not pay credit to either the American or Soviet political system or their leaders. Basically, both systems have gotten themselves into difficulties that preclude continuation of United States-Soviet conflict at a high level. For the Soviets the difficulty is a crisis of economics and morale that requires an attempt at some degree of economic reform and at least a pretense of political change. In the United States the development of political scandal in the executive branch coincides with the normal shift of power from a lame duck President to the Congress and possibly with a change in public opinion on the Soviet Union.

Such a trend toward improvement in relations has happened before but there has not been any fundamental change in either system. And weapons development and espionage proceed on both sides as usual. This is a lull. Making it last will be extremely difficult. The state of international politics is extraordinarily turbulent. In 1987 there were at least two new threats of war— between India and Pakistan, and between Greece and Turkey. Several other wars were underway, with the war in Afghanistan involving Soviet troops spilling over into Pakistan and the American-backed Contras trying to do Nicaragua serious injury. All this impedes any movement of the superpowers to get closer. In addition, the Western industrialized nations, though functioning, are facing numerous problems of the post-industrial age, and many of the developing countries cannot pay their foreign debt.

The power of the superpowers in the face of this difficult international situation is more limited than ever. Recently, it has been difficult for the United States to accept being only one member of quarreling family of new states, some of which seem anti-American. Blaming the Soviet Union for this new limitation was easier for some than accepting and working with the new conditions of international life. For the Soviet Union's part, although it has supported anti-Western forces in the Third World, it has come to realize the states that come out of these movements sometimes are strongly anti-Soviet. Anticolonialism can become anti-Sovietism. Both superpowers have armed to deter each other but cannot seem to use this "super" power for either inducing world or even regional stability or controlling ambitious lesser powers with their own expansionist agendas and mini-imperialisms. Neither superpower finds its own system being replicated in its Third World client-states.

The superpowers, then, are in a quandary. The United States finds it even more difficult to quiet the new fractious and violent international scene than it was to deter the Soviet Union. Its fleet in the Persian Gulf can keep the oil flowing but cannot begin to resolve the ancient and deadly feud among Moslems. Only a United States with a different internal sociopolitical life might begin to be able to cope with today's world. The USSR is even less able to be a calming force in the world, for several reasons: It has been a supporter of violent change for so long, it has not been able to develop a well-functioning welfare state with a materially satisfied citizenry, and it cannot, for reasons of domestic politics, easily take advantage of the high-technology and information "revolutions."

Apart from their international problems both peoples must learn to deal with their continuing rivalry as a permanent feature of life. While individual Russians and Americans can be friendly and even close, their governments are not individuals with the capacity to overcome all differences. However, rivalry can be combined with communication, some agreement, and even limited cooperation. Thus, the prospects are not totally bleak. However, hopes must be tempered by reason and experience. We cannot expect the Russian political elite to create a liberal democracy. This would cost them their political dominance and their many privileges, so very valuable in a country of shortages. At best, we can look forward to a further limitation of the Russian dictatorship. But this change will have to come from within the USSR; the United States cannot by itself bring this about through either pressure, persuasion, or example, though it can work for conditions that maximize normalization's chances.

We must not succumb to the temptation to overrate the Soviet leaders. The men who run the USSR are clever but they have done nothing of world-shaking import. Not since the 1920s have we seen any suggestion of generally applicable social or political originality in the Soviet system. It remains to be seen if Gorbachev can make the Soviet Union a major contributor to the world's development.

The Soviet Union will remain a problem for the United States, not because of the danger of communism, but because it rules too much of the non-Russian part of the world, has too much to defend and, hence, too great a fear of the outside world. It combats this fear by implicit and explicit intimidation, anti-Western sloganizing, expansionism, and exacerbation of conflict. Eventually, it will have to come to terms with its over-extension. Aspects of its foreign policy are inevitably irritants for the stability-seeking United States. Moreover, too many people in both countries still feel their systems are special and deserve special rights in the world. As a result, we shall continue to get in each other's way for some time, though probably in a less serious way than in the past.

At the moment, there is no international problem likely to throw the superpowers into a military confrontation. The worst situation imaginable is a new freeze in the relationship. We have lived through such ice ages before, but in these more complicated times, the superpowers have to make mutual adjustments. They cannot ignore each other. Being superpowers in common means they have still other similarities and even interests in common despite their continued rivalry.

What are the common interests on which a better relationship could be built? The avoidance of nuclear war is most fundamental and mentioned so often that it can lose its imperative truth. They both also face the common need of revitalizing their societies' productive power and reconstituting their people's confidence and morale. Societies beset by alcoholism and sloth and drug addiction and crime are tempting ruin. They both have been used by lesser powers. A climb down from the battlements of superpowerism is not a solution in itself, but it might provide opportunities for a general rethinking and reconstitution of the relationship. Both countries have some of the same major problems: how to get large, old economies to continue growing; how to minimize negative effects of postindustrial life such as drug addiction and juvenile delinquency; how to acquire and maintain the active support of the educated and foster their creativity; and how not to get taken in by Third World appeals and adventurism.

In improving the relationship, the United States must not give in to alarmist cries of "the Russians are coming." People who are bogged down in Afghanistan and have used their armies only against much smaller Communist countries in the past forty years are not going to attack another superpower except out of desperation. Driving the Soviets to that must also be avoided. Neither must the Americans resort to Soviet methods and abandon those traditional principles that have given their system an extraordinary strength and vitality. Disinformation and intimidation can bring no lasting solutions. Escapism and illusionism are to be avoided as well. There is nowhere to run or hide. The Soviet Union cannot be dealt with by stick-waving or by self-serving moralism. Yet it must not be overrated. The Soviet Union is no longer a revolutionary system. Its military is more a symbol of Russian culture and a force of last resort than a machine of conquest. And that weakness around Russia, which allowed it to expand, has now disappeared. China has reconstituted its power; Islam is in some process of revitalization, though still not united; and the peoples of Eastern Europe have lost their former illusions about communism and about Russia. Russia is in a weaker position in a new ball game much more difficult for it to play. That great previous Soviet economic growth that fueled its expansionism is now but a memory. Even when the USSR seemed an advancing monolith, it forced no war or total test of strength on the United States. The Soviets have "lost" more than the Americans have. China can never be replaced by minor Third World "victories." Moreover, Marxism has lost almost all of its pro-Sovietism. Where it remains, it is often anti-Soviet. It is almost impossible for the Soviets to replace Marxism with a better cover story that advances their interests as well as it did. Yet even if the Soviet Union seems more and more like an inadaptive dinosaur, remember, the dinosaur disappeared slowly and was dangerous for an era.

It must be generally recognized that the Soviet Union is only one problem facing the United States and that it is not the major threat to American well-being. Only in a war or if the Soviets could re-acquire China as an ally or take Europe, Africa, or the Middle East would the Soviet Union be "problem number one." Any of this is very unlikely. Containment has worked to a degree, as have the natural impediments to empire, but poor Soviet policy may have worked more in limiting the Soviet advance. The tide of the future in the Middle East and Africa is certainly not Sovietism. Islamic fundamentalism and military dictatorship are running far more strongly.

The powerful forces native to the world's regions must be addressed by the United States on their own terms. Latin America or parts of it may go through a new revolution and a strongly anti-American one. What would a new Chinese-Japanese special relationship mean for American interests? This is merely remote possibility now, but history does not stand still. The United States must develop a new vision of its needs and of the new, variegated world it has helped bring into being as well as a new foreign policy that helps the world to live, on the whole, peacefully and profitably with itself and also aids the United States in rectifying its domestic problems. This can be done without slighting military power. True power is well-rounded and never of a single nature. Geo-politics must be incorporated into political economy for the successful long haul.

History knows no examples of endless conflict between differing states or systems. The Crusades did end, as did the two hundred-year-wars between England and France and the once seemingly permanent Franco-German conflict. Some old conflicts continue, as in Ireland and between the Greeks and Turks, but these rest on bitter historical experiences very unlike the Soviet-American one.

American policy toward the Soviet Union should be patient, long-range, constructive, and firm. The United States should adopt policies that encourage a less harsh and more modern Soviet Union to emerge and that draw it into a more constructive participation in a new, less violent international system. We should act on the basis of a broader view of the Soviet Union that takes account of its weaknesses and peculiarities as well as its strengths and ordinary features. Demons can exist only in our minds. The Soviet Union is a finite, knowable, and progressively less unusual and dangerous entity. Arms control agreements are the necessary key for turning the lock that controls improvement in Soviet-American relations.

But the burden of change in policy lies not only on the United States. The Soviet Union will have to make it rather obvious that it is no longer militarily expansionist. Some reductions in conventional military force levels and changes in deployments are in order. Here a withdrawal from Afghanistan is essential. Gorbachev has begun it. Also required is less blatant Soviet conniving at using the misfortunes of the Third World for its own foreign policy designs. Less intimidation of its neighbors is also a necessity.

The Soviet Union will also have to reduce the harshness of its internal repression and allow some rather free flow of Jewish and other people abroad. Perhaps this is beginning. The United States cannot expect and will not get a total democratization. But a clear trend of reduction of Soviet expansion, manipulation, intimidation, and internal repression must become visible before Americans will be able to deal easily with the USSR and begin to treat it in a seminormal manner. American anti-Sovietism has been well-earned. Only its extreme aspects have been created by "cold warriors." Ironically, the Soviet Union could strengthen its influence in the world through these changes. Most Americans do not demand a weaker Soviet Union, only a different one.

Both superpowers must undergo some of the same general changes. For example, it is time to dump nostalgia for the past and pompous expectations of being Numero Uno. This is no longer possible in the world as it is. Neither the United States nor the Soviet Union will achieve any sort of domination over world affairs. We have seen that the predictions of Arabs "owning the world" turned out false, just as are the forecasts of Japan achieving global economic leadership. It is much more likely that both superpowers will remain truly significant powers, each in its own way, but that their power relative to that of other states will continue to decline slowly in the near future and that they will both find being superpowers increasingly a strain. That the international context will reduce both superpowers' power is increasingly clear. There will be still more nuclear powers and some regional superpowers. The United States and the USSR will have to cooperate more, both openly and implicitly, because of this rising potential threat. Their domestic politics will not change appreciably and neither will their views of each other. Their mutual ties will remain limited but will increase slightly through more realistic negotiation involving limited and slow progress in arms control. Their military competition will continue but will abate in tempo if only because of the horrendous cost and the dizzying complexity of new armaments. They will keep up their mutual propaganda, espionage, and active measures against one another and may even increase these forms of the competition for a time. Trade will increase somewhat, but there will be no significant growth for several years.

The future of the United States-Soviet relationship will see neither the big "bang" so many fear nor a whimper of despair from either side, but instead a mildly different, still conflictful, relationship with some increased hopes and satisfactions for both sides.

Index